PUBLICATION NUMBER FIVE OF THE
CONFERENCE ON LATIN AMERICAN HISTORY

SOVIET HISTORIANS ON LATIN AMERICA:
Recent Scholarly Contributions

SOVIET HISTORIANS ON LATIN AMERICA

Recent Scholarly Contributions

EDITED AND TRANSLATED FROM THE RUSSIAN,
WITH NOTES AND INTRODUCTION BY

RUSSELL H. BARTLEY

*Published for the Conference on Latin American History
by the University of Wisconsin Press*

Published 1978
The University of Wisconsin Press
Box 1379, Madison, Wisconsin 53701
The University of Wisconsin Press, Ltd.
70 Great Russell Street, London

Printed in the United States of America
for LC CIP information see the colophon
ISBN 0-299-07250-9

Publication of this book was made possible in part
by support from the Conference on Latin American History

Dedicated to the memory of
Vladimir Michailovich Miroshevskii (1900–1942),
Pioneer student of Latin America's historical past,
And to the late Adelaida Mikhailovna Zorina (1910–1977),
His devoted companion and disciple,
And distinguished historian of Cuba

CONTENTS

PREFACE

AN ESSENTIAL function of the scholarly professions is to promote communication and the exchange of views among their members and to facilitate the dissemination of research. This is, perhaps, to state the obvious, yet in point of fact the timeworn barriers of bias, parochialism, and intellectual inertia continue to constitute imposing obstacles to critical inquiry and scholarly dialogue. The historical profession is no exception, having on occasion manifested a disturbing lack of agility in surmounting these barriers.

The present volume is offered in the spirit of a partial palliative to such ills. It seeks, within the confines of a well-delimited subfield, to make known the labors of a group of professional historians who for reasons of language and ideology have remained largely isolated from the mainstream of non-Marxist scholarship. Specifically, this volume endeavors to familiarize Western historians of Latin America with the recent writings and research of Latin American specialists in the USSR.

The task is problematic, for despite the lack of any tradition of scholarship in this field, Soviet historians have produced a varied and already sizable body of scholarly literature. In preparing the present volume, I have attempted to provide an overview of this literature. To this end, it was deemed desirable to compile a collection of translations which would (1) reflect the development and priorities of Soviet historiography, (2) include original contributions to the literature, (3) offer examples of work by leading Soviet specialists in this field, and (4) span the main periods of Latin American history. As a result, materials which on the basis of other criteria might well have been selected for translation have here been omitted. Similarly, articles not necessarily representative of a given scholar's work have been included to comply with the stated objectives. An annotated bibliography has been appended to offset, in part, limitations imposed by the selection process.

It should be noted here that publication of this volume has been unavoidably delayed by the need to negotiate new press arrangements for the CLAH publications series. In the two years that have elapsed since the manuscript was first approved for inclusion in the series, numerous works on the history of Latin America have appeared in the Soviet Union. Accordingly, an effort has been made to include a few of these most recent titles in the annotated bibliography.

It has been my intention to provide those unfamiliar with Soviet scholarship some basis for forming their own judgements as to the merits of Soviet writing and research in the field of Latin American history. For this reason, I have refrained from all but the most general evaluations of Soviet historiography, preferring instead to leave such appraisals to the reader. In compiling this volume, however, I have been guided by the view that "attempts to indict all Soviet historical scholarship on the basis of the erroneous views of individual Soviet historians are untenable," for in the words of one Russian scholar, "Soviet authors have and continue to enrich creatively not only Soviet but world historical scholarship."* This holds as well for the scholarly literature on the history of Latin America.

Recognition of the need for expanded scholarly exchange among historians of differing ideological persuasions is reflected in the essentially collaborative nature of this volume. From the initial discussions in Moscow and Leningrad several years ago to the preparation of the final manuscript, there has been continuing contribution to the project by scholars from various countries. Appropriately, much of this has come from Soviet and American colleagues, who at various stages have offered valuable counsel and advice.

In the course of the project, there have been differences of opinion concerning content. Soviet colleagues, for example, felt strongly that the volume should contain not more than one contribution from any single author, so as to include writings by as many specialists as possible. In principle, I agreed with this view, although in three instances I chose to make exceptions, because of the special interest of specific materials. Both Soviet and American colleagues objected to some points of interpretation in the Introduction. There were also differences of opinion on matters of organization. Invariably, these views were given serious consideration, and wherever appropriate, modifications were made.

A book of this kind presents special technical problems. Stylistically, it was decided to adhere to a standard English-language format, as opposed to reproducing the somewhat different Soviet usages. This meant that footnotes frequently had to be expanded and personal names completed on first mention. Direct quotations from foreign sources were, insofar as possible, translated from or given in the original language, so as to avoid the inaccuracies of retranslating

---

*V. I. Salov, "Istoricheskii fakt i sovremennaia burzhuaznaia istoriografiia" [Historical fact and contemporary bourgeois historiography], *NNI*, no. 6 (November–December 1973), 55.

Russian translations. In the case of archival and other source materials unavailable to me this was, of course, not practicable.

Explanatory notes have not been rigorously systematized, although every effort has been made to anticipate and clarify confusing references in the translated materials. In a few instances, I have drawn on my own researches to expand points raised by the Soviet authors. These notes have been asterisked. Editorial changes within the translated texts, in turn, appear in brackets.

In citing Russian-language titles, I have employed a modified Library of Congress system of transliteration (see below). Titles have been translated only where deemed of interest to the Western reader. References to periodical titles have been abbreviated for reasons of space. The corresponding symbols are found below in the list of terms and abbreviations.

Preparation of this volume has entailed the professional and material assistance of numerous individuals and organizations. I must express very special gratitude to Professor Lewis Hanke, who from its inception supported the project with enthusiasm and personal commitment. His intervention at critical junctures proved decisive in seeing the volume to completion. I am similarly indebted to Dr. M. S. Al'perovich of the Institute of Universal History of the USSR Academy of Sciences, who, giving generously of his time, contributed invaluable advice and criticism, as well as an original essay prepared specially for this volume.

For financial support, I am indebted to the Graduate School of the University of Wisconsin—Milwaukee, the International Research and Exchanges Board (IREX), and the National Endowment for the Humanities (NEH). A UWM graduate faculty summer research grant in 1972 allowed me to consult with Soviet colleagues and to carry out preliminary bibliographic research in the USSR. A NEH grant the following year freed me from teaching responsibilities in order to prepare the manuscript, while a supplementary travel grant from IREX afforded me the opportunity to consult again with Soviet colleagues in the spring of 1973 and to complete the requisite review of the scholarly literature. In this connection, I should also like to express my appreciation to the UWM Department of History for facilitating my leave of absence during the first eight months of 1973.

Individual acknowledgements exceed the editor's capacity for comprehensive recall. Among those deserving special recognition are several contributors to the present volume: B. N. Komissarov, N. M. Lavrov, L. A. Shur, L. Yu. Slëzkin, and A. M. Zorina. Directly and indirectly, other Soviet colleagues, too, assisted the editor in his work, among them N. N. Bolkhovitinov, I. R. Grigulevich, and E. E. Litavrina. I am likewise obliged to J. V. Polišenský, Director of Charles University's Ibero-American Studies Center (Prague), and to Tadeusz Lepkowski, of the Institute of History of the Polish Academy of Sciences (Warsaw), for their helpful and constructive suggestions. Magnus Mörner, Director of the Institute of Latin American Studies, in Stockholm, also offered perceptive criticisms which were of value in preparing the final manuscript.

Colleagues at various universities in the United States contributed their time and professional experience to the project. I am particularly indebted to Benjamin Keen (Northern Illinois University), John J. Johnson (Stanford University), Friedrich Katz (University of Chicago), and the late John L. Phelan (University of Wisconsin—Madison), each of whom offered insightful counsel and advice. An expression of gratitude is also due several of my immediate colleagues at UWM, who at different stages of the project gave me the benefit of their professional talents. Here, I am in the special debt of Philip Shashko, James A. Brundage, David Healy, John F. McGovern, Ronald J. Ross, Roland N. Stromberg, and Walter B. Weare.

Competent technical assistance is an essential component of scholarly publication. I was especially fortunate in having the collaboration of Nucia Lodge, who in her capacity as a Russian-language consultant reviewed the translations included below. Equally deserving of credit are Mary Ann Bischel and Brigitte Taylor, whose combined efforts put this unusually complicated manuscript in final form.

Finally, I am indebted to Diana Bartley, whose patience and unstinting support saw this volume to fruition.

Russell H. Bartley

Milwaukee, Wisconsin
March 1974

TRANSLITERATION TABLE

THE DIFFICULTY of citing Russian-language works in their original Cyrillic form has made transliteration a standard practice of scholars writing in English. With minor modifications, the Library of Congress system for the natural and social sciences has been used in this volume.* The names of Soviet authors and editors have been transliterated accordingly; foreign scholars whose works have been published in the USSR appear in their original form. Capitalization in Russian-language titles follows current Soviet usage.

А а	A a	Р р	R r
Б б	B b	С с	S s
В в	V v	Т т	T t
Г г	G g	У у	U u
Д д	D d	Ф ф	F f
Е е	E e	Х х	Kh kh
Ё ё	Ё ё	Ц ц	Ts ts
Ж ж	Zh zh	Ч ч	Ch ch
З з	Z z	Ш ш	Sh sh
И и	I i	Щ щ	Shch shch
Й й	I i	— ъ —	"
К к	K k	— ы —	y
Л л	L l	— и —	'
М м	M m	Э э	E e
Н н	N n	Ю ю	Yu iu
О о	O o	Я я	Ya ia
П п	P p		

*See J. Thomas Shaw, *The Transliteration of Modern Russian for English-Language Publications* (Madison, Milwaukee, and London: The University of Wisconsin Press, 1967).

TERMS AND ABBREVIATIONS

AA	*American Anthropologist*
AAAPSS	*Annals of the American Academy of Political and Social Science*
AESC	*Annales: Économies, sociétés, civilisations*
AH	*Anuario de historia* (México)
AHR	*The American Historical Review*
AINAH	*Anales del Instituto nacional de antropología e historia* (México)
APSR	*American Political Science Review*
SEG	*Boletín de la Sociedad económica de Guatemala*
BZh	*Botanicheskii zhurnal*
CA	*Current Anthropology*
CAA	*Contributions to American Archeology*
CAAH	*Contribution to American Anthropology and History* (Carnegie Institution, Washington, D.C.)
CH	*Current History*
CHQ	*California Historical Quarterly*
delo (pl. dela)	record group
DP	*Departament politsii* (Department of Police)
d-vo	*deloproizvodstvo* (record group: official correspondence)
EHR	*English Historical Review*
FA	*Foreign Affairs*
fond	archival collection
GM	*The Geographical Magazine*
GR	*The Geographical Review*
HAHR	*The Hispanic American Historical Review*
HLAS	*Handbook of Latin American Studies*

HM	*Historia Mexicana*
HMAI	*Handbook of Middle American Indians*
HT	*History and Theory*
IA	*Istoricheskii arkhiv*
IAK	International Amerikanisten-Kongress
IAN	*Izvestiia Akademii nauk SSSR*
IMO	*Institut mezhdunarodnykh otnoshenii*
Ist. SSSR	*Istoriia SSSR*
IVGO	*Izvestiia Vsesoiuznogo geograficheskogo obshchestva*
JIAS	*Journal of Inter-American Studies*
JLAS	*Journal of Latin American Studies*
JMH	*Journal of Modern History*
JPE	*Journal of Political Economy*
karton	carton, box
LA	*Latinskaia Amerika*
LARR	*Latin American Research Review*
leg.	*legajo*
MS	*Morskoi sbornik*
MSQ	*Maya Society Quarterly*
Mzh	*Mezhdunarodnaia zhizn'*
NB LGU	*Nauchnyi biulleten' Leningradskogo gosudarstvennogo universiteta*
NGM	*The National Geographic Magazine*
NNI	*Novaia i noveishaia istoriia*
NT	*New Times* (Moscow)
NTNGPI	*Nauchnye Trudy Novosibirskogo gosudarstvennogo pedagogicheskogo instituta*
NWA	*New World Antiquity*
Nzh	*Nauka i zhizn'*
opis'	inventory list
PAPS	*Proceedings of the American Philosophical Society*
PMS	*Problemy mira i sotsializma*
razriad	category, grouping
RH	*Revista de Historia* (Buenos Aires)
RIB	*Revista Interamericana de Bibliografía*
RN	*Rasy i narody*
SA	*Scientific American*
SE	*Sovetskaia etnografiia*
SMAE	*Sbornik Muzeia antropologii i entografii*
SS	*Soviet Studies*
SShA	*SShA: Ekonomika, politika, ideologiia*
SSU	*Studies on the Soviet Union*

stol	department, section
SV	*Srednye veka*
TAPS	*Transactions of the American Philosophical Society*
Trudy	*Trudy arkhiva Akademii nauk SSSR*
UZIGPI	*Uchënye zapiski Ivanovskogo gosudarstvennogo pedagogicheskogo instituta*
UZKGPI	*Uchënye zapiski Kalininskogo gosudarstvennogo pedagogicheskogo instituta*
UZNNI	*Uchënye zapiski po novoi i noveishei istorii*
UZYGPI	*Uchënye zapiski Yaroslavskogo gosudarstvennogo pedagogicheskogo instituta*
VAN	*Vestnik Akademii nauk SSSR*
VG	*Voprosy geografii*
VIMK	*Vestnik istorii mirovoi kul'tury*
VLU	*Vestnik Leningradskogo gosudarstvennogo universiteta*
VMU	*Vestnik Moskovskogo gosudarstvennogo universiteta*
Vop. iazyk.	*Voprosy iazykoznaniia*
Vop. Ist.	*Voprosy istorii*
Vop. Ist. KPSS	*Voprosy istorii KPSS*
VS	*Vokrug sveta*
vyp.	vypusk (issue)
YULG	*The Yale University Library Gazette*
ZR	*Za rubezhom*

A dagger (†) has been used throughout the volume to identify works that are cited in full in the bibliography.

SOVIET HISTORIANS ON LATIN AMERICA:
Recent Scholarly Publications

1 INTRODUCTION

TWENTY YEARS ago, few specialists in the United States would have thought to look to the Soviet Union for serious scholarship in Latin American history. A great land mass and vast expanses of ocean lay between America and Europe's eastern periphery, rendering minimal early historical ties between the two distant regions. With the advent of the Soviet state and resultant articulation of the international communist movement, however, geography ceased to be an obstacle of consequence, as modern means of communication swiftly carried the revolutionary ideology of October to the farthest reaches of the globe. Soviet assistance to Republican Spain in the 1930s fired emotions on both sides of the Atlantic, and by the eve of the Second World War, Russia had irrevocably injected itself into the consciousness and realities of the peoples of the Western Hemisphere. In intensity its presence was sudden, for many disconcerting. It was, moreover, eminently political, and thus bore little apparent relation to the disciplined study of history.

Politics and the scholarly disciplines, however, are often closely related, and it was only a matter of time before Soviet academics turned a probing eye to Latin America's historical past. In the West as well as the East, the growth of Latin American studies has been due to both political and economic factors. These, observes one Western scholar, "are likely to promote the study of contemporary Latin America in the first place. But they also tend to favor the study of Latin America's past."[1]

The development of Soviet scholarship in this field has its own, not uninteresting, history. While it is generally recognized that "during the first years of its existence, the Soviet Union had too many other pressing preoccupations to spare much thought for Latin America,"[2] there were nonetheless scholarly, literary, and journalistic antecedents in this and preceding periods which, in more recent

3

times, have come to form the bases of an established field of historiographical endeavor. Indeed, the commonly held view that "Russia had no long-standing political, economic or cultural links with the area"[3] is not exact, for Russian interest in Latin America extends back at least to the eighteenth century and might legitimately be traced to an even earlier period. Russian-language adaptations of atlases and geographical treatises by Mercator, DeWitt, and other West European cartographers, for example, provided considerable descriptive information about Latin America to the enlightened of seventeenth-century Muscovy.[4] Publications of this nature received special attention during the reign of Peter the Great (1695–1725), whose own personal quest for geographical knowledge provided the impulse for the first Russian explorations of the New World.

In the course of the eighteenth century, Russian rulers more than once contemplated colonial ventures in Latin America, dissuaded only by more pressing involvements closer to home.[5] Rising interest in the Western Hemisphere, however, became increasingly apparent in Russian writings of the day. By mid-century, New World themes had begun to inspire such literary luminaries as M. V. Lomonosov (1711–65) and A. P. Sumarokov (1718–77), both of whom decried in verse the abandon with which Spain had plundered the New World. Lomonosov even extolled those "Russian Columbuses" who, scorning fate and struggling through floes of ice, would one day extend Russian power to America.[6] As the century progressed, more and more information about the New World circulated in the form of travel accounts and other descriptive works translated into Russian from French and German originals.[7] To these were added the accounts of Fëdor Karzhavin and Vasilii Baranshchikov, two Russian travelers who visited the West Indies in the 1780s and the first tsarist subjects to record travels in Latin America.[8]

As Russian New World interests extended into areas of trade and diplomacy in the late eighteenth and early nineteenth centuries, a corresponding interest was shown in the history and general socio-economic development of colonial Latin America. This at once produced and was reflected in numerous translations of scholarly works by foreign authors on the Iberian colonies. In 1767, for example, a two-volume translation of Antonio de Solís y Rivadeneyra's *Historia de la conquista de México* (Madrid, 1684) appeared in St. Petersburg.[9] William Robertson's *History of America* (London, 1777) was published in an abbreviated, one-volume translation in 1784.[10] On the eve of Latin American independence, a translation of Raynal's *Histoire philosophique et politique des établissements et du commerce des européens dans les deux Indes* (Amsterdam, 1770) was prepared and published by order of the tsarist government.[11] At about this same time, Alexander von Humboldt's monumental *Voyage aux régions équinoxiales du Nouveau Continent* (Paris, 1807–34) began to appear, attracting the attention of Tsar Alexander I, who in 1814 ordered a number of copies for his own personal use.[12] As early as 1809, the respected Muscovite monthly *Vestnik*

Evropy drew its readership's attention to Humboldt's fascinating geographical, political, and statistical notices on New Spain and the other Spanish possessions in America.[13] These notices underlay discussion of Latin American colonial matters in the Russian periodical press of the early nineteenth century, and by the mid-1830s had inspired the publication of an abbreviated, two-volume Russian translation of Humboldt's work.[14]

Following the troubled Napoleonic years, during which time the tsarist court became directly involved in the affairs of Latin America,[15] Russian interest in the former Iberian colonies continued at moderately increasing levels through the turn of the century. Although Russian publications on the New World never approached in scope or quantity works printed in the major countries of Western Europe, Russian journals and publishing houses did produce a steady, if modest, stream of titles dealing with the Hispanic world. Russian travel literature on Latin America appeared with growing frequency, while the periodical press of Moscow and St. Petersburg continued to carry articles on the newly independent republics of the Western Hemisphere. Interest in the history of Latin America was revealed in translations of Washington Irving's *The History of the Life and Voyages of Christopher Columbus* (1828),[16] William H. Prescott's *History of the Conquest of Mexico* (1843) and *History of the Conquest of Peru* (1847),[17] and Alfred Deberle's *Histoire de l'Amérique du Sud depuis la conquête jusqu'à nos jours* (1876).[18] The establishment of formal state relations with Brazil in 1828 stimulated occasional writings of a scholarly nature by Russian diplomats who had resided and traveled in South America. Worthy of special note are a lengthy politico-economic study of Brazil, Argentina, and Uruguay by Fëdor Smirnov, secretary of the Russian legation in Rio de Janeiro during the 1860s,[19] and a four-volume work on South America by A. S. Ionin, tsarist ambassador to Brazil in the 1880s.[20]

Formalization of diplomatic relations with Argentina in 1885, Uruguay in 1887, and Mexico in 1890 further stimulated Russian interest in Latin America. In addition to descriptions of New World realities, observes a Soviet specialist, accounts published at the turn of the century by Russian scholars, writers, and travelers who visited Latin America frequently contained information of an historical nature.[21] At the same time, Russian emigration to South America prompted studies on Brazil and Argentina, the principal recipients of this emigration,[22] while the researches of Russian scientists in various regions of the Western Hemisphere produced significant scholarship on such diverse subjects as the Mayan ruins of Yucatán, the climate in Central and South America, the geography and natural history of Argentina, customs and society in the River Plate, and the flora of Tierra del Fuego.[23]

In a related area, Russia also produced some limited historical scholarship on the Iberian Peninsula. Here, two names warrant special note: A. S. Trachevskii, who in 1872 published a volume on late eithteenth- and early nineteenth-century Spanish history;[24] and V. K. Piskorskii, who, in addition to a general survey of Spanish and Portugese history, wrote two monographic studies on the history of medieval Castile and Catalonia.[25] A second, revised edition of Piskorskii's general history of the Iberian Peninsula included two appended essays of note, one each on the sociopolitical evolution of nineteenth-century Spain and Portugal.[26] Other titles of varying scholarly significance appeared, too, in this period.[27] Although far from constituting an historical school, this fragile thread of scholarship nonetheless continued unbroken into the Soviet period, where it has served to complement the rapidly expanding field of Latin American history.[28]

The primary foundations on which serious historical investigation of Latin America's past might one day rest were thus laid before the advent of the Soviet state. While geography continued to militate against broad Russian involvement in the New World and, therefore, to discourage widespread popular interest in the region, published writings on Latin America reached the cultural centers of European Russia as they did those of Western Europe and the United States. Although there were no libraries of Spanish and Portuguese first editions such as might be found in Philadelphia, Boston, London, or Paris, Russian scholars with a knowledge of the major European languages did have access to much of the relevant literature.[29] And while there were no Russian Bancrofts, Prescotts, or Ticknors to inspire scholarly interest in Hispanic history and civilization, figures like Langsdorff, Ionin, and Piskorskii made analogous contributions to the bibliographic and documentary bases of future Soviet scholarship in this field.[30] By the early twentieth century, moreover, Russian holdings of Latin American materials were further augmented through publications exchanges with scholarly institutions in the New World. The Biblioteca Nacional, in Rio de Janeiro, for example, maintained exchange arrangements with Moscow University and with the public libraries of Odessa and St. Petersburg.[31]

The success of the October Revolution altered profoundly the future direction of historical scholarship in Russia. For the first time in history, the discipline of history became a central concern of the state. This development transcended mere censorship, to embrace the very foundations of Soviet society. Marxism, observed Lenin, "provides men with an integral world conception. . . . [It] has provided mankind, and especially the working class, with powerful instruments of knowledge."[32] "To know is to foresee," added M. N. Pokrovskii, "and to foresee is to be, or be able to be, in control. Thus, knowledge of the past gives us control over the future."[33] In the words of a contemporary non-Marxist scholar, "To be a Marxist . . . is to look at everything historically, to see the process of change in the depth of time, and to locate the tracks (*Gesetzmässigkeiten*, or laws . . .) of the past which project into the present and the future and determine the course of man's social evolution."[34] In Soviet perspective, history was midwife to the Revolution, steward and protector of the new social order. It demanded special deference and was the proper occupation only of those duly initiated in the finer points of dialectical and historical materialism. Consequently, the craft of history was removed from the hands of the independent practitioner.[35]

The difficult years immediately after 1917 saw a brief stand-off between scholars of Marxist and non-Marxist persuasions. Russian historical scholarship was deeply affected by the Revolution and the civil war that followed, but, in the words of one specialist, "the disruption caused by these events was more a result of the chaotic conditions of life than of the policies of the Soviet government."[36] Numerous non-Marxist historians remained in Russia following the Revolution, where they continued to write and teach, and even occupied important positions in the historical profession. While from the outset steps were taken to promote and institutionalize Marxist scholarship, over a decade passed before the Communist Party of the Soviet Union (CPSU) initiated measures to curb and ultimately eliminate non-Marxist historians. During this period, the "traditional" historians not only were tolerated "but in fact remained the principal source of scholarship except in those fields connected with the war and revolution in which the Communist Party was particularly interested."[37]

Soviet scholarship on Latin America in this period produced little of lasting value.[38] With the tightening of Party controls on the profession after 1928, however, this branch of historical inquiry began to develop perceptibly. This is partially explained by the central place which colonial and former colonial areas occupied in the Marxist-Leninist view of modern history. Lenin himself had cited the Latin American republics as examples of "dependent countries which, politically, are formally independent, but in fact, are enmeshed in the net of financial and diplomatic dependence" characteristic of contemporary times.[39] Latin America formed part of the larger picture of capitalist imperialism; its relationship to the leading exporters of finance capital was not entirely dissimilar to that of pre-Revolutionary Russia and its historical destiny was therefore identified with that of the new Soviet state.[40]

Translation was a significant component of the development of Latin American studies in the Soviet Union. If the rudimentary bibliographic foundations of scholarship in Hispanic history and civilization had been laid in the pre-Soviet period, an effort was now made to strengthen and broaden those foundations, particularly in the area of literature. Russian translations of prominent Latin American writers appeared with increasing frequency, including in some cases multiple editions. The verse of Darío, Martí, Guillén, Vallejo, Neruda, Mistral, Gutiérrez Nájera, and other lesser poets was also rendered into Russian. By the mid-1960s, Soviet readers had ready access to the prose of Fernández de Lizardi, Machado de Assis, Azuela, Rivera, Güiraldes, Gallegos, Alegría, Asturias, Amado, and others.[41] Works of an intrinsic historical interest, too, were translated, including Bernal Díaz del Castillo's *Historia verdadera de la conquista de la Nueva España,* Diego de Landa's *Relación de las cosas de Yucatán,* Bartolomé de las Casas' *Historia de las Indias,* and three volumes of Humboldt's *Voyage aux régions équinoxiales du Nouveau Continent.*[42]

With the awakened interest in Hispanic history and civilization, translations of interpretive works by foreign historians soon began to appear. In the immediate postwar period, for example, translations were published of Henry Bamford Parkes' *A History of Mexico* (1938) and Caio Prado Júnior's *Historia económica do Brasil* (1945).[43] Simultaneously, a slightly abbreviated version of Preston James' geography of Latin America appeared in Russian,[44] followed in 1951 by a two-volume translation of Altamira's *Historia de España y de la civilización española* (1900–1911).[45] William Z. Foster's *Outline Political History of the Americas* (1951) was translated two years later, and in 1960 a Russian-language version appeared of Alfred B. Thomas' general survey, *Latin America: A History* (1956).[46] These works were succeeded by translations of Rocha Pombo's *História do Brasil* (1905), Mariátegui's *Siete ensayos de interpretación de la realidad peruana* (1928), Philip Foner's *A History of Cuba and Its Relations with the United States* (1962–63), and Samuel Eliot Morison's *Admiral of the Ocean Sea: A Life of Christopher Columbus* (1942).[47]

The initial training of Soviet specialists in the field of Latin American history transpired in conditions of adversity and tension deriving from the politically unsettled conditions which obtained in the USSR during the first decades of its existence. The early elimination of traditional departments of history in Soviet universities, together with the creation of several institutional entities designed to prepare Marxist historians and promote Marxist historical scholarship, reflected the highly politicized circumstances in which Russian historians were subsequently to find themselves.[48] Under the influence of M. N. Pokrovskii (1868–1932), undisputed custodian of Soviet historiography in the twenties and early thirties, historical analysis turned on broad sociological formulations whereby the past was enlisted to serve the ends of present-day politics. History, in Pokrovskii's words, was "politics retrojected into the past."[49] Appropriately, it was Pokrovskii who in the period 1928–32 led the awaited offensive against the remaining "bourgeois" historians, more than a hundred of whom were arrested and sent into exile.[50]

This first academic purge ended in 1932, coinciding with the death of Pokrovskii. Ironically, it soon gave way to a purge of Pokrovskii's own disciples and the historical school which they represented. The sociological schematicism attributed to Pokrovskii was roundly scored for having presented historical facts "from the point of view of the present day, and not from the point of view of the conditions under which the historical events took place."[51] New emphasis was placed on the facts, personalities, and chronology of history, all of which seemed to suggest a closer approximation to scientific scholarship. In reality, this was only a prelude to a far more sinister manipulation of science by the heavy hand of Stalin. Indeed, history quickly degenerated into a crude cudgel of personal power which rendered the professional historian senseless, gravely affecting his ability to function in a scholarly capacity.

The first Soviet writings on topics of Latin American history appeared in the late twenties and early thirties. Characteristically, they exhibited the schematicism and sociologism of the Pokrovskii school and thus failed to achieve a place of permanent recognition in Soviet historiography.[52] The mid-thirties saw an initial turn toward "the concrete, chronological study of the salient events and facts of the history of the Latin American countries."[53] As in all branches of Soviet historiography, however, this trend was severely compromised by the political circumstances of the moment, and such contributions to scholarship as were made reflected a serious lack of direction. The gravity of the situation was placed in dramatic relief by the loss of two early students of Latin America's past, S. S. Pestkovskii (first Soviet ambassador to Mexico) and G. B. Skalov, both victims of the Stalinist purges.[54]

Despite these adversities, several Soviet scholars of note did emerge in the 1930s. Of particular significance for the development of Soviet scholarship in the field of Latin American history were Lev Israilevich Zubok (1894–1967), Aleksei Vladimirovich Efimov (1896–1971), Aleksandr Andreevich Guber (1902–71), and Vladimir Mikhailovich Miroshevskii (1900–1942). Zubok specialized in the history of the American labor movement, an interest which stemmed from his own participation in the movement while a resident of the United States; he also made an important contribution to the historiography of U.S. expansionism in the Caribbean basin.[55] Efimov, too, had a great interest in American history which ranged from problems of geographic discovery to the genesis of New World capitalism to methodological questions and the historiography of American history.[56] Guber specialized in the history of southeast Asia (Vietnam) and the Pacific basin (Indonesia and the Philippines), subsequently turning his attention to the broader problem of colonial and dependent countries, which led him also to write and teach in the area of Latin American history.[57] Following the Second World War, these three scholars trained a generation of specialists who were to establish Latin American history as an autonomous branch of Soviet historical scholarship.[58]

The leading pioneer in this field was V. M. Miroshevskii, who throughout his abbreviated career as a professional historian focused on the countries of Latin America. Active as a young man in the Bolshevik movement and the Ukrainian underground, Miroshevskii continued to serve the Party in various capacities until his death at the front in the summer of 1942. During the 1920s he gained experience as the editor (1922–25) of *Internatsional molodëzhi* (Moscow), official organ of the Communist Youth International, and the assistant editor (1925–27) of the provincial paper *Ural'skii rabochii* (Sverdlovsk). While occupied in this latter capacity, he also lectured on the history of the international labor movement at the Uralo-Siberian Communist University, in Sverdlovsk. Subsequently, he served as chairman of the department of international labor history at the Chinese Workers University, in Moscow, and in 1929 himself embarked on a course of advanced study in the historical division of the Institute of Red Professors, where he specialized in the history of Latin America.[59]

Amidst the many tribulations of the 1930s, from which he himself did not emerge unscathed, Miroshevskii managed to acquire a remarkable grounding in his field of interest. A knowledge of the major European languages facilitated his access to the relevant literature. As his studies progressed, Miroshevskii's interest gravitated toward the independence movement, as well as toward the cultural history of Latin America. In 1939, he offered a course in Latin American history at Moscow State University. That same year, he successfully defended a candidate's thesis on the antecedents to Spanish American independence, and as a result was admitted to doctoral candidacy in the then Institute of History of the USSR Academy of Sciences. In the eighteen months before the Second World War, he worked on his dissertation, which examined the role of the great powers in the emancipation of Spanish America.[60]

While fate denied Miroshevskii the opportunity to pursue his specialty to full fruition, he nonetheless left an indelible mark on this branch of Soviet historiography. "More than one generation of Soviet historians," writes M. S. Al'perovich, "has benefitted from his brilliant lectures and writings."[61] "His works marked the beginning of the systematic study of Latin America in the USSR," adds B. N. Komissarov.[62] Salient among these works was a volume published posthumously under the title *Liberation Movements in Spain's American Colonies from Their Conquest to the War of Independence (1492–1810).*† This work, in the opinion of a third Soviet specialist, represented "the best of Soviet historical scholarship in the Latin American area." Although nearly twenty years had passed since it first appeared, he affirmed that "even today we cannot but pay a tribute of high esteem to V. M. Miroshevskii, a pioneer of Soviet scholarly historiography of the Latin American countries...."[63]

Appearing in 1946, Miroshevskii's modest volume was the first "purely historical monograph by a Soviet Latin Americanist, written on a high scholarly and professional plane utilizing all available sources, including archival documents...."[64] This work was followed in 1948 by the posthumous publication of G. G. Manizer's volume on the Langsdorff expedition to Brazil† and by Zubok's lengthy study of U.S. imperialism in Middle America and the West Indies.† Other volumes appeared, too, although generally of an inferior quality. In addition, a limited number of articles were published, principally in the leading Soviet historical journal of the period, *Voprosy istorii.*

Thematically, most of these writings were narrow, focusing primarily on the imperialistic policies of the United States, secondarily on labor and peasant movements in Latin America. The "internal civil history" of the Latin American

† will be used throughout the volume to identify works cited in full in the bibliography.

countries was hardly studied at all; indeed, a majority of these countries remained outside the field of vision of Soviet researchers. Such a one-sided approach, states Al'perovich, "resulted in decisive measure from the situation created by the personality cult of Stalin, as well as from a lack of trained specialists and the limited number of available source materials."[65]

These obstacles notwithstanding, it was in the final years of the Stalin period that some of the most talented and influential scholars currently writing on problems of Latin American history in the Soviet Union completed their professional training.[66] In 1947, for example, N. M. Lavrov, present head of the Latin American sector of the Institute of Universal History of the USSR Academy of Sciences, defended a candidate's thesis on rural politics in the Mexican Revolution. That same year, A. M. Zorina defended a thesis on U.S. interests in Panama in the nineteenth century, and E. V. Ananova completed candidate's work on U.S.-Mexican relations during the presidency of Woodrow Wilson.[67]

In 1948, S. A. Gonionskii, until his recent death head of the division of American peoples of the Academy's Institute of Ethnography, defended a candidate's thesis on the U.S. role in the creation of the Republic of Panama.[68] Also that year, G. I. Ivanov, one of very few Soviet scholars subsequently to specialize in the colonial history of Latin America, completed a thesis on the Mexican *Reforma*.[69] Two theses were defended in 1949, one by B.T. Rudenko on American responses to the Mexican Revolution up to 1913, the second by M. S. Al'perovich on the same topic for the years 1913–17.[70] Between 1950 and 1954, candidates' theses were completed by E. L. Nitoburg on U.S. Cuban policy in the 1930s, A. I. Shtrakhov on Peronism, N. R. Matveeva on the Paraguayan War, L. Yu. Slëzkin on U.S. expansionism in South America in the depression years, V. I. Ermolaev on Argentine labor politics during the Second World War, and A. N. Glinkin on U.S. imperialist expansion in Brazil in the immediate postwar period.[71]

The death of Stalin, and more particularly the decision ratified by the 20th Congress of the CPSU in February 1956 to de-Stalinize Soviet life, provided a positive stimulus to the study of Latin American history in the USSR and to Soviet historical scholarship in general. Party leaders roundly scored the intellectual timidity of the Stalin era as "a cult of the individual alien to Marxism-Leninism" and exhorted Soviet scholars to become creative Marxist-Leninists in their approaches to the study of human history.[72] Dogmatism and uncritical thinking were to be expurgated from scholarship, and history was to be accorded the "profound, many-sided inquiry" necessary to comprehend the processes of societal evolution.[73]

Subsequent congresses of the CPSU, together with the Moscow Congress of Representatives of Workers and Communist Parties held in November 1960, provided additional guidelines for post-Stalin historical scholarship. The profession, observes a Western critic, "was to make a full commitment to the fight against capitalist and revisionist distortions of the historical process and to concentrate on the preparation of works dealing with communist construction, the developmental laws of the socialist system of states, the international labor movement, the crisis of capitalism and colonialism and the national liberation struggle in Asia, Africa and Latin America.''[74] As for Latin America, historians were now to concern themselves with the origins of contemporary socioeconomic turmoil, placing particular emphasis on the independence movement of the early nineteenth century. Imperialism, neocolonialism, and the role of foreign capital, too, constituted themes of central importance, as did the rise of organized labor, the spread of Marxist ideas, and the impact on Latin America of the Russian October Revolution.[75]

The ground was thus prepared for the striking development achieved in Soviet Latin American studies during the 1960s. It is perhaps well to observe in passing that this development was not in itself an outgrowth of the Cuban Revolution, although that important event clearly provided added impetus. As in the United States, where the spectacular increase in funding of Latin American research is frequently attributed to the Cuban experience, initial decisions providing augmented resources to area specialists were taken before analysts had any real appreciation of the historical significance of Batista's fall from power. In both cases, these decisions reflected long-term national imperatives which acquired new urgency with the emergence of a self-proclaimed socialist state in the Western Hemisphere.[76]

The initial infusion of specialists into the field in the early 1950s soon produced visible results. If in the late forties Soviet scholars were publishing an average of three works a year on Latin American history (including articles), by 1966 this figure exceeded eighty, including numerous monographs and collaborative works of book length.[77] At the same time, efforts were redoubled to train additional specialists. Of 219 persons listed in a 1971 directory of Soviet Latin Americanists, 59 held candidates' degrees in history, 16 were doctors of historical sciences.[78]

As new specialists completed their training, they occupied teaching and research positions not only in Moscow and Leningrad, the traditional centers of Russian culture and scholarship, but also in outlying cities like Ivanovo, Kalinin, and Kazan, in the Russian Soviet Federated Socialist Republic; Minsk, in White Russia; Kiev and Lvov, in the Ukraine; and Kishinëv, in Moldavia.[79] Many, too, were and continue to be employed in related but nonacademic positions.

The principal center of historical research on Latin America was the section of the modern and contemporary history of the countries of America, created in 1953 within the then Institute of History of the USSR Academy of Sciences, in Moscow. This section was subsequently reorganized into two separate units, one focusing on the United States and Canada, the other on Latin America.[80] Historical scholarship relating to Latin America was carried on, too, in the Moscow and

Leningrad branches of the Academy's Institute of Ethnography, as well as at various other institutions of higher learning.[81] In 1961, the growing significance attached to the countries of the Western Hemisphere led to the creation of an area institute within the Academy of Sciences to conduct research on problems of contemporary Latin America. This new institution was interdisciplinary in nature and provided additional stimulus to all aspects of Latin American studies in the USSR, including history.[82]

Rising institutional support for the study of Latin American history was accompanied by a parallel increase in opportunities for scholarly publication. While major Soviet publishing houses, including the Academy's own prestigious press, accepted with growing frequency historical manuscripts relating to Latin America, the same trend extended to the professional journals. In the early and mid-fifties, *Voprosy istorii* [Problems of history], a monthly journal published jointly by the USSR Academy of Sciences and the Soviet Ministry of Higher and Specialized Secondary Education, dedicated increasing space to Latin American topics. In 1957, the Academy's Institute of History began publishing *Novaia i noveishaia istoriia* [Modern and contemporary history], a bimonthly review which has since become the single most important periodical vehicle of Soviet historical scholarship on Latin America. From 1957 to 1961, the Academy published a second bimonthly review called *Vestnik istorii mirovoi kul'tury* [Bulletin of world cultural history]; similar in format to *Cahiers d' histoire mondiale* and in like fashion established to complement the work of UNESCO's International Commission for a History of the Scientific and Cultural Development of Mankind, it, too, accepted articles dealing with Latin American history. Soviet specialists in the field also found increasing access to the *Vestniki* [Bulletins] of Moscow and Leningrad State Universities, of the Academy's Institute of Ethnography, and of the All-Union Geographical Society, as well as to the *Uchënye zapiski* [Scholarly notes] of the state pedagogical institutes. And in 1969, the Academy's Latin American Institute initiated publication of a bimonthly review entitled *Latinskaia Amerika;* multidisciplinary in scope, this journal, too, opened its pages to Soviet specialists in Latin American history.[83]

Once the decisions were made to promote the study of Latin American history, the field developed with a clear internal logic. The first order of business was not to fill lacunae in research areas delineated by Western scholarship, but rather to begin elaborating an as yet nonexistent Marxist historiography of Latin America. This first of all entailed the writing of broad interpretive studies, including textbooks and related materials for reference and classroom use.[84] By the mid-1960s, almost all Soviet textbooks on world history contained chapters on Latin America, whereas ten years earlier the only such material extant were the chapters which Miroshevskii had contributed to the Academy's *Modern History of the Colonial and Dependent Countries.*[85] The first Soviet textbook devoted exclusively to Latin American history appeared in 1963 under the title *The History of the Latin American Countries in Recent Times.*[86] This volume has since been supplemented with historiographical surveys and other textbooks,[87] as well as numerous works of a more scholarly nature. Worthy of note in this latter category are a collection of articles on the Amerindian cultures, a general history of the discovery and exploration of Central and South America, and survey histories of Argentina, Brazil, Chile, Cuba, and Mexico.[88]

While laying the requisite bibliographic foundations of their newly established field, Soviet Latin Americanists also began to treat preferential themes of Marxist historical analysis: colonialism, imperialism, movements of national liberation, the formation of nation-states in conditions of developing capitalism, labor history, class and ideological conflict, and the international ramifications of the October Revolution. Collaborative works and monographs have been written on various aspects of pre-Columbian history, discovery, conquest and colonial administration, independence, national consolidation, the Catholic Church, the Mexican Revolution, imperialism, inter-American relations, and diverse problems in the modern history of Brazil, Chile, Colombia, Cuba, Paraguay, Puerto Rico, and Venezuela. As reflected in the annotated bibliography at the end of this volume, scholarly articles greatly expand the range of Soviet writings on Latin America to include standard topics of interest to Western historians, as well as those more directly associated with the central concerns of the Marxist scholar.

U.S. specialists in Latin American history first took note of Soviet contributions to the field in 1960, when *The Hispanic American Historical Review* published in its summer issue the now celebrated critical survey by I. R. Lavretskii (pen name of Iosif Romual'dovich Grigulevich), together with an introductory note by J. Gregory Oswald.[89] Based on a meager selection of sources and an excess of untested assumptions, Lavretskii presented the *HAHR* as a semi-official vehicle "to influence American public opinion in a direction useful to ruling circles of the U.S." and an instrument of "the millionaire Duke family," whose considerable financial interests extended into Mexico and Central America.[90] A survey of *HAHR* materials, Lavretskii wrote, "indicates that the official Latin Americanists of the U.S. falsify and distort the historical truth in order to benefit imperialism."[91]

Publication of the Lavretskii article sparked a heated exchange of views which itself reveals much about the nature of contemporary historiography as it relates to areas of international political concern. The Soviet Union, Oswald commented in his introductory note, seeks "to rally the un-committed areas of the world—including Latin America—to the acceptance of Soviet-style socialism. One of the means employed in this campaign is Soviet interpretation of the history of these areas." "To appreciate this purpose in Soviet historiography," he added, "one must realize that the study of history in the Soviet Union has more political than scholarly significance."[92] "Instead of responding to the essential criticism," Lavretskii replied, "Oswald makes a series of slanderous attacks on the Soviet Union and, in particular, on Soviet historical scholarship."[93]

According to Oswald, the Lavretskii article offered "deep insight into contemporary Soviet thinking on Latin American history." It suggested very strongly "that historical scholarship in the U.S.S.R. remains a branch of politics."[94] Professor Oswald, in Lavretskii's view, sought "to discredit Soviet historians." He accused them "of not being objective" and alleged that they "distort the facts to comply with Marxist-Leninist teachings." Yet nothing, Lavretskii declared, could be farther from the truth. "Soviet scholars have no need to fit anything to Marxism-Leninism, for the historical process itself confirms the strict scientific nature of Marxist-Leninist theory."[95]

Lavretskii also took issue with the notion that broadened research interests on the part of Soviet historians could somehow be equated with Soviet "intellectual and political penetration" of new areas of the world. Professor Oswald, he wrote, seemed to suggest that the study of Asia, Africa, and Latin America was a monopoly of the United States and other Western powers. As soon as historians of the Soviet Union manifest an interest in these areas, this is seen as evidence of "Soviet penetration."[96]

The subject matter of Soviet historical writings on Latin America likewise constituted an apparent obstacle to objective evaluation by Western critics. Oswald found objectionable Soviet preoccupation with "Yankee imperialism." "Yet was Yankee imperialism simply a myth, invented by Soviet historians?" Lavretskii queried rhetorically. "Have there in fact not been a hundred U.S. interventions in the countries of Latin America? Was there really no U.S. occupation of Cuba, Haiti, the Dominican Republic, and Nicaragua? And the Monroe Doctrine, 'dollar diplomacy', the 'big stick'—was all this, too, an invention of Soviet Historians?" Clearly not, Lavretskii declared. U.S. policy in Latin America had long consisted in preserving the continent "not for American ideals, but for American business." And that was the essence of imperialism.[97]

Over a decade has passed since this initial exchange, and in the interim many Western scholars have taken note of the growing Soviet output on Latin American history.[98] Appraisals of that output are varied, if not always informed, but among non-Marxist scholars there prevails an ingrained skepticism as to its real scientific value. Soviet specialists, writes Stephen Clissold, have shown "flexibility, amounting at times to acrobatic ingenuity, in offering acceptable Marxist interpretations of Latin American realities."[99] Whatever they think, states Magnus Mörner, Soviet specialists in Latin American history "have to make their products impregnable from an orthodox Marxist point of view."[100] "Just as in many other aspects of publication in countries east of the Elbe," asserts a third reviewer, "there is [among Soviet Latin Americanists] an ostrich-like avoidance of reality."[101]

Such suspicions notwithstanding, non-Marxist academics have come increasingly to recognize the scholarly potential of Soviet research and writing in the field of Latin American history. "It is obvious," concludes Charles Gibson in an oft-cited observation, "that the topics of Russian historiography, even when handled with the standard Russian formulae of interpretation, are worthy of our western attention.''[102] Soviet Latin Americanists, adds Lewis Hanke, ''now participate in international conferences, keep up-to-date on publications relating to Latin America that appear outside Russia, particularly in the United States, and Soviet interest in under-developed countries of the world, including those in Latin America, has evolved during the past decade into a major undertaking.''[103] ''We may conclude,'' writes Lawrence S. Thompson, ''that there are a number of sound students of Latin America in the Soviet Union, and that there are also a few charlatans who have their counterparts in English-speaking North America and western Europe.''[104]

For the non-Marxist, a balanced appraisal of Soviet historical scholarship on Latin America remains at best a difficult proposition. The ideological gulf separating him from his Marxist counterpart is as vast as it is deep—a monumental challenge to those who would build bridges of communication and intelligent dialogue. At the risk of offending otherwise conscientious, well-intentioned colleagues, it must be said that prevailing non-Marxist views of Marxist historiography reflect remarkable ignorance. ''It is one of the peculiar ironies of history,'' in the words of Erich Fromm, ''that there are no limits to the misunderstanding and distortion of theories, even in an age when there is unlimited access to the sources; there is no more drastic example of this phenomenon than what has happened to the theory of Karl Marx in the last few decades.''[105]

It is neither the purpose nor function of this introduction to present an apology for Marxist historiography. Still less is it the editor's wish to make light of historiographical aberrations disseminated under the imprimatur of Marxist orthodoxy. What is called for is a more considered approach to this question than has generally been the case in the past, when critics have felt entitled ''to talk about Marx without having read him, or at least, without having read enough to get an idea of his very complex, intricate, and subtle system of thought.''[106] The same applies to the writings of Lenin, which have added important dimensions to the basic interpretive principles first articulated by Marx. Continuing doubts and preconceptions about Soviet historical scholarship, write two prominent Soviet historians, ''are not due, of course, to anyone's ill intentions, but are rather the result of causes having profound sociological and epistemological roots.''[107]

Any serious appraisal of Soviet historiography must of necessity begin with a review of the basic tenets and conceptions of Marxism. One must understand, for example, that while Marxist theory does propound a total world view which in turn has certain methodological implications for the Marxist historian, it in no way negates the primacy of objective historical facts, nor the time-honored principles of testing and evaluating such facts. It does, of course, say a great deal about the weighing and ordering of facts in accord with the central precepts of Marxist thought, but as an operating principle, that hardly serves to differentiate Marxist from non-Marxist scholarship.[108] Imprecise notions concerning the role and place of economic determinism in Marxist historiography must likewise be discarded, for "the acceptance of necessity, of a strict causality in social development, in no way implies that there is nothing for mankind to do but march along a predefined route, submissively obeying the ineluctable laws of history."[109] The common belief that Marx, Engels, and Lenin claimed to have "explicitly forecast man's future actions" is totally erroneous, as is the correlative notion that Soviet historians do not take into account "the sociological, psychological, or even the theological aspects of human behavior which often perplex Western historians"—this because in their view "all history is economics; all economics Marxian."[110]

Having stated these qualifications, it is possible to make certain general observations about Soviet historical scholarship on Latin America as it has developed since the Second World War. On the negative side, one must lament the rigid organizational structure which so restricts the creative impulses of Soviet historians. Without wishing to debate the merits of the Marxist approach to history, nor the issue of how best to maintain the integrity of such an all-embracing world view in the area of historical interpretation, these are proper matters for the professional historian rather than the Party theoretician. While by definition the business of the latter is not wholly unrelated to the theory and practices of historical analysis, there nonetheless remains a wide gap between general theory and the insights gained from disciplined historical research. Unfortunately, the Soviet historical profession has not yet outgrown the adversary relationship of an earlier period between the individual scholar, inevitably drawn toward topics of personal preference, and the official party/state apparatus, ubiquitous in its imposed direction of scholarly research.[111]

The work of Soviet specialists in Latin American history has been hampered further by a lack of access to unpublished archival materials abroad. Indeed, only a very few Soviet historians have had an opportunity to pursue research in Latin America; to my knowledge, none has yet worked in the archives of Spain or Portugal. This has obliged Soviet historians to rely heavily on available published sources, including the now vast body of relevant non-Marxist literature. It has also moved them to search for pertinent Latin American materials in Soviet repositories, an effort in which they have achieved some notable successes.[112] Extensive use, for example, has been made of the tsarist diplomatic archives in treating topics of nineteenth-century Latin American history; unpublished travel accounts and analogous materials of that same period have also been used to good advantage.

On the positive side of the tally, one finds significant contributions, not the least of which is the development of scholarship in a field of historical inquiry where none existed. The reality of this is evident in the following translations. Indeed, as noted elsewhere, no general bibliography in the field would now be complete without reference to a growing number of Soviet works.[113]

Related to this is the systematic elaboration of a Marxist approach to the central problems of Latin American history, an approach which questions and challenges non-Marxist historical scholarship and in so doing furthers the general quest for objective historical knowledge. Soviet contributions in this broad sense of reinterpretation and scholarly polemic are numerous and span all periods of Latin American history. In addition, as suggested above, Soviet historians have produced some original archival research of merit, most notably, although not exclusively, on aspects of Russian New World interests. A subject that has not received adequate attention, despite the availability of key sources, is the history of the communist movement in Latin America and of individual Latin American communist parties.

On a rather different plane, the development of Soviet scholarship in the field of Latin American history has begun to arouse the interest of Latin Americans. As early as 1960, Juan Antonio Ortega y Medina concluded that "the Soviet contribution to [Mexican] historiography is important and of itself possesses great merit, objective as well as subjective."[114] In the intervening years, students from various Latin American countries have gone to the Soviet Union and other East European countries to study history. A few have pursued programs of advanced, professional training, which in addition to developing a capacity for Marxist analysis have provided these students with the requisite skills for serious historical scholarship.[115] Committed, in the words of one, to dispelling the image of Latin America as "the land of many poets and few scientists," this emergent generation of Latin American scholars promises to shake the foundations of established historiography and to combat the special interests which it serves. To the degree that this occurs, it will be the result, at least in part, of Soviet contributions to the field.

A comprehensive evaluation of these contributions already represents an imposing task, the parameters of which are readily discernible in the present volume. Paraphrasing an American commentator critical of Soviet scholarship, one can conclude that the increasingly balanced approach to area research in the USSR reflects a growing sophistication on the part of Soviet scholars. The intervening years since the 20th Congress of the CPSU "have provided researchers with more opportunities to study source material and even to visit the areas of their interest," while the partially eased atmosphere of de-Stalinization "has encouraged independent thinking and even open debates on matters of ideological importance."[116] Although examples of what another critic labels *suppressio veri* are still to be found, they are far less prevalent than in the past, and moreover, cannot be considered unique to Soviet scholarship. Such deficiencies as do still exist could be reduced through expanded dialogue; indeed, this same writer adds, scholarship in general would benefit greatly from "an honest exchange of information and views."[117] Contacts of this nature, remarks a third commentator, "would strengthen also in [American] scholars the need to be objective when faced with the certainty that neither of the two opposing sides possesses a monopoly of the truth, nor one hundred percent of the intellectual light."[118]

Several significant steps have been taken by American academics in recent years to prepare the way for serious scholarly exchange with Soviet Latin Americanists. As early as 1959, the Hispanic Foundation of the U.S. Library of Congress, in cooperation with that institution's Slavic and Central European Division, published a volume entitled *Latin America in Soviet Writings, 1945–1958: A Bibliography*. It was reprinted in 1960, and subsequently expanded into the first of a two-volume bibliography prepared by a special Library of Congress staff with financial assistance from the Ford Foundation and published under essentially the same title in 1966. Volume I spanned the years 1917–58; volume II updated entries to 1964.[119] This work revealed dramatically the rapidly widening scope of Soviet writings on Latin America. Indeed, observed Sergius Yakobson, "the volume of such materials has grown from a small base of three titles in 1918, to an all-time high of 898 in 1961."[120] While it suffered certain weaknesses, wrote a Soviet reviewer, this bibliography "might well serve as a reference point for preparing an analogous Soviet edition."[121]

A second major publication on Soviet Latin American research was proposed in 1963. After several revisions and editorial changes, this volume finally appeared in 1970 under the title *Soviet Image of Contemporary Latin America*.[122] Compiled and translated by J. Gregory Oswald and edited by Robert G. Carlton, with a foreword by Howard F. Cline and an introduction by Herbert S. Dinerstein, it represented an important effort to make available in English translation a representative selection of Soviet writings on Latin America. Like the present volume, it was issued as part of the official publications series of the Conference on Latin American History, and thus reflected the growing interest of U.S. historians in Soviet contributions to the historiography of Latin America.

While other volumes appeared on Soviet influence and interests in Latin America[123] and occasional translations of articles by Soviet Latin Americanists found their way into edited works,[124] scholarly journals in the United States also began to open their pages to Soviet specialists. In 1967, for example, the *Latin American Research Review* published an article on Latin American studies in the Soviet Union by V. V. Vol'skii, director of the Latin American Institute of the USSR Academy of Sciences.[125] In 1970, the same journal carried a statement by a leading Soviet historian, M. S. Al'perovich, outlining possible areas of fruitful dialogue between Marxist and non-Marxist specialists in Latin American history.[126] And in 1973, the *California Historical Quarterly* printed an important article by Soviet specialist L. A. Shur on Russian sources for the history of California in the first half of the nineteenth century.[127]

Growing bibliographic interest in Soviet Latin Americana was likewise reflected in the pages of the *Handbook of Latin American Studies*. In 1972, special contributing editors were named "to give the *Handbook* a broader balance in languages and countries such as the Scandinavian and Slavic groups. . . ."[128] This has produced markedly expanded, if not exhaustive, coverage of Soviet titles, and augurs well for future recognition of contributions to the field by scholars from the USSR and other socialist countries.

In addition to bibliographic and related publications calling attention to Soviet contributions to the scholarly literature on Latin America, parallel efforts have been made to promote direct exchange and contacts with Latin Americanists in socialist Europe. As early as 1966, the Conference on Latin American History (CLAH) extended an invitation to S. S. Mikhailov, then director of the Latin American Institute of the USSR Academy of Sciences, to address a CLAH luncheon meeting at the annual convention of the American Historical Association (AHA), in New York City, and thereafter to visit several Latin American studies centers in the United States. The invitation coincided, however, with the naming of Mikhailov as Soviet Ambassador to Brazil, and it was consequently re-extended to Mikhailov's successor, V. V. Vol'skii. Unable to attend the December meeting of the AHA, Vol'skii did travel to the United States during the first part of 1967 and had an opportunity to familiarize himself directly with various academic programs in the Latin American area.

As a result of the Vol'skii visit, the late Howard F. Cline, then director of the Hispanic Foundation, received an invitation from the USSR Academy of Sciences to spend a two-week period in the Soviet Union. Cline accepted the invitation and, following the 38th International Congress of Americanists held in mid-August 1968 in the Federal Republic of Germany, travelled to the USSR for a series of meetings and discussions with Soviet colleagues.

These visits improved the general climate for meaningful exchange and subsequent contacts increased noticeably. In January 1971, for example, Lewis Hanke spent two weeks in Moscow and Leningrad exploring possible avenues of future exchange with Soviet specialists in Latin American history. He had similar discussions with Czech and East German scholars during brief visits to Prague and Leipzig, recommending upon his return to the United States that additional invitations be extended by CLAH to appropriate Soviet and East European specialists. In the spring of 1972, the editor of this present volume spent a month in the USSR pursuing the talks initiated by Hanke. I returned a year later for another three weeks of discussions with Soviet colleagues, spending several days as well in Prague and Leipzig for additional talks with Czech and East German scholars.[129]

Since then, direct personal contacts between American, Soviet and East European specialists in Latin American history have expanded steadily. CLAH, through its Committee on Relations with the Socialist Countries and in cooperation with the International Research and Exchanges Board, has been instrumental in arranging several visits to the United States by colleagues from Poland, the

German Democratic Republic, and the USSR, as well as by Conference members to Eastern Europe and the Soviet Union. Soviet and East European academic institutions, in turn, have begun to extend invitations to and sponsor visits by Latin American specialists from the United States.

Opportunities for research and scholarly dialogue have thus been opened between Latin Americanists of otherwise competing social and political systems. Recognition by American academics of the increasing significance of Soviet and East European scholarship in the Latin American area is reflected in continuing CLAH efforts to promote professional ties with colleagues in the socialist countries. The present volume is a clear reflection of that recognition, for it underscores the need to follow more closely the work of numerous specialists heretofore ignored by Western scholars. It draws attention most especially to the field of history and to the relatively recent contributions of Soviet scholars to the historiography of Latin America.

NOTES

1 Magnus Mörner, "The Study of Latin American History Today," *LARR* 8, no. 2 (Summer 1973), 77.

2 Stephen Clissold, "Soviet Relations with Latin America Between the Wars," in J. Gregory Oswald and Anthony J. Strover, eds., *The Soviet Union and Latin America* (New York, Washington, and London, 1970), p. 15.

3 Ibid.

4 See L. S. Berg, *Istoriia russkikh geograficheskikh otkrytii* (Moscow, 1962), and Avrahm Yarmolinsky, *Russian Americana, Sixteenth to Eighteenth Centuries: A Bibliographical and Historical Study* (New York, 1943), pp. 5–26.

5 See, for example, L. A. Shur, *Rossiia i Latinskaia Amerika: Ocherki politicheskikh, ekonomicheskikh i kul'turnykh otnoshenii,*† and Ekkehard Völkl, *Russland und Lateinamerika, 1741–1841* (Wiesbaden, 1968).

6 Yarmolinsky, *Russian Americana*, pp. 38–39; Shur, *Rossiia i Latinskaia Amerika*, p. 12.

7 Yarmolinsky, *Russian Americana*, pp. 34–36.

8 Shur, *Rossiia i Latinskaia Amerika*, pp. 14–17.

9 Antonio de Solís, *Istoriia o pokorenii Meksiki*, 2 parts (St. Petersburg, 1767).

10 William Spence Robertson, *Istoriia o Amerike* (St. Petersburg, 1784).

11 Abbé Raynal, *Istoriia filosoficheskaia i politicheskaia o zavedeniiakh i torgovle Evropeitsev v obeikh Indiiakh*, 6 parts (St. Petersburg, 1806–9). A second edition was published in 1834–35. See, also, V. I. Moriakov, "Russkii perevod 'Istorii obeikh Indii' Reinalia."†

12 Russell Howard Bartley, "Russia and Latin American Independence, 1808–1826" (Ph.D. diss. Stanford University, 1971), p. 141.

13 Ibid. pp. 139–41.

14 A. von Humboldt, *Puteshestvie po Yuzhnoi Amerike*, 2 vols. (St. Petersburg, 1834–35).

15 See Russell H. Bartley, *Imperial Russia and the Struggle for Latin American Independence, 1808–1828* (Austin: The Institute of Latin American Studies, The University of Texas, forthcoming autumn 1977); Völkl, *Russland und Lateinamerika;* and L. Yu. Slëzkin, *Rossiia i voina za nezavisimost' v Ispanskoi Amerike.*†

16 Washington Irving, *Istoriia zhizni i putshestvii Khristofora Kolumba*, 4 vols. (St. Petersburg, 1836–37).

17 William H. Prescott, *Zavoevanie Meksiki Ferdinandom Kortetsom*, 2 vols. (St. Petersburg, 1885–86); idem, *Zavoevanie Peru* (St. Petersburg, 1886).

18 Alfred Deberle, *Istoriia Yuzhnoi Ameriki ot zavoevaniia do nashego vremeni* (St. Petersburg, 1899).

19 Fëdor Smirnov, *Yuzhnaia pri-atlanticheskaia Amerika: Politiko-ekonomicheskie ocherki*, s prilozheniem polikhromnykh vidov Brazilii, karty voennykh deistvii i tablits (St. Petersburg, 1872).

20 A. S. Ionin, *Po Yuzhnoi Amerike*, 4 vols. (St. Petersburg, 1892–1902).

21 M. S. Al'perovich, *Sovetskaia istoriografiia stran Latinskoi Ameriki,*† pp. 5–6.

22 See, for example, D. Antokolets, *Nekotorye dannye ob Argentinskoi Respublike* [Some facts about the Argentine Republic] (St. Petersburg, 1912); I. Gutman, *Zhizn' kolonistov v shtate San-Paulo v Brazilii* [The life of the colonists in the Brazilian state of São Paulo] (Riga, 1908); and I. A. Rebrin, *O pereselenii v Braziliiu* [On immigration to Brazil] (Khar'kov, 1909).

23 Shur, *Rossiia i Latinskaia America*, pp. 120–28.

24 A. S. Trachevskii, *Ispaniia deviatnadtsatogo veka* [Spain in the nineteenth century] (Moscow, 1872). This was the first of a projected two-volume work spanning the period 1788–1868; the second volume was not completed.

25 V. K. Piskorskii, *Istoriia Ispanii i Portugalii* [The history of Spain and Portugal] (St. Petersburg, 1902); idem, *Kastil'skie kortesy v perekhodnuiu epokhu ot srednikh vekov k novomu vremeni (1188–1520)* [The *cortes* of Castile in the transitional period from the Middle Ages to modern times (1188–1520)] (Kiev, 1897); idem, *Krepostnoe pravo v Katalonii v Srednie Veka* [Serfdom in Catalonia in the Middle Ages] (Kiev, 1907).

26 "Ocherk sotsial'no-politicheskoi evoliutsii Ispanii v XIX v.," and "Ocherk sotsial'no-politicheskoi evoliutsii Portugalii v XIX v.," in Piskorskii, *Istoriia Ispanii i Portugalii*, 2nd rev. ed. (St. Petersburg, 1909), pp. 215–51, 252–74.

27 See, for example, *Ispaniia s tochki zreniia istoricheskoi* [Spain from an historical point of view] (St. Petersburg, 1902).

28 This is reflected in the writings of E. E. Litavrina, who has produced some interesting work on the interaction of Spain and the Spanish American colonies in the sixteenth and seventeenth centuries. See Litavrina, "Iapanskii ekonomist XVI v. Tomas Merkado o prichinakh i sushchnosti 'revoliutsii tsen'" [The sixteenth-century Spanish economist Tomás Mercado on the causes and nature of the "price revolution"], in Z. V. Udal'tsova et al., eds., *Evropa v srednie veka: Ekonomika, politika, kul'tura* [Europe in the Middle Ages: economy, politics, culture] (Moscow, 1972), pp. 249–59; idem, "Ispaniia v epokhu velikikh geograficheskikh otkrytii"

[Spain in the age of the great geographic discoveries], in I. R. Grigulevich et al., eds., *Bartolome de Las-Kasas: K istorii zavoevaniia Ameriki,*† pp. 38–63; idem, "Memorial ispanskogo ekonomista Luisa Ortisa i zarozhdenie idei protektsionizma v Ispanii XVI v." [The *Memorial* of Spanish economist Luis Ortiz and the origin of protectionist ideas in sixteenth-century Spain], *SV,* vyp. 19 (1961), 142–59.

29 For an example of the variety of editions available to Russian scholars, see bibliography of Las Casas materials appended to I. R. Grigulevich et al., eds., *Bartolome de Las-Kasas: K istorii zavoevaniia Amerika,*† pp. 221–27.

30 On Georg Heinrich von Langsdorff, see below, B. N. Komissarov, "The Archive of the G. I. Langsdorf Expedition to Brazil"; on A. S. Ionin, see Shur, *Rossiia i Latinskaia Amerika,* pp. 89–100, and idem, "Materialy russkogo puteshestvennika i diplomata A. S. Ionina kak istochnik po istorii i etnografii stran Latinskoi Ameriki" [The papers of Russian traveler and diplomat A. S. Ionin as a source for the history and ethnography of the countries of Latin America], in I. R. Grigulevich et al., eds., *Ot Aliaski do Ognennoi Zemli,*† pp. 267–74.

31 Shur, *Rossiia i Latinskaia Amerika,* pp. 120–21.

32 V. I. Lenin, "The Three Sources and Three Component Parts of Marxism," in Lenin, *Collected Works,* XIX (Moscow, 1968), pp. 23–25.

33 "Introduction to M. Pokrovsky, *Russian History in Briefest Outline,*" in Marin Pundeff, comp. and ed., *History in the U.S.S.R.: Selected Readings* (San Francisco, 1967), p. 62.

34 Pundeff, *History in the U.S.S.R.,* p. 3.

35 For discussions in English of the transformation of the historical profession in the early years of the Soviet state, see Pundeff, *History in the U.S.S.R.;* Anatole G. Mazour, *The Writing of History in The Soviet Union* (Stanford, California, 1971); and Konstantin F. Shteppa, *Russian Historians and the Soviet State* (New Brunswick, New Jersey, 1962).

36 Cyril E. Black, ed., *Rewriting Russian History: Soviet Interpretations of Russia's Past,* 2nd rev. ed. (New York, 1962), p. 5.

37 Ibid., p. 7.

38 Al'perovich, *Sovetskaia istoriografiia stran Latinskoi Ameriki,* pp. 7–8.

39 V. I. Lenin, *Imperialism, the Highest State of Capitalism,* in Lenin, *Collected Works,* XXII, 263.

40 V. V. Vol'skii, "Leninizm i problemy revoliutsionnogo protsessa v Latinskoi Amerike," *LA,* no. 2 (March–April 1970), 9–10.

41 See, for example, José Joaquín Fernández de Lizardi, *Perikil'o Sarn'ento* (Moscow, 1964); Joaquim Maria Machado de Assis, *Don Kasmurro* (Moscow, 1961); Mariano Azuela, *Te kto vnizu* [Los de abajo] (Moscow, 1960; 2nd ed., 1961); José Eustacio Rivera, *Puchina* [La vorágine] (Moscow, 1935; 2nd ed., 1955; 3rd ed., 1957); Ricardo Güiraldes, *Don Segundo Sombra* (Moscow, 1960); Rómulo Gallegos, *Don'ia Barbara* (Moscow, 1959); Ciro Alegría, *V bol'shom chuzhom mire* [El mundo es ancho y ajeno] (Moscow, 1944); Miguel Angel Asturias, *Sen'or Prezident* (Moscow, 1959); Jorge Amado, *Gabriela, Khronika odnogo provintsial'nogo goroda* (Moscow, 1961). Amado has proven to be one of the most popular Latin American writers in the Soviet Union. Other translations of his works include *Beskrainie zemli* [Terras do sem-fim] (Moscow, 1955); *Krasnye vskhody* [Seara Vermelha] (Moscow, 1949; 2nd ed., 1961); *Podpol'e svobody* [Os subterrâneos da liberdade] (Moscow,

1954; 2nd ed., 1959), and *Zemlia zolotykh plodov* [São Jorge dos Ilhéus] (Moscow, 1948).

42 Bernal Díaz del Castillo, *Zapiski Soldata Bernalia Diaza*, 2 vols. (Leningrad, 1924–25); Diego de Landa, *Soobshchenie o delakh v Yukatane* (Moscow, 1955); Bartolomé de las Casas, *Istoriia Indii* (Leningrad, 1968); and Alexander von Humboldt, *Puteshestvie v ravnodenstvennoi oblasti Novogo Sveta v 1799–1804 godakh*, 3 vols. (Moscow, 1963–69).

43 Henry Bamford Parkes, *Istoriia Meksiki* (Moscow, 1949); Caio Prado Júnior, *Ekonomicheskaia istoriia Brazilii* (Moscow, 1949).

44 Preston James, *Latinskaia Amerika* (Moscow, 1949).

45 Rafael Altamira y Crevea, *Istoriia Ispanii*, 2 vols. (Moscow, 1951).

46 William Z. Foster, *Ocherk politicheskoi istorii Ameriki* (Moscow, 1953; 2nd ed., 1954); Alfred Barnaby Thomas, *Istoriia Latinskoi Ameriki* (Moscow, 1960).

47 José Francisco da Rocha Pombo, *Istoriia Brazilii* (Moscow, 1962); José Carlos Mariátegui, *Sem' ocherkov istolkovaniia peruanskoi deistvitel'nosti* (Moscow, 1963); Philip Sheldon Foner, *Istoriia Kuby i eë otnoshenii s SShA*, 2 vols. (Moscow, 1963–64); and Samuel Eliot Morison, *Khristofor Kolumb, moreplavatel'* (Moscow, 1968).

48 In Moscow and Leningrad, history departments were incorporated into newly created "social sciences faculties," where they remained essentially intact throughout this period; elsewhere in the country, historical research and teaching were abolished. (See Shteppa, *Russian Historians and the Soviet State*, p. 11.) The principal organizations for the promotion of Marxist scholarship were the Socialist (later Communist) Academy of Social Sciences (est. 1918), the Institute of Red Professors (est. 1921), and the Society of Marxist Historians (est. 1925), all under the direction of Pokrovskii. For more detail, see Pundeff, *History in the U.S.S.R.*, pp. 59–60; Shteppa, *Russian Historians and the Soviet State*, pp. 13–23.

49 Pundeff, *History in the U.S.S.R.*, p. 60.

50 Ibid., pp. 83–84.

51 Shteppa, *Russian Historians and the Soviet State*, p. 120.

52 Al'perovich, *Sovetskaia istorografiia stran Latinskoi Ameriki*, pp. 8–9.

53 Ibid., p. 9.

54 Ibid., p. 10.

55 Zubok emigrated to the United States from Odessa in 1913. Here he worked in industry, was active in the trade union movement, and participated in the founding of the American Communist Party. While in the United States, he pursued university studies through the Ph.D. He returned to the Soviet Union in 1924. For additional biographical data, see foreword to L. I. Zubok, *Ekspansionistskaia politika SShA v nachale XX veka* (Moscow, 1969). See also obituaries in *NNI*, no. 3 (May–June 1967) 188; and *Vop. Ist.*, no. 9 (September, 1967), 217.

56 For additional biographical data, see obituaries in *IVGO* 100 no. 4 (1972), 327–28; *NNI*, no. 6 (November–December 1971), 214–18; and *Vop. Ist.*, no. 12 (December 1971), 211.

57 At the time of his death, Guber was president of the International Committee of Historical Sciences. For additional biographical data, see obituaries in *NNI*, no. 4 (July–August 1971), 205–7, and *Vop. Ist.*, no. 9 (September 1971), 221.

58 Al'perovich, *Sovetskaia istoriografiia stran Latinskoi Ameriki*, p. 12.
59 For additional biographical data, see "Avtobiografiia" and other documents, in *Ist. SSR*, no. 3 (1967), 141–45, and B. N. Komissarov, "Iz istorii sovetskoi latino-amerikanistiki (Arkhiv V. M. Miroshevskogo)," *NNI*, no. 4 (July–August 1966), 132–35.
60 "Velikie derzhavy i voina za nezavisimost' Ispanskoi Ameriki," Lenin State Library (Moscow), Manuscript Department, fond 469, karton 1.
61 Al'perovich, *Sovetskaia istoriografiia stran Latinskoi Ameriki*, p. 10.
62 Komissarov, "Iz istorii sovetskoi latinoamerikanistki," p. 132.
63 Slëzkin, *Rossiia i voina za nezavisimost' v Ispanskoi Amerike*, pp. 17–18.
64 Al'perovich, *Sovetskaia istoriografiia stran Latinskoi Ameriki*, pp. 12–13.
65 Ibid., p. 16.
66 Soviet programs of graduate study in history lead to the Candidate of Historical Sciences degree, which is granted upon the successful defense of a candidate's thesis, roughly the equivalent of an American Ph.D. dissertation. The more advanced Doctor of Historical Sciences degree is reserved for established, publishing scholars; it is awarded upon the successful defense of a doctoral dissertation, which often appears first as a published book.
67 N. M. Lavrov, "Agrarnyi vopros v meksikanskoi revoliutsii 1910–1917 gg." (Moscow State University, 1947); A. M. Zorina, "Problema Panamskogo kanala vo vneshnei politike SShA v XIX veke" (Institute of History, USSR Academy of Sciences, 1947); E. V. Ananova, "Amerikano-meksikanskie otnosheniia v gody prezidenta Vudro Vil'sona (1913–1921)" (Moscow State Institute of International Relations, Ministry of Foreign Affairs of the USSR, 1947).
68 S. A. Gonionskii, "Zakhvat SShA zony Panamskogo kanala i sozdanie 'nezavisimoi' Panamskoi respubliki (Kolumbiisko-amerikanskie otnoshennia v 1900–1903 gg.)" (Moscow State Institute of International Relations, Ministry of Foreign Affairs of the USSR, 1948).
69 G. I. Ivanov, "Meksikanskaia reforma 50-kh - 60-kh gg. XIX veka i eë posledstviia (Iz istoriia razvitiia kapitalizma v Meksike)" (Leningrad State Pedagogical Institute, 1948).
70 B. T. Rudenko, "Imperialisticheskaia politika SShA v Meksike v 1910–1913 godakh (V period revoliutsii i pravitel'stva Madero v Meksike)" (Academy of Social Sciences, Central Committee of the CPSU, 1949); M. S. Al'perovich, "Meksikanskaia revoliutsiia i amerikanskii imperializm (1913–1917)" (Moscow State University, 1949).
71 E. L. Nitoburg, "Imperialisticheskaia politika SShA v Kube, 1933–36 gg. (Interventsiia pod maskoi 'dobrososedstva')" (Moscow State Pedagogical Institute, 1950); A. I. Shtrakhov, "Argentina i vtoraia mirovaia voina (Peronizm, kak argentinskaia raznovidnost' fashizma i bor'ba demokraticheskikh sil Argentiny protiv sil imperializma i argentinskoi reaktsii)" (Academy of Social Sciences, Central Committee of the CPSU, 1951); N. R. Matveeva, "Paragvai i paragvaiskaia voina 1864–1870 godov i politika inostrannykh derzhav na La Plate" (Moscow State University, 1952) L. Yu Slëzkin, "Imperialisticheskaia politika Soedinënnykh Shtatov v Yuzhnoi Amerike v gody mirovogo ekonomicheskogo krizisa (1929–1933)" (Moscow State University, 1952); V. I. Ermolaev, "Bor'ba rabochego klassa Argen-

tiny protiv imperializma za natsional'nuiu nezavisimost' i mir (1945–1951 gg.)"
(Academy of Social Sciences, Central Committee of the CPSU, 1953); A. N. Glin-
kin, "Imperialisticheskaia ekspansiia SShA v Brazilii (1945–1952)" (Moscow State
Institute of International Relations, Ministry of Foreign Affairs of the USSR, 1954).

72 M. S. Al'perovich, "Izuchenie istorii stran Latinskoi Ameriki," in N. M. Druzhinin
et al., eds., *Sovetskaia istoricheskaia nauka ot XX k XXII s'ezdu KPSS. Istoriia
Zapadnoi Evropy i Ameriki. Sbornik Statei* (Moscow, 1963), 152; S. S. Mikhailov,
"Izuchenie Latinskoi Ameriki v Sovetskom Soiuze (nekotorye itogi i predstoiashchie
zadachi)," *Vop. Ist.,* no. 4 (April 1962), 101.

73 Al'perovich, "Izuchenie istorii stran Latinskoi Ameriki," p. 152.

74 Hans Rogger, "Politics, Ideology and History in the USSR: The Search for Coexistence," *SS* 16, no. 3 (January 1965), 156.

75 Bartley, "A Decade of Soviet Scholarship in Brazilian History: 1958–1968," *HAHR*
50, no. 3 (August 1970), 448.

76 In the United States, both private foundations and government agencies had for some
time been providing increasing amounts of financial support for research and the
development of research centers relating to Latin America. (See Lewis Hanke, "The
Development of Latin American Studies in the United States, 1939–1945," *The
Americas* 4 [July 1947], 32–64.) Sustained interest in Latin American history was, in
the view of one specialist, "largely the result of U.S. political and economic expansion, the economic crisis of the 'thirties, the stresses and strains of World War II, and
the problems of economic growth, social change and political stability since 1945."
(Stanley J. Stein, "Latin American Historiography: Status and Research Opportunities," in Charles Wagley, ed., *Social Science Research on Latin America* [New
York and London, 1964], p. 89). As Latin America became increasingly identified in
the postwar period with the national interests of the United States, corresponding
steps were taken to promote scholarly research supportive of those interests. The
National Defense Education Act of 1958 marked the beginning of a decade of
unprecedented funding of Latin American and other area studies. Enactment of the
NDEA, in turn, reflected a response to the postwar world which at once antedated and
went beyond subsequent events in Cuba.

77 Al'perovich, *Sovetskaia istoriografiia stran Latinskoi Ameriki,* p. 17.

78 Akademiia nauk USSR, Institut Latinskoi Ameriki, *Sovetskie latinoamerikanisty.
Spravochnik* (Moscow, 1971).

79 Al'perovich, *Sovetskaia istoriografiia stran Latinskoi Ameriki,* p. 12. For examples
of historical research published outside Moscow and Leningrad, see Bibliography:
N. V. Korolëv, A. V. Gus'kov, G. I. Ivanov, N. R. Matveeva, and T. P. Sotnikova.

80 In the fall of 1968, the Institute of History of the USSR Academy of Sciences was
reorganized into two separate entities: The Institute of USSR History and the Institute
of Universal History. The latter includes a section of United States and Canadian
history, and a section of Latin American history. For more detail, see Z. S. Be-
lousova, "Ob osnovnykh napravleniiakh nauchno-issledovatel'skoi raboty Instituta
vseobshchei istorii," *NNI,* no. 6 (Novermber–December 1969), 164–66.

81 In contrast with the American system, Soviet academe reflects a division of labor: in
general, research is the province of the Academy of Sciences, teaching the primary
function of the university. There are, of course, many exceptions.

82 A similar but more elaborate institute was established in 1968 to coordinate research on the contemporary United States. Since January 1970, it has published a monthly journal entitled *SShA: Ekonomika, politika, ideologiia* [USA: economics, politics, ideology], which occasionally carries articles relating to Latin America; a recent number included an interesting study of the Mexican-Americans: V. A. Skroznikova, "Chikanos—amerikantsy meksikanskogo proiskhozhdeniia" [Chicanos—Americans of Mexican origin], *SShA*, no. 6 (June 1973), 30–41.

83 *Latinskaia Amerika* carries articles in all the social science disciplines, as well as interviews, memoirs and travel accounts, political documents, translations, cultural notes, and book reviews. This journal represents a major publication effort and is indicative of the notable progress achieved by Soviet specialists in the Latin American studies area. A quarterly edition is published in Spanish.

84 Two significant reference works published in the late 1950s are Efimov and Tokarev, eds., *Narody Ameriki,* vol. II, Tsentral'naia i Yuzhnaia Amerika,† and E. N. Lukshova, *Yuzhnaia Amerika: Fizicheskaia geografiia* [South America: a physical geography] (Moscow, 1958).

85 V. Miroshevskii, "Latinskaia Amerika i Vest Indiia" [Latin America and the West Indies], in Adakemiia nauk SSSR, Institut istorii, *Novaia istoriia kolonial'nykh i zavisimykh stran,* vol. I (Moscow, 1940), pp. 68–81, 364–98, 731–60.

86 V. G. Revunenkov, *Istoriia stran Latinskoi Ameriki v noveishee vremia* (Moscow, 1963).

87 See, for example, I. S. Galkin et al., eds., *Istoriografiia novogo vremeni stran Evropy i Ameriki* [Historiography of the countries of Europe and America in modern times] (Moscow, 1967); idem, *Istoriografiia novoi i noveishei istorii stran Evropy i Ameriki* [Historiography of the modern and contemporary history of the countries of Europe and America] (Moscow, 1968); M. S. Al'perovich and L. Yu. Slëzkin, *Novaia istoriia stran Latinskoi Ameriki†;* and idem, *Obrazovanie nezavisimykh gosudarstv v Latinskoi Amerike (1804–1903)* [The founding of independent states in Latin America (1804-1903)] (Moscow, 1966).

88 A. V. Efimov and I. A. Zolotarevskaia, eds., *Kul'tura indeitsev: Vklad korennogo naseleniia Ameriki v mirovuiu kul'turu* [The culture of the Indians: the contribution of the aboriginal population of America to world culture] (Moscow, 1963); I. P. Magidovich, *Istoriia otkrytiia i issledovaniia Tsentral'noi i Yuzhnoi Ameriki†;* V. I. Ermolaev et al., eds., *Ocherki istorii Argentiny†;* M. S. Al'perovich et al., eds., *Ocherki istorii Brazilii†;* idem, *Ocherki istroii Chili†;* L. Yu. Slëzkin, *Istoriia Kubinskoi respubliki†;* M. S. Al'perovich and N. M. Lavrov, eds., *Ocherki novoi i noveishei istorii Meksiki, 1810–1945.†*

89 See J. Gregory Oswald, "A Soviet Criticism of *The Hispanic American Historical Review,*" *HAHR* 40, no. 3 (August 1960), 337–39; and I. R. Lavretskii, "A Survey of *The Hispanic American Historical Review, 1956–1958,*" ibid., 340–60. Both of these articles have been reprinted in Howard F. Cline, comp. and ed., *Latin American History: Essays on Its Study and Teaching, 1898–1965,* 2 vols. (Austin and London, 1967), I, 142–56. The Lavretskii article originally appeared in Russian as "Obzor 'Ispano-amerikanskogo zhurnala' za 1956–1958 gody," *Vop. Ist.,* no. 12 (December 1959), 94–107.

90 Lavretskii, *HAHR,* pp. 340–41.

91 Ibid., p. 360.

92 Oswald, *HAHR*, p. 337.
93 I. R. Lavretskii, "Replika professoru Dzh. Gregori Osval'du," *Vop. Ist.*, no. 2 (February 1971), 206.
94 Oswald, *HAHR*, p. *339*.
95 Lavretskii, "Replika," p. 207.
96 Ibid.
97 Ibid., pp. 207-8.
98 See, for example, Bartley, "A Decade of Soviet Scholarship in Brazilian History, *pp. 445-66*; Jean-Pierre Berthe, "L'historiographie soviétique et l'Amérique latine," *AESC*, 21e Anné, no. 1 (January–February 1966), 235-36; Roland T. Ely, "El panorama interamericano visto por investigadores de la URSS," *JIAS* 8, no. 2 (April 1966), 294-317; Juan A. Ortega y Medina "Bartolomé de las Casas y la historiografía soviética," *HM* 16, no. 3 (January–March 1967), 320-40; idem, "Crítica y contracrítica en torno a la historiografía soviética," *AH*, Año 5 (1965), 261-90; J. Gregory Oswald, "Contemporary Soviet Research on Latin America," *LARR* 1, no. 2 (Spring 1966), 77-96; idem, "The Development of Soviet Studies on Latin America," *SSU*, new series 7, no. 3 (1968), 70-83; Edward B. Richards, "Marxism and Marxist Movements in Latin America in Recent Soviet Historical Writings," *HAHR* 41, no. 4 (November 1965), 577-90.
99 Book review by Stephen Clissold in *JLAS* 4, part I (May 1972), 146.
100 Mörner, "The Study of Latin American History Today," p. 78.
101 Book review by Lawrence S. Thompson in *RIB* 22, no. 4 (October–December 1972), 412.
102 Charles Gibson, general introduction to section on history, *HLAS*, no. 26 (Gainesville, Florida, 1964), p. 39.
103 Lewis Hanke, "Studying Latin America: The Views of an 'Old Christian'," *JIAS* 9, no. 1 (January 1967), 49.
104 Thompson, *RIB* 22, no. 4 (October–December 1972), 413.
105 Erich Fromm, *Marx's Concept of Man*, with a translation of Marx's *Economic and Philosophical Manuscripts* by T. B. Bottomore (New York, 1964), p. 1.
106 Ibid., p. 5.
107 M. J. Gefter and V. L. Malkov, "Reply to a Questionnaire on Soviet Historiography," *HT* 6, no. 2 (1967), 182.
108 For Soviet writings on Marxist historiography, see articles on historiography ("Istoriografiia") and historical method ("Metodologiia istorii") in *Sovetskaia istoricheskaia entsiklopediia*, VI, 455-514, and IX, 387-401, respectively; in English, see Gefter and Malkov, *HT* 6, no. 2 (1967), 180-207; G. Glezerman and G. Kursanov, eds., *Historical Materialism: Basic Problems* (Moscow, 1968); K. Marx, F. Engels, and V. Lenin, *On Historical Materialism: A Collection*, comp. T. Borodulina (Moscow, 1972); and A. Spirkin and O. Yakhot, *The Basic Principles of Dialectical and Historical Materialism* (Moscow, 1971). See also, Howard Selsam, David Goldway, and Harry Martel, eds., *Dynamics of Social Change: A Reader in Marxist Social Science. From the Writings of Marx, Engels and Lenin* (New York, 1970).
109 Gefter and Malkov, *HT* 6, no. 2 (1967), 188.
110 Adlai E. Stevenson, preface to *A Soviet View of the American Past*, ed. with an

introduction by O. Lawrence Burnette, Jr., and William Converse Haygood (Madison, Wis., 1960).

111 On the internal workings of the Soviet historical profession, see Nancy Whittier Heer, *Politics and History in the Soviet Union* (Cambredge, Mass., and London, 1971).

112 For a brief statement in English on Latin American source materials available to Soviet historians, see Russell H. Bartley and Stuart L. Wagner, *Latin America in Basic Historical Collections: A Working Guide* (Stanford, Calif., 1972), pp. 124–26.

113 Bartley, "A Decade of Soviet Scholarship in Brazilian History," p. 466.

114 Ortega y Medina, *Historiografía soviética iberoamericanista*, p. 192.

115 One example is Enrique Semo, co-editor of the Mexican historical journal *Historia y sociedad*. Semo received his postgraduate training at Humboldt University, in East Berlin, where in 1971 he defended his doctoral dissertation on the economic origins of Mexico ("Die ökonomischen Ursprünge der mexikanischen Nation, 1521–1759"). This study was subsequently published by Editorial Era under the title *Historia del capitalismo en México: Los orígenes, 1521–1763* (Mexico, 1973).

116 Thomas Perry Thronton, eds., *The Third World in Soviet Perspective: Studies by Soviet Writers on the Developing Areas* (Princeton, 1964), p. 5.

117 Book review by Ronald Hilton, in *HAHR* 49, no. 3 (August 1969), 581.

118 Ely, "El panorama interamericano visto por investigadores de la URSS," p. 317.

119 Leo Okinshevich, comp., and Robert G. Carlton, ed., *Latin America in Soviet Writings: A Bibiliography*, 2 vols. (Baltimore, 1966).

120 Ibid., I, xii–xiii.

121 B. N. Komissarov, "Latinskaia Amerika v sovetskoi bibliografii i istoriografii," *LA*, no. 3 (May–June 1971), 205. See translation below: "Latin America in Soviet Bibliography and Historiography."

122 Published by the University of Texas Press, Austin and London.

123 See, for example, Oswald and Strover, eds., *The Soviet Union and Latin America;* and Stephen Clissold, ed., *Soviet Relations with Latin America, 1918–1968: A Documentary Survey* (London, New York, and Toronto, 1970).

124 See, for example, V. Afanasiev, "The Literary Heritage of Bartolomé de las Casas," in Juan Freide and Benjamin Keen, eds., *Bartolomé de las Casas in History: Toward an Understanding of the Man and His Work* (DeKalb, Ill., 1971), pp. 539–78.

125 Victor V. Vol'skii, "The Study of Latin America in the U.S.S.R.," *LARR* 3, no. 1 (Fall 1967), 77–87.

126 M. S. Al'perovich, "Soviet Historiography of the Latin American Countries," *LARR*, 5, no. 1 (Spring 1970), 63–70.

127 Leonid A. Shur, "Russian Travel Notes and Journals as Sources for the History of California, 1800–1850" (trans. with an introductory note by James R. Gibson]. *CHQ* 52, no. 1 (Spring 1973), 37–63.

128 "Editor's Note," *HLAS*, no. 34 (Gainesville, Fla., 1972), p. xii.

129 Generous financial support for these trips was provided by the International Research and Exchanges Board (IREX), the National Endowment for the Humanities, and the Graduate School of the University of Wisconsin—Milwaukee. Additional funds have been provided by IREX to help cover CLAH invitations to Soviet and East European scholars.

2 PRINCIPAL TRENDS IN SOVIET RESEARCH ON THE HISTORY OF LATIN AMERICA

M. S. AL'PEROVICH

THE STUDY of the history of the Latin American countries,[1] as well as of other problems relating to this broad region, is one of the newest branches of Soviet scholarship. In pre-Revolutionary Russia it was in fact scarcely developed at all and therefore naturally lacks the same deep, established traditions as Russian Oriental, Medieval, and Byzantine studies or the modern history of France, England, and other European states. Interest in Latin America grew noticeably in our country following the Great October Socialist Revolution, but during the first decades of the Soviet regime research on this area was disorganized and unsystematic, restricting itself to the elucidation of isolated questions, while scholars who studied Latin American problems were literally few in number (S. S. Pestkovskii, G. M. Dashevskii, G. M. Yakobson, G. B. Skalov, V. M. Miroshevskii).

Some relative progress was made in this field of historical scholarship only at the end of the Great Patriotic War (1941–45), but initially it was quite insignificant. Although the circle of scientific research establishments and institutions of higher learning which in some degree began to give attention to Latin America expanded, and the number of specialists and volume of publications (including historical literature) increased slightly, the quantity of published works was still not great and the topics treated were extremely limited. Suffice it to say that in the second half of the 1940s an average of no more than three publications (primarily articles) appeared annually. Of the three monographs which appeared in this period, two came out posthumously, one (G. G. Manizer's book on the first Russian scientific expedition to South America†) completed in 1917, the second (V. M. Miroshevskii's study of anticolonial movements in Spanish

---

This article was prepared by the author for inclusion in the present volume and is published here for the first time.

America prior to the war of independence†) before the war. From 1949 to 1951 not a single book was published, while in the first half of the 1950s there were periods when for an entire year a single work at most would appear.

A change, both quantitative and qualitative, as well as in the scope of topics treated, occurred in the mid-fifties, becoming especially noticeable in the late fifties and early sixties. This "turn" of Soviet historians to Latin America was by no means sudden and unexpected. It developed over a long period of time and was brought about by numerous circumstances.

One of the primary reasons stemmed from the developing internal demands of Soviet historical scholarship, which could not achieve an objective, thorough study of the history of human society from a Marxist-Leninist perspective while ignoring the past of an entire continent where in different historical epochs exceedingly important events had occurred which significantly affected the destiny of the world. At the same time, the revolutionary upheavals and sharpening of class and political struggle experienced by the Latin American peoples contributed to a growth of interest in the area among Soviet historians. During the 1950s alone there was the revolution in Bolivia (1952), the bloody suppression of the Guatemalan revolution (1954), the fall of the Vargas regime in Brazil (August 1954), the overthrow of the Perón government in Argentina (1955), and the fall of dictatorships in Colombia and Venezuela (1957–1958). This decade ended with an event of worldwide historical significance: the triumph of the Cuban Revolution. Also of great importance was the appearance at this time of Latin Americanists trained in the postwar period, a majority of them as students of V. M. Miroshevskii, A. A. Guber, L. I. Zubok and A. V. Efimov.

An essential role was played by the augmentation of sources available to scholars and the publication of some of these sources in Russian translation.[2] Especially noteworthy is the publication of materials relating to the history of the Cuban Revolution: official documents of the Revolutionary government of Cuba, the speeches and addresses of Fidel Castro, the memoirs and works of Raúl Castro, Camilo Cienfuegos, Ernesto Guevara, and other leaders of the Revolution.[3] Of considerable interest is the publication of materials pertaining to Latin America uncovered in Soviet archives: documents of the tsarist government, diplomatic dispatches, the notes and diaries of Russian seamen and travelers.[4] Among those items which have been published, specific mention can be made of the previously unknown correspondence of Francisco de Miranda with the Russian Ambassador to England, S. R. Vorontsov, and his son, M. S. Vorontsov (dating from 1791 to 1800),[5] and portions of the unpublished diaries of G. I. Langsdorf, participants in his expedition N. G. Rubtsov and Hercule Florence, and F. F. Matiushkin, F. P. Litke, F. P. Vrangel, and others.[6] Broad possibilities have been opened to historians with the description of materials from the first Russian expedition to Latin America.[7]

Under the influence of these factors, favorable conditions developed which over the past fifteen or twenty years have permitted Soviet scholars to achieve certain successes in the study of Latin America, including its history. The object of the present article is to give a very generalized overview of the development of historical writing on the Latin American countries, in the USSR, from the latter half of the 1950s to the beginning of the 1970s (through 1973),[8] that is, in the period when this development became more productive, regular, intensive, and purposeful. The article seeks to show on which problems Soviet Latin Americanist historians have worked in this period and to describe the basic directions of their research. With this in mind, the author has intentionally omitted from his brief review literature dealing strictly with political, economic, geographic, juridical, philosophic, and other questions, which would itself require special treatment,[9] although he of course realizes that thematic distinctions are highly fluid, relative, and in many cases exceedingly vague. At the same time, even within these chronological and problematical limitations the article (itself of restricted length) makes no claim whatsoever to bibliographic completeness. It is not our aim to list all Soviet publications for the years indicated above,[10] but rather to elucidate the basic trends in the development of this branch of historical studies and to describe the range of questions addressed in general works, monographs, individual studies, and scholarly articles printed in various collections, journals, and other periodical publications.

The study of Latin American history in the Soviet Union is today concentrated in several scientific research establishments and institutions of higher learning. The most important scholarly centers of Latin American studies are found in Moscow. First among them is the Latin American Institute of the USSR Academy of Sciences, which has been in existence since 1961. While concerned primarily with contemporary problems, it also gives attention to historical topics. In the Academy's Institute of Universal History there is a special sector devoted to the modern and contemporary history of the Latin American countries, which until 1968 formed part of the Institute of History. A broad program of historico-ethnographic research is carried on by the American sector of the Academy's Institute of Ethnography. In recent years, the study of the ancient civilizations of Latin America has occupied a special place in the activities of the Institute of Archeology. Latin American problems, including those relating to the recent past, also enter the sphere of interests of several other academic institutes: the Institute of World Economics and International Relations, the Institute of the International Labor Movement, and the Institute of Economics of the World Socialist System.

Noteworthy among the institutions of higher learning in Moscow in which Latin American history is studied are Moscow State University, the Academy of Social Sciences attached to the Central Committee of the CPSU, the Moscow State Institute of International Relations, Patrice Lumumba Peoples' Friendship University, and the Moscow State Pedagogical Institute. In Leningrad, Latin

Americanist historians are concentrated mainly in the Leningrad branch of the Institute of Ethnography and Leningrad State University. Various aspects of Latin American history are also studied by specialists working in the universities and pedagogical institutes of many other cities of the Russian Federation (Ivanovo, Kalinin, Saratov, Ul'ianovsk, Kazan, Kostroma, Yaroslavl, Novosibirsk, Tomsk), the Ukraine (Kiev, L'vov), White Russia (Minsk), Moldavia (Kishinëv), Transcaucasia (Tbilisi, Baku), the Northern Caucasus (Groznyi, Nal'chik), Central Asia (Alma-Ata), the Baltic (Riga, Tartu), etc.

As for the publication of historical literature devoted to Latin America, first place belongs to the "Nauka" [Science] press. In addition, books in this field are issued by such publishing houses as Politicheskaia Literatura [Political Literature], Mysl' [Thought], Mezhdunarodnye Otnosheniia [International Relations], Prosveshchenie [Enlightenment], Vysshaia Shkola [Upper School], Molodaia Gvardiia [Young Guard], the Moscow University Press, etc. Articles, essays, communications, notes, reviews, and other materials appear more or less regularly in the monthly journal *Voprosy istorii* (organ of the Historical Section of the Academy of Sciences and the Ministry of Higher and Specialized Secondary Education of the USSR) and in the journals *Novaia i noveishaia istoriia, Latinskaia Amerika, Sovetskaia etnografia,* and *Sovetskaia arkheologiia* (published bimonthly by the Institutes of Universal History, Latin America, Ethnography, and Archeology, respectively), and occasionally in the bulletins of Moscow and Leningrad State Universities, the proceedings of the All-Union Geographic Society, and the scholarly notes of various universities, pedagogical institutes, and other institutions.

One of the most important conditions for promoting the study of Latin American history in the USSR is the training of teachers and research specialists. This training takes place in universities and in pedagogical and several other kinds of institutes. All students enrolled in the history faculties of these institutions must attend lectures on the main problems of Latin American history, which are included in the general courses on modern and contemporary history. However specialization in this field of historical scholarship is undertaken mainly in such major universities as those of Moscow, Leningrad, and Kiev, and at the Moscow State Institute of International Relations. It begins in the third year of study. The student who specializes in Latin American history takes three years of lectures and seminars. During this period he is obliged to prepare a written report on a topic of his choice or selected by his advisor, as well as a course paper and, finally, a graduation thesis.

If during his years of study the student proves capable and shows an inclination for independent research, he may upon graduation continue at the university as a post-graduate or pursue graduate studies in some scientific research institute. In either case, the applicant must go through a competition based on oral entrance examinations and a written paper. Individuals accepted for graduate study must in the course of three years pass candidate's exams and prepare a dissertation under the direction of a qualified specialist in the field. The dissertation must be defended publicly at a meeting of the academic council before two official examiners, in addition to whom anyone is free to intervene. The awarding of the degree is decided by secret ballot.[11]

The young scholar who receives the candidate of sciences degree can undertake independent research at one of the scientific establishments or teach at an institution of higher learning. In the latter case, he is eligible to hold the position of assistant, senior instructor, and eventually docent. The more advanced specialist is awarded the degree of doctor of sciences. For this he must prepare and successfully defend a doctoral dissertation which is correspondingly more demanding than the candidate's dissertation. The doctor of sciences who is engaged teaching may hold the rank of professor at a university or other academic institution.

A marked improvement in the training of Latin Americanists and in the teaching of Latin American history has resulted to a large degree from the appearance of textbooks in this discipline. University texts were published on the contemporary history of the Latin American countries by V. G. Revunenkov in 1963† and on the modern history of the region by M. S. Al'perovich and L. Yu. Slëzkin in 1970.† In 1966, the latter two authors also wrote an essay, "The Founding of Independent States in Latin America," for teachers and the general public.[12] S. A. Gonionskii's *Essays on the Recent History of the Latin American Countries*† was addressed to this same audience.

Of fundamental significance was the publication of several collective survey works prepared by the Institute of Ethnography of the USSR Academy of Sciences,[13] which together with the ethnic composition, life, and culture of the contemporary population of Latin America also show the development of the Indian civilizations before the European conquest, elucidate the distinctive features of Spanish and Portuguese colonization, and trace the founding and subsequent evolution of the Latin American nations. A work by O. A. Zhidkov (1967) treats the administrative and legal history of the region's countries.[14] The role of the church and work of the clergy from the arrival of the conquerors to the mid-twentieth century are described in I. R. Grigulevich's (Lavretskii) book *Shadow of the Vatican Over Latin America* (1961).[15]

Great attention is given to the preparation of survey works covering either in part or its entirety the history of the major Latin American states. A considerable contribution to the compilation of such works was made during the 1960s by the Institute of History of the USSR Academy of Sciences, whose members, together with other authors, wrote surveys of the modern and contemporary history of Mexico and the general history of Argentina, Brazil, and Chile.† These surveys, written collectively, contain a systematic account of the salient events of the historical past of the countries cited. They represent the first attempt not only in

Soviet historiography, but perhaps in Marxist historiography in general, to summarize the main stages of the history of the leading Latin American states.

In 1966, two analogous works appeared on Cuba: the Institute of History published L. Yu. Slëzkin's *A History of the Republic of Cuba,*† which spans the period from the founding of the republic to the early 1960s (1902–62), while the Peoples' Friendship University published N. A. Krasheninnikova's study of the history of the Cuban state and its legal institutions.[16] At the end of 1973, S. A. Gonionskii's book appeared on the history of Colombia (from pre-Columbian times to the early 1970s).[17] A. N. Glinkin has shed light on the contemporary history of Brazil during and following the Second World War (1939–59).† In 1972, N. S. Leonov published a work entitled *Aspects of the Political History of Twentieth-Century Central America.*[18]

Among Soviet studies of the ancient civilizations which existed on the American continent before its discovery and conquest by the Europeans, note must be made first of works relating to the geo-cultural area usually called Mesoamerica. For many years the Mayan civilization has attracted special attention, with the greatest contributions having been made by the Leningrad scholars Yu. V. Knorozov and R. V. Kinzhalov.

The first of these scholars is known far beyond the borders of our country for his efforts to decipher the written language of the Mayas. Already in the mid-fifties he reported the preliminary results of his investigations in this area,[19] the results and summary of which comprise the fundamental work published by him in 1963, *Maya Indian Writing.*† Based on a thorough analysis, Knorozov reached the theoretically important conclusion that this writing was of a hieroglyphic nature analogous to the writing systems of ancient China, Sumer, and Egypt. Proceeding on the basis of this idea, in 1960 a group of researchers at the Institute of Mathematics of the Siberian branch of the USSR Academy of Sciences undertook an experiment to decipher the written language of the Mayas with the aid of the computer.[20] Although the results obtained by the scholars in Novosibirsk were exposed both in the Soviet and foreign press to serious criticism,[21] they nonetheless confirmed "hand"-deciphered data and demonstrated the possibility of using contemporary computer techniques to decipher ancient writing systems.

Pursuing his research, Yu. V. Knorozov has in recent years published a number of articles on the Mayan calendar. In 1971, following earlier books on the art of ancient America (1962) and of the ancient Mayas (1968),[22] R. V. Kinzhalov published a solid monograph entitled *The Culture of the Ancient Maya.*†

This topic has also found reflection in the works of the younger generation. The Moscow archeologist V. I. Guliaev, however, already in his first major work which appeared in 1968[23] and especially in his book *The Oldest Civilizations of Mesoamerica,*† examines a broader historico-regional complex which in addition to the Mayas includes the civilizations of Teotihuacán and Monte Albán. He gives considerable attention to the Olmec problem, as well as to the question of pre-Columbian contacts between ancient America and the Old World. This latter question is also discussed in the volume *Archeology of the Old and New Worlds*.[24]

Interest is shown, too, in the ancient Indian cultures of South America. It is reflected in monographs by S. A. Sozina on the Chibcha-Mwiskas† and V. A. Bashilov on the ancient civilizations of Peru and Bolivia.† The socio-economic nature of the Tawantinsuyu state and ancient Peruvian writing system are analyzed in the articles of V. A. Kuz'mishchev.[25] The journal *Sovetskaia etnografiia* has published materials on the native population of several islands in the Caribbean before Spanish intrusion, for example Jamaica and Haiti.[26]

The discovery and conquest of Latin America is treated in a work by the noted specialist in historical geography I. P. Magidovich which draws a very complete picture of European penetration of the West Indies, Mexico, and Central and South America.† The nature of the European conquest of America is revealed in a collection of articles prepared by the Institute of Ethnography of the USSR Academy of Sciences on the four-hundredth anniversary of the death of the great sixteenth-century Spanish humanist Bartolomé de las Casas.† Two of these articles—"Bartolomé de las Casas in His Youth" and "The Literary Legacy of Bartolomé de las Casas and Aspects of the History of Its Publication"—belong to the pen of the Leningrad historian V. L. Afanas'ev, who in that same year [1966] published still another work on Las Casas,† and in 1968 a lengthy study entitled *Bartolomé de las Casas and His Time*.† Early in 1972, O. S. Tomanovskaia published an article "Bartolomé de las Casas and the Origin of Negro Slavery in the West Indies".† The discovery and conquest of Brazil are described in L. Yu. Slëzkin's book *Land of the Holy Cross*.†

The social, economic, and other problems of the three-century colonial period of Latin American history have been studied relatively little to date. Suffice it to say that, strictly speaking, there is a total of one book on this vast period—A. D. Dridzo's historico-ethnographic study *The Jamaican Maroons,*† which embraces approximately a century and a half—from the mid-seventeeth to the late-eighteenth century. Colonial studies appear predominantly in article form. Some treat of individual countries. Thus over a ten-year period (1964–73), G. I. Ivanov (Ivanovo) published a series of works on Mexico in the sixteenth through eighteenth centuries.† The evolution of the socio-economic structure and plantation slave system of colonial Brazil, and the history of the Negro Palmares Republic, have been examined by Zh. D. Smirenskaia,[27] B. I. Koval (see below, ch. 6),† and A. M. Khazanov.† The author of the present article, in turn, has analyzed the distinctive features of the exploitation of the native population of the Spanish colonies.† I. R. Grigulevich and L. G. Kritskii have studied the influence of the Catholic Church, the activities of the inquisition, and the role of the

Jesuit order in Latin America of the sixteenth to nineteenth centuries.[28] Among works dealing with popular movements in the colonial period, mention must be made above all of S. A. Sozina's documentary study (1973) of the Tupac Amaru uprising of the 1780s.† Somewhat earlier (1971) Yu. A. Zubritskii wrote on this same subject.[29] The struggle of the Negro slaves for freedom and the fall of slavery in the British West Indies is the subject of the researches of B. N. Foinitskii.[30]

One of the most important tasks of Soviet Latin Americanists is to study the history of the democratic liberation movement in Latin America; of the region's revolutionary struggle for freedom and national independence and against colonialism, foreign imperialism, and local oligarchies. While working on a broad range of questions relating to the development of the Latin American liberation movement in the nineteenth and twentieth centuries, Soviet historians manifest in particular a profound interest in the war of independence of the first quarter of the past century (1810–26). Increased attention to this topic is explained by its significance for a proper understanding of the complex processes of national formation and the founding of nation states in Latin America, the nature of the socio-economic and political development of the Latin American countries, and the causes of their dependency on foreign capital.

All this makes it most essential to study thoroughly a whole complex of questions relating to the preconditions, motive forces, course, social essence, historical significance, and consequences of the independence struggle of the Latin American peoples in the late eighteenth and early nineteenth centuries. The more so, as for a long time there has predominated in our historical literature a tendency to view this struggle not as a broad national movement, but exclusively as the work of a small group of "creole separatists" who supposedly lacked popular support.

An important landmark signalling a new approach and the beginning of a critical reexamination of the one-sided views and appraisals of the past was the publication in late 1956 of a collaborative article by four authors (M. S. Al'perovich, V. I. Ermolaev, I. R. Lavretskii [Grigulevich], S. I. Semënov) entitled "On the War of Independence in the Spanish American Colonies."† A number of theoretical questions were raised in this article concerning an appraisal of the nature, motive forces, and historical significance of the war of independence. The authors criticized several points of view expressed earlier in Soviet and foreign literature, specifically the characteristics attributed to Bolívar, San Martín, Francia, and other figures.

A significant stimulus to research in this area was the 150th anniversary of the beginning of the war of independence in Spain's American colonies, widely observed in 1960 by the Soviet academic community. In particular, this signal historical event was the object of a celebration in the Hall of Columns of the Palace of Unions, a special expanded meeting of the Academic Council of the

Institute of History, a scientific session of the Institute of World Economy and International Relations of the USSR Academy of Sciences, and other anniversary celebrations.[31]

In 1964, a collective work appeared [edited by N. M. Lavrov et al.] entitled *The War of Independence in Latin America (1810–1826),*† which contained articles on general problems of the independence war, its development in individual regions of the continent (the River Plate, Chile), the preconditions and development of the struggle for independence in Brazil, the policies of the United States and the European powers toward the revolutionary movement in Latin America, and other questions. That same year, the author of the present article published a monograph entitled *Mexico's War of Independence (1810–1824),*† and subsequently a brief study of the Spanish American revolution of the first quarter of the nineteenth century.† In addition, a series of articles was published treating various aspects of the independence movement of the late eighteenth and early nineteenth centuries and its historical preconditions both on a continent-wide scale[32] and in individual countries and regions, for example Haiti, the River Plate, Venezuela, Central America, and Cuba.[33] As for the study of the international aspects of the war of independence, fundamental significance attaches to an article by N. N. Bolkhovitinov, which argues that in the early 1820s there was no real threat of armed intervention in Latin America by the Holy Alliance [see below, ch. 9].

It goes without saying that in approaching concrete problems and events, in characterizing the level of colonial development, the degree of maturity of bourgeois relations and the role of social and economic factors, scholars differ in the nuances of their views. But whatever the individual differences, works by Soviet authors on this topic possess several features in common: "Soviet historians," observed A. A. Guber, "see the fundamental causes of the war for independence in internal processes, in the economic development and changes which took place in the Spanish colonies at the end of the eighteenth century. Their analysis of the birth of capitalist relations in the specific conditions of the Spanish colonial regime and of the artificial obstacles to the development of trade and industry created by those conditions, of the formation of a local bourgeoisie, etc.... leads them to the conclusion that in the course of the war for independence the imperatives of a bourgeois revolution came to the fore as the order of the day."[34]

The history of the Latin American countries from the war of independence of 1810–1826 to the end of the last century has been examined hardly at all. Among the few studies that do exist on this period are two books, one by N. V. Potokova on the Mexican-American War of 1846–1848,† the other, by A. B. Belen'kii, on the struggle under the leadership of Benito Juárez against the French intervention of the 1860s.[35] Events relating to other countries are discussed in articles on socio-economic processes in Brazil, the peculiarities of the genesis of capitalism in Cuba, the War of Federation of 1859–1863 in Venezuela, the activities of the Argentine radicals in the 1870s–'90s, the actions of Ecuadorian Indians, and the first and second wars of the Pacific.[36] Between 1962 and 1971, N. R. Matveeva (Kalinin) published a series of articles describing Paraguay's relations with England and the United States in the 1840s and '50s, as well as the political situation in the River Plate following the Paraguayan War of 1864–70.[37] An overview of the rise of labor organizations and Marxist groups in Latin America was given in 1959 by V. I. Ermolaev [see below, ch. 15].

A notable place in Soviet scholarship on Latin America is occupied by the study of the revolutionary movement of the late nineteenth and early twentieth centuries, above all the Cuban struggle against the Spanish colonialists (1895–98) and the Mexican Revolution of 1910–17.

A pioneer in research on this important period of Cuban history is A. M. Zorina, who published a monograph describing the socio-economic and political preconditions, motive forces, and objectives of the independence movement and the role of the Cuban Revolutionary Party founded by José Martí.[38] The Minsk scholar O. S. Ternovoi provides an analysis of the sociopolitical views and philosophical outlook of the leader and ideologue of the Cuban revolutionary movement of the 1880s and '90s in his book *José Martí*.[39] In 1969, a work appeared by V. I. Shishkina entitled *The socio-political views of José Martí*.†

Soviet historians have for some time shown serious interest in the Mexican Revolution. In the second half of the 1940s and the first half of the 1950s this was the subject of several dissertations and articles. For many years it has been studied by N. M. Lavrov, B. T. Rudenko, the author of the present article, and others. Their works analyze the causes, historical objectives and development of the Revolution in Mexico and the configuration of class forces which evolved in its course. Special interest is given to evaluating the nature of the Revolution and elaborating scientifically its periodization.

It should be noted that several conclusions of Soviet scholars have been cited also in foreign historiography, in particular their appraisal of the Mexican Revolution as a bourgeois-democratic revolution and their definition of its chronological limits (1910–17). At the same time, as this problem was studied in increasing depth and with greater precision there emerged certain differences of opinion. One such issue is the precise role and place in the Mexican Revolution of Ricardo Flores Magón and the movement which he headed.

S. A. Gonionskii's work, published in 1958,† narrates the separation of Panama from Colombia and the simultaneous seizure of the Canal Zone by the United States.

The interwar period, replete with important events, has begun to be studied only relatively recently. Suffice it to say that right up until the mid-1960s Soviet historical scholarship on these decades had produced one short study by N. M. Lavrov on the labor and national-liberation movement of the Latin American countries in this period (1956)[40] and a few articles. Recently it has expanded significantly, due in the first place to the publication of a series of works on the history of Mexico. The most important of these are N. S. Larin's monograph on the "cristeros" uprising of 1926–29† and A. F. Shul'govskii's book *Mexico at a Critical Juncture of Its History,*† which examines the complex processes unfolding in the country during the 1930s, especially during the Cárdenas administration. In 1971, two articles appeared by A. A. Sokolov, one on the attitude of the Mexican Regional Labor Confederation toward the regime of "revolutionary *caudillismo*" (1920–28),† the second on the activities of the Mexican Communist Party in the years 1919–29.†[41]

Of the South American states, Argentina and Chile have received comparatively more attention than the others. In 1969 a work by A. I. Stroganov, *The Struggle for a United Labor and Popular Front in Argentina in the Years 1933–1936,* was published;[42] subsequently, in 1972, this same author published an article on the labor policies of the first Irigoyen government.[43] Previously in Soviet historical literature V. I. Ermolaev had written on the founding of the Argentine Communist Party and Party activities in the 1920s and '30s.† In 1967, A. V. Gus'kov published two articles on the experience of the Chilean Communists during the 1930s.† And, in 1973, F. A. Garanin's book *the Popular Front in Chile*† came out.

The revolutionary movement in Cuba in the years 1917–25 is the topic of a work by A. M. Zorina.† A number of articles deal with aspects of Brazilian history during the Vargas regime, Colombia in the 1920s and '30s, the Sandino movement in Nicaragua, and the attitude of the Latin American countries toward the League of Nations.[44]

It is unquestionably the postwar period that has most attracted the attention of Soviet Latin Americanists. Among the problems they have studied, a prominent place is occupied by the economic processes of the past decade. Published books examine the distinctive features and forms of capitalist development, in particular the state capitalism of Mexico and Brazil, the role of petroleum resources in the economic and political evolution of the Latin American countries, and the tendencies of these countries to integrate.[45] A work by A. M. Sivolobov (1966) analyzes the process of the development of capitalism in Latin American agriculture, the position of different classes and political parties on the agrarian question, forms of the peasant movement, and the economic bases for a union of the working class and the peasantry.[46] In 1968, a collective of scholars from the Latin American Institute issued a work entitled *The Agrarian Question and Problems of the Liberation Movement in the Countries of Latin America.*[47] Published monographs provide an overview of agrarian reforms throughout the region, together with studies of land relations in Brazil, agrarian transformations in Peru, and the course of the struggle for agrarian reform in Chile.[48]

N. N. Razumovich's book *Who Rules and How in Latin America* gives an idea of the political systems of the Latin American countries.[49] A number of works contain descriptions of political parties and movements. Among them is the volume *Political Parties of Latin America,* which gives a picture of the origins, development, and current composition of these parties.[50] The role of Christian Democracy on the continent is examined by S. I. Semënov.[51] Other studies elucidate the ideology and policies of the Venezuelan Democratic Action Party from 1945 to 1968,† the program and activities of the Christian Democrats in Chile, the evolution of the bourgeois parties of Cuba in the years 1945–58, and the Peronist movement in Argentina.[52]

Special attention is given to the study of the position of the Latin American proletariat and of the labor and Communist movement since the Second World War. On these questions there is a work by a group of authors entitled *The Proletariat of Latin America,* M. V. Danilevich's monograph *The Working Class in the Liberation Movement of the Latin American Peoples,* Yu. I. Vizgunova's volume *The Working Class of Contemporary Mexico,* B. I. Koval's book *History of the Brazilian Proletariat,* † which appeared in 1968 (the chronological limits of this book span the period 1857–1967), and a short study by V. I. Ermolaev and A. F. Shul'govskii entitled *The Labor and Communist Movement in Latin America.*[53] Published articles discuss the posture of a number of Latin American Communist Parties with respect to the national-liberation movement (Koval) and to Catholic labor organizations,[54] and describe individual stages in the struggles of the Communist Parties of Argentina, Chile, Cuba, Mexico, and Uruguay in the 1950s and '60s.[55] A majority of materials dealing with the activities of these parties have been published in topical collections issued by the Academy of Social Sciences attached to the Central Committee of the CPSU.[56]

Developments within the Latin American clergy are examined in I. R. Grigulevich's book *The "Insurrectionary" Church in Latin America.*† This same author has described the religious cults of the Antilles.[57] V. P. Andronova has shown the influence of the church on education, and, taking Colombia as an example, has studied its place and role in public life.[58]

A collective work entitled *The Latin American Countries in Contemporary International Relations* spans, roughly, the decade from the mid-1950s to the mid-1960s.[59] There are several monographs on the Organization of American States and the evolution of the inter-American system, the problem of international recognition of new governments in Latin America, and the creation and subsequent transformation of the Organization of Central American States.[60]

Among the numerous publications dealing with the events of the postwar years a prominent place is occupied by works on revolutionary Cuba. The historical preconditions of the Cuban Revolution are shown in a brief study by E. A. Grinevich, which ends with the revolution of 1952 and the establishment of the

Batista dictatorship.† Collective works were prepared and issued on the fifth and tenth anniversaries of the triumph of the Cuban Revolution in which various aspects of this remarkable phenomenon are discussed.[61] Since 1959, a number of volumes have been written on the Cuban Revolution.[62] The gestation of the preconditions of the Revolution and its economic, social, military, international, and other aspects are discussed also in articles.

The accession to power of the Popular Unity government in Chile under the leadership of Salvador Allende has in recent years stimulated heightened interest in the contemporary history of that country. Scholars who are studying Chilean problems have focused their attention primarily on the struggle to unify democratic and anti-imperialist forces from the mid-1950s to the early 1970s.[63]

In the years 1968–73, monographs were also published on the role of the army in the political life of Brazil,[64] the sociopolitical problems of Central America, the development of Venezuela in the period 1945–58, the political struggle in Colombia from 1946 to 1957,† the revolution of 1952 and subsequent events in Bolivia, the Stroessner dictatorship in Paraguay, and the independence movement of the population of the English, French, and Dutch possessions in the Caribbean since the Second World War.[65] Important problems of the postwar history of Argentina, Peru, Colombia, Venezuela, and Puerto Rico are discussed in collections of works by young scholars and graduate students published by the Institutes of History and Latin America of the USSR Academy of Sciences.[66] A series of articles examining the nature of the dictatorial regimes in Central America and the West Indies includes characterizations of the dictatorships of Trujillo in the Dominican Republic, Duvalier in Haiti, and the Samoza "dynasty" in Nicaragua.[67]

Considerable attention has been given to the Latin American policies of the United States and the European powers at various historical stages: the early twentieth century, the period of the world economic crisis of 1929–33, during and immediately following the Second World War, and the 1960s and early 1970s.[68]

Special studies have been devoted to pan-Americanism, the "New Frontier" policies of the Kennedy administration, and the military policy of the United States in the region.[69]

Several works discuss the economic expansion of the United States, the Federal Republic of Germany, and the member states of the European Economic Community in Latin America.[70] In 1970, a collective of authors published a book entitled *U.S. Neocolonialism in Latin America.*[71] B. I. Gvozdarev, Yu. P. Eliutin, and others have written on the "Alliance for Progress."[72] N. V. Korolëv has traced the struggle of the imperialist powers for control over Latin America from the late nineteenth century to the early 1960s.†

Among studies of U.S. policies in individual Latin American countries primacy is given to an analysis of U.S. relations with Cuba, summarized by E. L.

Nitoburg in a study spanning the century and a half from 1810 to 1960.[73] The period of struggle for Cuban independence (1895–98) is examined from this perspective by L. Yu. Slëzkin and L. S. Vladimirov in their monographs on the Spanish-American War.† K. S. Shustov's book *The Pearl of the Antilles and the Yankees* spans the prolonged period from 1899 to 1952.[74] The more limited scope of E. L. Nitoburg's work *The Policies of American Imperialism in Cuba, 1918– 1939*† permitted the author to state in greater detail many important facts. The period 1957–61 is examined in a study entitled *The Secret War Against Revolutionary Cuba*, by V. Listov and Vl. Zhukov.[75] Anatolii A. Gromyko recounts the Caribbean crisis of 1962.†

Also the subject of thorough study are U.S. policies toward the Dominican Republic, Puerto Rico, and Nicaragua in the late nineteenth and early twentieth centuries,[76] the position of the United States with regard to the second War of the Pacific of 1879–84,[77] etc.

Of particular significance is the appearance in Soviet literature of works on the history of the culture, social thought, and ideology of the Latin American countries. In this connection, one must stress above all the study of the spread of Marxist-Leninist ideas in Latin America and their influence on the area's development. This problem is dealt with in a collection entitled *K. Marx and Latin America*.[78] A major contribution to the elaboration of this topic was the all-Union conference of scholars on Leninism and Latin America, held in April 1971.[79]

The conceptions of the prominent Peruvian Marxist thinker José Carlos Martiátegui have attracted the special attention of the scholarly community. Subjecting to criticism earlier characterizations (particularly those of V. M. Miroshevskii) of the views of this eminent propagandist of Marxist ideas in South America as petty bourgeois, "populist," "liberal," and utopian,[80] authors writing in the 1950s and '60s have given an objective analysis of his world view and ideological legacy as well as his role in the revolutionary movement in Peru.[81] Mariátegui's multifaceted activities and his ideas on a variety of questions (the independence movement, the role of the Indian community, the development of a national culture, literature and art, etc.) have received exceedingly full treatment in a collection of articles published on the seventieth anniversary of his birth.[82]

Diverse material is contained in the collaborative works *Problems of Ideology and the National Culture of the Latin American Countries*,† *Culture of the Indians*, and *The Culture and Life of the American Peoples*.[83] I. R. Grigulevich's book on the cultural revolution in Cuba represents the first attempt to analyze and summarize the basic achievements of the Cuban Revolution in the field of culture in the period 1959–64.[84]

It is only natural and logical that Soviet scholars should develop an interest (especially pronounced in the past decade) in the history of political, diplomatic, economic, cultural, scientific, and other ties between our country and the states of Latin America. A fundamental step in this direction was taken in the relatively brief survey by L. A. Shur, *Russia and Latin America,*† which offers a general picture of the development of Russo-Latin American relations from the sixteenth century to the Great October Socialist Revolution. Specific periods in these relations are examined in L. Yu. Slëzkin's monograph *Russia and the War of Independence in Spanish America*† and in the book by the Kishinëv scholar N. V. Korolëv, *The South American Countries and Russia,*† which spans the years 1890–1917.[85] Many articles have been published on the expedition of academician G. I. Langsdorf to Brazil (1821–29), the expedition of the Petersburg Academy of Sciences to Cuba and Mexico (1840–43), and the Russian scientific expedition of 1914–15 to South America, as well as on Russian seamen and travelers who in the late-eighteenth and nineteenth centuries visited various Latin American countries; the travel notes, diaries, and other materials of these visitors have been analyzed as sources for the history and ethnography of Brazil, California, Peru, Cuba, and other countries by L. A. Shur, B. N. Komissarov, B. V. Lukin, N. A. Smirnova, and Yu. Ya. Gerchuk.[86]

Somewhat less developed is the history of Soviet-Latin American relations, which is treated in studies by A. I. Sizonenko spanning the years 1924–70.† In 1967 a collection was published under the title *The USSR and Latin America.*† Articles by A. E. Ioffe† and V. M. Marchenko cover the 1920s and '30s.[87] As for ties between the Soviet Union and individual Latin American countries, the historical literature touches on the activities of the first diplomatic representatives of the USSR in Mexico[88] and on Soviet-Cuban relations.[89] In recent years, Soviet scholars have also shown interest in the history of cultural and scientific ties between Latvia and Latin America and in Ukrainian immigration to Argentina and Brazil at the turn of the nineteenth century.[90]

Historiographical studies, in their vast majority articles, treat an increasingly wide range of problems. They include a critical analysis by A. I. Shtrakhov of conservative-clerical conceptions of the Spanish colonial regime in the River Plate,† a review of foreign works on Russo-Latin American relations by Ya. M. Svet and L. A. Shur,† and A. A. Guber's analysis of studies by Soviet historians on the independence movement in Latin America†; other topics include North American historiography of the U.S. war against Mexico in 1846–48, U.S. Latin American policy during and following the Second World War, the Cuban Revolution, and the Dominican events of 1965.[91] Textbooks on historiography contain essays on the development of historical scholarship in Argentina, Chile, Brazil, Cuba, and Mexico.[92] One of several important historiographical works is A. A. Matlina's book *A Criticism of the Concept of "Peaceful Controlled Revolution" in Latin America.*[93]

Historical problems occupy an important place in the collective works *Latin America, Past and Present,*† *The Independence Movement in Latin America,*† and *From Alaska to Tierra del Fuego,*† as well as in country-survey volumes prepared by the Latin American Institute and the Institute of Ethnography of the Academy of Sciences (in some cases jointly): *Cuba* (1961), *Brazil* (1963),

Ecuador (1963), *Chile* (1965), *Venezuela* (1967), *Mexico* (1968), *Guiana* (1969), and *Peru: 150 Years of Independence* (1971).[94]

The Life of Outstanding People series, published by the Young Guard press, includes biographies of Simón Bolívar, Francisco de Miranda, Benito Juárez, Pancho Villa, Ernesto Che Guevara,† Columbus, Tiradentes, José Martí, Julio Antonio Mella, and Augusto César Sandino.[95] Short studies have appeared, too, on the lives and activities of Luis Emilio Recabarren and Camilo Cienfuegos.[96] A distinctively original treatment of the complex and contradictory figure of Bolívar is found in a book by V. I. Gusev, which was published in a massive edition of 200,000 copies.[97]

Semipopular works on the rise and fall of the Mayan civilization, the state of the "Olmec problem," the destiny and legacy of Christopher Columbus, and the discovery and conquest of Colombia[98] have also been published in large editions (the first two numbering 100,000 each, the third and fourth 65,000 and 60,000 respectively), thus testifying to a growing popular interest in Latin American topics.

In sum, one can state that Soviet Latin Americanists have, relatively speaking, been most successful in treating certain historical aspects of the ancient Indian civilizations, the independence movement of the late eighteenth and early nineteenth centuries, Russian relations with Latin America in the last century, and U.S. policies toward Latin America in the era of imperialism. Rather full treatment has been accorded the history of Mexico in the nineteenth and twentieth centuries and especially the Mexican Revolution of 1910–17, the historical development of Cuba from the late nineteenth century to the present—above all the Cuban Revolution and its consequences—the contemporary history of Chile, mainly in the period of the Popular Unity government (1970–73), and, in considerable measure, the history of Argentina, Brazil, and Colombia.

It goes without saying that these problems have been far from exhausted and many important questions remain to be resolved. But special attention must be given to those areas of Latin American history where the "blank spots" are far greater: the colonial era, the period between the wars of independence and the end of the nineteenth century, the twenty-year period from the First to the Second World War, and even to some degree the postwar years. Besides those countries which have been relatively well studied are others such as Peru, Uruguay, Ecuador, and the states of Central America and the West Indies, whose history remains, in essence, for Soviet Latin Americanists to investigate.

NOTES

1 Insasmuch as the concept of "Latin America" is a relative one, it is well to specify that in using this term we understand the aggregate of countries which occupies the

territory of South, Central, and a part of North America (south of the Río Grande), as well as the islands of the West Indies. The author derives this definition from the fact that all of these countries were discovered, conquered, and colonized by Latin peoples, namely the Spaniards, the Portuguese, and in part the French, although subsequently (seventeenth through nineteenth centuries) some of them became colonial possessions of England, Holland, Denmark, and the United States.

2 Diego de Landa, *Soobshchenie o delakh v Yukatane* [Relación de las cosas de Yucatán] (Moscow and Leningrad, 1955); *Popol-Vukh: Rodoslovnaia vladyka Totonikapana* [Popol Vuh: Título de los señores de Totonikapán] (Moscow and Leningrad, 1959); *Puteshestviia Khristofora Kolumba: Dnevniki, pis'ma, dokumenty* [The voyages of Christopher Columbus: journals, letters, documents], 4th ed. (Moscow, 1961); Bartolomé de las Casas, *Istoriia Indii* [Historia de las Indias] (Leningrad, 1968); Ya. M. Svet, ed., *Otkrytie velikoi reki Amazonok: Khroniki i dokumenty XVI veka o puteshestviiakh Fransisko de Orel'iany* [Discovery of the great river Amazon: sixteenth-century chronicles and documents on the travels of Francisco de Orellana] (Moscow, 1963); Walter Raleigh, *Otkrytie obshirnoi, bogatoi i prekrasnoi Gvianskoi imperii s pribavleniem rasskaza o velikom i zolotom gorode Manoa* [The discovery of the large, rich, and beautiful empire of Guiana, with a relation of the great golden city of Manoa] (Moscow, 1963); Alexandre Olivier Exquemelin, *Piraty Ameriki* [The buccaneers of America] (Moscow, 1968); Juan Bautista Alberdi, *Prestuplenie voiny* [El crimen de la guerra] (Moscow, 1960); José Martí, *Izbrannoe* [Selected works] (Moscow, 1956); idem, *Severo-amerikanskie stseny* [Escenas norteamericanas] (Moscow, 1963); A. R. Burgete, ed., *Progressivnye mysliteli Latinskoi Ameriki (XIX-Nachalo XX v.)* [Progressive thinkers of Latin America (19th and early 20th centuries)] (Moscow, 1965); José Carlos Mariátegui, *Sem' ocherkov istolkovaniia peruanskoi deistvitel'nosti* [Siete ensayos de interpretación de la realidad peruana] (Moscow, 1963); G. S. Gurvich, ed., *Konstitutsii gosudarstv Amerikanskogo kontinenta* [The constitutions of the states of the American continent], 3 vols. (Moscow, 1957-1959); *Programmnye dokumenty kommunisticheskikh i rabochikh partii stran Ameriki* [Program documents of the communist and labor parties of America] (Moscow, 1962).

3 N. N. Razumovich, ed., *Osnovnye zakonodatel'nye akty Kubinskoi Respubliki* [Basic legislative enactments of the Republic of Cuba] (Moscow, 1962); Fidel Castro, *Rechi i vystupleniia* [Speeches and addresses] (Moscow, 1960); idem, *Rechi i vystupleniia, 1961-1963* [Speeches and addresses, 1961-1963] (Moscow, 1963); idem, *Nashe delo pobezhdaet: Rechi i vystupleniia, 1963-1964* [Our casue triumphs: speeches and addresses, 1963-1964] (Moscow, 1965); idem, *Sila revoliutsii v edinstve* [The strength of the Revolution lies in unity] (Moscow, 1972); idem, *Budushchee prinadlezhit internatsionalizmu* [The future belongs to internationalism] (Moscow, 1973); Ernesto "Che" Guevara, *Partizanskaia voina* [Guerrilla warfare] (Moscow, 1961); idem, *Boliviiskii dnevnik* [Bolivian diary] (Moscow, 1968); idem, *Epizody revoliutsionnoi voiny* [Revolutionary war episodes] (Moscow, 1973); *Ot S'erra-Maestry do Gavany* [From the Sierra Maestra to Havana] (Moscow, 1965).

4 N. N. Bolkhovitinov, comp., "Otnoshenie Rossii k nachalu voiny Latinskoi Ameriki za nezavisimost'" [The attitude of Russia toward Latin America's war of independence], *IA,* no. 3 (May–June 1962), 120–31; "Russkie diplomaty o voine za

nezavisimost' v Latinskoi Amerike" [Russian diplomats on the war of independence in Latin America], *NNI*, no. 1 (January–February 1966), 112–21; "Otnosheniia Rossii so stranami Tsentral'noi Ameriki vo vtoroi polovine XIX veka" [Russian relations with the countries of Central America in the second half of the nineteenth century], *NNI*, no. 4 (July–August 1972), 106–19; Yu. P. Dzagurova et al., "Dva dokumenta o kubinskom osvoboditel'nom dvizhenii, 1934–1935," *IA*, no. 5 (September–October 1960), 208–10; "Iz geroicheskogo proshlogo kubinskogo naroda" [From the heroic past of the Cuban people], *MZh*, no. 3 (March 1964), 150–60; A. A. Guber, ed., "Agressiia SShA na Kube, 1898–1912 gg.," *IA*, no. 3 (1961). A valuable collection of documents on the history of the Cuban revolutionary movement, primarily from the late 1920s through the mid-'30s, is housed with the foreign holdings of the State Museum of the Revolution of the USSR [see bibliography: E. L. Nitoburg, "Dokumenty po istorii osvoboditel'nogo dvizheniia na Kube"].

5 See Bibliography: B. V. Lukin, "Sviazi Mirandy s rossiiskoi diplomaticheskoi missiei v Londone."

6 B. N. Komissarov, comp., "Braziliia v opisaniiakh uchastnikov russkoi ekspeditsii 1821–1829 godov"†; idem, "Iz dnevnika uchastnika russkoi nauchnoi ekspeditsii v Braziliiu v 1821–1829 gg." [From the diary of a participant in the Russian scientific expedition of 1821–1829 to Brazil], *LA*, no. 5 (September–October 1972), 144–60, and no. 1 (January–February 1973), 142–61; L. A. Shur, "Braziliia nachala XIX v. v neopublikovannom 'Zhurnale krugosvetnogo plavaniia' M. I. Ratmanova" [Early nineteenth-century Brazil in the unpublished "Journal of a Voyage Around the World" by M. I. Ratmanov], *LA*, no. 3 (1969), 176–84; idem, *K beregam Novogo Sveta*.†

7 See Bibliography: D. E. Bertel's, B. N. Komissarov, and T. I. Lysenko, comps., L. A. Shur, ed., *Materialy ekspeditsii akademika Grigoriia Ivanovicha Langsdorfa v Braziliiu v 1821–1829 gg.*

8 The earlier period (through 1966) is discussed in M. S. Al'perovich, *Sovetskaia istoriografiia stran Latinskoi Ameriki.*†

9 See, for example, E. S. Dabagian, "50 let sovetskoi latinoamerikanistiki (bibliograficheskii ocherk)" [Fifty years of Soviet Latin American studies (bibliographic essay)], in V. V. Vol'skii, ed., *SSSR i Latinskaia Amerika*†; S. S. Mikhailov, "Izuchenie Latinskoi Ameriki v Sovetskom Soiuze" [The study of Latin America in the Soviet Union], *Vop. Ist.*, no. 4 (April 1962), 98–106; idem, "Nekotorye voprosy izucheniia Latinskoi Ameriki" [Some problems of Latin American studies], *NNI*, no. 2 (March–April 1964), 29–36; V. V. Vol'skii, "Sovetskaia latinoamerikanistika: Nekotorye itogi i zadachi" [Soviet Latin American studies: some results and tasks], *LA*, no. 3 (May–June 1971), 6–16.

10 This is not necessary, since in addition to the bibliographic data contained in the above-mentioned works and in E. S. Dabagian's review, "Raboty sovetskikh uchënykh v 1965–1969 gg. po istorii stran Latinskoi Ameriki" [The works of Soviet scholars on the history of Latin America, 1965–1969], in *Raboty sovetskikh istorikov za 1965–1969 gg.* (Moscow, 1970), pp. 192–207, a complete bibliography of books and articles on Latin America published in the period 1946–1970 is found in the multivolume guide *Latinskaia Amerika v sovetskoi pechati* [see below, pp. 59–60]. In English, see Leo Okinshevich, comp., and Robert G. Carlton, ed., *Latin America in*

48 | M. S. AL'PEROVICH

Soviet Writings: A Bibliography, 2 vols. (Baltimore, 1966). In the present volume, as well, there is a selected annotated bibliography of Soviet works compiled by Professor R. Bartley.

11 On the training of Soviet Latin American specialists, see V. V. Vol'skii, "The Study of Latin America in the U.S.S.R.," *LARR* 3 no. 1 (Fall 1967), 87.

12 M. S. Al'perovich and L. Yu. Slëzkin, *Obrazovanie nezavisimykh gosudarstv v Latinskoi Amerike (1804–1903)* (Moscow, 1966).

13 S. A. Tikarev and I. A. Zolotarevskaia, eds., *Indeitsy Ameriki* [The Indians of America] (Moscow, 1955); A. V. Efimov and S. A. Tokarev, eds., *Narody Ameriki*†; A. V. Efimov, I. R. Grigulevich, and S. A. Gonionskii, eds., *Natsii Latinskoi Ameriki.*†

14 O. A. Zhidkov, *Istoriia gosudarstva i prava stran Latinskoi Ameriki* (Moscow, 1967).

15 I. R. Lavretskii, *Ten' Vatikana nad Latinskoi Amerikoi* (Moscow, 1961).

16 N. A. Krasheninnikova, *Istoriia gosudarstva i prava Kuby* (Moscow, 1966).

17 S. A. Gonionskii, *Kolumbiia* (Moscow, 1973).

18 N. S. Leonov, *Nekotorye problemy politicheskoi istorii Tsentral'noi Ameriki XX stoletiia* (Moscow, 1972). 1972).

19 Yu. V. Knorozov, *Sistema pis'ma drevnykh maiia.*†

20 E. V. Evreinov, Yu. G. Kosarev, and V. A. Ustinov, *Primenenie elektronnykh vychislitel'nykh mashin v issledovanni pis'mennosti drevnykh maiia* [The application of electronic computers in research on ancient Mayan writing], 3 vols. (Novosibirsk, 1961); idem, "Vychislitel'naia tekhnika v istoriko-filologicheskikh issledovaniiakh (Analiz drevnykh rukopisei maiia s pomoshch'iu elektronnoi matematicheskoi mashiny)" [Computer techniques in historico-philological investigations (An analysis of ancient Mayan manuscripts with the aid of the electronic computer)], *VAN*, no. 1 (1962), 80–83. See, also, *VAN*, no. 4 (1961), 64–67.

21 See Yu. V. Knorozov, "Mashinnaia deshifrovka pis'ma maiia" [Computer deciphering of Mayan writing], *Vop. iazyk.*, no. 1 (1962), 91–99; *VAN*, no. 11 (1963), 143–44; U. Schlenther, "Kritische Bemerkungen zur kybernetischen Entzifferung der Maya-Hieroglyphen," *Ethnographisch-archäologische Zeitschrift*, no. 2 (1964), 111–39; idem, *Die geistige Welt der Maya* (Berlin, 1965), pp. 130–50.

22 R. V. Kinzhalov, *Iskusstvo drevnei Ameriki* (Moscow, 1962); idem, *Iskusstvo drvnykh maiia* (Leningrad, 1968).

23 V. I. Guliaev, *Amerika i Staryi Svet v dokolumbovu epokhu.*†

24 V. I. Guliaev, "K voprosu ob aziatskikh vliianiiakh na drevnie tsivilizatsii Tsentral'noi Ameriki (Sovremennoe sostoianie voprosa)" [On the question of Asian influences on the ancient civilizations of Central America (the present state of the problem)], in N. Ya. Merpert and P. M. Kozhin, eds., *Arkheologiia Starogo i Novogo Sveta* (Moscow, 1966), pp. 251–68.

25 V. A. Kuz'mishchev, "Govoriashchie uzly Tauantinsuiiu" [The quipu of Tahuantinsuyo], *LA*, no. 6 (November–December 1971), 104–22; idem, "Eshchë raz ob inkakh (k voprosu o sotsial'no-ekonomicheskoi prirode gosudarstva Tauantinsuiiu" [More on the Incas (the socio-economic nature of the government of the Tahuantinsuyo)], *LA*, no. 2 (March–April 1973), 129–50.

26 A. D. Dridzo, "K voprosu o chislennosti indeitsev Yamaiki pered nachalom

kolonizatsii" [On the size of the Indian population of Jamaica at the onset of colonization], *SE*, no. 3 (May–June 1966), 139–44; L. S. Shteinbaum and E. G. Aleksandrenkov, "Etnicheskie gruppy indeitsev Bol'shikh Antil'skikh i Bagamskikh ostrovov na rubezhe XV-XVI vv." [Indigenous ethnic groups of the Greater Antilles and Bahamas at the turn of the 15th century], *SE*, no. 3 (May–June 1971), 103–12.

27 Zh. D. Smirenskaia, "Ob evoliutsii sotsial'no-ekonomicheskoi struktury Severo-Vostoka Brazilii v XVI-XVIII vv." [The evolution of the socio-economic structure of Northeast Brazil in the 16th–18th centuries], SV, vyp. 35 (1972), 174–95.

28 Idem, "Krushenie iezuitskogo ordena v kolonial'noi Amerike" [The demise of the Jesuit order in America], *NNI*, no. 5 (September–October 1973), 85–101, and no. 6 (November–December 1973), 128–38; L. G. Kritskii, "Ispanskaia tserkov' i rol' katolitsizma v Latinskoi Amerike v XVI–XIX vekakh" [The Spanish church and the role of Catholicism in Latin America in the 16th–19th centuries], *Vop. Ist.*, no. 4 (April 1973), 90–102.

29 Yu. A. Zubritskii, "Velikoe vosstanie" [The great uprising], in *Peru: 150 let nezavisimosti* [Peru: 150 years of independence] (Moscow, 1971), pp. 29–55.

30 B. N. Foinitskii, "Iz istorii padeniia plantatsionnogo rabstva v britanskoi Vest-Indii" [From the history of the decline of plantation slavery in the British West Indies], *NTNGPI*, vyp. 22 (1968), 48–68.

31 On the commemoration of this important historical date, see *VAN*, no. 7 (July 1960), 113–14; *Vop. Ist.*, no. 8 (August 1960), 172–74; G. A. Mel'nikova and L. V. Pegusheva, "150-letie voiny za nezavisimost' stran Latinskoi Ameriki v SSSR" [The USSR and the 150th anniversary of the Latin American war of independence], *VIMK*, no. 5 (September–October 1961), 151–58. The proceedings of the above-mentioned session of the Institute of World Economy and International Relations were published as a separate volume: V. Ya. Arvin and M. V. Danilevich, eds., *Natsional'no-osvoboditel'noe dvizhenie v Lationskoi Amerike na sovremennom etape* [The present stage of the national-liberation movement in Latin America] (Moscow, 1961).

32 V. I. Ermolaev, "Nekotorye voprosy osvoboditel'noi bor'by amerikanskikh kolonii Ispanii i Portugalii (K 150-letiiu nachala voiny za nezavisimost' 1810–1826 gg.)"†; A. A. Guber and N. M. Lavrov, "K 150-letiiu voiny za nezavisimost' Latinskoi Ameriki"†; M. S. Al'perovich, "Velikaia frantsuzskaia revoliutsiia XVIII veka i ispanskie kolonii v Amerike."†

33 For more detail on the study of these problems, see A. A. Guber, "Problemy natsional'no-osvoboditel'noi bor'by v Latinskoi Amerike (1810–1826 gg.) v trudakh sovetskikh istorikov."†

34 Ibid., p. 34.

35 A. B. Belen'kii, *Razgrom meksikanskim narodom inostrannoi interventsii.*†

36 V. M. Goncharov, "Dakilema, velikii Dakilema..." [Daquilema, the great Daquilema...], *LA*, no. 3 (May–June 1972), 122–29; idem, "Indeitsy v liberal'noi revoliutsii Eloia Al'faro" [The Indians in the liberal revolution of Eloy Alfaro], *LA*, no. 3 (May–June 1973), 122–30; B. I. Koval, "K voprosu o sotsial'no-ekonomicheskom razvitii Brazilii v seredine XIX veka"†; V. I. Petukhov, "Nastuplenie inostrannykh monopolii v Yuzhnoi Amerike posle Tikhookeanskoi voiny 1879–1884 godov"†; idem, "Posledniaia interventsiia Ispanii v Yuzhnoi Amerike (1863–1866)"†; T. N. Shavlokhova, "Federal'naia voina v Venesuele"†; G. S.

Vasilevich, "Burzhuaznyi radikalizm v Argentine v 70–90-e gody" [Bourgeois radicalism in Argentina in the 1870s–'90s], *VMU*, no. 6 (November–December 1971), 38–51; A. M. Zorina, "K voprosu o genezise kapitalizma na Kube v XIX veke."†

37 N. R. Matveeva, "Braziliia i strany La Platy posle Paragvaiskoi voiny, 1864–1870"†; idem, "Kolonial'naia ekspansiia Anglii v Paragvae"†; idem, "O prichinakh voenno-morskoi ekspeditsii SShA protiv Paragvaia v 1858–1859 gg." [Reasons for the U.S. naval expedition against Paraguay in 1858–1859], *UZKGPI* 62 (1971), 39–68; idem, "Pervye popytki ustanovleniia otnoshenii SShA s Paragvaem."†

38 A. M. Zorina, *Iz geroicheskogo proshlogo kubinskogo naroda.*†

39 O. Ternovoi, *Khose Marti* (Moscow, 1966).

40 N. M. Lavrov, *Rabochee i natsional'no-osvoboditel'noe dvizhenie v stranakh Latinskoi Ameriki na pervom etape obshchego krizisa kapitalizma* [The labor and national-liberation movement in Latin America during the first phase of the general crisis of capitalism] (Moscow, 1956).

41 A. A. Sokolov, "Meksikanskaia regional'naia rabochaia konfederatsiia i rezhim 'revoliutsionnogo kaudil'izma' (1920–1928 gg.)"†; idem, "Meksikanskaia kommunisticheskaia partiia v bor'be za edinstvo rabochego dvizheniia strany (1919–1929 gg.)."†

42 A. I. Stroganov, *Bor'ba za edinyi rabochii i narodnyi front v Argentine v 1933–1936 gg.* (Moscow, 1969).

43 Idem, "Rabochaia politika pravitel'stva Irigoiena v Argentine (1916–1922 gg.)" [Labor policy of the Irigoyen adminstration in Argentina (1916–1922)], in *Problemy novoi i noveishei istorii* [Problems of modern and recent history] (Moscow, 1972), pp. 132–48.

44 N. P. Kalmykov, "Rabochaia politika pravitel'stva Zh. Vargasa v period 'Novogo gosudarstva' (1937–1945 gg.)" [The labor policy of the G. Vargas administration during the Estado Novo period (1937–1945)], *LA*, no. 3 (May–June 1971), 65–83; B. I. Koval, "Iz istorii revoliutsionnykh boev 1935 goda v Brazilii" [From the history of the revolutionary conflicts of 1935 in Brazil], *NNI*, no. 2 (March–April 1962), 15–28; V. M. Pchela, "Proniknovenie amerikanskogo kapitala v Kolumbiiu v 20-e gody XX v. i ego vliianie na sotsial'no-ekonomicheskoe razvitie strany" [The penetration of American capital in Colombia in the 1920s and its influence on the country's socioeconomic development], in *Problemy novoi i noveishei istorii stran Evropy i Ameriki* (Moscow, 1972), pp. 98–121; idem, "Rabochii klass Kolumbii i politika A. Lopesa" [The Colombian working class and the policies of A. López], *LA*, no. 4 (July–August 1972), 51–58; N. S. Larin [pseud.], "Iz istorii osvoboditel'noi bor'by naroda Nikaragua protiv vooruzhënnoi interventsii SShA v 1927–1933 godakh"†; Yu. A. Zubritskii, "Sandino i kharakter ego dvizheniia" [Sandino and the nature of his movement], *Trudy Universiteta druzhby narodov* [Transactions of the Peoples' Friendship University] 32 (istoriia), vyp. 1 (1968), 130–46; I. S. Ivanov, "Strany Latinskoi Ameriki i Liga natsii" [The Latin American countries and the League of Nations], *LA*, no. 5 (September–October 1973), 125–36,

45 I. K. Sheremet'ev, *Gosudarstvennyi kapitalizm v Meksike* [State capitalism in Mexico] (Moscow, 1963); L. S. Nosova, *Gosudarstvennyi kapitalizm v Brazilii* [State capitalism in Brazil] (Moscow, 1971); S. S. Mishin, *Protsess kontsentratsii kapitala v*

Brazilii [The process of capital concentration in Brazil] (Moscow, 1972); Z. I. Romanova, *Problemy ekonomicheskoi integratsii v Latinskoi Amerike* [Problems of economic integration in Latin America] (Moscow, 1965); M. L. Chumakova, *Integratsionnye protsessy v stranakh Tsentral'noi Ameriki* [Processes of integration in the countries of Central America] (Moscow, 1972); V. V. Vol'skii, *Latinskaia Amerika, neft' i nezavisimost'* [Latin America, oil and independence] (Moscow, 1964), published in Spanish as *América Latina, petróleo e independencia* (Buenos Aires, 1966).

46 A. M. Sivolobov, *Ekonomicheskie problemy soiuza rabochego klassa i krest'ianstva v stranakh Latinskoi Ameriki* [Economic problems of uniting the working class and peasantry in the countries of Latin America] (Moscow, 1966).

47 Yu. G. Onufriev, ed., *Agrarnyi vopros i problemy osvoboditel'nogo dvizheniia v stranakh Latinskoi Ameriki: Sbornik statei* [The agrarian question and problems of the liberation movement in the countries of Latin America: a collection of articles] (Moscow, 1968).

48 E. V. Kovalev, *Agrarnye reformy v stranakh Latinskoi Ameriki* [Agrarian reform in the countries of Latin America] (Moscow, 1973); A. M. Sivolobov, *Agrarnye otnosheniia v sovremennoi Brazilii* [Agrarian relations in contemporary Brazil] (Moscow, 1959); V. I. Leonov, *Revoliutsionnye agrarnye preobrazovaniia v Peru* [Revolutionary agrarian reforms in Peru] (Moscow, 1973); A. D. Galkina, *Chili: Bor'ba za agrarnuiu reformu* [Chile: the struggle for agrarian reform] (Moscow, 1972).

49 N. N. Razumovich, *Kto i kak pravit v Latinskoi Amerike: Politicheskaia sistema stran Latinskoi Ameriki* [Who rules and how in Latin America: the Latin American political system] (Moscow, 1967).

50 G. N. Kolomiets et al., *Politicheskie partii stran Latinskoi Ameriki* (Moscow, 1965).

51 S. I. Semënov, *Khristianskaia demokratiia i revoliutsionnyi protsess v Latinskoi Amerike* [Christian Democracy and the revolutionary process in Latin America] (Moscow, 1971).

52 E. S. Dabagian, *Natsional-reformizm v sovremennoi Vanasuele*†; I. N. Zorina, *Revoliutsiia ili reforma v Latinskoi Amerike: Kritika reformizma chiliskoi khristianskoi demokratii* [Revolution or reform in Latin America: criticism of Chilean Christian Democratic reformism] (Moscow, 1971); B. S. Nikiforov, *Kuba: Krakh burzhuaznykh politicheskikh partii (1945–1958)* [Cuba: the collapse of the bourgeois political parties (1945-1958)] (Moscow, 1973); I. E. Shokina, *Peronistskoi dvizhenie v sovremennoi Argentine* [The Peronist movement in contemporary Argentina] (Moscow, 1969).

53 V. I. Ermolaev and A. F. Shul'govskii, *Rabochee i kommunisticheskoe dvizhenie v Latinskoi Amerike (s Oktiabria do nashikh dnei)* [The labor and communist movement in Latin America (from the October Revolution to the present)] (Moscow, 1970).

54 B. I. Koval, ''Problemy natsional'no-osvoboditel'nogo dvizheniia v programmnykh dokumentakh kompartii stran Latinskoi Ameriki'' [Problems of the national-liberation movement in the official documents of the Latin American Communist Parties], *NNI,* no. 2 (March–April 1964), 95–107; I. R. Lavretskii [pseud.], ''Katolicheskoe rabochee dvizhenie i politika kommunisticheskikh partii Latinskoi Ameriki'' [The Catholic labor movement and the policy of the Latin American Communist Parties], *Vop. Ist. KPSS,* no. 8 (August 1961), 70–89.

55 A. V. Viatkin, "Kommunisticheskaia partiia Argentiny v bor'be za edinstvo rabochego klassa (1956–1960 gg.)" [The Communist Party of Argentina in the struggle for working class unity (1956–1960)], in A. A. Guber, ed., *Bor'ba za edinyi rabochii i antiimperialisticheskii front v stranakh Latinskoi Ameriki* [The struggle for a united labor and antiimperialist front in Latin America] (Moscow, 1963), pp. 16–123; N. V. Miachin, "Bor'ba Kommunisticheskoi partii Chili za sozdanie fronta natsional'nogo osvobozhdeniia (1956–1960 gg.)" [The struggle of the Communist Party of Chile for the creation of a national-liberation front (1956–1960)], ibid., pp. 124–219; M. I. Mokhnachev, "Sliianie revoliutsionnogo dvizheniia na Kube v edinyi patrioticheskii, antiimperialisticheskii potok (1951–1958 gg.)" [The development of the revolutionary movement in Cuba into a unified patriotic, antiimperialist current 1951–1958)], ibid., pp. 120–307; O. Konstantinov, "Novyi etap rabochego i kommunisticheskogo dvizheniia Meksiki" [A new stage in the labor and Communist movement of Mexico], in *Voprosy mezhdunarodnogo rabochego i natsional'no-osvoboditel'nogo dvizheniia na sovremennom etape: Sbornik statei* [Questions of the contemporary international labor and national-liberation movement: a collection of articles] (Moscow, 1963), pp. 61–167; N. F. Kolobashkin, "Bor'ba Kommunisticheskoi partii Urugvaia za sozdanie demokraticheskogo fronta natsional'nogo osvobozhdeniia (1955–1962 gg.)" [The struggle of the Communist Party of Uruguay for the creation of a democratic front of national liberation (1955–1962)], in A. A. Guber and Yu. N. Chubarov, eds., *Natsional'no-osvoboditel'naia bor'ba narodov na sovremennom etape* [The national-liberation struggle in its present stage] (Moscow, 1966), pp. 150–91.

56 *Voprosy mezhdunarodnogo rabochego i natsional'no-osvoboditel'nogo dvizheniia na sovremennom etape;* Guber and Chubarov, eds., *Natsional'no-osvoboditel'naia bor'ba narodov na sovremennom etape.*

57 I. R. Lavretskii [pseud.], *Bogi v tropikakh* [Gods in the tropics] (Moscow, 1967).

58 V. P. Andronova, *Tserkov' i prosveshchenie v Latinskoi Amerike* [The church and education in Latin America] (Moscow, 1972); idem, *Kolumbiia: Tserkov' i obshchestvo* [Colombia: church and society] (Moscow, 1970).

59 A. N. Glinkin, V. V. Vol'skii and B. I. Gvozdarev, eds., *Strany Latinskoi Ameriki v sovremennykh mezhdunarodnykh otnosheniiakh* (Moscow, 1967).

60 B. I. Gvozdarev, *Organizatsiia amerikanskikh gosudarstv* [The Organization of American States] (Moscow, 1960); idem, *Evoliutsiia i krizis mezhamerikanskoi sistemy* [Evolution and crisis of the inter-American system] (Moscow, 1966); M. I. Lazarev, *Dvortsovye perevoroty v stranakh Latinskoi Ameriki (mezhdunarodno-pravovoe priznanie novykh pravitel' stv)* [Palace coups in Latin America (the recognition of new governments in international law)] (Moscow, 1967); M. L. Chumakova, *Organizatsiia tsentral'noamerikanskikh gosudarstv* [The Organization of Central American States] (Moscow, 1970).

61 A. V. Efimov et al., eds., *Piat' let kubinskoi revoliutsii* [Five years of the Cuban Revolution] (Moscow, 1963); V. V. Vol'skii et al., eds., *Kuba: 10 let revoliutsii* [Cuba: 10 years of the Revolution] (Moscow, 1968).

62 See, for example, K. M. Obyden, *Kuba v bor'be za svobodu i nezavisimost'* [Cuba in the struggle for freedom and independence] (Moscow, 1959); V. V. Andrianov, *Svobodnaia Kuba* [Free Cuba] (Moscow, 1960); P. G. Kokhreidze, *Kuba: Zaria*

pervogo ianvaria [Cuba: the dawning of January first] (Tbilisi, 1963); N. N. Klymko, *Sotsialistychni peretvorennia no Kubi* [Socialist reforms in Cuba] (Kiev, 1964); B. M. Merin, *Svobodnaia Kuba* [Free Cuba] (Moscow, 1964); N. N. Razumovich, *Gosudarstvennye preobrazovaniia revoliutsionnoi Kuby* [Governmental reforms in Revolutionary Cuba] (Moscow, 1964).

63 Yu. N. Korolëv, *Chili: Problemy edinstva demokraticheskikh i antiimperialisticheskikh sil (1956–1970 gg.)* [Chile: problems of uniting the democratic and antiimperialist forces (1956–1970)] (Moscow, 1973); M. F. Kudachkin, *Chili: Bor'ba za edinstvo i pobedu levykh sil* [Chile: the struggle for the unity and triumph of the forces of the left] (Moscow, 1973). See, also, K. M. Obyden, "Chiliiskaia revoliutsiia: Uspekhi i problemy" [The Chilean revolution: achievements and problems], *NNI*, no. 2 (March–April 1973), 20–38.

64 Yu. A. Antonov, *Braziliia: Armiia i politika (istoricheskii ocherk)* [Brazil: the army and politics (an historical outline)] (Moscow, 1973). For a more general discussion of this topic, see A. F. Shul'govskii, *Latinskaia Amerika: Armiia i osvoboditel'noe dvizhenie* [Latin America: the army and the liberation movement] (Moscow, 1972).

65 B. M. Merin, *Tsentral'naia Amerika: Problemy sotsial'no-politicheskogo razvitiia* [Central America: problems of socio-political development] (Moscow, 1973); E. V. Demushkina, *Venesuela posle vtoroi mirovoi voiny: 1945–1958* [Venezuela following the Second World War: 1945–1958] (Moscow, 1969); N. G. Il'ina, *Politicheskaia bor'ba v Kolumbii (1946–1957)*†; Yu. A. Fadeev, *Revoliutsiia i kontrrevoliutsiia v Bolivii* [Revolution and counterrevolution in Bolivia] (Moscow, 1969); V. A. Kharitonov, *Paragvai: Voenno-politseiskaia diktatura i politicheskaia bor'ba* [Paraguay: the military-police dictatorship and the political struggle] (Moscow, 1970); A. S. Koval'skaia, *Na puti k svobode* [On the path to freedom] (Moscow, 1973).

66 *Argentina 60-kh godov* [Argentina in the 1960s] (Moscow, 1973); R. F. Ivanov and M. S. Al'perovich, eds., *Rabochee i natsional'no-osvoboditel'noe dvizhenie v stranakh Ameriki* [The labor and national-liberation movement in the countries of Latin America] (Moscow, 1966).

67 E. V. Ananova, "Dominikanskaia tragediia" [The Dominican tragedy], *NNI*, no. 4 (July–August 1965), 34–52 and no. 6 (November–December 1965), 64–80; S. A. Gonionskii, " 'Papasha Diuval'e'—besnovatyi tiran Gaiti" ['Papa Duvalier''— raging tyrant of Haiti], *NNI*, no. 2 (March–April 1966), 44–55; S. I. Lukina, "Gaitianskii narod v bor'be protiv diktatury Diuval'e" [The Haitian people against the Duvalier dictatorship], *LA*, no. 2 (March–April 1973), 40–53; S. A. Gonionskii, "Dinastiia tiranov Somosa" [The tyrannical Somoza dynasty], *NNI*, no. 1 (January– February 1973), 136–45 and no. 2 (March–April 1973), 128–37.

68 S. A. Gonionskii, *Latinskaia Amerika i SShA (1939–1959)* [Latin America and the USA (1939–1959)] (Moscow, 1960); L. I. Zubok, *Ekspansionistskaia politika SShA v nachale XX veka* [U.S. expansionist policies in the early 20th century] (Moscow, 1969); L. Yu. Slëzkin, *Politika SShA v Yuzhnoi Amerike, 1929–1933*†; K. S. Tarasov, *SShA i Latinskaia Amerika (voenno-politicheskie i voenno-ekonomicheskie otnosheniia)* [The United States and Latin America (military-political and military-economic relations)] (Moscow, 1972).

69 M. V. Antiasov, *Sovremennyi panamerikanizm: Proiskhozhdenie i sushchnost' doktrin panamerikanskoi "solidarnosti"* [Contemporary Pan-Americanism: the origin

and nature of the doctrines of Pan-American "solidarity"] (Moscow, 1960); G. A. Kumanev and G. K. Seleznev, *Amerikanskaia politika "novykh rubezhei" v Latinskoi Amerike (1961-1971 gg.)* [The American "new frontiers" policy in Latin America (1961-1971)] (Moscow, 1972); V. N. Selivanov, *Voennaia politika SShA v stranakh Latinskoi Ameriki* [U.S. military policy in Latin America] (Moscow, 1970).

70 Z. I. Romanova, *Ekonomicheskaia ekspansiia SShA v Latinskoi Amerike* [The economic expansion of the United States in Latin America] (Moscow, 1963); Yu. M. Grigor'ian, *Ekonomicheskaia ekspansiia FRG v Latinskoi Amerike* [The economic expansion of the Federal Republic of Germany in Latin America] (Moscow, 1965); E. Ya. Sheinin, *Ekonomicheskaia ekspansiia gosudarstv chlenov EES v Latinskoi Amerike* [The economic expansion of the member states of the EEC in Latin America] (Moscow, 1969).

71 B. I. Gvozdarev, ed., *Neokolonializm SShA v Latinskoi Amerike* (Moscow, 1970).

72 B. I. Gvozdarev, *"Soiuz radi progressa" i ego sushchnost'* [The "Alliance for Progress" and its nature] (Moscow, 1964); Yu. P. Eliutin, " 'Soiuz radi progressa'— novoe orudie imperialisticheskoi politiki SShA v Latinskoi Amerike" [The "Alliance for Progress"—a new instrument of U.S. imperialist policy in Latin America], *NNI*, no. 3 (May–June 1963), 36–48.

73 E. L. Nitoburg, *Pokhishchenie zhemchuzhiny* [The stolen pearl] (Moscow, 1968).

74 K. S. Shustov, *Zhemchuzhina Antill i ianki (Kuba i imperializm SShA), 1899-1952* [The Pearl of the Antilles and the Yankees (Cuba and U.S. imperialism), 1899-1952] (Alma-Ata, 1967).

75 V. Listov and Vl. Zhukov, *Tainaia voina protiv revoliutsionnoi Kuby* [The secret war against revolutionary Cuba] (Moscow, 1966).

76 V. G. Zhukov and V. V. Listov, *"Bol'shaia dubinka" nad Santo-Domingo* [The "big stick" over Santo Domingo] (Moscow, 1969); Yu. P. Gorokhov, *Dominikanskaia Respublika i amerikanskii imperializm* [The Dominican Republic and American imperialism] (Moscow, 1970); N. T. Poiarkova, *Kolonial'naia politika SShA v Puerto-Riko†*; A. P. Moskalenko, *Puerto-Riko—koloniia SShA* [Puerto Rico: an American colony] (Moscow, 1972); idem, "Zakhvat Puerto-Riko v 1898 godu i prevrashchenie ego v koloniiu SShA" [The seizure of Puerto Rico in 1898 and its conversion into an American colony], *NNI*, no. 3 (May–June 1968), 81–87; N. S. Leonov, "Iz istorii amerikanskoi interventsii v Nikaragua" [From the history of the American intervention in Nicaragua], *LA*, no. 2 (March–April 1972), 124–41.

77 V. Smolenskii, "SShA i Tikhookeanskaia voina 1879-1884 gg." [The United States and the War of the Pacific, 1879-1884], *NNI*, no. 3 (May–June 1967), 16–30.

78 V. V. Vol'skii, ed., *K. Marks i Latinskaia Amerika* [Karl Marx and Latin America] (Moscow, 1970).

79 V. Vol'skii et al., eds., *El leninismo y América Latina* (Moscow, 1971).

80 See V. Miroshevskii, " 'Narodnichestvo' v Peru: K vopruso o roli Kh. K. Mariategi v istorii latinoamerikanskoi obshchestvennvoi mysli" ["Populism" in Peru: the role of José Carlos Mariátegui in the history of Latin American social thought], *Istorik-marksist*, no. 6 (1941), 78–86.

81 S. I. Semënov and A. F. Shul'govskii, "Rol' Khose Karlosa Mariategi v sozdanii Kommunisticheskoi partii Peru"†; V. N. Kuteishchikova, "Rol' Khose Karlosa Mariategi v razvitii natsional'noi kul'tury Peru" [The role of José Carlos Mariátegui

in the development of Peruvian national culture], *VIMK*, no. 6 (November–December 1960), 3–19; V. G. Korionov, "Vydaiushchiisia borets za torzhestvo idei marksizma-leninizma v Latinskoi Amerike" [A prominent champion of the ideas of Marxism-Leninism in Latin America], *NNI*, no. 6 (November–December 1965).

82 *Khose Karlos Mariategi: Plamennyi borets za torzhestvo idei marksizma-leninizma v Latinskoi Amerike* [José Carlos Mariátegui: ardent champion of the ideas of Marxism-Leninism in Latin America] (Moscow, 1966).

83 A. V. Efimov and I. A. Zolotarevskaia, eds., *Kul'tura indeitsev: Vklad korennogo naseleniia Ameriki v mirovuiu kul'turu* [Culture of the Indians: the contribution of the native American population to world culture] Moscow, 1963); R. V. Kinzhalov, ed., *Kul'tura i byt narodov Ameriki* [Culture and life of the American peoples] (Leningrad, 1967).

84 I. R. Grigulevich, *Kul'turnaia revoliutsiia na Kube* [The cultural revolution in Cuba] (Moscow, 1965).

85 See, also, V. F. Sukhomlinov, "Ob ustanovlenii russko-brazil'skikh otnoshenii"†; R. Sh. Ganelin, "Iz istorii ekonomicheskikh sviazei Rossii s Meksikoi i Braziliei v seredine XIX veka".†

86 See in this volume, L. A. Shur, ch. 7, and B. N. Komissarov, ch. 11. See also, B. V. Lukin, "Etnograficheskie svedeniia o Peru serediny XIX v. v dnevnike L. I. Shrenka" [cited below, ch. 7 n. 45]; idem, "Ekspeditsiia Peterburgskoi Akademii nauk v Meksiku i na Kubu" [An expedition of the Petersburg Academy of Sciences to Mexico and Cuba], *VAN*, no. 7 (July 1966), 109–12; N. A. Smirnova, "Vtoraia russkaia ekspeditsiia v Yuzhnuiu Ameriku 1914–1915 gg., eë materialy i kollektsii" [The second Russian expedition to South America (1914–1915), papers and collections], *SE*, no. 6 (November–December 1966), 98–112; Yu. Ya. Gerchuk, "Etnograficheskie nabliudeniia russkogo puteshestvennika F. A. Karzhavina v Amerike" [The ethnographic observations of the Russian traveler F. V. Karzhavin in America], *SE*, no. 1 (January–February 1972).

87 V. M. Marchenko, "Pervye shagi sovetskoi diplomatii v ustanovlenii politicheskikh i ekonomicheskikh sviazei so stranami Latinskoi Ameriki v 20-e–30-e gody" [The first steps of Soviet diplomacy in the establishment of political and economic ties with the countries of Latin America during the 1920s–1930s], *VLU*, no. 2 (seriia istorii, iazyka i literatury), vyp. 1 (1966), 54–61; idem, "Sovetsko-meksikanskie diplomaticheskie i torgovye otnosheniia v 20-e i 30-e gody" [Soviet-Mexican diplomatic and trade relations in the 1920s and '30s], in *Problemy otechestvennoi i vseobshchei istorii* [Problems of Russian and world history] (Leningrad, 1969), pp. 183–94.

88 A. I. Sizonenko, *V strane atstekskogo orla: Pervye sovetskie polpredy v Meksike* [In the country of the Aztecan eagle: the first Soviet ambassadors to Mexico] (Moscow, 1969).

89 *Sovetskii Soiuz i Kuba: 15 let bratskogo sotrudnichestva* [The Soviet Union and Cuba: 15 years of fraternal cooperation] (Moscow, 1973); A. D. Bekarevich and N. M. Kukharev, *Sovetskii Soiuz i Kuba: Ekonomicheskoe sotrudnichestvo* [The Soviet Union and Cuba: economic cooperation] (Moscow, 1973).

90 See, for example, A. D. Dridzo, "Latyshi v Latinskoi Amerike" [Letts in Latin America], *LA*, no. 1 (January–February 1970), 99–106; idem, "Iz istorii kul'turnykh i nauchnykh sviazei Latvii i Latinskoi Ameriki" [From the history of cultural and

scientific ties between Latvia and Latin America], in *Iz istorii estestvoznaniia i tekhniki Pribaltiki* [From the history of natural science and technology in the Baltic] (Riga, 1968), I, 261–68; A. A. Strelko, "Pervye immigranty-ukraintsy na latinoamerikanskom kontinente" [The first Ukrainian immigrants on the Latin American continent], *LA*, no. 4 (July–August 1972), 87–93.

91 N. V. Potokova, "Amerikano-meksikanskaia voina 1846–1848 godov" [The Mexican-American War of 1846–1848], in G. N. Sevost'ianov, ed., *Osnovnye problemy istorii SShA v amerikanskoi istoriografii* [Fundamental problems of U.S. history in American historiography] (Moscow, 1971), pp. 315–62; A. I. Kedrov, "Politika SShA v Latinskoi Amerike v gody vtoroi mirovoi voiny v traktovke amerikanskikh burzhuaznykh istorikov" [U.S. policies in Latin America during the second world war as presented by American bourgeois historians], *Vop. Ist.*, no. 11 (November 1961), 172–82; E. V. Ananova and A. A. Matlina, "Politika SShA v Latinskoi Amerike" [U.S. policy in Latin America], in G. N. Sevost'ianov, ed., *Amerikanskaia istoriografiia vneshnei politiki SShA, 1945–1970* [American historiography of U.S. foreign policy, 1945–1970] (Moscow, 1972), pp. 302–48; L. Yu. Slëzkin, "Istoriografiia kubinskoi revoliutsii (vozniknovenie i stanovlenie)"†; Yu. P. Gorokhov, "Amerikanskaia burzhuaznaia istoriografiia dominikanskikh sobytii 1965 g.," *LA*, no. 2 (March–April 1973), 187–93.

92 See above, ch. 1, n. 87, vols. edited by I. S. Galkin et al.

93 A. A. Matlina, *Kritika kontseptsii "mirnoi reguliruemoi revoliutsii" dlia Latinskoi Ameriki* [A criticism of the concept of "peaceful controlled revolution" in Latin America] (Moscow, 1971).

94 A. V. Efimov and I. R. Grigulevich, eds., *Kuba: Istoriko-etnograficheskie ocherki* [Cuba: historico-ethnographic essays] (Moscow, 1961); A. V. Efimov et al., eds., *Braziliia: Ekonomika, politika, kul'tura* [Brazil: economy, politics, culture] (Moscow, 1963); A. V. Efimov et al., eds., *Ekvador: Istoriko-etnograficheskie ocherki* [Ecuador: historico-ethnographic essays] (Moscow, 1963); S. A. Gonionskii et al., eds., *Chili: Politika, ekonomika, kul'tura* [Chile: politics, economy, culture] (Moscow, 1967); A. F. Shul'govskii et al., eds., *Meksika: Politika, ekonomika, kul'tura* [Mexico: politics, economy, culture] (Moscow, 1968); I. R. Grigulevich et al., eds., *Gviana* [Guayana] (Moscow, 1969); A. F. Shul'govskii, ed., *Peru: 150 let nezavisimosti* (Moscow, 1971).

95 I. R. Lavretskii, *Bolivar* (Moscow, 1960); idem, *Miranda* (Moscow, 1965); idem, *Khuares* (Moscow, 1969); idem, *Pancho Vil'ia* (Moscow, 1962); Ya. M. Svet, *Kolumb* (Moscow, 1973); O. K. Ignat'ev, *Tiradentis* (Moscow, 1966); L. I. Vizen, *Khose Marti: Khronika zhizni povstantsa* [José Martí: chronical of the life of an insurgent] (Moscow, 1964); Yu. V. Pogosov, *Mel'ia* (Moscow, 1968); S. A. Gonionskii, *Sandino* (Moscow, 1965).

96 V. I. Ermolaev and Yu. N. Korolëv, *Rekabarren—velikii grazhdanin Chili* [Recabarren—a great citizen of Chile] (Moscow, 1970); A. M. Zorina, *Kamilo S'enfuegos—geroi kubinskoi revoliutsii* [Camilo Cienfuegos—hero of the Cuban Revolution] (Moscow, 1966).

97 V. I. Gusev, *Gorizonty svobody* [Freedom's horizons] (Moscow, 1972).

98 V. Kuz'mishchev, *Taina zhretsov maia* [The mystery of the Mayan priests] (Moscow, 1968); V. I. Guliaev, *Idoly priachutsia v dzhungliakh* [The idols hide in the jungles]

(Moscow, 1972); Ya. M. Svet, *Sevil'skaia zapadnia (Tiazhba o kolumbovom nas-ledstve)* [The Sevillian trap (dispute over the legacy of Columbus)] (Moscow, 1972); S. A. Sozina, *Na gorizonte—El'dorado* [El Dorado on the horizon] (Moscow, 1972). In this same genre are books by A. Lielais on the discovery and conquest of Central and South America published in Latvian in 1967 and 1969, in Riga; for Russian translations, see A. Lielais, *Karavelly vykhodiat v okean* [The caravelles are putting to sea] (Riga, 1969); idem, *Konkistadory* [The conquistadores] (Riga, 1973).

3 LATIN AMERICA IN SOVIET BIBLIOGRAPHY AND HISTORIOGRAPHY

B. N. KOMISSAROV

IN THE past decade, the study of Latin American problems has occupied a prominent place in Soviet scholarship. The triumph of the Cuban Revolution and the growth of the national-liberation struggle of the Latin American peoples has prompted [Soviet] scholars to initiate a profound and thorough study of the countries lying to the south of the Rio Grande. Interest in these countries has been further motivated by the expansion of Soviet-Latin American diplomatic, economic, and cultural relations. The actual growth of Soviet Latin American studies, even if judged solely by numbers of works published, is impressive. Whereas from 1946 to 1948, for example, there appeared an average of three works a year devoted to the history of Latin America, in 1966 more than eighty books and articles were published.[1] It is not, however, simply a question of the quantity of publications. In the words of the prominent American specialist Charles Gibson, in recent years "Soviet research has reached a point where a Latin Americanist who cannot read Russian finds himself at a disadvantage."[2]

The considerable growth in the number of Soviet publications pertaining to Latin America and the increased interest in Latin American problems in the USSR necessitated the compilation of Russian bibliographic works on this subject. The first, highly successful steps in this direction were taken by the All-Union State Library of Foreign Literature (AUSLFL). Here, a major effort was undertaken to produce bibliographies of the Latin American literatures, in the course of which much valuable experience was gained in compiling fundamental bibliographic guides of this kind.

In the 1950s and '60s, AUSLFL published in its Writers of Foreign Countries series a number of bibliographic guides to the writings of such major literary, social, and political figures of nineteenth- and twentieth-century Latin America

Originally published as "Latinskaia Amerika v sovetskoi bibliografii i istoriografii," *LA*, no. 3 (May–June 1971), 202–8.

as José Carlos Mariátegui, Nicolás Guillén, Pablo Neruda, Miguel Ángel Asturias, and Jorge Amado.[3] Included in the guides are the works of these writers and poets published in the original and in Russian and other translations, as well as literature about the authors themselves. The bibliographic sections of the guides include brief essays on the life and work of these representatives of Latin American culture.

A significant achievement of AUSLFL was the publication of a bibliography entitled *Latin American Belles Lettres in the Russian Press*.[4] Compiled by L. A. Shur, this book clearly showed how old and deep was Russian interest in the literature of Latin America. This bibliography has elicited positive responses both in the Soviet Union and abroad. Thus, for example, professor Lawrence S. Thompson of the United States has written in the *Revista Interamericana de Bibliografía:* "There are, to be sure, a few [European] centers of Latin American studies, notably in Gothenburg, Stockholm, Hamburg, Berlin, and Leipzig; and now Mr. Shur is adding Moscow to this group, introducing the Soviet capital to this field with a solid, meticulously compiled bibliography."[5]

In 1966, AUSLFL published a continuation of this bibliography spanning the years 1960–64.[6] The appearance of this volume was very timely. The number of Russian translations of the works of Latin American writers and poets increased markedly in the early 1960s. It is enough to note that the bibliography published in 1960 was almost the same size as the guide which appeared in 1966, despite the fact that the first volume contained entries spanning almost two centuries, while the second covers a mere five years.

In 1963, on the fifth anniversary of the triumph of the Cuban Revolution, the Latin American Institute (ILA) of the USSR Academy of Sciences (established in 1961) and AUSLFL jointly issued a bibliography entitled *Cuba in the Soviet Press*.[7] This volume listed the titles of books and articles on the political situation, history, economics, culture, literature, and art of Cuba published in the USSR from 1959 to 1963.

In 1964, ILA issued a bibliography entitled *Latin America in the Soviet Press* in which an effort was made to include works appearing from 1946 through 1962.[8] The following year a second volume of this bibliography was published covering the years 1963–64;[9] a third volume appeared in 1967 listing works published in 1965–66;[10] a fourth, issued in 1969, covered the years 1967–68.[11] (The second, third, and fourth volumes were prepared jointly by the Institute of Scientific Information and the Central Library for the Social Sciences of the USSR Academy of Sciences.) Taken as a whole, these volumes give a broad idea of the books and articles devoted to the politics, history, economics, and culture of the Latin American countries which have been published in the USSR during a twenty-year period or more.

The organization of these volumes is in each case identical. First are described works of a general nature, then those pertaining to individual countries and the dependent territories. Under each rubric publications are grouped by year, and under each year they are arranged alphabetically by author and title. These volumes are not of equal value, however, for each amplifies and continues the preceding one. Thus in the first, the section labeled "General Works" contains no subheadings, whereas in subsequent volumes it is divided into several parts ("Latin American Studies," "Reference Works," "Contemporary Latin American Issues," etc.), which naturally facilitates use of the bibliography. The professional quality of the first volume is rather low. There are many omissions, while at the same time information is included about works which have nothing to do with a stated topic. For example, of D. Ya. Tsukernik's various articles on the discovery of America published in the years 1952–62, only one is listed in the index, while Yu. Slepukhin's novel *At the Edge of the Sunset* is included in the section on Argentina (no. 647). We find many articles on the history and ethnography of Brazil, Cuba, Mexico, and other countries in the "General Works" section, whereas articles of a general nature are located in sections devoted to individual countries. One frequently encounters distortions in the names of authors, as well as mistakes and inaccuracies in the titles of books and articles.

In the second, third, and fourth volumes, bibliographic descriptions have certainly been executed with greater care. Works on economic geography and geology have been included in the fourth volume. From one volume to the next, auxiliary indices are improved. In the third and fourth volumes, in addition to a well-compiled author index and an alphabetical index of edited works, there is a useful section entitled "Reviews of Foreign Books."

Publication of the bibliography *Latin America in the Soviet Press* is an important step toward the compilation of a complete Soviet annotated bibliography of all works on Latin America appearing in the USSR. The lack of such a work is acutely felt. In 1932, a guide to Soviet literature on the countries of Latin America (up to and including 1932) was published in the journal *Revoliutsionnyi Vostok* [The Revolutionary East], but this guide is defective from a bibliographic point of view; it does not meet present-day needs, and is wanting in accuracy.[12] Literature on the history, economics, and ethnography of the continent appearing in the USSR between 1932 and 1945 has in general not yet been described by Soviet bibliographers.

An effort has been made by the American bibliographer Leo Okinshevich to compile the titles of works on Latin America published in the USSR. His two-volume bibliography, which appeared in 1966, seeks to reflect all books and articles on Latin America printed in the USSR in the years 1917–64.[13] The compiler has not limited himself to a description of works devoted to history, economics, and culture, but has also included information about writings on industry, agriculture, geology, military affairs, medicine, etc. Okinshevich's guide is organized thematically, comprising twenty-five sections. Such an abundance of sections makes use of the book extraordinarily difficult. Its greatest shortcoming is the compiler's subjective appoach to the classification and appraisal of listed works and his failure to distinguish between items of primary and secondary importance. For example, works of history are listed not only in the section labeled "History" but in others as well, for example "Politics and Government," "Foreign Relations," "Society and Social Conditions"; writings of a literary nature are included under "Languages and Literatures," "International Cultural Relations," etc. It should be noted that the foreword to the bibliography gives no notion of the development of Latin America studies in the USSR. It reflects a certain tendentiousness in appraising the aims of this branch of Soviet scholarship and in explaining the significance of the growing scale of research on Latin American problems in the USSR over the past ten years.

Despite these shortcomings, however, Okinshevich's work will undoubtedly aid the foreign reader to gain a better grasp of the ever-growing volume of works by Soviet Latin Americanists. The Okinshevich bibliography might well serve as a reference point for preparing an analagous Soviet edition.

Among the numerous books and articles on Latin America published in the USSR, an important place belongs to works of an historical nature. The first Soviet historical works devoted to the Latin American countries appeared as early as the 1920s. Associated with the beginnings of Soviet Latin American studies were such prominent researchers as S. S. Pestkovskii, G. M. Dashevskii, G. M. Yakobson, V. M. Miroshevskii, G. B. Shalov, and others. In the postwar years, and especially since the late 1950s, there has appeared in our country a school of specialists in Latin American history worthy of note for their numerous quality publications. The task of interpreting the evolution of Soviet Latin American studies and of summarizing their development has fallen to M.S. Al'perovich, author of the study *Soviet Historiography of the Latin American Countries*[14] and of numerous works on various problems of modern Latin American history and historiography, including several articles on the study of the history of the Latin American countries in the USSR.[15]

In the first section of his study,* Al'perovich writes about the initial growth of interest in the history of the Latin American countries in the USSR; the institu-

---

*What follows is a review and criticism of Al'perovich's important historiographical essay on Soviet scholarship in this field, published in 1968, a brief portion of which appeared in English translation with introductory commentary by the editor of the present volume. See Russell H. Bartley, "On Scholarly Dialogue: The Case of U.S. and Soviet Latin Americanists," *Latin American Research Review* 5, no. 1 (Spring 1970), 59–62; and M. S. Al'perovich, "Soviet Historiography of the Latin American Countries," *loc. cit.,* pp. 63–70. The final chapter of Al'perovich's study, together with another historiographical essay by the same author, appeared a year later in Spanish translation under the title *Historiografía Soviética Latinoamericanista* (Caracas: Publicaciones de la Escuela de Historia, Facultad de Humanidades y Educación, Universidad Central de Venezuela, 1969). The complete study was published in Prague in a two-part, not entirely felicitous Spanish translation entitled "La historia de los países latinoamericanos y su estudio en la Unión Soviética," *Ibero-Americana Pragensia,* Año II (1968), 181–207 and Año III (1969), 241–64.

tions which were at that time concerned with Latin American problems; the treatment of these problems in the pages of Soviet scholarly and sociopolitical journals, and about the work of individual Latin Americanist scholars. Al'perovich has correctly noted that only in the late 1920s did Soviet researchers begin to treat problems of Latin American history proper, while the turn toward the specific study of the salient events in the civil history of Latin America came only in the mid-1930s. In the prewar period, the researches of Soviet Latin Americanists failed to move beyond an elaboration of isolated problems. They were not of a planned and systematic nature, and at times suffered from serious errors of fact and theory. This resulted both from a lack of many important materials in the libraries of the USSR and from an uncritical use of sources and non-Marxist literature; it was also the result of a severe lack of trained specialists in the Latin American area. Only on the eve of the Great Patriotic War [the Second World War] was a first effort made by V. M. Miroshevskii to summarize the highlights of Latin American history from a Marxist perspective.

One must note in passing that in appraising the pioneers of Soviet Latin American studies the author of this study has accorded insufficient space to the period 1917–45—in all, five pages. Meanwhile, students and young scholars [in the USSR] studying the history of Latin America show great interest in the initial period of Soviet Latin American studies, yet they still have available to them only a few specialized works and publications on this subject.[16]

In the second section of [Al'perovich's] essay, the author discusses the study of Latin American history in the USSR in the years 1946–55, soberly characterizing the shortcomings of works from this period. In the first postwar decade, articles were written and dissertations defended on various, primarily foreign policy aspects of Latin American history; L. I. Zubok published his fundamental monograph on U.S. policy in the Caribbean in the years 1900–1939; and a more intensive training of specialists in Latin American history was undertaken not only in Moscow and Leningrad but in several other republican and provincial centers as well. Nonetheless, as rightly noted by Al'perovich, the scope of published works was extremely limited, and in these works "the Latin American peoples were in fact depicted more often than not as simple objects of the aggressive policies of American imperialism."[17]

The second section of Al'perovich's study is unquestionably successful. One might object, however, to the author's having mentioned here the monographs of G. G. Manizer and V. M. Miroshevskii, which, while they appeared in the latter half of the 1940s, were completed long before—the first in 1917, the second in 1939. Moreover, in discussing Manizer's book on the expedition of academician G. I. Langsdorf to Brazil in 1821–29, the author fails to note that this valuable work was prepared for publication and annotated by N. G. Shprintsin (1904–63). Unfortunately, nowhere in the study do we find this researcher's name, although her articles and publications on the Indian and Negro population of Brazil are of considerable significance, not only for ethnographers but also for historians. They substantially augment the documentary basis for research on nineteenth- and early twentieth-century Brazilian history.[18]

In the third and largest section of his work. Al'perovich examines the development of Soviet historiography of Latin America in the years 1956–66. In these years, a great quantity of books and articles on the history of the Latin American countries appeared in the USSR, and, naturally, the author was unable to dwell on all publications. He has given an overview of survey works, monographs, and other investigations which appeared as separate books and pamphlets, as well as articles whose content was not reflected in the books and pamphlets covered by the study. The author has appraised textbooks on the recent history of the Latin American countries, the fundamental work *Peoples of America,* and the outline histories of Mexico, Argentina, and Brazil, which came out in the early 1960s; he has noted various edited volumes prepared by the Institute of Ethnography and the Latin American Institute on individual countries of the continent, together with other works. In providing information on specific researches, Al'perovich proceeds chronologically, summarizing data on works dealing with problems of special concern to Soviet Latin Americanists: the history of the ancient American civilizations; some important aspects of the history of the great geographic discoveries of the fifteenth and sixteenth centuries; the war of independence in Latin America during the first quarter of the nineteenth century (1810–26)[19]; the history of Russo-Latin American relations; the recent history of the national-liberation, democratic and workers movement in the Latin American countries; and so on.

It is most significant that the author has accorded basic attention to those questions which stimulate debate. Objectively and with great tact Al'perovich writes about the essential differences of view expressed by Soviet Latin Americanists in seeking to resolve certain scholarly problems. Thus, the reader learns of the debates connected with the deciphering of the Mayan writing system, with research on the history of the discovery of America, with the study of the life and work of Peruvian Marxist José Carlos Mariátegui, and with other problems.

Al'perovich has raised the important question of sources for the history of nineteenth- and twentieth-century Latin America published in the USSR, correctly noting that thus far only materials pertaining on the whole to isolated aspects of Cuban history have appeared in print. It is too bad, however, that in touching on this problem the author fails to mention an interesting dimension of the work of Soviet Latin Americanists, which consists in the search for and investigation of Russian sources for the history and ethnography of Latin America. The works of Soviet researchers appearing in recent years have shown that our archives house numerous and valuable documents bearing on Latin America's past. An effort has even been made to classify Russian sources for the

history and ethnography of the Latin American countries. The further study of
these documents and their publication is an important task of [Soviet] Latin
Americanists.

The concluding section of this study, which shows the place of Soviet historiography of Latin America in world historical scholarship, is to our view the
most successful.[20] The author quotes statements by several prominent bourgeois
specialists on Soviet Latin American studies, offers interesting thoughts on the
nature of criticism to which the works of Soviet scholars are subjected in the
capitalist countries, provides summary information on translations of their books
and articles abroad, and dwells as well on other, as yet unresolved, problems.

M. S. Al'perovich's interesting and useful essay, as well as the bibliographic
works examined above, are indicative of the considerable achievements of Soviet
Latin American studies, which deservedly attract the increasing attention of
scholars from other countries.

NOTES

1 M. S. Al'perovich, *Sovetskaia istoriografiia stran Latinskoi Ameriki,*† p. 17.

2 Ibid., p. 68. [HLAS, no. 26 (1964), p. 39.]

3 L. A. Shur, comp., *Khose Marti: Bibliograficheskii ukazatel'* [José Martí: a bibliographic guide] (Moscow, 1955); I. M. Levidova, comp., *Nikolas Gil' en: Bibliograficheskii ukazatel'* [Nicolás Guillén: a bibliographic guide] (Moscow, 1955); L. A.
Shur, comp., *Pablo Neruda: Bibliograficheskii ukazatel'* [Pablo Neruda: a bibliographic guide] (Moscow, 1960); Yu. A. Pevtsov, comp., *Migel' Ankhel' Asturias:
Bibliograficheskii ukazatel'* [Miguel Angel Asturias: a bibliographic guide] (Moscow,
1960); L. A. Shur, comp., *Nikolas Gil' en: Bibliograficheskii ukazatel'* [Nicolás Guillén: a bibliographic guide] (Moscow, 1964); L. A. Shur, comp., *Zhorzhi Amadu:
Bibliograficheskii ukazatel'* [Jorge Amado: a bibliographic guide] (Moscow, 1965).

4 L. A. Shur, *Khudozhestvennaia literatura Latinskoi Ameriki v russkoi pechati: An-
notirovannaia bibliografiia russkikh perevodov i kriticheskoi literatury na russkom
iazyke, 1765-1959* [Creative literature of Latin America in the Russian press: an
annotated bibliography of Russian translations and critical literature in Russian,
1765-1959] (Moscow, 1960).

5 *RIB* 10, no. 4 (October–December 1960), 401.

6 L. A. Shur, *Khudozhestvennaia literatura Latinskoi Ameriki v russkoi pechati: An-
notirovannaia bibliografiia russkikh perevodov i kriticheskoi literatury na russkom
iazyke, 1960-1964* [Creative literature of Latin America in the Russian press: an
annotated bibliography of Russian translations and critical literature in Russian,
1960-1964] (Moscow, 1966).

7 E. V. Braginskaia and L. A. Shur, comps., *Kuba v sovetskoi pechati: Bibliografiia
knig i zhurnal'nykh statei o sovremennom politicheskom polozhenii, istorii,*

ekonomike, kul'ture i iskusstve Kuby, 1959–1963 [Cuba in the Soviet press: a bibliography of books and journal articles on the contemporary politics, history, economics, culture, literature and art of Cuba, 1959–1963] (Moscow, 1963).

8 E. V. Ananova et al., eds., *Latinskaia Amerika v sovetskoi pechati: Bibliografiia knig i zhurnal'nykh statei na russkom iazyke o sovremennom politicheskom polozhenii, istorii, ekonomike i kul'ture stran Latinskoi Ameriki, 1946–1962* [Latin America in the Soviet press: a bibliography of books and journal articles in Russian on the contemporary politics, history, economics, and culture of the Latin American countries, 1946–1962] (Moscow, 1964).

9 Z. G. Borob'eva, S. A. Kolomiitseva, and K. A. Surova, comps., *Latinskaia Amerika v sovetskoi pechati: Annotirovannyi bibliograficheskii ukazatel' knig i statei na russkom iazyke o sovremennom politicheskom polozhenii, ekonomike, kul'ture i istorii stran Latinskoi Ameriki, 1963–1964* [Latin America in the Soviet press: an annotated bibliographic guide to books and articles in Russian on the contemporary politics, economics, culture, and history of the Latin American countries, 1963–1964] (Moscow, 1965).

10 Z. G. Borob'eva, I. M. Kaptsova, and K. A. Surova, comps., *Latinskaia Amerika v sovetskoi pechati: Annotirovannyi bibliograficheskii ukazatel' knig i statei na russkom iazyke o sovremennom politicheskom polozhenii, ekonomike, kul'ture, geografii i istorii stran Latinskoi Ameriki, 1965–1966* [Latin America in the Soviet press: an annotated bibliographic guide to books and articles in Russian on the contemporary politics, economics, culture, and history of the Latin American countries, 1965–1966] (Moscow, 1967).

11 Z. G. Borob'eva and K. A. Surova, comps., *Latinskaia Amerika v sovetskoi pechati: Annotirovannyi bibliograficheskii ukazatel' knig i statei na russkom iazyke o sovremennom politicheskom polozhenii, ekonomike, kul'ture, geografii i istorii stran Latinskoi Ameriki, 1967–1968* [Latin America in the Soviet press: an annotated bibliographic guide to books and articles in Russian on the contemporary politics, economics, culture, geography, and history of the Latin American countries, 1967–1968] (Moscow, 1969).

12 *Revoliutsionnyi Vostok,* nos. 3–4 (1932), 346–64.

13 Leo Okinshevich, comp., *Latin America in Soviet Writings: A Bibliography.* Vol. I: 1917–1958; Vol. II.: 1959–1964. Edited by Robert G. Carlton (Baltimore, 1966).

14 Al'perovich, *Sovetskaia istoriografiia stran Latinskoi Ameriki.*

15 M. S. Al'perovich, "Izuchenie istorii Latinskoi Ameriki v Sovetskom Soiuze (Kratkii obzor)" [The study of Latin American history in the Soviet Union (a short review)], in *Latinskaia Amerika v proshlom i nastoiashchem* [Latin America, past and present], V. V. Vol'skii et al. (Moscow, 1960), pp. 450–63; idem, "Izuchenie istorii stran Latinskoi Ameriki" [The study of the history of the Latin American countries], in *Sovetskaia istoricheskaia nauka ot XX k XXII s'ezdu KPSS: Istoriia Zapadnoi Evropy i Ameriki* [Soviet historical science from the 20th to the 22nd Congress of the CPSU: the history of Western Europe and America], ed. N. M. Druzhinin et al. (Moscow, 1963), pp. 151–70; idem, "Issledovanie problem istorii Latinskoi Ameriki" [Research on problems of Latin American history], *VAN,* no. 12 (1964), 24–29. See, also, S. S. Mikhailov, "Izuchenie Latinskoi Ameriki v Sovetskom Soiuze (nekotorye itogi i predstoiashchie zadachi) [The study of Latin America

in the Soviet Union (some results and future objectives)], *Vop. Ist.*, no. 4 (1962), 98–106; idem, "Izuchenie problem Latinskoi Ameriki" [The study of Latin American problems], *VAN*, no. 5 (1962), 54–59; idem, "The Study of Latin America in the Soviet Union," in *The Third World in Soviet Perspective. Studies by Soviet Writers on the Developing Areas*, ed. Thomas Perry Thornton (Princeton, 1964), pp. 88–102; idem, "Nekotorye voprosy izucheniia Latinskoi Ameriki" [Some problems in the study of Latin America], *NNI*, no. 2 (1964), 29–36; V. V. Vol'skii, "The Study of Latin America in the USSR," *LARR* 3, no. 1 (Fall 1967), 77–87; E. S. Dabagian, "50 let sovetskoi latinoamerikanistiki" [Fifty years of Soviet Latin American studies], in V. V. Volskii, ed., *SSSR i Latinskaia Amerika: 1917–1967,*† pp. 176–209; idem, "Raboty sovetskikh uchënykh v 1965–1969 gg. po istorii stran Latinskoi Ameriki" [Works of Soviet scholars on the history of the Latin American countries, 1965–1969], in *Raboty sovetskikh istorikov za 1965–1969 gg. (Sbornik, izdannyi k XIII Mezhdunarodnomu kongressu istoricheskikh nauk)* [Works of Soviet historians during 1965–1969 (collection published for the 13th International Congress of Historical Sciences)]. ed. A. A. Guber (Moscow, 1970), pp. 192–207.

16 See B. V. Lukin and A. M. Chernikov, "Proekt sovetskoi akademicheskoi ekspeditsii v Yuzhnuiu Ameriku (K istorii sovetsko-latinoamerikanskikh nauchnykh sviazei) [Proposed Soviet academic expedition to South America (toward a history of Soviet-Latin American scientific ties)], *VAN*, no. 7 (1963), 101–3; B. N. Komissarov, "Arkhiv V. M. Miroshevskogo" [The V. M. Miroshevskii Archive], *Gosudarstvennaia biblioteka SSSR im. V. I. Lenina: Zapiski otdela rukopisei* [USSR Lenin State Library: notes of the Manuscript Department], vyp. 28 (1965), 33–44; idem, "Iz istorii sovetskoi latinoamerikanistiki (Arkhiv V. M. Miroshevskogo)," [From the history of Soviet Latin American studies (the V. M. Miroshevskii Archive)], *NNI*, no. 4 (1966), 132–35; see, also, *Ist. SSSR*, no. 3 (1967), 141–45.

17 Al'perovich, *Sovetskaia istoriografiia stran Latinskoi Ameriki*, p. 16.

18 For a list of the scholarly works of N. G. Shprintsin, see *SE*, no. 3 (1964), 139–40.

19 Works by Soviet authors on the history of Latin America's struggle for national independence in the years 1810–1826 have stimulated considerable interest abroad. Academician A. A. Guber presented a special paper on this subject in September 1969, at the Fifth Congress of Soviet and English Historians, in London. See A. A. Guber, "Problemy natsional'no-osvoboditel'noi bor'by v Latinskoi Amerike (1810–1826 gg.) v trudakh sovetskikh istorikov" [Problems of the national-liberation struggle in Latin America (1810–1826) in the works of Soviet historians], *NNI*, no. 1 (1970), 32–38.

20 Part of this section (pp. 72–79) was published in the United States in a translation by R. Bartley. See M. S. Al'perovich, "Soviet Historiography of the Latin American Countries," *LARR* 5, no. 1 (Spring 1970), 63–70.

ON THE DISCOVERY OF AMERICA

A. V. EFIMOV

IT PERHAPS seems strange that the history of the discovery of America has occupied a prominent place in recent scholarly and popular publications, and that on 17 August 1964 the U.S. House of Representatives should have passed a special resolution on this subject. New facts are of less significance for a correct dating of geographic discovery than how one understands the problem itself. Resolution of the problem depends on this general conception and on the overcoming of certain biases.

Has it only recently become clear that almost five centuries before Columbus the Norsemen reached (or almost reached) the northeastern shores of America?

Norse voyages in the Atlantic have long been known, and it is generally recognized that these people inhabited Iceland and Greenland. Now it has been shown that they settled on the island of Newfoundland as well, from where they could easily have reached the [North] American continent. Information about these Norse voyages has come primarily from the Icelandic sagas *Erik the Red* and the *Tale of the Greenlanders*. We now have additional evidence at our disposal.

Beginning in 1953, the Norwegian writer and traveler Helge Ingstad systematically explored the coast of North America from Rhode Island to Newfoundland. He reached the conclusion that the mysterious Cape Vinland mentioned in the sagas was Cape Meadows [Bauld] in the extreme north of Newfoundland. There, near the fishing village of L'Anse-aux-Meadows, Ingstad found the remains of an ancient Norse settlement. Since 1961 he has been excavating the site and has found numerous artifacts which he has identified as Norse.[1] The noted American archeologists [Henry B.] Collins and [Junius B.] Bird have verified and con-

Originally published as "Vopros ob otkrytii Ameriki," in *Iz istorii velikikh russkikh geograficheskikh otkrytii* (Moscow, 1971), pp. 11–20.

firmed Ingstad's data. Thus, the arrival of the Norsemen in America around the year 1000 A.D., of which the sagas speak, has now been confirmed archeologically.

On 17 August 1964, the U.S. House of Representatives adopted the following resolution:

> Whereas Lief Erikson did make the original discovery by non-native Americans of the North American Continent in about the year 1000 anno Domini, and subsequently explored portions thereof; and
> Whereas proof of this historical fact rests solidly, not only on two independent accounts in the Norse sagas, but on archeological discoveries and evidence from the archives of European libraries; and
> Whereas the fact of this discovery is further supported by the writings of numerous historians, and in encyclopedias and textbooks for school use; and
> Whereas it is fitting that due recognition should be accorded to the historic exploit in early American history: Now, therefore, be it
> *Resolved by the Senate and House of Representatives of the United States of America in Congress assembled,* That the President of the United States is authorized and requested to officially proclaim October 9 in each year as Leif Erikson Day, and to issue annually a proclamation calling upon officials of the Government to display the flag of the United States on all Government buildings on such day, and inviting the people of the United States to observe such day in schools, churches, and other suitable places with appropriate ceremonies and activities.[2]

The President of the United States endorsed this recommendation.

To Ingstad's discoveries have been added the findings of the so-called Basel map of 1440, which antedates Columbus and on which America, as noted by several scholars, is depicted as an island.[3] The map comes up in connection with Leif Erikson's discovery. In the view of its researchers, scholars from Yale University and the British Museum, this is a copy of an original map of the early twelfth century, executed in 1440.

Yet the Spanish writer and scholar Salvador de Madariaga, an authority on the history of the discoveries of Columbus, has come out in defense of Columbus' honor, emphatically declaring the map to be a fraud prepared for mercenary ends.[4] Subsequently, Icelandic scholar Björn Thorsteinsson, Genoese scholar Gaetano Ferro, Italian professor Aminatore Fanfani, English professor E. G. R. Taylor, and others have joined those who hold that this map has no scientific significance and that a number of outstanding scholars have been deceived by it.[5]

The noted specialist on the history of geographic discovery R. A. Skelton admits the possibility of doubting the authenticity of the Basel map. He writes that the delineations of Iceland and Southern Greenland on that map

> persuade us that they must have been drawn from experience and copied from a map-model, probably first prepared in the 13th or early 14th century, before the decline of the Norse settlements in Greenland. ... The outline of Vinland, which must reflect

even older information, going back to the 12th century at latest, seems to be constructed wholly from the oral or written data of the sagas, and not from any map reflecting experience.[6]

Those who would deny the Vikings primacy in the discovery of America have been joined by the Danish researcher Count Eigil Knuth. In his opinion, the Basel map reflects only an old Norwegian tradition about "Vinland," but in no way demonstrates that the Vikings reached America.[7] The controversy over the presence of the Norsemen in America after Leif Erikson, therefore, continues. E. G. R. Taylor thus recognized as authentic information contained in the letter of an Italian sailor, Nicolò Zeno (published in 1558 by one of his descendants), about the voyage of a fisherman from the Faeroe Islands to Markland (supposedly on the Labrador Peninsula) around the year 1354. There this fisherman found a Norse colony.[8]

Before Ingstad, more than fifty authors had written about Vinland, placing it in the most diverse spots.[9] Now, it seems, the location of Vinland has been established, yet sufficient problems remain to be resolved. For example, it was long thought that the name Vinland meant "wine (or grape vine) country." The Swedish philologist [Sven] Söderberg, with whom Ingstad agrees, traces Vinland back to the old Scandinavian word *vin,* meaning "pasture." However, professor Gwyn Jones has called attention to the fact that in this meaning, the word *vin* had already in the eleventh century fallen out of use in Norwegian lands.[10]

The problem of America's discovery is far from exhausted by the debates about the Vikings. Spanish historians are reviving the version of America's discovery in 1484 by the Spanish mariner Alonso Sánchez de Huelva. Torcuato Luca de Tena has written on this in the Madrid newspaper *ABC,* citing old chronicles and poems of the sixteenth and seventeenth centuries. The Andalusian captain Sánchez de Huelva set out from Spain to England. A storm [supposedly] diverted his ship to the West Indies, where he was received by certain "painted people." On the return voyage, he is said to have stopped at Madeira or Pôrto Santo and been given shelter by Columbus, who in fact lived there until 1484.[11]

It is said that adventurers and seekers of fortune from Portugal, Spain, and Ireland reached America in the sixth, seventh, and ninth centuries, that Basque fisherman had visited the Newfoundland banks since the year 1000, and that in the twelfth century Polynesians visited the territory of present-day Peru.[12] There is information that Arabs from Madagascar reached a transoceanic country with "red-skinned inhabitants," where they met fellow countrymen who had arrived there previously.[13] Here, however, the eminent authority on the manuscripts of Arab geographers I. Yu. Krachovskii, at my request, checked the works of Idrīsī for such information and came to the categorical conclusion that there was none.

It is, of course, difficult to believe the folk tale about St. Brendan, the father superior of an Irish monastary who, in the sixth century A.D., having prayed on the back of a whale, gathered his monks, sailed into the unknown on a ship guided by an angel, and discovered America. The whale and the angel, of course, are folkloric adornments, but it is significant that the manuscript about this sixth-century voyage should appear only in the eleventh century.

Recently, the Italian linguist Mario Gattoni Celli announced to the Institute of Etruscan Studies [Florence] that over 3000 years ago, in the twelfth century B.C., Etruscan-type people emigrated to America and that the customs and religious ceremonies of the Akawayo Indians [Amerindian group native to the region of the Guianas] are extremely close to the customs and ceremonies of the Etruscans.[14]

In Chinese sources, mention is made of the voyage of five Buddhist monks to the country of Fusan at the beginning of the Christian era.[15] Just what this country was has long been debated—a score of historians vehemently argue that this was America, and in particular California or Mexico; an equal number disagree. Yet Henri Cordier, after examining the arguments pro and con, reached the conclusion that Fusan certainly could not be America, since in the monks' account reference is made to an ocean current to the east of Fusan, which must have been the Kuroshio [Japan Current]. Consequently, Fusan was most likely Japan or some other islands of the Pacific Ocean.

The noted American archeologist Froelich G. Rainey has reported on flint implements found while excavating in Alaska. They are supposed to date back to around 6000 B.C. and are of the same type as instruments found earlier in the Aleutian Islands and on the east coast of Japan.[16]

The husband and wife team Betty J. Meggers and Clifford Evans, of the Smithsonian Institution, in Washington, D.C., have studied pottery found in Ecuador which they believe dates from the period 3000–2300 B.C. In its construction and ornamentation it is similar to Japanese pottery of the neolithic Jomon culture. Inasmuch as the Ecuadorian pottery is later than the Japanese, Meggers and Evans have concluded that these artifacts were brought to Ecuador from the Japanese islands roughly 4500 years before Columbus. One cannot rule out that in the future this version may come to signify for South America what Ingstad's discovery means for North America.

Adducing data on the resemblance of a series of features of the ancient material culture of Ecuador and Asia, and citing examples of distant voyages in ancient times from Asian countries and the possibility of surviving unexpected protracted drifts at sea, archeologist [Emilio] Estrada and Betty Meggers contend it can no longer be argued that

> either the means or the opportunity to make a transpacific journey from Asia to America was lacking; indeed, all things considered, it is surprising that so little serious attention has been paid by scholars in either hemisphere to this problem. It is our hope that the evidence here will stimulate New World archeologists to watch for similar complexes in other areas and will lead archeologists in Asia to follow out the clues and to pin down the region from which the people came.[17]

Drawing on the results of earlier research, Estrada and Evans have established that the Valdivia ceramic culture of the northern coast of Ecuador is atypical for the New World 3000 years B.C., the time from which it dates. However, they write,

> there is a remarkable similarity between the Valdivia culture and early middle Jomon of southern Japan.... Furthermore, the dates in Japan fall between approximately 3000 and 2000 B.C., making the two cultures contemporary. We consequently feel that however radical it may seem to postulate a transpacific contact as early as 3000 B.C., this is the only conclusion that adherence to the principles of comparative analysis will allow.[18]

The article further states that around 200 B.C. there appears in the highly developed Bahía culture a complex of unique ritual traits which "are not of equivalent antiquity elsewhere in the New World [but] are widespread and earlier on the western side of the Pacific. To equate their appearance with the arrival of a vessel from Asia seems the most reasonable way to account for them."[19] Summing up, Meggers writes:

> The first appearance of pottery making in Mesoamerica seems to be independent and perhaps slightly later than in South America, although it is dangerous to accept present evidence as final. The lack of comparability both in vessel shape and in technique and motif of decoration suggests that the source is not South America. Some archeologists favor an origin by diffusion from Asia either overland via North America, or directly, by sea.[20]

Recently, Meggers and Evans have found that with archeological advances, ever-increasing similarities are being discovered in the civilizations of Asia and America.[21] In their view, this can lead to only one conclusion: some 4500 years before Cortés reached Mexico, "a boatload of inadvertent voyagers from Japan strayed ashore in the New World." Apparently, the people of the Japanese Jomon culture 3000 years B.C. lived much as the inhabitants of the Ecuadorian and Peruvian coast of that time. But Jomon culture pottery was the result of several thousand years of development, while the pottery of Valdivia has no antecedents in America. Moreover, it is most probable that on being carried out to sea the ancient Japanese fishermen, like the modern Micronesians, felt at home there and were able to survive for a long time. Landing on the shores of Ecuador, they could without much trouble adjust to the local population, for they were of an approximately equal level of cultural development.[22]

The authors thus suggest the possibility of ancient transoceanic contacts and the influence of developed Asiatic cultures on the civilizations of the New World.[23] The above-mentioned archeological finds failed at first to evoke a broad response in the press. Only recently, in connection with the Norse discovery of America, have they attracted attention. Many people began to wonder if the first Columbuses were not ancestors of the contemporary Japanese, living 4500-5000 years ago?

This gave rise to much controversy, the nature of which is not hard to determine. Thus in New York [John Napoleon] La Corte, president of the Italian

Historical Society of America, stated that "the day (Columbus Day) when the world honors the man who opened the doors of America to colonization turns out to be a most disagreeable day." Pennsylvania Supreme Court Justice Michael A. Musmanno* called the idea that ancestors of the Japanese discovered America "the ravings of a madman." "And how did [Meggers and Evans] prove the Japanese landed here 5000 years ago?" he asks. "By the presence of a fragment of pottery. I am surprised because of the color of the pottery that they did not say it was a Communist who discovered America."[24]

When new evidence appears on early visits to America, the question raised is that of initial discovery. Yet what if we attempt not simply to compare information about separate appearances of people from other continents in pre-Columbian America, but rather examine the whole progression of information on early visits to America?

It is possible, even probable, that not all of this data is reliable, but it is difficult to suppose that all of it is the fruit of the flushed imaginations of mariners, chroniclers, archeologists, linguists, ethnographers, and historians. Rather, one can reach another conclusion—that from its earliest stages the history of America evolved in a less-isolated manner than normally thought; that separate ties between America and other parts of the world, as well as separate, perhaps local influences from abroad could have occurred even in pre-Columbian times.[25] In this regard, the bold voyages of Thor Heyerdahl and his companions are profoundly significant.

I take the liberty of expressing the conviction that with the further progress of science, especially archeology, linguistics, and ethnography, there will be more and more information on this subject, information, moreover, of greater historical validity than folklore and chronicles. Data concerning episodic visits to America, interesting as it is and even were it entirely reliable, would not lead us to a solution of the problem of when America was discovered. The difficulty lies in the fact that discovery of an inhabited region is a two-sided act, that is, a first encounter of peoples from different continents and countries, the beginning or new stage of relations between their inhabitants, and, on the other hand, the discovery of an uninhabited geographic object, that is, its initial discovery.[26]

The voyages of the Vikings influenced the destinies of America and of the Norsemen themselves only to a small degree. The discovery of an inhabited America by Columbus initiated wide contacts between the peoples of America and non-American countries; it initiated the colonization of America by the Europeans, and opened a new stage in the history of America and of the world.

But if one considers only the initial discovery of America, then the primacy of Columbus disappears. For we, unlike Hegel, do not divide mankind into historical and nonhistorical peoples, nor do we hold that before a certain time people had no history and only later, in the course of development, rose to a higher, now

*In the original Russian version of this article, the author mistakenly identified Musmanno as a U.S. Supreme Court justice.

historical stage. And consequently, the vast, still uninhabited continents of America were discovered by those who first settled them. As is known, remains of anthropoid apes have not been found in either of the Americas. Man came to America from outside 35,000–12,000 years ago. America was discovered and settled during the Pleistocene by proto-Mongoloids, who perhaps came overland from Asia across the area where the Bering strait was later formed. The waves of migration from Asia to America, moreover, could well have included ethnic components from the more southerly regions of Asia. Ties between the population of Asia and America before its colonization were sustained not only by migrations but also by way of trade, armed raids, and so on.

Moreover, the discovery of America was not a momentary act but rather a prolonged, multistaged process.[27] The discovery of this or that specific point is one thing, but it is quite another to discover a vast continent, and in the case of America, two immense land masses. To discover simultaneously all of America was simply impossible—the staged nature of this process was inevitable. Even the initial discovery of the vast uninhabited American continent by the Mongoloids was merely the beginning of its discovery and settlement, of a prolonged movement from Alaska to Patagonia and the archipelago of Tierra del Fuego.

Naturally, geographic discoveries by peoples lacking a written language cannot usually be established with precision and can be appraised only on the basis of indirect data—archeological, anthropological, etc. Those peoples who already in the early stages of their class development possessed a written language—the Phoenicians, Egyptians, Greeks, Romans, Chinese, and Indians—as the peoples of medieval Europe, Africa, and Asia, recorded geographic discoveries in chronicles, literary monuments, and accounts, in primitive unscaled maps, and later in scaled maps with graticules (initially of little precision). Among such peoples, geographic discovery usually contributed only to their immediate culture, sometimes embracing neighboring peoples as well, while information about discoveries made in distant regions was as a rule incidental, incomplete, and sometimes hearsay.

In the fifteenth century, however, there emerges the universal science of the western world, which acquires a single language: Latin. The great discoveries of that time, particularly geographic discoveries, were described in this language. But even after they had been scientifically established, there were not a few historical circumstances in which discoveries of one or another object were repeated. The Canary Islands, for example, were known to the ancient Greeks and Romans, and also to the Africans, yet in the fourteenth century they were again discovered by a mixed Luso-Italian expedition. Pitcairn Island was discovered by the Polynesians roughly in the thirteenth century, and again in 1767 by [Philip] Carteret, commander of the British sloop *Swallow*. The inhabitants of the Hawaiian and Gilbert Islands discovered and settled a series of islands in central Polynesia in about the fifth century A.D., yet over a thousand years later discovery of these islands is attributed to the Englishman, [Samuel] Wallis.[28] The southern extremity of the African continent was known to the Arabs, Indonesians, Indians, and probably also to the ancient Carthaginians, many years before the arrival of Bartolomeu Dias and Vasco da Gama.

I have addressed myself often to the problem of multistaged geographic discovery in my writings on the history of geographic discovery.[29] There it is shown that the discovery of America was not a momentary act but rather a process. Columbus never was in North America; it was discovered by John Cabot (Giovanni Caboto), while in the first half of the eighteenth century northwestern America was discovered independently by "Russian Columbuses." Scores of Columbuses and thousands of their companions discovered, described, mapped, and studied America. But if one speaks of the first discoverers, then undoubtedly they were the ancestors of the present-day Indians and Eskimos.

The idea of initial discovery as initial settlement can be found in several older works. Thus in 1912, professor Konrad Kretschmer wrote in *Geschichte der Geographie:* "In America already before 1492 there lived millions of people; consequently, for them it was not necessary to be the first to discover America. . . . The concept of discovery is relative." Or there is the analogous opinion expressed by the traveler and thoughtful theoretician of geographic discovery, Vilhjalmur Stefansson: "Africa and Asia could never be discovered by man, for he originated in one or the other of them. . . . These men, Asiatic or African, discovered Europe at least a million years ago."[30]

And yet, even if all the world's scientists were to conclude that America was first discovered by its original inhabitants, the Congress of the United States, at least as presently constituted, could not in all likelihood adopt a resolution establishing a national holiday in honor of the discovery of America by the proto-Mongolids. It is not difficult to imagine what would happen if some congressman from, say, the forty-ninth state, Alaska, were to propose that America be considered to have been discovered by the ancestors of the present-day Indians and Eskimos. Some gentleman from one of the southern states—Texas or Alabama, for example—might then rise from his seat and say: "What, America discovered by colored people? This we cannot allow!"

To establish the fact of geographic discovery, therefore, requires a surmounting of certain unscientific biases, recognition of all peoples as historical, a repudiation of all nationalistic and racial prejudices which might obscure the question, and exposure of the ulterior motives behind pseudoscientific sensations. What we are here calling for in a positive way is a determination of the theoretical content of the concept of "geographic discovery," a differentiation between discoveries of uninhabited and inhabited geographic entities, and an historical approach not only to separate discoveries but to discoveries in continuum, to the entire, sometimes multistaged process of geographic discovery and exploration.

NOTES

1 See, for example, Helge Ingstad, "Vinland Ruins Prove Vikings Found the New World," *NGM* 126, no. 5 (November, 1964), 708-34. (An abbreviated translation of this richly illustrated article appeared in *NzH*, no. 7 [1965]). For an appraisal of this discovery, see M. A. Kogan, "Vinland naidën: Novye dannye o normannakh v Amerike," *IVGO* 97, vyp. 5 (1965); Gwyn Jones, *The Norse Atlantic Sage* (London, New York, and Toronto, 1964), pp. vi, 85-86, 91-92; also G. I. Anokhin, "Kto zhe otkryl Ameriku?" *Priroda*, no. 10 (1965).

2 *Congressional Record,* 88th Congress, Second Session, vol. 110, pt. 15, August 13, 1964, to August 19, 1964 (pp. 19277 to 20538), 19877.

3 This map was published by Alexander O. Vietor in *YULG* 37, no. 1 (July 1962), 8-12. It is the work of Henricus Martellus Germanus.

4 *ZR,* no. 46 (1965), 26.

5 See M. A. Kogan, "O tak nazyvaemoi karte Vinlanda," *IVGO,* no. 6 (1966); idem, "K voprosu o ieil'skoi karte," *IVGO* 100, vyp. 3 (1968), 252-55.

6 R. A. Skelton, "The Vinland Map and the Tartar Relation," *GM* 38, no. 9 (January 1966), 668.

7 *Daily Worker,* 13 October 1965; see also: *ZR,* no. 17 (1966), 27-28.

8 E. G. R. Taylor, "A Fourteenth-Century Riddle—And Its Solution," *GR* 54, no. 4 (October 1964), 573-76. A popular version of this same article appeared in *GM* 37, no. 9 (January 1965), 709-12.

9 Kogan, "Vinland naidën," *IVGO* 97, vyp. 5 (1965). It is interesting that up to 1942 there were no fewer than forty different conjectures about the location of Atlantis (J. Imbelloni and A. Vivante, *Les levres d' Atlantide* [Paris, 1942]).

10 Jones, *The Norse Atlantic Saga.*

11 Philip Benjamin, "Columbus's Crew Won't Change," *The New York Times,* 12 October 1965, p. 58. [Efimov here corrects the *Times* article, which erroneously states that in 1484 Columbus was living in the Canary Islands.-RHB]

12 For a critique of various views on the striking likeness of the languages and customs of the tribes of Oceania and South America, see A. V. Efimov and S. A. Tokarev, eds., *Narody Ameriki,* 2 vols. (Moscow, 1959), I, 11-17; II, 285 ff.†

13 This version was advanced by American historian A. V. Babin (Russian by origin) in his work *Istoriia SASSh* (St. Petersburg, 1907).

14 *ZR,* no. 46 (1965), 26.

15 N. I. Bichurin, *Sobranie svedenii o narodakh obitavshikh v Srednei Azii v drevnie vremena,* ed. A. N. Bernshtam and N. V. Kiuner, 3 vols. (Moscow, 1950-1953), II, 45-48.

16 *ZR,* no. 46 (1965), 26; no. 5 (1971).

17 Emilio Estrada and Betty J. Meggers, "A Complex of Traits of Probable Transpacific Origin on the Coast of Ecuador," *AA* 63, no. 5 (October 1961), 936.

18 Emilio Estrada and Clifford Evans, "Cultural Development in Ecuador," in Betty J. Meggers and Clifford Evans, eds., *Aboriginal Cultural Development in Latin America: An Interpretative Overview* (Washington, D.C.: The Smithsonian Institution, 1963), pp. 79-80.

19 Ibid., p. 84.

20 Betty J. Meggers, "Cultural Development in Latin America: An Interpretative Overview," in Meggers and Evans, eds., *Aboriginal Cultural Development in Latin America,* p. 144.

21 Betty J. Meggers and Clifford Evans, "A Transpacific Contact in 3000 B.C.," *SA* 214, no. 1 (January 1966), 28-35.

22 Ibid., pp. 28, 34-35.

23 Ibid., p. 35. Professor Nobuo Naora of Waseda University (Tokyo), commenting on this article by Meggers and Evans, admits the possibility that ancient Japanese could have reached America by means of drifting rafts (*ZR*, no. 9 [1969], 28, with a reference to *The Mainichi Daily News of Tokyo*); see, also, G. Zhuikov, "More Discoverers of America," *NT*, no. 9 (2 March 1966), 27-28.

24 *Daily Worker,* 13 October 1965; Zhuikov, "More Discoverers of America," p. 28. [On this subject, see Michael A. Musmanno, *Columbus WAS First* (New York: Fountainhead Publishers, 1966).]

25 A number of authors hold to the idea of a pre-Columbian history of ties between America and other continents. Professor E. F. Greenman, for instance, has published a study on the ancient ties of America and Europe, "The Upper Palaeolithic and the New World," *CA* 4 no. 1 (February 1963), 41-91. Drawing on a large group of Palaeolithic pictorial representations, the author hypothesizes about the existence of ties between the ancient cultures of Europe and America. The weakness of his conception is the lack of attention paid to the findings of physical anthropology. S. R. Varshavskii has spoken of ties between pre-Columbian America and other continents, too, notably in a paper which he read before the Moscow branch of the Geographic Society of the USSR in 1964. See also *VS*, no. 12 (1961); *NWA* 8 (1961), 101-5.

26 Initial discovery need not be only initial arrival. Thus, for example, the island of Vize was discovered in theory by V. Yu. Vize in 1924 and placed on the map on the basis of an analysis of the movement of ice and winds, while it was actually found where the scholar had indicated in 1930.

27 The idea of recurring geographic discoveries is contained in a paper by professor J. L. Giddings entitled "Seven Discoveries of Bering Strait," *PAPS* 106, no. 2 (April, 1962), 89-93. A critique of his idea was given by me in a paper at the 8th International Congress of Anthropological and Ethnographic Sciences, in Moscow (see *Vop. Ist.,* no. 3 [1965]).

28 Te Rangi Khiroa, *Moreplavateli solnechnogo voskhoda* (Moscow, 1950), p. 74.

29 See, for example, *Ocherki istorii SShA* (Moscow, 1957); *SShA: Puti razvitiia kapitalizma* (Moscow, 1969); and the introduction to *Atlas geograficheskikh otkrytii v Sibirii i Severo-Zapadnoi Ameriki v XVII-XVIII vv. (Moscow, 1964).*

30 Vilhjalmur Stefansson, ed., *Great Adventures and Explorations* (New York, 1947), p. ix. See also H. Plischke, *Entdeckungsgeschichte von Alterum bis zur Neuezeit* (Leipzig, 1933), p. 7: "The penetration of man from known into still unknown regions of the earth, and also into still unknown human groups, is in geography and ethnography called discovery—primitive peoples investigate only that which lies in their immediate proximity, while the range of discoveries of cultured peoples is far wider."

5 INDIAN SOURCES FOR THE HISTORY AND ETHNOGRAPHY OF HIGHLAND GUATEMALA

(The Tenth to the Sixteenth Centuries)

R. V. KINZHALOV

THE HISTORY and culture of the indigenous peoples of southwestern Guatemala before the Spanish conquest have not especially attracted the attention of Americanists. During the initial development of Americanist studies (about a century ago), the history of this region was treated in several works by the French scholar Charles Étienne Brasseur de Bourbourg, particularly in his fundamental monograph *Histoire des nations civilisées du Mexique et de l'Amérique Centrale.*[1] In this work, Brasseur used for the first time (and thereby introduced into the scholarly literature) written sources which he had found in the archives of Guatemala, Mexico, and Spain. A number of them are of major significance (for example, *Popol Vuh, Anales de los Cakchiqueles,* etc.) and the work of this enthusiastic Americanist cannot be overestimated. The magnificent Mayan culture discovered in the Guatemala lowlands through the travels of John Lloyd Stephens and Frederick Catherwood and the explorations of Désiré Charnay, Alfred P. Maudslay, and others so eclipsed in its unassuming sister that the latter had almost completely been forgotten. At the very end of the nineteenth century, the attention of scholars was again drawn to the descendents of the classical Mayas in the highlands of Guatemala by Otto Stoll, Karl Theodor Sapper, G. Berendt, and other travelers, geographers, ethnographers, and linguists.

This awakening of interest, however, was confined to a series of investigations of the geography, languages, and ethnography of individual Indian peoples of the area, and to the publication of several sources. The history and culture of the Guatemalan highlands in the pre-Hispanic period remained (and remains), as before, the Cinderella of Americanist studies. It is still not possible to name one

Originally published as "Indeiskie istochniki po istorii i etnografii narodov gornoi Gvatemaly v X–XVI vv.," in Grigulevich et al., eds., *Ot Aliaski do Ognennoi Zemli,*† pp. 222–33.

major investigation nor a single monograph in this field. Even in the large work of the well-known Guatemalan scholar José Antonio Villacorta Calderón, the history of this region is allotted an exceedingly small place.[2] To a considerable degree, such a situation is explained by the fact that since Brasseur's time the quantity of written sources has hardly grown at all. Documents of great scientific value still lie unpublished in the archives of Guatemala and in the scientific institutions of the United States. The archeological investigation of this region is totally inadequate, which makes it difficult to compare data from written sources with the material culture.

Moreover, even the published written sources have scarcely been studied; there exist neither reviews, nor classifications,[3] nor published summaries. In the present study, an effort is made to examine a group of written sources for the ancient history of the Guatemalan highlands; it is the most important group, yet at the same time the most difficult to interpret, namely documents in indigenous languages. This group is relatively small and can be compared neither on the basis of diversity nor quantity of information with, for example, the pre-Hispanic sources available for the history of the central highlands of Mexico. Nonetheless, its study is a matter of prime importance, for it contains invaluable material relating to the history and ethnography of the period in question. Only through this group of documents can the scholar learn about forms of land tenure, varieties of tribute, the organization of society, Indian religion in its various aspects, slavery, the terms of kinship, and so on.

Although the Spanish chroniclers repeatedly mention the hieroglyphic manuscripts of the Indians of highland Guatemala,[4] not one of them has come down to us. The reasons for this are the same as in the case of the Mayan peoples of the lowlands: the barbarity and fanaticism of the Spanish monks and conquerors. Considering the peculiarities of climate, we have no grounds on which to hope for the discovery of hieroglyphic manuscripts preserved together with their owners since before the coming of the Spanish conquerors.[5]

The written sources that have survived to the present can be divided into several groups. The first, and numerically the smallest, corresponds to several pictographic manuscripts of Mexican origin which refer to the region in which we are interested. We are able to name only two such sources, but it is entirely probable that once the Mixtecan codices are deciphered, their number will increase. The first is the celebrated *Lienzo de Tlaxcala,* done by Indian masters between 1550 and 1556. It contains information on the military actions of the Spanish conquerors in Zapotitlán, Quezaltenango, Atitlán, Izcuintepec, and Cuauhtlemallan. Unfortunately, this manuscript has been preserved only in an eighteenth-century copy.[6] The second source, the Porfirio Díaz Codex, cannot yet be tied with sufficient precision to any specific people of ancient Mexico, for it has inscriptions in the Cuikatec language and refers to the culture of the Cuikatecs, yet in its artistic features it is closer to the style of the Vatican Codex

B. Most probably, therefore, it is a copy from the Spanish period of a pre-Hispanic manuscript executed somewhere in the eastern part of Mixtec territory. This document begins by describing the departure of some kind of military or trading expedition from Guatemala to the isthmus of Tehuantepec, its return to the point of departure, and a battle in the vicinity of Quezaltenango.[7]

The second group of sources is more numerous and embraces all memorials written in indigenous tongues by means of the Latin alphabet. (It must immediately be noted that the time of writing does not necessarily indicate post-conquest origins of the source.) All of these documents fall into three clear subgroupings, each with distinctive features in an ideological sense, as well as of theme and composition. The first subgroup is closest in content to the medieval European chronicles: it comprises genealogical histories, records of various events and the like, written by members of the Indian nobility. It is known that immediately following the conquest, the Spanish conquerors went to great lengths to win over the native aristocracy. In order to strengthen their own position in the conquered country, they used the indigenous nobility as an instrument for the exploitation of the common populace. This led to the practice of preserving the rights of the descendents of the former rulers to land and other forms of property; of issuing special certificates of nobility; of marriage between Spaniards and Indian "princesses"; and so forth. This moved the descendents of the former indigenous aristocracy to record the history of their people and the customs of their ancestors. In central Mexico, we can count dozens of such authors: Fernando de Alva Ixtlixóchitl, Juan Bautista Pomar, Alvarado Tezozómoc, Domingo Chimalpain Cuauhtlehuanitzin, and others. In the Guatemalan highlands, there were incomparably fewer. We know of only one such chronicle which can be compared to the written monuments of central Mexico: the *Anales de los Cakchiqueles*. Other sources, as for example the *Historia Quiché* by Juan de Torres and *Guerras de los Quichés y los Cakchiqueles* (the first is the largest and most interesting), represent widely dispersed *títulos*.

The *Anales de los Cakchiqueles*, known also as the *Memorial de Soloá* or *Memorial de Tecpán-Atitlán*, was composed soon after the Spanish conquest. Some member of the noble Cakchiquel family of Xahilá (perhaps the father of Francisco Hernández Arana, who is mentioned below) wrote down in his native tongue, but already in the Latin alphabet, the legends and history of his people. It is possible that some other members of his family helped him in this, adding, perhaps even inserting in their own hand, various events. The first such co-author who later (ca. 1560) began regularly to keep records of the times was Francisco Hernández Arana (born circa 1505), grandson of the Cakchiquel ruler Hunyg. This manuscript gradually turned into a unique diary of life in the Indian community of Sololá, recording the dates of the births and deaths of the settlement's inhabitants, the names of official personages, land disputes, fires and earthquakes, the arrival of noble guests, community expenses, solar eclipses, assistance to needy members of the community, etc. The last entry in which the name Francisco Arana is mentioned is dated December 1581. In 1583, a new name appears in the text—that of Francisco Díaz, a descendant of the Cakchiquel ruler Oxlahuh Tzíi. He kept the record until 1604, when the text of the annals suddenly ends.[8] It is possible that a number of the concluding pages were lost.

The *Memorial de Sololá* is one of the most valuable written sources for the history of the Cakchiquels and the Quichés. The information contained in the first part helps to understand the political history of the peoples of highland Guatemala before the Spanish conquest, as well as their social organization. Materials contained in the second part vividly elucidate the appearance of the Spaniards in the country, the dramatic events of the conquest, and the gradual consolidation of the colonial system.

This written monument has its own history, although not as involved as that of *Popol Vuh*. Somewhere in the early seventeenth century, the notes of Francisco Hernández Arana and Francisco Díaz were transcribed by a single hand (in all probability, by a professional scribe) and were placed in the library of the monastery of San Francisco (Guatemala City), which exercised spiritual steward-ship over the local populace. This manuscript, comprising forty-eight folio pages, represents for us the primary text, since the original from which it was transcribed has vanished without a trace. At the end of the seventeenth century, the *Anales de los Cakchiqueles* were used by Francisco Vázquez, a Francis-can historian in Guatemala, who included several quotations in his work. In citing the manuscript, Vázquez called it "the Indian papers," apparently consid-ering it to be a collection of *títulos*.[9]

In 1844, the young Guatemalan historian Juan Gavarrete was sent to the San Francisco monastery to organize its archive. Assiduously collecting and copying all documents of interest for the history of his country (it is known, for example, that he personally copied Fr. Francisco Ximénez' six-volume *Historia de la Provincia de San Vicente de Chiapa y Guatemala,* a total of some 2200 pages), Gavarrete encountered the *Anales* manuscript and appreciated its historical sig-nificance. When Brasseur de Bourbourg arrived in Guatemala in 1855, Gavarrete informed him of the manuscript. Brasseur made a rough French translation of it, but, as Adrían Recinos pointedly expressed, kept the original with that same facility with which he acquired other similar documents.[10] Upon leaving Guatemala, Brasseur gave a copy of his translation to Gavarrete, who translating it back into Spanish, published it in 1873 under the title given this memorial by the French scholar, *Memorial de Tecpán-Atitlán*.[11]

Brasseur made wide use of the *Anales de los Cakchiqueles* in writing his *Histoire des nations civilisées du Mexique et de l'Amérique Centrale* and even included in this work substantial quotations from his translation, but published neither the translation itself nor the complete text. The first French translation of this source was the fragment published in 1838 by the well-known collector of old documents on the history of America Henri Ternaux-Compans.[12] After Brasseur's death, his collection of ancient manuscripts was sold at auction in Paris, in 1884. The original *Anales de los Cakchiqueles* and Brasseur's translation were acquired by the well-known Americanist Daniel G. Brinton, who a year later published his own English translation of the memorial, which at a number of points differs from the interpretations of Brasseur.[13] To the translation were added the original text in Cakchiquel, a lengthy introductory article, and brief commentaries. Brinton translated far from the entire manuscript; rather only forty-eight of the ninety-six pages, those which to his view contained the most interesting material. A limited knowledge of the Cakchiquel language prohibited him from surmounting all the difficulties contained in the text, and Brinton himself felt that this publication should be viewed not as a finished work but rather as raw material for investigation.

After studying *Popol Vuh*, Professor Georges Raynaud of the Sorbonne prepared a partial French translation (to 1589) of the *Anales de los Cakchiqueles*.[14] A Spanish translation this version made by Miguel Angel Asturias and J. M. González de Mendoza was published in 1927, in Paris.[15] A second edition of this latter translation appeared in the translators' homeland in 1937. Three years earlier, in Guatemala, José Antonio Villacorta issued his own edition of the *Anales;* in it was reproduced the entire text in Cakchiquel, accompanied by a Spanish translation.[16] Unfortunately, the latter is merely an inferior copy of the Brinton translation. Moreover, Villacorta's attempt to phoneticize proper and place names proved most unsuccessful. In 1946, C. N. Teletor attempted to translate that part of the *Anales* which Brinton had omitted, this being a kind of local court journal.[17] This was undoubtedly a later part of the document, although it occupied the first seventeen pages of the *Anales.*

The first fairly authoritative Spanish translation of this important memorial was published in 1950 by the Guatemalan scholar Adrián Recinos.[18] Some years later, an English translation of the Recinos edition was published by Oklahoma University—unfortunately, in a substantially abbreviated form.[19] Here, information is given on life in Sololá during the early colonial period, including materials which permit us to understand better some aspects of the social life of the Cakchiquels before the Spanish conquest. Finally, in 1952, a phototypographic edition of the original manuscript itself was published, housed now in the library of the University of Pennsylvania Museum.[20] Thanks to this edition, scholars no longer need depend on the old Brinton edition, in which the Cakchiquel text is not always faithfully reproduced.

The previously unpublished chronicle of the town council of San Juan Amatitlán constitutes a brief record of events in the colonial period and in content is therefore similar to the second part of the *Anales de los Cakchiqueles.* It is interesting to note that while eighteen of its pages are written in the language of the Pokomans and fourteen in Pipil, it was written by one man, a secretary named Francisco, son of the ruler Don Juan.

Another subgroup of sources written in Indian languages comprises *títulos*. This kind of source appeared soon after the Spanish conquest, when in one community or another representatives of noble families compiled familial or community histories (in their native tongue, but using the Latin alphabet), in which were indicated the boundaries of their landholdings. These documents were often used in court proceedings involving land disputes between Indian communities and by Spanish landholders who sought to annex communal lands. Such detailed títulos were kept in almost every village. Only in the last quarter of the nineteenth century, when, in the interests of furthering capitalist development, Guatemalan president Justo Rufino Barrios launched an attack on inalienable communal Indian lands, were the títulos voided of legal force. As a result of this decision, a great number of valuable historical documents disappeared, since in most communities the títulos ceased to be kept. On the other hand, some Indian communities decreed that in the future these manuscripts would be shown to no one, and for this reason, although carefully preserved by the village elders, they are not available to the scholar. Thus, for example, in the village of San Pedro Solomá (department of Huehuetenango), such a título is brought out once a year, on the day of the local saint. During the ceremonial procession, the second *alcalde* solemnly carries it before a statue of the saint in a locked chest wrapped in red velvet. After this, the document is again returned to its hiding place.[21]

There does not even exist a precise list of those highland Guatemalan villages where such documents are still preserved, but fragmentary data from travelers, historians, and ethnographers permit us to assume that a certain number of them are preserved in the areas inhabited by the Quichés and the Mams. According to Karl Sapper, at the beginning of the present century they were also preserved in isolated Xahil villages, as well as among the Poconchí and Kekchí of Baja and Alta Verapaz.[22] The greatest quantity of títulos, apparently, have been preserved in the department of Huehuetenango, in the villages of San Juan Ixcoi, San Pedro Solomá, Santa Eulalia, San Mateo Ixtatán, Todos Santos, and Cabricán.[23] A document from the latter supposedly dates from the time of Philip II.

Of all the documents of this sort at our disposal, the most complete and interesting are the *Títulos de Totonicapán* and the *Historia Quiché*, by Juan de Torres. The origin and history of the first título are as follows. In 1834, the Indians who lived in Totonicapán addressed a petition to the governor of the department of Sacapulas, Santiago Solórzano. Their petition consisted of a request that the priest of Sacapulas, Dionisio José Chonay, translate an important document from Quiché into Spanish. When Chonay had carried out the governor's commission, the Indians turned the original document and its translation over to the local court, asking that "two comprehending persons" examine the document and verify the accuracy of the translation. The Indians' wish was fulfilled, but by order of the court a copy of the translation remained in the court archive. In translating the document, Chonay abbreviated it. This is made clear by his letter to Santiago Solórzano, which is appended to the translation.

Finding himself in Totonicapán in 1860 during his second visit to Guatemala, Brasseur de Bourbourg uncovered Chonay's translation and made a copy of it. This copy is today the only one available, for, despite all efforts to find them, neither the original document nor Chonay's translation have thus far been discovered.[24] Following Brasseur's death, the copy passed into the hands of the French Americanist Comte de Charencey, who published it together with his own translation in French.[25] In 1950, the text was republished by Recinos as an appendix to his edition of the *Anales de los Cakchiqueles.*[26] In this same edition, the Guatemalan scholar published an additional Quiché document of the sixteenth century—*Origen de los Señores de Zapotitlán,* similar in spirit to the *Título de Totonicapán.* Both of these documents were compiled in the second half of the sixteenth century by some personage of the ruling Quiché line of Kavek.

The other título of interest is the *Historia Quiché,* by Juan de Torres, a descendant of the ruling Ekoamakib line of the Tams. At the end of the manuscript is the date of compilation: 12 October 1580. Unfortunately, the *Historia Quiché* comes to us from a copy made at the beginning of the last century (September 1812); it was acquired by the well-known collector of Mayan language materials William Gates somewhere in Guatemala, and today is preserved in Princeton (USA). It contains valuable information on the history of the Tam tribe and on the genealogy of its rulers. The *Historia Quiché* was first published by Recinos in 1957.[27]

In this edition, the Guatemalan scholar collected other like documents in the Quiché language housed in the archives and libraries of scientific institutions in Guatemala and the United States. These are testaments of Indian nobility, various títulos, *probanzas,* etc. Some of them, such as the *Título de Totonicapán,* are preserved only in Spanish translations. Among the most interesting and significant of these documents are the *Títulos de Ixciun* (1558, Ni-Hay line), *Guerras comunes de los Quichés y los Cakchiqueles* (1554, Zibak line?), *Título de Francisco Izkin* (1558, Ni-Hay line), *Testamento de Xpantzay* (1554, Zibak?).[28] A manuscript in the form of a notebook entitled *Título de Ahpopkeham (Título de Ahpopkamha?),* which is preserved by the Indians of San Andrés Xehul (near Totonicapán) and mentioned by the Guatemalan chronicler Francisco Antonio de Fuentes y Guzmán, is evidently the same kind of document.[29] In describing the conquest of Quezaltenango by the Spaniards, Fuentes bases himself on data drawn from this source. It is most likely that the "Tzutuhila Manuscript" repeatedly cited in the works of Brasseur de Bourbourg was this very same título. Brasseur, for his part, had in his possession the *Título de los Señores de Sacapulas,*[30] but, unfortunately, this document has not come down to us.

To date, only one of the títulos in other Indian languages of Guatemala has been published. It is written in Pokom (1565) and is preserved in San Cristóbal Kahkoh. A more detailed copy of this document dating from the early seventeenth century was also found there.[31] Judging from this copy, the Pokomana wandered for a long time in the territory of the Chols, where they tarried in the lands of the Akahal tribe, settling in Kahkoh only after the Spanish conquest. A testament in the Kekchí language dated in 1565 was published by E. P. Dieseldorf.[32]

It is known that at the beginning of the colonial period the Spanish authorities sent out questionnaires for the purpose of gathering all information on the history and culture of the subjugated peoples which might be of use to them. This was done in order to expand, and consequently, to heighten the exploitation of the country's indigenous population, since in the responses to the questionnaires there frequently figured data on the natural riches of the area and the means for their utilization, as well as on taxes paid by the population to their former rulers. Such reports (relaciones), which we place in the third subgroup, frequently constitute important historical sources. As far as I know, there exists only one such report from the area of Guatemala in which we are interested. It was compiled by a former Tzutuhil noble and the unpublished original is housed in the University of Texas library, in the United States.[33]

The few literary pieces of the Indian peoples of highland Guatemala which have come down to us can also be used as historical sources. The scholar will be moved to do so by two circumstances: the first and most important is the scarcity and fragmentary nature of all the other written Indian sources enumerated above; the second is the close tie between pre-Hispanic literary works and the historical tradition. Unfortunately, this kind of material is even sparser than the former. Virtually the only pieces extant in this category are the Quiché epos, Popol Vuh, and the texts of a few dramatic dance presentations.

Popol Vuh was discovered by the Dominican monk Francisco Ximénez, who from 1701 to 1703 was the father superior of a church in the small Guatemalan town of Santo Tomás Chuvila, or Chichicastenango.[34] A good knowledge of the Quiché language and a fervent interest in Guatemala's pre-Hispanic past permitted him to appreciate fully the importance and significance of the literary memorial which he had found. Ximénez transcribed the Indian text, translated it, and repeatedly used it in his writings on the history of ancient Guatemala. The subsequent fate of the manuscript, its publication and study, as well as the significance of this epos as an historical source, are related in an article accompanying the Russian translation of Popol Vuh, to which we refer the reader.[35] The Indian text was last published in 1944 by the German scholar Leonhard Sigmund Schultze-Jena.[36]

Several researchers have reported that until recently a manuscript of an epic work representing either a variation of *Popol Vuh* in Kekchí, or an independent Kekchí epos, was preserved in the village of San Pedro Karcha, in the highlands of Guatemala.[37] One must not lose hope that this literary monument may still be uncovered.

In 1850, that same indefatigable Brasseur de Bourbourg received from a descendant of the former ruler, Bartoló Sis, living in the village of Rabinal a written text of the dramatic dance presentation, *Rabinal Achi* (Warrior of Rabinal). Despite the late date of the copy, this work undoubtedly is a Quiché literary monument from the pre-Hispanic period and, in all probability, was composed in the second half of the fifteenth century. It tells of a combat between the son of the ruler Rabinal, Rabinal Achi, and Kunen Keche Achi, son of the ruler of a neighboring city-state. The drama ends with the latter's death on the sacrificial altar of Rabinal. In different places *Rabinal Achi* gives a vivid notion of the characteristic features of the social structure and daily life of the Quichés and neighboring peoples in the second half of the fifteenth century.[38]

We know of two other dramas in the Quiché language, which, in all probability, have historical content. The first, entitled *Xahoh Kiche Vinak* (Dance of the Quiché People), according to Brasseur de Bourbourg was still being presented in his day.[39] The subject of this dramatic work was the adventures of the Cakchiquel ruler's son, who in the guise of a magician penetrated the palace of the ruler Kumarkaaha; the drama ends with his death on the sacrificial altar. Of the second dramatic dance piece, *Alit,* we know virtually nothing beyond the title, the name of its heroine, the Indian princess Alit Sispua, and the place of action (Rabinal).[40]

The *Ordenanzas* of religious confraternities (primarily of the seventeenth century) and the calendars of the soothsayers descended from the former priests (eighteenth century) are of recognized value for research on the ethnography of the Indian peoples of highland Guatemala before the Spanish conquest. Along with notions borrowed from Catholicism, these materials contain data on the old [Indian] religion, calendar, and customs. Unfortunately, not one of these documents has yet been published.

Finally, a wealth of material on the ethnography and, in part, the history of the period in question is to be found in early dictionaries of the Indian languages compiled by the clergy. Although formally they can be considered Spanish-language sources, the scattered terms and fragments of ancient texts to be found in them are nonetheless of exceptional interest, inasmuch as they contain wide information gathered among the Indians. Thus, based on material in D. Zúñiga's dictionary (ca. 1608), Suzanne W. Miles was able to write a study on the social structure of the Pokomans.[41] The dictionaries of the Quiché, Cakchiquel, and Tzutuhil languages compiled by Fr. Francisco Ximénez, Pedro de Guzmán, Tomás Coto, D. de Basseta, Fr. Varela, and others have not yet been studied in this respect.

NOTES

1 Charles Étienne Brasseur de Bourbourg, *Histoire des nations civilisées du Mexique et de l'Amérique Centrale durant les siècles anteriéurs à Christophe Colomb,* 5 vols. (Paris, 1857-59).

2 José Antonio Villacorta Calderón, *Prehistoria e historia antigua de Gautemala*

3 An attempt to classify the Quiché-language sources is made in the following article: Munro S. Edmonson, "Historia de las tierras altas mayas, según los documentos indígenas," in *Desarrollo cultural de los mayas,* ed. Evon Z. Vogt and Alberto Ruz L. (Mexico, 1964), pp. 255-78.

4 Antonio de Herrera y Tordesillas, *Historia general de los hechos de los castellanos en las islas i tierra firme del Mar Océano* (Madrid, 1726-1730), III, lib. IV, cap. 18 (manuscript in Q'umarkaah); Francisco Ximénez, *Historia de las provincia de predicadores de San Vicente de Chiapas y Guatemala,* 3 vols. (Guatemala, 1929-1931), I, 108 (Cakchiquel); Alonso de Zorita, *Breve y sumaria relación de los señores de la Neuva España: Nueva colección de documentos para la historia de México* (Mexico, 1892) III, 225-26. (Q'umarkaah manuscript over 800 years old?)

5 Manuscript remains found in excavated tombs in San Agustín and Nebaj [See A. V. Kidder, "Notes on the Ruins of San Agustín Acasaguastlán, Guatemala," *CAAH* (Carnegie Institution), no. 15 (Washington, D.C., 1935), 112; A. Ledyard Smith, *Excavations at Nebaj, Guatemala,* Carnegie Institution of Washington publication no. 594 (Washington, D.C., 1951), p. 186] are too fragmentary to permit a judgment on their contents. Hieroglyphic inscriptions on walls of an earlier period in this region have not yet been decipered. See *HMAI,* vol. II, p. 111.

6 *Códex Colombiano (Lienzo de Tlaxcala)* (Mexico, 1892), pp. 66-175.

7 *Códice Porfirio Díaz: Antigüedades mexicanas...'* ed. A. Charvero (Mexico, 1892), pp. 1-29.

8 It should be noted that in the old translations, the word Xahila was arbitrarily added to the name Francisco Hernández Arana and to that of Francisco Díaz—Gebutá Keh. In reality, Hernández Arana was probably of the Xahila line, but he himself never mentions this. Gebutá Keh has no relationship to Francisco Díaz, he is someone else.

9 Francisco Vázquez, *Crónica de la provincia del Santísimo nombre de Jesús de Guatemala,* 4 vols. (Guatemala, 1937-1944), vol. I, ch. 21.

10 Adrián Recinos and Delia Goetz, trans., *The Annals of the Cakchiquels* (Norman, Oklahoma, 1953), p. 7.

11 "Memorial de Tecpán Atitlán, escrito por Don Francisco Hernández Arana Xahilá y continuado por Don Francisco Díaz Xebutá Queh," *BSEG* 3 (1873-1874), 29-43.

12 Henri Ternaux-Compans, "Requête de plusieurs chefs indiens d'Atitlan á Philippe II," in *Voyages, rélations et memoires originaux... Recueil de pièces relatives a la conquête du Mexique* (Paris, 1838,), pp. 415-28.

13 Daniel G. Brinton, *The Annals of the Cakchiquels.* The original text with a translation, notes, and introduction (Philadelphia, 1895).

14 Georges Raynaud, *Les dieux, les héros et les hommes de l'ancien Guatémala d'après le Livre du Conseil* (Paris, 1927).

15 *Anales de los Xahil de los indios cakchiqueles,* trans. Miguel Angel Asturias and J. M.

González de Mendoza (Paris, 1927, 2nd ed. Guatemala, 1937; 3rd ed. Mexico, Biblioteca del Estudiante Universitario no. 61, 1946).

16 Francisco Hernández Arana Xajilá and Francisco Díaz Gebutá Quej, *Memoriales de Tecpán Atitlán (Anales cakchiqueles)*, Texto y traducción revisados con notas sobre la lingüística guatemalteca por J. A. Villacorta (Guatemala, 1934).

17 C. N. Teletor, *Memorial de Tecpán Atitlán (Última parte)* (Guatemala, 1946).

18 Adrián Recinos, ed., *Memorial de Solalá: Anales de los cakchiqueles. Seguido de Título de los señores de Totonicapán* (Mexico, 1950).

19 *The Annals of the Cakchiquels: Title of the Lords of Totonicápán* (Norman, 1953).

20 Ernst Mengin, ed., "Memorial de Tecpán-Atitlán (Sololá): Anales de los cakchiqueles. Historia del antiguo Reino del Cakchiquel dicho de Guatemala," *Corpus Codicum Americanorum Medii Aevi*, vol. IV (Copenhagen, 1952).

21 Fr. Termer, *Zur Ethnologie und Ethnographie des Nördlichen Mittelamerika* (Hamburg, 1930), p. 399.

22 K. Sapper, *Título del Barrio de Santa Ana, Agosto 14 de 1565* (Stuttgart, 1906), p. 375.

23 Termer, *Zur Ethnologie und Ethnographie*, p. 399.

24 Ibid., pp. 399–400.

25 H. de Charencey, *Título de los Señores de Totonicápán, escrito en lengua Quiché, el año de 1554, y traducido al castellano el año 1834, por Padre Dionisio-José Chonay, indígena, cura de Sacapulas. Titre de Genéalogique des Segneurs de Totonicapán* (Alençon, 1875).

26 *Memorial de Sololá* (Mexico, 1950).

27 Adrián Recinos, *Crónincas indígenas de Guatemala* (Guatemala, 1957), pp. 23–67.

28 Ibid., pp. 71–181.

29 Francisco Antonio de Fuentes y Guzmán, *Recordación florida: Discurso historial y demonstración natural, material, militar y política del reyno de Guatemala*, 3 vols (Guatemala, 1932–1933), III, 159–62.

30 Charles Étienne Brasseur de Bourbourg, *Popol Vuh: Le Livre Sacré et les mythes de l'antiquité américaine...* (Paris, 1861), p. 261.

31 Sapper, *Título del Barrio de Santa Ana*, pp. 373–97.

32 E. P. Dieseldorf, "Kedchi Will of 1565," *MSQ*, no. 1 (1932), 65–68.

33 "Releción del pueblo y cabecera de Atitlán," ms., 1585.

34 On the life in Guatemala of Francisco Ximénez, see J. Rodríguez Cabal, *Apuntes para la vida del M. R. Padre presentado y predicador general Fr. Francisco Ximénez* (Guatemala, 1935).

35 R. V. Kinzhalov, "Kniga naroda kiche," in *Popol'-Vukh: Rodoslovnaia vladyka Totonikapana* (Moscow-Leningrad, 1959), pp. 159–87.

36 Leonhard Sigmund Schultze-Jena, *Popol Vuh, Das Heilige Buch der Quiche— Indianer von Guatemala* (Stuttgart and Berlin, 1944).

37 K. Sapper, *Uber den Charakter und die geistige Veranlagung der Kekchi-Indianer*. Festschrift Eduard Seler (Stuttgart, 1922), p. 435; Termer, *Zur Ethnologie und Ethnographie*, p. 400; E. P. Dieseldorf, *Extracto del libro antigue que conserva la confradía de Carcha*, XIV, IAK, vol. II, pp. 399–402.

38 To date, the only known Quiché text of *Rabinal Achi* is that published by Brasseur as

an appendix to his Quiché grammar; see Charles Étienne Brasseur de Bourbourg, *Grammaire de la langue quiché* (Paris, 1862). An appraisal of the drama as an historical source is given in R. V. Kinzhalov, "Drama kiche 'Rabinal'-Achi'," *VIMK*, no. 5 (1961), 92–96.

39 Brasseur de Bourbourg, *Histoire des nations civilisées . . .* , II, 543–45.
40 A. Barrera Vázquez, "Indioma Quiché," *AINAH* 1 (1945), 187.
41 Suzanne W. Miles, "The Sixteenth-Century Pokom-Maya. A Documentary Analysis of Social Structure and Archaeological Setting," *TAPS*, vol. 47, pt. 4 (Philadelphia, 1957), pp. 733–81.

6 COLONIAL PLANTATION SLAVERY AND PRIMARY CAPITAL ACCUMULATION IN WESTERN EUROPE

(Based on sources from the History of Brazil)

B. I. KOVAL

CHAPTER TWENTY-THREE of the first volume of *Capital* contains an extraordinarily important observation: "In fact, the veiled slavery of the wage-workers in Europe needed, for its pedestal, slavery pure and simple in the new world."[1] Usually, these words are understood to mean in the first instance the international slave trade.[2] Actually, Marx's inference is considerably broader, embracing the entire complex of phenomena associated with so-called primary accumulation in Western Europe. As is known, the most essential phases of this process are, on the one hand, the expropriation of the mass of direct producers and the formation of a free labor market, and, on the other, the concentration of the means of production and wealth in the hands of the nascent bourgeoisie who use them as capital. Among the "principal phases" of the primary accumulation of capital in Western Europe Marx included the seizure of colonies, particularly those where from the outset production rested on a slaveholding, plantation base.

It is known that, for a variety of reasons, in the English possessions of the North American south, in the Portuguese colony of Brazil, in French and Spanish Santo Domingo (Haiti), in Dutch Surinam, on the island of Cuba, and in several other colonies of the New World, slavery gained a dominant position in the sixteenth to eighteenth centuries. As an example of how slave labor on the colonial periphery served as the "foundation" of West European capitalism, Marx repeatedly cited Brazil,[3] whose economic history in the era of Portuguese colonial rule gives the clearest idea of the international interrelationship between slavery and capital in the sixteenth through eighteenth centuries. Brazil was discovered by the Europeans in 1500 and until 1822 constituted a feudal Portuguese colony deprived of all rights. Six to eighteen million Indian and Negro

Originally published as "O roli plantatsionnogo rabstva v koloniiakh dlia pervonachal'nogo nakopleniia kapitalov v Zapadnoi Evrope (Na materialakh istorii Brazilii)," *SV*, no. 23 (1963), 198–215.

slaves labored on Brazilian plantations in the course of the sixteenth through nineteenth centuries, slaveholding having existed legally in that country until May 1888.[4] Slavery has left a profound mark on the entire socio-economic and political history of Brazilian society.

In hundreds of studies devoted to the history of the plantation economy, bourgeois historiography has amassed factual material of great value, yet has been unable to resolve the problem of slavery. The majority of bourgeois scholars hold to a fallacious "exchange conception" of the origin of capitalism, denying class struggle, exaggerating the role of geography, and so forth. This holds not only for the most serious survey works of well-known Brazilian authors (Rocha Pomba, Calmon, Simonsen, Pandia Calógeras, Werneck Sodré),[5] but also for specialized studies on the history of slavery in Brazil penned by such leading scholars as Ramos, Perdigão Malheiro, Rodriguez, Freyre, Moraes, and others.[6] The first to provide a really scientific formulation of the problem of slavery as a whole and to evaluate the role of the slaveholding plantation in the genesis of capitalism was Karl Marx, in his book *The Poverty of Philosophy*, published in 1845. Marx repeatedly dealt with this topic, expanding and developing his conceptions in a number of works written subsequently.

Unfortunately, in Marxist historical literature there are no specialized works devoted to the role of colonial plantation slavery in the primary accumulation of capital in the countries of Western Europe. In large measure, this can be explained by the fact that the socio-economic history of the former colonial and dependent countries, particularly the countries of Latin America, has not been raised in direct connection with the process of primary capital accumulation in the metropolises. This means that the problem of the genesis of capitalism in Western Europe and America has largely been ignored and that the economic role of slavery in this process is not taken seriously into consideration. The book by English [sic] scholar Eric Williams,* *Capitalism and Slavery,* published in Russia in 1948, does not alter the situation, since the author, following other scholars, limits his analysis of the problem exclusively to the slave trade.[7]

Several aspects of the history of plantation slavery in the New World and its role in the formation of international capitalism have been discussed in a series of monographs and articles belonging to the pens of Marxist scholars. In the first instance, one must mention the works of William Z. Foster,[8] as well as those of Brazilian economist Caio Prado Júnior.[9] Of notable interest, too are isolated articles by Soviet historians.[10] For all practical purposes, however, the problem raised in *Capital* has not yet been investigated in Marxist historical scholarship.

Nevertheless, the interrelationship between plantation slavery and the development of capitalism is not merely a question of abstract theoretical interest,

---

*The author is in error here. Eric Williams is a Trinidadian who was educated in England and later became the first prime minister of independent Trinidad and Tobago.

for the thorough study of this question is important from a practical point of view, as well. In order to develop correct tactics in dealing with the national bourgeoisie, for example in Brazil, it is necessary to know how capitalism developed in a given country and what were the specific features of its economic history. For present-day Brazil the problem of slavery is not simply a forgotten echo of the distant past. Slavery itself was abolished there only seventy-five years ago, and in the countryside many vestiges of the slaveholding order are still preserved today. Moreover, capitalist relations in Brazil evolved in conditions of a dominant slaveholding plantation economy, and as a result, especially in the countryside, they have retained its specific imprint, which must also be taken into account in analyzing the development of productive forces and relations of production in the country. And finally, the formation of the Brazilian proletariat was in the first decades closely tied to the life and labor of the slave class. Even before the abolition of slavery in 1888, the nascent Brazilian bourgeoisie, as the West European bourgeoisie before, exploited extensively the labor of Negro slaves and simultaneously the wage labor of free workers. In other words, even in our day and age the problem of slavery has not lost its relevancy for Brazil.

Until only very recently, forced labor was widespread in many countries of the world. In Nepal, for example, slavery was formally outlawed only in 1926, and in Iran in 1929, while in Ethiopia slaveholding officially existed right up to 1942. It is no secret that in some areas of Africa and Asia it survives in one form or another at present.[11] A special United Nations committee, as noted in one of its resolutions in 1951, "unanimously agreed that slavery, even in its crudest form, still exists in the world today."[12]

The awakening of the peoples of the former dependent countries to a new life, the progressively rapid disintegration of the colonial system of imperialism, and the growing role of Africa, Asia, and Latin America in the life of mankind present Soviet scholarship with the task of seriously studying the economic and political history of these states, and of elucidating Marx's famous formulation, according to which the exploitation of colonies served in its own way as the basis for the establishment of capitalism in Western Europe. Based on the example of Brazil, the present article seeks to describe the role of the colonial slave plantation in the so-called primary accumulation in Europe, and also, in this connection, to show the change in the nature of slavery itself as a specific economic category. The problem raised here is examined only in a most general and preliminary manner. The author's aim is to call the attention of scholars to this fundamentally important subject and, based on the example of colonial Brazil, to express his opinion on several possible approaches to the problem.

The founders of Marxism-Leninism always recognized the important role of slavery in the history of human society. Engels underscored that, with the help of this "almost bestial means,"[13] man broke away from the world of beasts, making possible for the first time a social division of labor. The enslavement of one man by another represented the crudest, most primitive form of exploitation.

By slavery sometimes is meant only its ancient form ("classical" slavery), which confuses slavery as a specific economic category with the slaveholding system. But these, of course, are not the same thing. It is known that some economic institutions are capable of serving means of production other than those peculiar to them. Slavery belongs to this category. It appeared already within the primitive communal system long before the triumph of the slaveholding system. Germany, Russia, and a number of other countries knew only primitive, undeveloped slaveholding relations, and, although slavery did exist there, these states passed to a feudal order, in fact having bypassed the slaveholding formation. On the other hand, the disintegration of the slaveholding system did not automatically bring with it an end to slavery. Even many centuries after the final disintegration of the slaveholding system in those countries where it achieved its greatest height, the institution of slavery continued to survive in one form or another and in varying degrees, successfully serving the needs of feudalism, and especially those of the capitalist system. Slavery proved capable of serving, or in the words of Engels, "accompanying,"[14] without exception all the antagonistic socio-economic formations.

In contrast with several other economic categories, slavery changes its form rather easily depending on different conditions: history has known patriarchal slavery, ancient slavery, plantation slavery, latent slavery in the form of peonage, and so on. The diversity of forms, however, does not change its essence. In every age it represents the most primitive and barbarous "form of subjugation and class rule."[15] Marx considered slavery "the lowest, most shameless form of human enslavement ever encountered in the annals of history."[16] Slavery, as is known, rests on a system which "unites" people and the means of production in such an elementary way that, like cattle, the workers themselves as "living bearers of *work capacity* still *belong directly to the objective conditions of production* and in this capacity are themselves appropriated. . . ."[17] Precisely the simplicity of the connection between people and the means of production, despite the correspondingly low productivity of labor, made slavery an exceedingly vital economic phenomenon. Here is why forced slave labor was widely adopted not only in the ancient world but also in a later era.

In the vast, undominated lands of the New World, where from the very beginning of colonization a plantation economy emerged requiring substantial amounts of human labor, only slaves could be forced to work for the white colonists without compensation. The first step of the colonists who came to America, however, was an attempt to enslave the native population and in that way to solve the problem of a labor force. The highpoint came with the direct seizure of lands belonging to the Indian tribes. Assimilating Brazilian lands, which were insolently declared property of the crown, the Portuguese colonizers viewed the 800,000 Indians living in this territory as a "natural" appendage thereof and considered their enslavement perfectly reasonable.[18] To this end, there were even special slaving marches, the so-called *bandeiras*. The expeditions of armed *bandeirantes* not only seized new land, to which bourgeois historiography has accorded primary attention,[19] but also fulfilled another, perhaps even more important mission—"the natural appropriation of an alien labor force by means of direct physical coercion."[20] By and large most bourgeois historians shamefully ignore this point,[21] although it is not always possible to do so. Thus according to the calculations of [John A.] Crow, in the fifteen-year period from 1614–39 alone the *bandeirantes* of São Paulo enslaved over 300,000 Indians.[22] In consequence of the severe violence, the native population was to a large degree exterminated; many millions of Indians were killed, while those who remained fled to isolated areas in the interior.

The problem of a labor force, however, was not completely solved by means of the enslavement of Indians. A solution was found in the organization on an unprecedented scale of the international slave trade. The extensive and continuous importation of slaves from abroad was assured primarily at the expense of Africa, which, in Marx's figure of speech, was turned into a "preserve for hunting blacks."[23] According to the very authoritative calculations of Professor W. E. Du Bois, the population of Africa was reduced as a result of this by more than 100 million people.[24] Precisely African black slaves comprised the mass base of Brazil's laboring population. During the seventeenth and eighteenth centuries, slave labor was the basic productive force in Brazilian society.

Bourgeois scholars usually divide the development of the Brazilian economy into cycles corresponding to a basic product of the national economy. As the first such cycle they unanimously cite the so-called brazilwood era,[25] which was followed by sugar, then gold, and finally coffee. Such a scheme only superficially reflects reality, for it essentially ignores the development of the productive forces and relations of production in the country, focusing attention on the circulation of goods between colony and metropolis rather than on the methods whereby these goods are produced. If one examines the history of Brazil's economic development in the colonial period precisely from this latter point of view, he can only come to the conclusion that, despite differences in the methods of slave exploitation from the extraction of brazilwood to the plantation production of sugar cane and coffee to the mining of gold and precious stones, the essence of the system remained unchanged: slave labor was dominant throughout. With each successive stage, or "cycle," the slaveholding system expanded and developed along an ascending line. Even greater masses of slaves were exploited, and methods of oppression became progressively more refined.

As a result, in the seventeenth and eighteenth centuries slaves surpassed in numbers all other segments of Brazilian society taken together and constituted an absolute majority of the population, exclusive of Indians pushed far into the interior of the country and thereby removed from any active participation in the country's socio-productive system. In 1789, of the colony's 3.2 million inhabitants around 2 million were slaves,[26] to whom fell the bulk of all social labor. In these conditions, even land tenure was possible only as a component part of the ownership by certain individuals of the persons who were themselves the direct producers.[27] It was no coincidence, for example, that often the value of the slaves constituted more than half the value of an entire plantation, including the land.[28] In such circumstances, ownership of slaves was equivalent to the possession of basic wealth. In Brazilian society the slave himself was most valuable as a medium of exchange, as "humanized money."[29]

Based on a thorough study of the specifics of the colonial slaveholding economy, Marx reached an extraordinarily important theoretical conclusion. In his economic manuscripts of 1857–58 he wrote: "In the person of the slave is abducted a direct instrument of production. However, the production of that country for which it is abducted must then be organized so as to permit the use of slave labor, or (as in South America and elsewhere) a mode of production must be created which corresponds to slave labor."[30]

This exceptionally important conclusion of Marx, which unfortunately was for a long time ignored, should not, of course, be extended mechanically to all the countries of South America, for in a number of the Spanish colonies slavery was of secondary importance. Conditions there fully "permitted" the application of slave labor, even to very considerable degrees, but the principal role was nonetheless played by other (feudal and semifeudal) forms of exploitation. In those colonies (Brazil, Cuba, Surinam, Santo Domingo) where slaveholding became a decisive force and the slave class was predominant, a corresponding mode of production had inevitably to triumph.

Of course, there was a fundamental difference between these New World colonies and ancient Rome, although in both instances the prevailing relations of production were those of slavery. Yet, it is known that quite often "one and the same economic base—one and the same with respect to basic conditions—due to an endless variety of empirical circumstances, natural conditions, race relations, external historical influences, etc., can manifest endless variations and gradations which can be understood only through an analysis of these empirically given circumstances,"[31] alike only in their main features. This was roughly the case in Brazil, where the slaveholding system took on its own special, original form. The analogy with classical slavery holds only in that the basis of productive labor was in both cases slave labor, although there appears to have been some juridical differences as well.[32] From an economic point of view, Brazilian slave production contrasted with the era of antiquity above all in its plantation form. In Brazil during the sixteenth through eighteenth centuries, the great slave plantations represented the most typical economic units and accounted for the bulk of society's productive labor. Precisely this circumstance makes it possible to focus on the specific plantation form of slavery. The principal distinction of this form lies in the fact that it emerged as the result of a new historical era, specifically under the direct influence of the process of so-called primary accumulation in Western Europe, which exercised a great influence on the world, including the colonies.

It is sometimes forgotten that following the bourgeois revolution in the Netherlands and England, the possessions of feudal Spain and Portugal in fact became economic colonies not only of their mother countries but of nascent West European capitalism as well. And while political control lay entirely in the hands of the courts of Madrid and Lisbon, it would be a serious mistake to underestimate the role of the young West European bourgeoisie (in the first place, of course, the English) in the exploitation of the New World. In the case of Brazil, this situation acquired with the passage of time the character of a permanent economic factor. In his work *Imperialism, the Highest Stage of Capitalism,* V. I. Lenin underscored this point: "Portugal is an independent sovereign state, but in fact, for over two hundred years, since the war of Spanish Succession (1701–14), it has been an English protectorate. England has protected Portugal and its colonial possessions in order to strengthen its own position in the struggle against its rivals, Spain and France. In return, England has received trade advantages and improved conditions for the exportation of goods and especially capital to Portugal and its colonies...."[33] Typically in the seventeenth century, over 65 percent of the total vlaue of English imports from Portugal comprised goods of Brazilian origin.[34]

Nascent capitalism in the leading countries of Western Europe shunned no means for its own enrichment, not even those which would appear to be historically defunct. Thus capital revived and infused new life into the institution of slavery, which had long ago disappeared in Europe, and laid the basis for the extensive trade in [African] blacks.[35] The propagation of a colonial slaveholding order was as typical of feudal Spain and Portugal as it was of bourgeois England and Holland. In both cases, slavery was considered the most advantageous and convenient system of plantation organization and colonial dominion. This was explained by the fact that developing world commodity production required the rapid incorporation of colonies into its sphere of influence, and at the time the most effective method for achieving this end in plantation colonies was the extensive use of slaves, who could be forced to work in any conditions.

Precisely for this reason, it became the immediate task of the conquerors upon seizing new lands to "appropriate" by force the people who lived in these lands.[36] Marx expressed this idea most graphically in his well-known words that the direct slavery of blacks in Surinam, Brazil, Santo Domingo, and the southern states of North America, like machines and credit, served as the specific basis for the development of bourgeois production in Europe. Without slavery there would have been no cotton, and without cotton, contemporary industry would be inconceivable. It was precisely slavery that enriched many colonies, and they in turn facilitated the formation of world trade, which represented an indispensable condition for the development of heavy industry.[37] Thus emerged the direct interconnection of two historically antagonistic categories, slavery and capital, wherein the first operated primarily in the form of colonial plantation slavery, while the second became ever more distinctly productive (industrial) in nature.[38]

Not everywhere, of course, did slavery put down deep roots, but wherever large plantations were created, slave labor became dominant. Newly revived in its plantation form, slavery was to play, and in practice actually played, an auxillary role in the fierce struggle of nascent West European capitalism against obsolescent feudalism, appreciably contributing to the realization of so-called accumulation.

The interconnection in the process of primary accumulation between the categories of slavery and capital was manifested simultaneously in several aspects. The first and most tangible stage was the slave trade. The infamous trade in human beings was initiated by feudal Portugal. Already in 1441 the first party of African slaves was conveyed to Lisbon, which soon became a major center of the world slave trade. After 1562, English traders were included in the "business." In 1672, the British government, feeling that "the slave trade would promote the well-being of the nation,"[39] created a special "Royal African Company." By the Peace of Utrecht in 1713, England received a monopoly in the supply of slaves to America. In *Capital* Marx gave a great deal of attention to the slave trade, underscoring that for a number of British cities, particularly Liverpool and others, it served as the basic method of primary accumulation.[40]

Actually, the slave trade provided European merchants with enormous profits. The Portuguese crown, reserving for itself a given rate of return on each slave sold in Brazil, received in a single year over 25,000 cruzeiros.[41] According to incomplete official records, Dutch traders made over 600,000 gilders from trafficking in human beings during the thirty years of their dominion in the northeast of Brazil (1620–54).[42] Especially large profits were made by English traders, who exported almost four times as many slaves from Africa as all other foreign merchants taken together.[43] Profits from the sale of black slaves frequently reached and exceeded 300 percent in the sixteenth through eighteenth centuries.[44] Thus man, turned slave, became the primary monetary medium, a form of capital that bore interest.

The horrors of the slave trade and its role in the establishment of West European capitalism have been fairly cogently outlined in the historical literature, and consequently there is no need to dwell on this in any detail.[45] It is more important to underscore that the entire life of the colonial slaveholding plantation was totally dependent on a constant replenishment of the work force from outside sources. This is explained by the fact that "in the slave system money spent for the purchase of a work force acts as a monetary form of fixed capital which is reimbursed only gradually in the course of the slave's active life."[46] And this means that each master tried to cover his expenses as quickly as possible, and, consequently, to exact a maximum of surplus labor from the slave in a minimum period of time. In the sixteenth through eighteenth centuries this tendency, which had played an important role in the ancient world as well, acquired the nature of fundamental economic law. In order to meet this demand, it was necessary to reduce all expenses for the maintenance of slaves to a minimal level. Expenditures for the maintenance of a slave were roughly three to four times lower that what was required, amounting to about £4 sterling per year.[47] This circumstance, in turn, precluded the possibility of raising the already exceedingly low productivity of slave labor. Income from the economy, therefore, was achieved first by means of the severest exploitation, and second, by the simultaneous employment of large masses of slaves.

The internal contradiction of the slaveholding economy contained in the attempt to secure a maximum of surplus product, on the one hand, and in the impossibility of assuring this increase by the most effective means, that is, by raising the productivity of slave labor, on the other, occasioned a generally low level of reproduction. Indeed, more often than not it was a matter of simple replacement. The over-all development of slave production occured not primarily as the result of the growth of internal forces but rather of the continually growing influx of ever new masses of slaves from without. That large-scale replenishment was possible in the system of plantation slavery only through external sources is incontestably demonstrated by so striking a fact as the impossibility of assuring the reproduction of the work force within the limits of the plantation itself (or even the country) through natural increase. The latter played no appreciable role, for the simple reason that the reduction of maintenance costs to a minimum, combined with the exceedingly low productivity of labor, inevitably led to the appropriation by the planters not only of surplus labor but also of much if not all essential labor, which in normal conditions would be used to support children, that is, to assure a full natural, indeed widescale, reproduction of the work force. Here, too, of course, one must take into account that portion of labor which is essential for the renewal of the normal physical and spiritual forces of the slave himself and his mate.

But for the colonial plantation this variant was totally precluded. In Brazil and other colonies the life of the slaves was so terrible and the degree of exploitation so great that the active life of a slave did not exceed seven years.[48] while the

Population groups	Birth rate %	Death rate %	Increase %
Free			
Whites	4.04	2.83	+1.21
Mulattoes	3.67	2.75	+0.92
Indians	4.08	3.70	+0.28
Negroes	4.76	5.38	−0.62
Slaves			
Mulattoes	3.81	6.00	−2.19
Negroes	2.91	6.86	−3.95

death rate was almost twice the birth rate. Official figures on death and birth rates by population groups during the final year of Portuguese colonial rule in Brazil (1821) provide a vivid picture of this.[49]

From the table it is seen that the birth rate among slaves was significantly lower, while the death rate was 2.5 times higher, than among the free population. Even among the free but black-skinned population more people died than were born. As for the Mulatto slaves and especially the Negro slaves, had it not been for the regular importation of slaves from abroad they would have literally died out in one or two generations. The greatest gap between slaves and whites is observed in relation to the death rate (6.86 : 2.83), and not the birth rate (4.04 : 2.92). In other words, natural increase as an internal source did not play a material role in the reproduction of the work force in the conditions of the colonial plantation, the entire life of which consequently depended on the international slave trade—the primary external source for replenishing slaves. Through and in the slave trade, therefore, was realized the direct interconnection between the slaveholding plantation and West European capital. For Brazil this had even greater significance, as what was being purchased were the living bearers of labor themselves—people.

But however great the significance of the slave trade, to limit an analysis of the interconnection between slavery and capital to the slave trade would be incorrect, for the very purchase and sale of slaves falls into the sphere of circulation, although for Brazil, given the specific nature of these goods, the slave trade was actually fused with production. The slave, however, could not act as the proprietor of his own labor, and consequently in colonial Brazil the conditions were lacking for the conversion of money into capital. Even the extraction of exchange value in its monetary form through the production of gold and silver[50] did not yet mean that the colony produced capital itself. For the colony, gold and silver were not in the main capital, their monetary form notwithstanding, but rather an ordinary article of trade which was produced for the world market; in the best of cases the precious metals were converted into treasure. But as soon as gold reached Europe, it could immediately be used as capital. This is why Marx says, "Treasure acquired outside Europe by means of direct pillage, native enslavement and killing flows into the metropolis, where it is converted into capital."[51] In this "metallic link" between America and Europe[52] lies the essential aspect of the interconnection between slavery and capital, no less important than the slave trade.

According to Calogeras, from 1700 to 1801 Brazilian slaves produced over one thousand tons of pure gold worth 600 million contos.[53] In the first half of the eighteenth century alone, notes Roberto Simonsen, Europe took from Brazil more than 50 percent of all the gold acquired by Europeans in the three hundred years spanning the sixteenth through eighteenth centuries.[54] According to Humboldt, twice as much gold was received from Brazil than from all the Spanish colonies together (6,290,000 Castilian gold marks as against 3,625,000),[55] and also a greater amount of diamonds (worth £10 million sterling)[56] and other precious stones. In the historical literature one can find the most diverse, often contradictory data on the output of precious metals,[57] but what matters is the general conclusion. It is that indeed the titanic labor of slaves in Brazil and the other colonies of the New World engendered that torrent of gold which abundantly reared West European capitalism.

The torrent of gold and precious stones which gushed from Brazil undoubtedly enriched, too, the ruling elites of feudal Portugal—the royal court[58] and its favorites, merchants and large landowners—but it was precisely Brazilian gold that in the final analysis ruined Portugal. Engels observed that the pursuit of gold, "while at first undertaken in feudal and semifeudal forms, nonetheless by its very nature was incompatible with feudalism."[59] In the case of backward Portugal, this was especially apparent. The gold was not kept in the state coffers of a debilitated Portugal, but rather passed into the hands of the English, French, and Dutch bourgeoisie.[60] Portugal merely served as a pump supplying accidentally accumulated gold nuggets, which evidently were insufficient for the successful accumulation of capital in Portugal itself, where moreover they were on the whole expended unproductively. This circumstance, in turn, was noted by Adam Smith, who underscored that as a result of the almost total reexport of gold to England, both Portugal and Spain, while possessing the richest and largest mines in the world, proved to be "the most wretched countries of Europe."[61] Marx underscored that in countries where money appears not from circulation but is found in a corporal form," like gold, the nation grows poor, while those who must work in order to provide the Spaniards with money "develop the sources of wealth and actually enrich themselves."[62] A similar situation obtained also in

Portugal, which imported at almost no cost an enormous quantity of gold from Brazil that was then converted into capital, but on English soil.

But not just the gold and silver extracted in the colonies by slaves were converted into capital in Europe. All other goods produced by slaves underwent this same miraculous conversion. As is known, it is of practically no importance to the buyer on the market who produced the goods or where—worker, peasant or slave—since there is no difference between goods of differing origin as consumer values. All these goods enter into the process of capital circulation. Nascent capitalism, therefore, readily "appropriates" with the aid of the world market those goods and that surplus product (and in a number of cases a good part of the essential product, as well) which were produced in countries dominated by precapitalist forms of production. The market completely erases their origin. This is why the labor of Brazilian slaves played an important role in the development of a world market, not only assuring Europe of gold but contributing to the growth and strengthening of capital itself, to the ripening of conditions for the industrial revolution and the triumph of the capitalist mode of production. Brazilian goods were traded on the world market by Portuguese merchants who received a monopoly on the sale of colonial goods from the king. More than half of all Portuguese exports to other countries comprised goods of Brazilian origin—coffee, cotton, brazilwood, sugar, etc.[63] It was not by chance that Marx included these goods among the fifteen "primary articles of trade."[64]

The historical literature contains a variety of statistics on the amount of goods exported to Europe which were produced by slaves in Brazil. Most exact and generally accepted are the calculations of Roberto Simonsen, who pointed out that in the years 1500–1822 Europe exported from Brazil goods valued at more than £536 million sterling (sugar, 300, gold and diamonds, 170, hides, 15, brazilwood, 15, tobacco, 12, cotton, 12, rice, 4, coffee, 4, etc.)[65] It must be said that for Brazil this signified plain robbery, since because of its colonial dependency and the low productivity of slave labor it was obliged to give up not only the entire aggregate surplus product but also a large part of the essential product. At the end of the eighteenth century, the exportation of goods from Brazil was two times greater than imports,[66] which precluded any possibility of accumulating even commercial capital.[67]

Thus, the labor of millions of slaves on colonial plantations was a great aid to early West European capitalism, serving as the "basis" for strengthening and developing the new capitalist mode of production. Therein lies the essence of the process of the so-called primary accumulation in Western Europe.

The multifaceted interconnection of the slave plantation with international capital influenced more and more each year on the nature of slavery itself. As a result of the industrial revolution in Western Europe during the final third of the eighteenth century and the first quarter of the nineteenth century, the slaveholding plantation once and for all came to depend on capital and was turned into a "commercial system of exploitation."[68] Now its main objective was to produce as many goods as possible for the capitalist market, which meant increasing the mass of surplus labor. It was no longer a question of forcing slaves to produce a given quantity of useful products, but rather of producing surplus value itself.[69] For the planter who produced a good, the absolute value of that good was immaterial except insofar as it concerned the West European capitalist. Both were interested only in surplus value as embodied in a good and realized through the good's sale—surplus value created by slave labor. Based on slavery, with its primitive instruments and exceedingly low productivity, it was practically impossible to reduce essential work time and thereby increase surplus work time, with a corresponding increase in surplus value. The only alternative was a simple lengthening of the work day and the forced introduction of excessive labor. Marx pointed out that as a result of the capitalist pursuit of surplus value "the excessive labor of the Negro, which in individual cases could cost him his life after seven years' work, became a factor of a deliberate and calculating system."[70] A direct reflection of this was the extraordinarily rapid growth of goods exported from the colonies in the late eighteenth and early nineteenth centuries. The number of slaves on the plantations of the Brazilian province of Bahia, for example, remained almost unchanged, while the export of goods which they produced grew three times over a twenty-year period (1780–1800).[71] General exports from the country grew twofold in the final quarter of the eighteenth century and were valued at £3 million sterling.[72] Data on Brazil's foreign trade at the turn of the eighteenth century attest to the rapidly increasing output of the plantation economy. This was especially striking following the declaration of free trade in 1808 by the regent, João VI. According to official statistics, in 1812 Brazil exported goods valued at 6.5 thousand contoreis, in 1816 exports were valued at 19.9 thousand, and in the year of the declaration of independence (1822) they reached 42,000 contoreis.[73] Thus in a single decade the increased exploitation of slaves (just as of other groups of workers) greatly increased the product created and exported abroad.

All this attests to the fact that the fundamental goal of the slave plantation became, as a result of its subordination to international capital, the production of surplus value. Inasmuch as the landowner, who possessed all the instruments of production, including land and the slave producers themselves, was at the same time the planter, in the plantation economy rent and profit were likewise one and the same. The planters directly extracted from the slaves all surplus labor embodied in the surplus product. The capitalist mode of production itself did not exist on Brazilian plantations, but "a corresponding mode of thought was introduced there from the capitalist countries,"[74] in consequence of which a dominant role was played by profit as such, without breaking it down into its different forms. Increasingly the plantation developed into a kind of capitalist economy, although the system for exploiting the direct producers was not capitalistic, since the goods produced represented not their labor, but rather themselves and their labor together. Such a deformed system, wherein productive relations remained pre-capitalistic while the primary goal had become the capitalist pursuit of profit, was described by Marx as the specific condition of "the formal subordination of labor to capital."[75] That "capitalist graft" which slavery experienced in modern times consisted, in our opinion, precisely in this subordination. The real nature of the whole labor process was not revolutionized, the slave did not turn into a hired worker; rather, his labor already served to produce surplus value, albeit primarily the absolute surplus value extorted from the slaves through excessive exploitation.[76] What is important here is that at first the subordination of the slaveholding plantation to capital took the form of an international division of labor, since in the colonies in the sixteenth through eighteenth centuries capitalist relations had for all practical purposes not been developed. Thus, in a second type of colony, i.e. plantations, which from the outset were designed to produce goods for the world market, there emerged a unique form of production, in which the planters acted as bourgeoisified slaveholders. "The mode of production introduced by them did not arise out of slavery but was grafted thereto."[77] Marx explained the possibility of such an anomaly by the fact that "in the conditions of a worldwide market resting on free labor," the owners of colonial plantations, uninterested in radically changing the production process and unable to abandon the slave trade, nonetheless adjusted to the new conditions and were themselves "infected" by the quest for surplus value.[78] Yet inasmuch as free wage labor, that is, the basis of capitalist production, was here missing, one can speak, as Marx underscored, only of a "formal" outward resemblance to capitalist production. The analogy pertains only to the production of surplus value, as the nature of productive relations was different.

Developing from the very beginning in close dependence on the emerging world capitalist market, the colonial plantation economy, including that of Brazil, formed a common sphere of circulation with West European capital and in connection with this acquired an exceptionally high commodity form. In contrast to the ancient era, the exploitation of slaves now pursued entirely different ends, namely the creation of a maximum amount of goods for sale on a world market in order to receive profits. In Brazil, commercial and loan capital, which gave the plantation a capitalist nature, found in this connection a much greater field of action than in the ancient world. Its limitation and "antediluvian nature" notwithstanding, loan capital, possessing, in the words of Marx, "the mode of exploitation characteristic of capital without capital's characteristic mode of production,"[79] greatly influenced the plantation, although it did not itself directly enter the sphere of production. In other words, slave production in the colonies experienced considerable influence of the times, acquiring a number of specific new features previously absent or only contemplated. The ways of exploiting slaves became more refined. This, of course, could not escape the attention of bourgeois scholars, although the assessment which many of them have made of the slave plantation is erroneous. Thus, a number of bourgeois scholars view the dominant productive relations in colonial Brazil as some special form of capitalism that sprouted from colonial soil. As early as the end of the last century G. F. Knapi wrote that, in his view, "the slaveholding plantation economy in Brazil" is nothing more than "the first, earliest step" of a capitalist form of production, "a capitalist enterprise."[80] Another German scholar, K. Grünberg, also argued that the plantation form of slavery "is the very earliest trial of this (capitalist–B.K.) form of industrial enterprise."[81] The well-known contemporary Brazilian historian and journalist Nelson Werneck Sodré, for example, is inclined to view the plantation slaveholding economy also as some original "colonial form of capitalism."[82] These scholars have thus come to the conclusion that under the influence of nascent capitalism in Western Europe, slavery completely lost its specific nature and changed in a radical manner, becoming one of the forms which capitalism took on colonial soil.

The basis of such erroneous interpretations of the plantation slaveholding economy obviously lies in the fact that, having observed the influence of nascent capitalist relations on plantation production in the colonies, these bourgeois scholars were still incapable of understanding correctly that real interconnection between slavery and capital which was formed in the world arena during the seventeenth and eighteenth centuries. They have erroneously taken the subordination of slave labor to international capital as some "colonial form" of capitalism itself. To support this position the fact is occasionally cited that some planters let their most skillful slaves out for hire (in Brazil these slaves were called *escravos de serviço*).[83] But such a presentation of the problem is unconvincing, for slaves did not become free wage laborers as a result of such a transfer, although in a number of cases they did receive wages from the new master. In point of fact there occurred only a temporary change of masters, "wage slaves" changed hands, but not for a minute did they therefore cease to be slaves.[84] This was one of numerous ways in which planters exploited their human capital,[85] which, of course, had nothing to do with the capitalist form of hired labor.

To be exact, one must also distinguish between other forms of hired plantation labor. Overseers, day laborers (*jornaleiros*),[86] tailors, barbers, construction workers, etc., were hired for temporary jobs by wealthy city-dwellers or planters. However, they all served the needs of the slave-owning class, and their labor, despite the fact that it was wage labor, bore no relation to the capitalist form of hire. In *Anti-Dühring,* Engels observed that "wage labor, which already conceals within itself the complete embryo of the capitalist mode of production, has existed since ancient times; in isolated, chance forms it existed for centuries next to slavery. But only when the necessary historical conditions had been created could this embryo develop into a capitalist mode of production."[87] Such conditions did not yet exist in the colonies in the sixteenth through eighteenth centuries. As trade and usury in themselves cannot be viewed as the embryo of capitalism, although without commercial-monetary relations the latter could not appear and exist, so, too, wage labor which serves precapitalist modes of production cannot be considered the beginning of the existence of a proletariat. This is why the presence of wage labor in colonies dominated by slavery was in no way symptomatic of the beginning of capitalism.

In Brazil and other colonies, yearly expenses for the maintenance of a slave were roughly two times lower than the earnings of a free worker.[88] Such low cost of slave labor offset with interest its low productivity. In sum, the exploitation of slaves proved economically more advantageous than the use of free wage earners. In this regard one must keep in mind that however widely wage labor may have been used on a plantation, it did not because of this cease to be a slaveholding operation, nor did it acquire capitalist features, for the dominant form of labor remained slave labor. The more slaves who worked on plantations, the more extensively overseers had to be hired.[89] It was precisely with the aid of the overseer's lash that the planter secured the slave's extraordinary effort, forcing from him additional surplus product in order to keep pace with the demands of the times, when the pursuit of profit literally infected the entire world. In these conditions, the production of surplus product in response to the demands of increasingly bourgeois slaveholding planters, as well as of West European capitalists, became the underlying economic law of the slaveholding plantation.

Such was the influence of capital on slave production in Brazil. This influence tended to be progressive in nature, creating the preconditions for the further development of productive forces in the colony based on high market production. However, the international collaboration of the slave economy with capital gradually encountered opposition from monopolies manifested in the efforts of Portuguese feudal lords to impart their own particular feudal spirit to the economic institutions of the colony. In conditions of a "formal" subordination of slavery to capital, such a feudalization of slavery would in essence signify a step backward, opposing the development of productive forces in the colony, on the one hand, and denying the "foundation" for the triumph of the capitalist system in the advanced West European countries, on the other. These were two sides of a single socio-economic process occurring throughout the world—the decline of feudalism and the conception, consolidation, and triumph of the new capitalist mode of production. However paradoxical, to this end the temporary revival of the slaveholding plantation in the colonies proved indispensable.

NOTES

1 K. Marx, *Capital*, I, in K. Marx and F. Engels, *Sochineniia* [cited hereafter as *Sochineniia*], XXIII, 769. In the English edition, this passage appears in chapter 31, "Genesis of the Industrial Capitalist."

2 Such an interpretation, for example, can be found in E. L. Bondarenko, *Pervonachal'noe nakoplenie kapitala* (Moscow, 1959), pp. 23-25.

3 K. Marx, *The Poverty of Philosophy*, in *Sochineniia*, IV, 135; K. Marx to P. V. Annenkov, 28 December 1848, in *Perepiska K. Marksa i F. Engel'sa s russkimi politicheskimi deiateliami* (Moscow, 1951), pp. 16–17; K. Marx, introduction to economic manuscripts of 1857–1858, in *Sochineniia*, XII, 724.

4 Arthur Ramos, *The Negro in Brazil* (Washington, 1939), p. 6.

5 José Francisco de Rocha Pombo, *História do Brasil*, 10 vols. (Rio de Janeiro, 1905); Pedro Calmon, *História social do Brasil*, 3 vols. (São Paulo, 1937–1939); Roberto C. Simonsen, *História econômica do Brasil, 1500–1820*, 2 vols. (São Paulo, 1937); Nelson Werneck Sodré, *Introdução á revolucão brasileira* (Rio de Janeiro, 1958).

6 Ramos, *The Negro in Brazil;* Gilberto Freyre, *Casa grande e senzala* (Rio de Janeiro, 1933); Agostinho M. Perdigão Malheiros, *A escravidão no Brazil*, 2 vols. (Rio de Janeiro, 1944); Evaristo de Moraes, *A escravidão africana no Brazil* (São Paulo, 1933); Nina Rodrigues, *Os africanos no Brasil*, 2nd edition (São Paulo, 1945); Donald Pierson, *Negroes in Brazil: A Study of Race Contact at Bahia* (Chicago, 1942); Aires de Mata Machado Filho, *O negro e o garimpo em Minas Gerais* (Rio de Janeiro, 1943); L. A. Costa Pinto, *O negro no Rio de Janeiro* (Rio de Janeiro, 1955); Luiz Vianna Filho, *O negro na Bahia* (Rio de Janeiro and São Paulo, 1946).

7 Eric Williams, *Kapitalizm i rabstvo* (Moscow, 1948).

8 William Z. Foster, *Ocherk politicheskoi istorii Ameriki* (Moscow, 1953); idem, *Negritianskii narod v istorii Ameriki* (Moscow, 1955).

9 Caio Prado Júnior, *Ekonomicheskaia istoriia Brazilii* (Moscow, 1949); idem, *Formação do Brasil contemporáneo, Colônia* (São Paulo, 1961).

10 See, for example, L. Yu. Slëzkin, "Revoliutsiia negrov-rabov na ostrove San-Domingo"†; V. I. Ermolaev, "Nekotorye voprosy osvoboditel'noi bor'by amerikanskikh kolonii Ispanii i Portugalii".†

11 A. E. Pasherstnik and I. D. Levin, *Priunuditel'nyi trud i rabstvo v stranakh kapitala* (Moscow, 1952), p. 236.

12 United Nations, Economic and Social Council, Official Records, Annexes. Thirteenth Session, 30 July–21 September 1951 (Geneva), Document E/1988, Report of the *Ad Hoc* Committee on Slavery (2nd session), 4 May 1951, p. 5.

13 F. Engels, *Anti-Dühring*, in *Sochineniia*, XX, 186.

14 F. Engels, *Proiskhozhdenie sem'i, chastnoi sobstvennosti i gosudarstva* [The Origin of the Family, Private Property, and the State] (Moscow, 1953), p. 182.

15 Engels, *Anti-Dühring*, p. 187.

16 K. Marx, "The London 'Times' on the princes of Orleans in America," in *Sochineniia*, XV, 335.

17 K. Marx, *Formy, predshestvuiushchie kapitalisticheskomu proizvodstvu* (Moscow, 1940), pp. 32–33.

18 João Pandiá Calógeras, *Formação histórica do Brasil* (São Paulo, 1938), p. 37.

19 Bourgeois historians, as a rule, exaggerate the heroism of the *bandeirantes,* romanticizing their activities in every way possible. A striking example of unlimited praise of the *bandeirantes* is the two-volume study by the prominent Brazilian scholar Affonso de Escragnolle Taunay, *História das bandeiras paulistas* (São Paulo, 1951)

20 Marx, *Capital,* II, in *Sochineniia*, XXIV, 544.

21 The fundamental work of Basílio de Magalhaes, *Expansão geográfica do Brasil colonial* (Rio de Janeiro, 1944).

22 John A. Crow, *The Epic of Latin America* (New York, 1946), p. 405.

23 Marx, *Capital*, I, in *Sochineniia*, XXIII, 760.

24 W. E. Du Bois, *The Negro* (New York, 1951), p. 156. Compare *Narody Afriki* (Moscow, 1959), p. 21.

25 Name given in Brazil to a variety of commercial wood. The exploitation of *paubrasil* was especially significant in the sixteenth century, but it continued to play an important role throughout the entire colonial period. Portugal annually took up to 700 tons of *paubrasil* from the colony; 25 percent of the receipts from its sale were for the exclusive benefit of the royal treasury. For more detail, see Simonsen, *História econômica do Brasil*, I, 100; II, 222.

26 See Simonsen, *História econômica do Brasil*, II, 55.

27 See Marx, *Capital*, III, in *Sochineniia*, XXV, pt. 2. p. 184.

28 See Simonsen, *História econômica do Brasil*, I, 137.

29 See *Arkhiv Marksa i Engel'sa*, IV (Moscow, 1935), 105.

30 Marx, introduction to economic manuscripts of 1857–1858, in *Sochineniia*, XII, 724.

31 Marx, *Capital*, III, in *Sochineniia*, XXV, pt. 2, p. 354.

32 It is very difficult to clarify the legal status of slaves in Brazil, as all documents pertaining to the slave trade were, by popular demand, ceremoniously destroyed immediately following the abolition of slavery in May 1888.

33 V. I. Lenin, *Polnoe sobranie sochinenii*, XXII, 251.

34 Alan K. Manchester, *British Preëminence in Brazil, Its Rise and Decline: A Study in European Expansion* (Chapel Hill, 1933), pp. 230–31.

35 See F. Engels, *Dialektika prirody* (Moscow, 1955), p. 142; *Arkhiv Marksa i Engel'sa*, IV, 225.

36 Marx, *Capital*, III, in *Sochineniia*, XXV, 353.

37 See Marx, *The Poverty of Philosophy*, in *Sochineniia*, IV, 135. See, also, K. Marx, to Annenkov, 28 December 1846, in *Perepiska K. Marksa i F. Engel'sa*, pp. 16–17.

38 According to Marx, as is known, industrial capital serves not only to appropriate surplus value or surplus product but also to create them, whether in agriculture or industrial activity. See Marx, *Capital*, II, in *Sochineniia*, XXIV, 65.

39 Lujo Brentano, *Istoriia razvitiia narodnogo khoziaistva Anglii*, III (Moscow and Leningrad, 1930), 78.

40 See Marx, *Capital*, I, in *Sochineniia*, XXIII, 769.

41 Simonsen, *História econômica do Brasil*, I, 209.

42 *Relatorio apresentado a Asambleia general ordinaria realisada em 31 Mayo de 1937* (Rio de Janeiro, 1937), p. 196.

43 J. S. Redding, *They Came in Chains* (New York, 1950), p. 17.

44 Williams, *Kapitalizm i rabstvo*, p. 55.

45 The above-mentioned works by Simonsen, Calmon, Ramos, Pandiá Calógeras, Taunay, and other scholars contain a wealth of factual material on the slave trade. See, also *An Essay on the Slavery and Commerce of the Human Species, Particularly the African*, translated from a Latin dissertation, which was honored with the first prize at the University of Cambridge, for the year 1735 (London, 1738); H. A. Wyndham, *The Atlantic and Slavery* (London, 1935); W. E. DuBois, *The Negro;* idem, *Black Folk, Then and Now* (New York, 1945); Frank Tannenbaum, *Slave and Citizen: The*

Negro in the Americas (New York, 1947); Dieudonné Rinchon, *La traité et l'escla-vage des Congolais par les Européens: Histoire de la déportation de 13 millions 250.000 noirs en Amérique* (Brussells, 1929); Christopher Lloyd, *The Navy and the Slave Trade: The Suppression of the African Slave Trade in the 19th Century* (London and New York, 1949).

46 Marx, *Capital*, II, in *Sochineniia*, XXIV, 544.

47 Celso Furtado, *Formação econômica do Brasil* (Rio de Janeiro, 1959), p. 58.

48 Marx, *Capital*, I, in *Sochineniia*, XXIII, 247. This is the active life span of a slave, according to bourgeois scholars; see, for example, Simonsen, *História econômica do Brasil*, I, 204.

49 See *Diccionário histórico, geográphico e etnográphico do Brasil*, I (Rio de Janeiro, 1922), pp. 282–83.

50 Gold was first found in the province of Minas Gerais, in 1694; before long over 100,000 slaves were working in the gold fields of this region (by 1735). At the end of the eighteenth century, there were 555 active mines here, some of which were ex-ploited by 100,000 slaves at one time. See Simonsen, *História econômica do Brasil*, II, 93–94.

51 Marx, *Capital*, I, in *Sochineniia*, XXIII, 763.

52 See *Arkhiv Marksa i Engel'sa*, IV, 229.

53 Pandiá Calógeras, *Formacão histórica do Brasil*, p. 60.

54 Roberto C. Simonsen, *Brazil's Industrial Evolution* (São Paulo, 1939), p. 12.

55 Manchester, *British Preëminence in Brazil*, p. 38.

56 Simonsen, *História econômica do Brasil*, II, 82.

57 Ample statistical data on this question are contained in the following special studies: Henri Landrin, *Traité de l'or, monographie: Histoire naturelle, exploitation, statis-tique, son role en économie politique et ses divers emplois* (Paris, 1863); United States Senate, 67th Congress, 4th Session, Gold and Silver Statistics, persuant to S. Res. 469 (28 August 1923), Series 3 (Washington, 1923); Émile Levasseur, *La Question de l'or* (Paris, 1858); Jacques E. Mertens, *La Naissance et le développement de l'étalon-or, 1696–1922* (Louvain: Institut des Recherches Économiques, Université de Louvain, 1944); L. D. Edie, "Gold Production and Prices before and after the World War," *Indiana University Studies*, XV, no. 78 (March 1928).

58 By a decree of 1695, the royal government created special foundries (*casas de fun-dação*) in Brazil, where gold nuggets were smelted into ingots, one-fifth of which went to the royal treasury (*quintos reais*). For more detail on this, see Manuel S. Cardozo, "The Collection of the Fifths in Brazil, 1695–1709," *HAHR* 20, no. 3 (August 1940), 359–79.

59 F. Engels, *O razlozhenii feodalizma i vozniknovenii natsional'nykh gosudarstv*, in *Sochineniia*, XXI, 408.

60 In accord with a treaty of 1703, Portugal was obliged to export to England from £400,000 to £1,000,000 in gold bars, thus seeking to offset its trade deficit with England by means of Brazilian gold. See Manchester, *British Preëminence in Brazil*, pp. 31, 40; Marcus Cheke, *Dictator of Portugal: A Life of the Marquis of Pombal, 1699–1783* (London, 1938), p. 7.

61 Adam Smith, *Issledovanie o prirode i prichinakh bogátstva narodov* [Wealth of Nations] (Moscow and Leningrad, 1935), p. 212.

62 *Arkhiv Marksa i Engel'sa*, IV, 225.

63 Simonsen, *História econômica do Brasil*, II, 222.
64 Marx, *Capital*, III, in *Sochineniia*, XXV, pt. 2, p. 97.
65 Simonsen, *História econômica do Brasil*, II, 222.
66 See *Diccionário histórico, geográphico e etnográphico do Brasil*, I, 540.
67 The extent of real accumulation, that is, of productive and commodity capital, is given by export-import statistics. See Marx, *Capital*, III, in *Sochineniia*, XXV, 514.
68 Marx, *Capital*, I, in *Sochineniia*, XXIII, 769.
69 Ibid., p. 247.
70 Ibid.
71 Simonsen, *História econômica do Brasil*, II, 196, 206.
72 Ibid., p. 270.
73 *Anuario estadístico do Brasil*, Ano XVI (Rio de Janeiro, 1955), pp. 276–77. The dynamics of Brazilian exports, expressed in pounds sterling, developed at a rate two times lower (1812, 1,233,000; 1816, 2,330,000; 1822, 4,030,000). This was explained by the fact that, in those years, Brazilian currency depreciated at a considerably quicker rate: in 1808, 1 milreis equalled 70 English pence, while in 1822 only 40 pence. See João Roberto Moreira, *Educação e desenvolvimento no Brasil* (Rio de Janeiro, 1960), p. 41; Simonsen, *História econômica do Brasil*, II, 347.
74 Marx, *Capital*, III, in *Sochineniia*, XXV, pt. 2., p. 368.
75 *Arkhiv Marksa i Engel'sa*, II (VII), 101.
76 Ibid.
77 Marx, *Teoriia pribavochnoi stoimosti* [The Theory of Surplus Value] (vol. IV of *Capital*), pt. 2 (Moscow, 1957), pp. 297–98.
78 See Marx, *Formy, predshestvuiushchie kapitalisticheskomu proizvodstvu*, p. 51.
79 Marx, *Capital*, III, in *Sochineniia*, XXV, pt. 2, p. 147.
80 G. F. Knapi, "Rabstvo i svoboda v sel'skom trude," in *Istoriia truda v sviazi s istoriei nekotorykh form promyshlennosti* (St. Petersburg, 1897), pp. 191–92.
81 Karl Grünberg, "Sostoiane lichnoi zavisimosti," in *Istoriia truda v sviazi s istoriei nekotorykh form promyshlennosti*, p. 173.
82 Werneck Sodré, *Introdução a revolução brasileira*, p. 21.
83 On this group of slaves, see Prado Júnior, *Formação do Brasil contemporâneo, Colônia*, p. 220.
84 Marx, "Wage Labor and Capital," in *Sochineniia*, VI, 433.
85 Compare K. Marx, *Ob osvobozhdenii krepostnykh krest'ian v Rossii*, in *Sochineniia*, XII, 695.
86 On the existence of groups of day-laborers, see, for example, *An Essay on the Commerce and Products of the Portuguese Colonies in South America, especially the Brazils*, trans. from the Portuguese of J. J. da Cunha de Azevedo Coutinho, Bishop of Fernambuco, and fellow of the Royal Academy of Sciences of Lisbon, many years a resident of South America (London, 1807), p. 135.
87 Engels, *Anti-Dühring*, p. 282.
88 Furtado, *Formação econômica do Brasil*, p. 58.
89 Marx referred directly to this in *Capital*, III, in *Sochineniia*, XXV, pt. 1, p. 422.

7 RUSSIAN TRAVELERS OF THE EIGHTEENTH AND NINETEENTH CENTURIES: SOURCE MATERIALS ON THE GEOGRAPHY, HISTORY, AND ETHNOGRAPHY OF LATIN AMERICA

L. A. SHUR

THE PAPERS of Russian travelers who visited the Latin American countries in the eighteenth and nineteenth centuries have only comparatively recently attracted the attention of scholars. The present intensification of interest in this area is a result of the broad and multifaceted development of ties between the Soviet Union and distant Latin America. These materials are of primary interest as a source for the geography, history, and ethnography of the Latin American countries.[1]

If the accounts, travel notes, and diaries of West European travelers who visited Latin America at the end of the eighteenth and in the first half of the nineteenth century (Humboldt, Bonpland, María Graham, Spix and Martius, Eschwege, and many others) have long been widely used as sources for the study of the geography, history, ethnography, and culture of the Latin American countries, scholars have not made use of analogous Russian materials. The first scholar to consider using the materials of Russian travelers for such study was N. G. Shprintsin.[2] The value of the ethnographic observations of Russian seamen who sailed around the world at the beginning of the nineteenth century was recognized by B. A. Lipshits,[3] while B. N. Komissarov has written on the notes and diaries of Russian sailors who witnessed the war of independence in Latin America.[4] The need for organized study and use of the papers of Russian travelers to Latin America has been pointed out by the author of the present article.[5]

The first steps in this direction have already been taken. It is therefore possible to present preliminary results and to raise some questions for further study. The primary task remains to identify as fully as possible all Russian travelers who

Originally published as "Materialy russkikh puteshestvennikov XVIII–XIX vv. kak istochnik po geografii, istorii i etnografii stran Latinskoi Ameriki," *IVGO* 100, no. 3 (1968), 230–36.

visited Latin America in the eighteenth and nineteenth centuries. No one has yet managed to do this in an exhaustive manner.

The second and no less complex task is to locate the published and unpublished notes, diaries, and letters of Russian travelers in the archives and book repositories of the Soviet Union (as well as abroad). These materials have not yet been collected by anyone. A part of the notes of Russian travelers have been lost in the pages of forgotten Russian periodical publications of the last century, or buried in archives, often in the most unlikely collections. Therefore, the work undertaken by our researchers in recent years cannot, even in any significant part, be considered finished or complete. Not even all the printed sources have yet been found, not to mention manuscript sources, only a small part of which are known to us. One can confidently predict that in the process of further research many new and valuable materials will be found.

The next essential stage of work is the analysis of sources and their comparison with other materials of a similar kind belonging, for example, to foreign travelers of that time, in order to establish the significance of a given source for the study of the history and ethnography of the Latin American countries in a given historical period. In general, this effort has not yet been undertaken, and therefore the articles which have come out in recent years on Russian sources relating to Latin America should be considered merely as preliminary reports on materials found.

The documentary materials of Russian travelers who visited Latin America can be classified into several groups. First of all, one must isolate the materials of eighteenth-century Russian travelers. The first Russian known to have reached far-away [Latin] America was Nikifor Poluboiarinov. His account of a trip to India was uncovered by V. A. Divin.[6] En route to India aboard the English ship *Speaker,* Poluboiarinov stopped in Brazil in July and August 1763. In his journal he described Rio de Janeiro; he also left sketches of Brazilian fish, birds, and reptiles.

In the 1780s, V. Baranshchikov and F. V. Karzhavin visited Latin America. As early as 1950, A. V. Efimov called attention to the book *The Misadventures of Vasilii Baranshchikov, Citizen of Lower Novgorod, in Three Parts of the World, America, Asia, and Europe, from 1780 to 1787,* which contains interesting information about the Antilles islands.[7] F. V. Karzhavin, a writer and translator, was the first Russian to visit Cuba, this in 1782. It is known that during the many years he traveled in America, Karzhavin kept a diary. Upon his return to Russia, he prepared a book about his American adventures. The fate of this manuscript, however, is unknown. Perhaps further archival investigations will help to uncover it.[8]

An important group of sources are the documentary materials accruing from nineteenth-century Russian circumnavigations of the world. The best-known and most-studied part of these materials are the official travel accounts written by the commanding officers, which usually were published following an expedition's return to Russia. These books contain information on the life and customs of the peoples of Latin America; on the history, contemporary political situation, and culture of those countries which the seaman visited. In addition to the ships' captains, travel accounts were sometimes published by naval officers who sailed on the voyages. Yet even these printed materials have scarcely been used by researchers as a source for the history and ethnography of those Latin American countries visited by Russian round-the-world voyagers. Thus, for example, in the essays on the history of Argentina, Brazil, and Mexico prepared by the Institute of History of the USSR Academy of Sciences and published in 1960–62,† Russian sources were not taken into account. Only most recently have Soviet historians who study the countries of Latin America begun in some measure to use the better-known materials of Russian travelers. For example, the published travel notes of I. F. Kruzenshtern, Yu. F. Lisianskii, V. M. Golovnin, M. P. Lazarev, O. E. Kotzebue, and other Russian mariners of the early nineteenth century are analyzed in L. Yu. Slëzkin's book *Russia and the War of Independence in Spanish America.*[9]

Despite an apparent awareness of the sources for the history of Russian circumnavigations of the world, the notes of several Russian travelers which appeared in print remain unknown to scholars. Thus, for example, in the historico-geographical literature the view prevails that the account of the round-the-world voyage of the transport *Krotkii,* commanded by F. P. Vrangel in the years 1827–29, was not published. Only excerpts of Vrangel's notes were included in *Severnyi arkhiv,* in 1828.[10] Few were aware that an account of the *Krotkii*'s voyage around the world belonging to the pen of P. Nizovtsev, an artillery sergeant, was published in 1903 by the Kronshtadt daily, *Kotlin.* Nizovtsev included in his notes exceedingly interesting details about the final event of the war of independence in Latin America—the royalist surrender in January 1826 of the fortress of Callao (Peru), Spain's last stronghold in South America.[11]

While the principal published accounts of the best-known Russian circumnavigations of the nineteenth century are more or less familiar to researchers and have been placed at the disposition of scholars (although they have not been used as a source for the history and ethnography of Latin America), the matter of unpublished materials is far more complicated. Almost all Russian naval officers on these voyages kept diaries and travel notes and wrote letters home. Until the 1860's, diaries and notes were with rare exceptions (for example, "Pamiatnik"—the diary of E. Kiselev, a sailor who took part in the Bellingshausen voyage of 1819–1821) kept only by officers. From the seventies and eighties on, travel notes were frequently kept by sailors as well. To date, however, these materials, lost in archives and the manuscript departments of libraries, remain for the most part unknown to scholars.

A series of as yet unused materials from Russian round-the-world voyages housed in the archives of Leningrad has been noted by A. I. Andreev,[12] A. N. Mikhailova,[13] and B. G. Ostrovskii.[14] Notes and diaries of Russian sailors which were not written with a view to publication are especially significant as a source for the history and ethnography of Latin America, since they often contain far more material on Latin America than the published accounts of ships' captains. The unofficial nature of such materials is most apparent in the authors' frankness; the Decembrist sentiments of progressive Russian youth is reflected in many diaries, notes, and letters from young Russian officers of the early nineteenth century.

Comparatively recently, the manuscript diaries of F. F. Matiushkin and F. P. Litke, who realized their first round-the-world voyage aboard the sloop *Kamchatka* under the command of V. M. Golovnin, were discovered and have attracted the attention of scholars. Matiushkin's journal was extensively used for the first time by Yu. V. Davydov in his book *Wandering the Seas,*[15] Litke's diary has been put at the disposition of scholars by B. N. Komissarov.[16] Both of these diaries serve as splendid sources for the study of the history, ethnography, and culture of Brazil and Peru at the beginning of the nineteenth century. In the "Brazilian" and "Peruvian" notes of Matiushkin and Litke,* much space is devoted to the national-liberation struggle of the Latin American peoples against the Spanish colonial yoke. Litke wrote, for example: "The Peruvian patriots . . . await only the rout of crown forces in Chile before declaring themselves independent. Mexico certainly will follow the example of Peru. Thus Spain is on the verge of losing all her possessions in the New World."[17]

Not long ago, we discovered two unknown letters written during the round-the-world voyage of the sloop *Apollon* by the Decembrist sailor M. Küchelbecker.[18] In these letters, which date from 1822–23 and are addressed to his mother, Küchelbecker shares his impressions of the voyage, relating the arrival in Kamchatka, the sloop's passage to Novo-Arkhangel'sk and then to San Francisco (California) to winter over. Küchelbecker describes California and recalls the Spanish missionaries who exploited the Indians. He writes, too, of the revolutionary events in Mexico, particularly the declaration of Agustín de Iturbide emperor of the country.

The papers of Russian travelers are housed not only in Soviet archives but in foreign repositories too. Not long ago, letters and a diary of an unknown Russian officer who took part in the first [Russian] round-the-world voyage under the command of I. F. Kruzenshtern were found in the manuscript department of the Bibliothèque Nationale, in Paris.[19] We were able to establish that the letters and diary belonged to M. I. Ratmanov. Some of the letters were addressed to N. M.

---

*The Latin American portions of these journals have since been published. See L. A. Shur, *K beregam Novogo Sveta: Iz neopublikovannykh zapisok russkikh puteshestvennikov nachala XIX veka.*†

Karamzin.* The Ratmanov diary found in Paris is the third journal of which we are aware; two others are housed in the Central Naval Archives and the manuscript department of the State Public Library, both in Leningrad.

Another group of sources comprises the materials of the Russian-American Company, whose possessions bordered on Mexico (at Ross, not far from San Francisco). The company carried on extensive trade not only with Mexico but also with other Latin American countries along the Pacific coast, especially Peru and Chile.‡ Company agents traveled repeatedly to Mexico, as well as elsewhere in Latin America. Naturally, therefore, official company documents (reports, correspondence) and the notes, diaries, and letters of company employees who visited Latin America are without question of interest as sources. This group of sources complements the documentary materials accruing from the Russian voyages of circumnavigation, for as is known, almost all Russian round-the-world expeditions were connected with Russian America.

Published sources for the history of the Russian-American Company are fairly well known. They have been enumerated in the works of S. B. Okun,[20] A. A. Preobrazhenskii,[21] and others. A significant portion of the company's archival materials preserved in Soviet archives were brought to light by Okun.[22] Less well known to scholars are the Russian-American Company archives that were located in Novo-Arkhangel'sk [Sitkha] and after 1867 transferred to the United States. As early as 1943, A. I. Andreev pointed out the great value of these archives.[23] Only recently, however, has the Central Archival Administration [of the USSR] received a microfilm copy of the Russian-American Company papers from the United States.[24] It is possible that some of these documents, too, are of interest as a source for the history and ethnography of Latin America.

The private papers of Russian-American Company employees were dispersed after the company's liquidation; part of them have been lost. In recent years, some private archives of company officials have been found and reviewed by A. I. Andreev,[25] A. A. Preobrazhenskii,[26] and especially S. N. Markov.[27] The published and archival materials of the Russian-American Company have been used in the works of A. I. Andreev,[28] S. B. Okun,[29] S. N. Markov,[30] and others. However, as a source for the history and ethnography of the Latin American countries they have not yet attracted the attention of scholars. Of particular interest here is the study of documents from the archives of K. T. Khlebnikov, F. P. Vrangel, and other agents of the Russian-American Company, who on numerous occasions were in Mexico and elsewhere in Latin America.

---

*Nikolai Mikhailovich Karamzin (1766–1826), influential Russian historian and writer.

‡That agents of the Russian-American Company indeed effected commercial transactions in the Spanish colonies is a certain fact; the extent of such transactions, however, remains to be documented. On this topic, see, for example, Ekkehard Völkl, *Russland und Lateinamerika, 1741– 1841* (Wiesbaden, 1968).

The archive of K. T. Khlebnikov, a writer and well-known official of the Russian-American Company, is now housed in the State Archives of Perm [Gosudarstvennyi arkhiv Permskoi oblasti]. The holdings of this archive have been described and in part used by B. N. Vishnevskii.[31] Of especial value in the Khlebnikov archive are numerous papers pertaining to California, where he was obliged to travel frequently on company trade matters.

The F. P. Vrangel archive, housed in the Central State Historical Archives of Estonia [Tsentral'nyi gosudarstvennyi istoricheskii arkhiv Estonskoi SSR], in Tartu, was first described briefly by A. I. Andreev, in 1943.[32] A portion of these materials have been used by Yu. V. Davydov in a short book entitled *Ferdinand Vrangel,*[33] and also by V. M. Pasetskii.[34] Among the many manuscripts in this archive, perhaps the most interesting is the diary we uncovered of Vrangel's voyage from Sitkha to St. Petersburg (1835–36), in which he describes his trip across Mexico from the Pacific to the Atlantic Ocean.* Vrangel's diary presents a canvas of Mexican life. It served as the basis for a short travel essay which was published in St. Petersburg, in 1836.

Many archives of Russian-American Company officials have not been used by scholars, while some have not yet been found. Thus, for example, in the works of S. N. Markov[35] and N. A. Chernitsyn[36] on I. A. Kuskov, renowned agent of the Russian-American Company and founder of Fort Ross, in California, use has not been made of the Kuskov papers, which are housed in the manuscript department of the Lenin State Library [in Moscow]. The larger part of these materials comprises the business correspondence of A. A. Baranov with Kuskov. This archive contains documents bearing on the founding of Fort Ross and on efforts to initiate trade relations with the Spaniards in California.[37]

Among the papers of Russian travelers, a special group is made up of the writings of Russian scientists who visited Latin America in the nineteenth century, beginning with the first Russian expedition to South America under the leadership of G. I. Langsdorf (1821–29) and ending with the scientific travels of A. I. Voeikov (1874), N. M. Al'bov (1895–97), S. K. Patkanov (1895), and others. This group of materials has in part already been introduced into the scholarly literature. Thus, for example, in various of her writings N. G. Shprintsin made use of the Langsdorf materials as a source for the study of the ethnography of Brazil.[38] At the present time, B. N. Komissarov is studying the papers of the Langsdorf expedition as a source for the history of early nineteenth-century Brazil.[39]

Many documentary materials of Russian scholars who visited Latin America have not yet been found. The geographer P. A. Chikhachev, for example, visited Chile and Argentina in 1837. A brief description of his trip appeared in 1844 in

*This journal has since been published. See L. A. Shur, *K beregam Novogo Sveta.*†

the journal *Otechestvennye zapiski.** Chikhachev's papers, however, have thus far not been uncovered.

In addition to Russian expeditions and individual scholars who undertook geographic and ethnographic investigations in the Latin American countries, one must keep in mind the Russian scientific expeditions sent to the Russian-American Company possessions, in Alaska. The 1830s and '40s saw a flowering of ethnographic research on Russian America.[40] Inasmuch as the Russian American Company held Fort Ross until 1841, naturally there is also among the ethnographic and historical materials of the Russian expeditions which worked in Alaska information about California and the Indians and Spanish settlements of that region. Great credit for collecting such materials belongs to I. G. Voznesenskii, a zoologist and ethnographer who spent several years in Russian America. Voznesenskii's biography and a review of his papers can be found in the works of K. K. Gil'zen,[41] M. V. Stepanov,[42] B. A. Lipshits,[43] and E. E. Blomkvist.[44] Many of Voznesenskii's ethnographically valuable drawings relate to California. Of no less interest are his unpublished travel journals, which include notes about not only California but also Brazil and Chile, where he stopped en route to Russian America. None of these materials, however, has yet attracted the attention of students of the ethnography and history of Latin America.

Several Russian scholars visited Latin American countries in the nineteenth century while on scientific expeditions to the Far East. In 1853–54, for example, the Russian botanist and ethnographer L. I. Shrenk visited Rio de Janeiro, Callao, and Lima while on an expedition to study the Amur river area. Shrenk's diaries remain unpublished, although B. V. Lukin has established that Shrenk's Latin American notes contain interesting ethnographic observations.[45]

The papers of Russian travelers who visited Latin America in the eighteenth and nineteenth centuries constitute the largest part of Russian sources pertaining to the geography, history, and ethnography of Latin America. Precisely for this reason, the primary task at the present time is, insofar as possible, to bring to light all such materials extant in archives and book repositories. Until this is done, any analysis of these sources, or even their use, will not prove very productive, for it is essential first to work out a general picture of existing Russian sources for the history and ethnography of Latin America. Once the Russian sources have been identified, published, and introduced into the scholarly literature, it will be possible to evaluate their real place in the general

---

*An English translation of this account appeared several years ago in the United States. See Platon Alexandrovich Chikhachev, *A Trip Across the Pampas of Buenos Aires (1836–1837),* trans. from the Russian by Jack Weiner, University of Kansas, Center of Latin American Studies, Occasional Publications no. 8, (Lawrence, Kansas, 1967).

body of available sources on the history and ethnography of the Latin American countries.

NOTES

1 Unpublished and printed Russian sources on Latin America can tentatively be divided into the following three broad areas: (a) travel notes, diaries, memoirs, and letters of Russian travelers who visited Latin America in the eighteenth and nineteenth centuries; (b) official dispatches of Russian diplomats in the Latin American countries (envoys, chargés d'affaires, consuls) sent to the ministry of foreign affairs, in St. Petersburg; and (c) documentary materials housed in Soviet archives relating to Latin America but which did not originate with any Russian expedition to Latin America. See L. A. Shur, "Russkie puteshestvenniki v Chili v XIX v (O russkikh istochnikakh po istorii i etnografii Chili)" [Russian travelers in Chile in the nineteenth century (on Russian sources for the history and ethnography of Chile)], in S. A. Gonionskii et al., eds., *Chili. Politika, ekonomika, kul'tura. Sbornik statei* (Moscow, 1965), pp. 338–39.

2 N. G. Shprintsin, "Ekspeditsiia akademika G. I. Langsdorfa v Braziliiu v pervoi chetverti XIX veka" [The expedition of G. I. Langsdorf to Brazil in the first quarter of the nineteenth century], *SE*, no. 1 (1936), 109–20; idem, "Materialy russkikh ekspeditsii v Yuzhnuiu Ameriku, khraniashchiesia v arkhive AN SSSR" [Materials from Russian expeditions to South America in the archives of the USSR Academy of Sciences], *SE*, no. 2 (1947), 187–94; idem, introduction and notes to G. G. Manizer, *Ekspeditsiia akademika G. I. Langsdorfa v Braziliiu (1821–1828)*†; idem, "Pervaia russkaia ekspeditsiia v Braziliiu" [The first Russian expedition to Brazil], in I. P. Gerasimov et al., eds., *Voprosy geografii* (Moscow and Leningrad, 1956), pp. 344–49.

3 B. A. Lipshits, "Etnograficheskie issledovaniia v russkikh krugosvetnykh ekspeditsiiakh pervoi poloviny XIX v." [Ethnographic investigations on Russian round-the-world expeditions of the first half of the nineteenth century], in V. K. Sokolova, ed., *Ocherki istorii russkoi etnografii, fol'kloristiki i antropologii* (Moscow, 1956), pp. 299–322.

4 B. N. Komissarov, "Braziliia pervoi chetverti XIX veka v opisaniiakh russkikh moreplavatelei"†; idem, "Russkie moreplavateli o voine Ispanskoi Ameriki za nezavisimost'" [Russian mariners on Spanish America's war of independence], in Lavrov et al., eds., *Voina za nezavisimost' v Latinskoi Amerike (1810–1826,*† pp. 301–11. On the linguistic materials of the 1821–1829 Russian expedition to Brazil, see O. K. Vasil'eva-Shvede, "Lingvisticheskie materialy russkoi ekspeditsii v Braziliiu 1821–1829 gg.," *NB LGU*, no. 14/15 (1947), 36–42.

5 L. A. Shur, "Russkie puteshestvenniki na Kube v XVIII–XIX vv." [Russian travelers in Cuba in the eighteenth and nineteenth centuries], in Efimov and Grigulevich, eds., *Kuba: Istoriko-etnograficheskie ocherki,*† pp. 274–301; idem, "Kul'turnye i literatur-

nye sviazi Rossii i Brazilii v XVIII–XIX vv."†; idem, *Rossiia i Latinskaia Amerika*†; idem, "Russkie puteshestvenniki v Chili v XIX v.," in Gonionskii et al., eds., *Chili*.

6 V. A. Divin, "Dnevnik puteshestviia michmana Nikifora Poluboiarinova v Indiiu v 1763–1764 gg." [The diary of warrant officer Nikifor Poluboiarinov's voyage to India in 1763–1764], *Voprosy istorii estestvoznaniia i tekhniki*, vyp. 3 (1957), 204–5.

7 A. V. Efimov, *Iz istorii velikikh russkikh geograficheskikh otkrytii v Severnom Ledovitom i Tikhom okeanakh (XVII–pervaia polovina XVIII v.)* [From the history of the great Russian geographic discoveries in the Arctic and Pacific Oceans (seventeenth to the first half of the eighteenth century)] (Moscow, 1950), p. 14.

8 Shur, "Russkie puteshestvenniki na Kube," pp. 274–77.

9 L. Yu. Slëzkin, *Rossiia i voina za nezavisimost' v Ispanskoi Amerike,* † pp. 348–50.

10 N. N. Zubov, *Otechestvennye moreplavateli-issledovateli morei i okeanov* [Russian seamen-explorers of the seas and the oceans] (Moscow, 1954), p. 196.

11 Shur, "Russkie puteshestvenniki v Chili," p. 344.

12 A. I. Andreev, "Novye materialy o russkikh plavaniiakh i otkrytiiakh v Severnom Ledovitom i Tikhom okeaniakh v XVIII–XIX vv." [New materials on Russian voyages and discoveries in the Arctic and Pacific Oceans in the 18th and 19th centuries], *IVGO* 75, vyp. 5 (1943), 34–36.

13 A. N. Mikhailova, "Rukopisnye materialy po istorii russkogo voenno-morskogo flota" [Manuscript materials for the history of the Russian navy], *MS*, no. 3 (1946), 114–28; nos. 8–9 (1946), 116–20.

14 B. G. Ostrovskii, "O pozabytykh istochnikakh i uchastnikakh antarkticheskoi ekspeditskii Bellingsgauzena-Lazareva" [Forgotten sources and participants of the Bellingshausen-Lazarev expedition to Antarctica], *IVGO* 81, vyp. 2 (1949), 239–49.

15 Yu. Davydov, *V moriakh i stranstviiakh* (Moscow, 1959).

16 Komissarov, "Braziliia pervoi chetverti XIX v.," loc, cit.; idem, "Dnevnik puteshestviia F. P. Litke na shliupe *Kamchatka* v 1817–1819 gg." [Diary of the voyage of F. P. Litke aboard the sloop *Kamchatka* in 1817–1819], *IVGO* 96, vyp. 5 (1964), 414–19.

17 L. A. Shur, *K beregam Novogo Sveta,*† pp. 121–22.

18 Manuscript Department, Lenin State Library, fond 449, karton 2, delo 18. The letters of M. K. Küchelbecker have been prepared by us for publication.

19 Bibliothèque Nationale (Paris), Department of Manuscripts, "Slave," nos. 103(1), 104. The author expresses his deep appreciation to Mr. A. Zvigil'skii for a microfilm copy of this manuscript.

20 S. B. Okun, *Rossiisko-amerikanskaia kompaniia* [The Russian-American Company] (Moscow and Leningrad, 1939).

21 A. A. Preobrazhenskii, "Dokumenty po istorii Rossiisko-amerikanskoi kompanii" [Documents on the history of the Russian-American Company], *IA*, no. 2 (1959), 229–34.

22 Okun, *Rossiisko-amerkianskaia kompaniia*.

23 A. I. Andreev, "Ob arkhive Rossiisko-amerikanskoi kompanii" [On the archives of the Russian-American Company], *IVGO* 75 vyp. 3 (1943), 61–62.

24 G. E. Baskakov, V. V. Ievlev and V. F. Kokhov, "Dokumenty Rossiisko-amerikanskoi kompanii v Natsional'nom arkhive SShA" [Russian-American Company documents in the U.S. National Archives], *Ist. SSSR*, no. 5 (1963), 212–16.

25 A. I. Andreev, "Materialy o Rossiisko-amerikanskoi kompanii i eë deiateliakh (Rukopisnoe otdelenie GPB)" [Materials on the Russian-American Company and its agents (The manuscript department of the State Public Library)], *IVGO* 75, vyp. 5 (1943), 55–59; idem, ed., *Russkie otkrytiia v Tikhom okeane i Severnoi Amerike v XVIII–XIX vv: Sbornik materialov* [Russian discoveries in the Pacific Ocean and North America in the eighteenth and nineteenth centuries: a collection of materials] (Moscow and Leningrad, 1944); idem, "Russkie otkrytiia v Tikhom okeane i v Severnoi Amerike v XVIII v. (Obzor istochnikov i literatury)" [Russian discoveries in the Pacific and in North America in the eighteenth century (a review of the sources and literature)], in idem, ed., *Russkie otkrytiia v Tikhom okeane i Severnoi Amerike v XVIII v.* (Moscow, 1948), pp. 5–76.

26 Preobrazhenskii, "Dokumenty po istorii Rossiisko-amerikanskoi kompanii"; idem, "Kollektsiia G. V. Yudina v Gosudarstvennom arkhive Krasnoiarskogo kraia" [The G. V. Yudin collection in the Krasnoiarsk territorial State archives], in *Arkheograficheskii ezhegodnik za 1958* (Moscow, 1960), pp. 267–92.

27 S. N. Markov, "Arkhivy 'Kolumbov rossiiskikh'" [Archives of the "Russian Columbuses"], *Omskaia oblast'*, no. 7 (1940); idem, "Klady 'Kolumbov rossiiskikh': Dokumenty o russkoi morskoi slave" [Hidden treasures of the "Russian Columbuses": documents on Russian maritime glory], *MS*, no. 8–9 (1944), 76–81; no. 10 (1944), 81–88.

28 Andreev, *Russkie otkrytiia v Tikhom okeane i Severnoi Amerike;* idem, "Russkie otkrytiia v Tikhom okeane i v Severnoi Amerike."

29 Okun, *Rossiisko-amerikanskaia kompaniia.*

30 S. N. Markov, *Russkie na Aliaske* [Russians in Alaska] (Moscow, 1946); idem, *Letopis' Aliaski* [Alaskan chronicle] (Moscow, 1948).

31 B. N. Vishnevskii, "Materialy arkhiva K. T. Khlebnikova, predstavliaiushchie interes dlia istorii geografii" [Materials from the K. T. Khlebnikov archive pertaining to the history of geography], *IAN,* seriia geografii, vyp. 5 (1953), 87–88; idem, "Puteshestvennik Kirill Khlebnikov i ego nauchnoe nasledie" [The traveler Kirill Khlebnikov and his scientific legacy], in *Na Zapadnom Urale: Sbornik statei* (Perm, 1956), pp. 119–34; idem, *Puteshestvennik Kirill Khlebnikov* [The traveler Kirill Khlebnikov] (Perm, 1957).

32 A. I. Andreev, "Arkhiv Vrangelia" [The Vrangel archive], *IVGO* 75, vyp. 5 (1943), 36–37.

33 Yu. Davydov, *Ferdinand Vrangel* (Moscow, 1959).

34 V. M. Pasetskii, *O chëm sheptalis' poliarnye maki* [The whisperings of the Arctic poppies] (Moscow, 1965).

35 Markov, "Klady 'Kolumbov rossiiskikh'"; idem, *Russkie na Aliaske;* idem, *Letopis' Aliaski.*

36 N. A. Chernitsyn, "Issledovatel' Aliaski i Severnoi Kalifornii Ivan Kuskov" [Ivan Kuskov, explorer of Alaska and northern California], in *Letopis' Severa* (Moscow), III, 108–21; idem, "Portrety I. A. Kuskova i ego zheny" [Portraits of I. A. Kuskov and his wife], in *Letopis' Severa,* IV, 244–46.

37 Manuscript Department, Lenin State Library, fond 204, karton 32, dela 8–12, 24–27, 30–32, 36, etc. For a brief review of the I. A. Kuskov archive, see *Zapiski Otdela rukopisei Gosudarstvennoi biblioteki SSSR im. V. I. Lenina,* vyp. 13 (1952), 25–29.

38 N. G. Shprintsin and M. V. Krutikova, "Indeitsy guato" [The Guato Indians], *IVGO* 80, vyp. 5 (1948), 500–506; N. G. Shprintsin, "Polozhenie indeitsev i negrov Brazilii (Po materialam russkikh ekspeditskii)" [The situation of the Indians and Negroes in Brazil (according to the records of Russian expeditions)], *Kratkie soobshcheniia Instituta etnografii AN SSSR*, VII (Moscow, 1949); idem, "Pervaia russkaia ekspeditsiia v Braziliiu."

39 B. N. Komissarov, "Novyi russkii istochnik po istorii i etnografii Brazilii 20-kh godov XIX v. (Zapiski N. G. Rubtsova)" [A new Russian source for the history and ethnography of Brazil in the 1820s (The notes of N. G. Rubtsov)], *SE*, no. 3 (1963), 172–76; idem, "Braziliia v opisaniiakh uchastnikov russkoi ekspeditsii 1821–1829 godov"†

40 M. V. Stepanova, "Iz istorii etnograficheskogo izucheniia byvshikh russkikh vladenii v Amerike" [From the history of ethnographic research on the former Russian possessions in America], *SE*, no. 3 (1947), 141–44.

41 K. K. Gil'zen, "Il'ia Gavrilovich Voznesenskii," *SMAE* 3 (Petrograd, 1916), 1–14.

42 M. V. Stepanova, "I. G. Voznesenskii i etnograficheskoe izuchenie severo-zapada Ameriki" [I. G. Voznesenskii and ethnographic research on the American Northwest], *IVGO* 76, vyp. 5 (1944), 277–79.

43 B. A. Lipshits, "Etnograficheskie materialy po severo-zapadnoi Amerike v arkhive I. G. Voznesenskogo" [Ethnographic materials on the American Northwest in the archive of I. G. Voznesenskii], *IVGO* 82, vyp. 4 (1950), 415–20.

44 E. E. Blomkvist, "Risunki I. G. Voznesenskogo (Ekspeditsiia 1839–1849 gg.)" [The drawings of I. G. Voznesenskii (The expedition of 1839–1849)], in *SMAE* 13 (Leningrad, 1951), 230–303.

45 B. V. Lukin, "Etnograficheskie svedeniia o Peru serediny XIX v. v dnevnike L. I. Shrenka" [Ethnographic notices on mid-nineteenth-century Peru in the diary of L. I. Shrenk], *SE*, no. 1 (1965), 124–33.

8

THE CONGRESS OF AIX-LA-CHAPELLE
AND THE PACIFICATION
OF SPAIN'S COLONIES IN AMERICA:
THE POSITION OF TSARIST RUSSIA

L. YU. SLËZKIN

BY MID-1818, the results of Spain's foreign policy were truly catastrophic. While she was squandering her insignificant, painfully acquired resources on an increasingly unsuccessful war with the Spanish American patriots, England and the United States sought to expand their trade with the insurgent colonies.[1] In so doing, they at the same time prejudiced Spain's prestige and efforts in the overseas possessions, for they violated her interdictions and frustrated attempts to organize a blockade of the South American coast. The Portuguese took the Eastern Bank from Spain (even before this it had not in fact belonged to Spain), converting it into a province of Brazil (even while talks were under way to settle the dispute). The United States seized Florida, disguising the annexation after the fact by signing a treaty of concession (February 1819). Russia, on whom Spain so counted, in essence defaulted on the warship deal,* strengthened its position on the boundaries of California, discounting Spanish claims to the Ross territory, and advised Madrid that in its dispute with the Americans it had only one option—to cede Florida, without carrying the affair to a military defeat in the self-delusion of receiving desired outside assistance.

The war with the insurgent colonies brought Spain not only reverses on the field of battle. This war drained her economically, rendering her powerless in the face of all who encroached on her overseas possessions or failed to recognize her claims. The resolution of this situation lay either in a final desperate effort to

---

Excerpted from a monograph by the same author entitled *Rossiia i voina za nezavisimost' v Ispanskoi Amerike,*† pp. 166–77.

*This refers to the controversial cession of eleven Russian warships to Spain in the course of 1817–18. One view current at the time and also held subsequently by some historians maintains that the ceded ships were destined for service against the Spanish American insurgents and consequently demonstrated active Russian support of the Spanish Crown in the matter of colonial pacification.

suppress the insurrection militarily or in a reconciliation with the colonies. The Spanish government decided on the first course of action. In Cádiz, a military expedition was intensively prepared—the largest of any sent thus far in the war. However, a lack of money, the embezzlement of state property, and the negligence of officials and officers hampered the effort. The expedition's ships were unable to sail for at least a year. In the meantime, one could only expect still further complications in America. Therefore, Madrid again turned to the idea of mediation. Spanish statesmen and diplomats never abandoned the thought that somehow they would manage to persuade the great powers to support Spain's military efforts. A new initiative was occasioned by the initial preparations of the Quadruple Alliance for a congress (usually called the Congress of the Holy Alliance), at which the future status of France was to be considered. The point of departure from which Madrid wished to initiate the new movement toward the desired goal was again the doctrine of legitimacy.

Already in the spring of 1818 [Francisco de] Zea Bermúdez, the Spanish envoy to Russia, inquired of the Russian ministry of foreign affairs whether it might not be possible for representatives of the Spanish king to attend the coming congress and to include the matter of the Spanish colonies on the agenda. After consultation with the allied powers, Zea Bermúdez was informed that the Spanish government's proposal had been flatly rejected by the cabinets of Vienna, London, and Berlin, who, as [Dmitrii Pavlovich] Tatishchev was advised on 15 (27) April, had agreed beforehand to discuss no matters at the congress which "went beyond the jurisdiction" of the forthcoming meeting.[2] In this dispatch to Tatishchev, it was also pointed out that by its own conduct the Spanish government had itself impeded any progress whatsoever in the pacification of the colonies and in terminating its conflict with Portugal. It was once again stated that under no circumstances should Spain count on separate aid from Russia.[3] A day after this dispatch was sent to Tatishchev, it was followed by another (a copy of instructions to the Russian envoy to the United States), in which was stated the following:

> In taking part in the mediation (should it take place), the Emperor is far from wishing to use his influence to the end that the colonies, by submitting to the metropolis, should as before be subservient to the mercantile system and serve the ephemeral trading interests of Cádiz. . . . The Emperor will not cease to insist that the colonies receive *from their metropolis* a form of government based on the principles of national representation and the freedoms attached thereto.[4]

In June 1818, Zea Bermúdez again raised the colonial question with the Russian ministry of foreign affairs.[5] In response (in the document it is not indicated with whom he talked), he was advised that if Spain wished to involve the allied powers in the resolution of this matter, then she must at last propose her own concrete plan for the pacification of the colonies.[6] To the question of just what form the plan should take, the Spanish envoy was told that this was Spain's business and not for foreign governments to think about. As for general ideas, the plan should, in Russia's view, include amnesty for the insurgents and the full equality of rights for Spanish Americans vis-à-vis Spaniards (the legal integration of the overseas possessions and the metropolis)—in other words, the elimination of the colonial regime. Thus the aspirations of the patriots of Spanish America would be satisfied and the sovereignty of the king of Spain over his overseas subjects would be maintained. "Enjoying an absolute equality of civil, political, and commercial rights with the European Spaniards, his American subjects could claim nothing further, except absolute independence, to which the European powers can under no circumstances legally consent and which they are unable to support."[7]

Thus the government of St. Petersburg insistently and not for the first time advised Ferdinand VII to effect constitutional reforms in Spanish America. Furthermore, the document under consideration coincides almost textually with the corresponding articles of the Spanish constitution of 1812. This advice given to Madrid was, as in every other case, a continuation of a Russian policy directed at the "improvement" of the regime of the Spanish monarchy in the name of its salvation, in the present instance for the salvation of Ferdinand VII's rights" in the revolted colonies. Not recognizing (in accordance with the protectionist system of the Holy Alliance) the right of the colonies to rebel, but considering the inexorable fact of their successes, Russia pressed Ferdinand VII to sanction, himself, the liberties already achieved by the patriots in the war, thereby not only maintaining some authority over them but giving the appearance as well of a voluntary step by a beneficent king. On the surface, everything would have the more or less convincing form of legality in the spirit of the principles of legitimacy.[8]

This kind of logic reached the extreme that, in the face of further patriot successes, in order to maintain appearances when there was no longer any hope for more, Ferdinand VII was advised ultimately to sanction colonial independence (perhaps receiving in return from the patriots some privileges for Spain, for example in trade). The course of events led to such thoughts. But at this point in our investigation we have reached only the second half of 1818. The war in Spanish America was at its height. Spain was readying a new expedition to reinforce her troops. Not only in Spain, but also in the insurgent colonies themselves by no means everyone repudiated the idea of maintaining some ties between the old metropolis and the rebel governments (particularly the creation in these states of a monarchy headed by Spanish princes).[9] The republican United States, meanwhile, did not go beyond recognizing the Spanish American patriots as combatants, flatly rejecting their petitions for recognition of the insurgent colonies' independence ("in the present stage of the conflict").[10] In light of the foregoing, one can argue that during the period under consideration the position of Russian diplomacy in the Spanish American question was, for all its adherence to legitimacy, quite sober. Primary in determing this position was the insurmountable force of the insurrection in the Spanish colonies.

Encountering obstacles to its participation in the congress of allies and comprehending that by simply referring to the "legality" of its rights it would obtain nothing, the Spanish government, in a circular dated 18 June 1818, announced its proposed basis for mediation of the powers in its dispute with the colonies: (1) amnesty for the insurgents—from the moment of their surrender; (2) equal rights with Spaniards for the inhabitants of Spanish America in the obtainment of jobs and honors; (3) the regulation of the trading interests of the overseas provinces in accord with principles to meet the new conditions and the relations of these provinces with Europe (4) the King's agreement to proposed conditions of mediation, provided they were in accord with his dignity.[11]

The Madrid proposals were a very long way from meeting the demands of the English memorandum or the advice given Zea Bermúdez not long before in St. Petersburg. London immediately requested that the Spanish government clarify, above all, "the nature of the intervention which the Mediating Powers are expected to undertake."[12] In a return memorandum given Castlereagh by the Spanish ambassador, San Carlos, it was stated that should the conditions of mediation fail to satisfy "some rebels," the king of Spain would "expect effective assistance in compelling them to accept these conditions."[13]

Everything returned to its starting point. This simplified matters for the powers not wishing to deal with Spanish affairs at the congress. Once again England and Austria[14] spoke out against the attendance of Ferdinand VII or his representatives. Russia and France were ready to support Spain's request for an invitation to the congress,[15] but were not willing to bring the matter to a head in a decisive confrontation with England and Austria, who already in the spring had pronounced themselves negatively; all the more so, as St. Petersburg and Paris were going to the congress with the intention of putting an end to the occupation of French territory. It would be difficult for London and Vienna to yield on this latter question, and as a result it made no sense for Russian and French diplomacy to irritate them by forcing lesser issues, the discussion of which they wished to avoid.[16] Spain remained outside the congress doors.

The congress opened at Aix-la-Chapelle on 30 September 1818. There it was decided that the occupation forces would quit the territory of France, and that a portion of the latter's indemnity payments would also be eliminated. The French government was accepted into the Holy Alliance.[17] On the initiative of the English delegation, an exchange of views was also held (off the record and without an official protocol) on the matter of the insurgent Spanish colonies.

The principle of peaceful mediation in the war between Spain and her colonies put forth by Castlereagh met with no objections from any quarter. The first discussions (22-25 October) centered on the advisability of a preliminary declaration of the powers' decision to resort only to peaceful mediation. Adopting the principle of peaceful mediation, Capo d'Istria objected (as in turn did Pozzo di Borgo and Liven) to the issuance of a preliminary declaration by the powers, feeling that this would weaken the position of Spain at the talks. Richelieu expressed the view that without the participation of a representative from Spain it would be difficult to take any decision on the matter at hand. And no resolution was adopted.[18] Then, with Capo d'Istria's support, Richelieu presented to the participants of the congress a "Note on the conduct of talks concerning the pacification of the revolted Spanish colonies." In this document, regret was expressed that Spain had not yet presented to the powers her own plan for the pacification of the colonies, nor spelled out the means by which she intended to implement such a plan. It was further suggested that it would be advisable to invite the United States (which exercised no little influence on the insurgent colonies) to take part in the mediation,[19] in particular to the end of averting the apparent possibility that the United States might recognize the independence of Buenos Aires. It was also proposed that the Duke of Wellington be empowered to undertake talks with Spain on behalf of the participants of the congress in order to clarify her position and possibilities in the matter of colonial pacification.[20]

Both Castlereagh and Wellington, the latter arriving a short time later, objected to talking with Spain before she had taken a definite stand, and also to inviting the United States. It was at last decided that in the event Spain agreed to Wellington's mediation and herself took the initiative in proposing such mediation, the Duke would be sent to Madrid for the talks.[21] Summing up the discussion, Castlereagh wrote on 2 November 1818:

> There seemed a general concurrence that force could under no circumstances be employed, and that Spain must, as a preliminary measure, confer upon her South American Provinces, which had remained faithful, the full extent of advantage which the Mediators were to be authorized to propose to the Provinces in revolt.[22]

Castlereagh broached the colonial question in one of his meetings with Alexander I. The Tsar agreed completely with the English minister that the application of sanctions should not be one of the conditions of mediation, if indeed it were to take place. Alexander instructed his ministers and representatives abroad accordingly.[23] Thus, in the discussions at the Congress of Aix-la-Chapelle on the problems of mediation between Spain and her colonies, the Russian government, on this occasion, adopted without reservations the point of view of England.

Interrupting the narration, we ought here to touch upon some questions of historiography and sources which fall within the sphere of our research and cannot be treated adequately in the brief space of a footnote.

In foreign historical literature, there exists an interpretation which holds that the "Note on the conduct of talks concerning the pacification of the revolted Spanish colonies" presented at the congress was drawn up according to a Russian draft (allegedly uncovered in the archives of the Russian ministry of foreign affairs). Such an interpretation (with emphasis on the French origin of the Note) is present, for example, in Robertson's book *France and Latin-American Independence*.[24] This is surprising, since in the previously published book by Webster, *The Foreign Policy of Castlereagh*,[25] this version is convincingly refuted based on documents housed in English archives and on the authority of Perkins, who demonstrated the French origin of the Note.

Robertson's interpretation comes from Cresson.[26] But, as in other documentary citations, Cresson does not give exact data on the source, indicating only that the document he mentions relates to the Congress of Aix-la-Chapelle. A thorough search permits the author of the present article to affirm that no Russian draft of the "Note on the conduct of talks" exists. In the Russian Foreign Policy Archives there is a clean, undated, unsigned, and uncorrected copy of the Note. As seen from Webster's citations, such a copy also exists in English archives (and also, probably, in the archives of the other participants in the congress), which is only natural, together with other documents presented at the congress.

The Note to which we have referred is sometimes called the "Russo-French" or "Franco-Russian" note, which is permissible, inasmuch as the Russian representatives supported Richelieu, who introduced it, thus allowing one to view it as a joint document.

The question of who wrote and instigated the presentation of this document at the Congress of Aix-la-Chapelle, and also the matter of its precise content, acquire major significance. In foreign historical scholarship, the contents of the "Note on the conduct of talks" have long been described incorrectly. We find a distortion of its text in Robertson's book, where it is stated that the Note proposed armed intervention by the European powers in the affairs of the insurgent Spanish colonies.[27] He repeats this in his article "Russia and the Emancipation of Spanish America."[28] His mistaken assertion passed into Maurice Bourquin's book.[29] In *The Foreign Policy of Castlereagh*, Webster states that in the Note it was proposed, in the event of mediation, to conceal the powers' accord not to resort to force, which, in Webster's words, made Castlereagh very angry.[30]

Neither version corresponds to the truth. This is shown by a careful study of the Note's text. It is remarkable that none of the authors who find in it aggressive principles has even once cited such important passages! Most often they all quote Cresson. But in the passage which Cresson includes in his book, nothing speaks of proposed intervention by the powers and nothing suggests such an idea! Such an idea never even occurred to Wellington. In his point-by-point response to the Note, he found no place to mention the provisions attributed to this document and which would have attracted his attention at the outset. Even supposing that the Note itself and Wellington's response thereto for some reason proved to be unknown to these scholars in originals or in copies (although Webster, while not quoting them, does refer to them in *The Foreign Policy of Castlereagh*), they could have familiarized themselves in detail with the Note's contents in the documentary collection published by Polovtsov, in 1908.[31] Here, too, we fail to encounter the propositions attributed to the Note. Nor are they in the summary of the Note made by Castlereagh in his letter to [Earl] Bathurst, which was published by Webster in his collection of documents.[32]

Thus, all the "horrors" attributed to the Note, and the effort to tie Russia as closely to it as possible, are the fruit either of misunderstanding or of a conscious falsification—that falsification which, as noted by us earlier, served to obscure Russia's role in the matter of the insurgent Spanish colonies.* Robertson, for example, wrote that the Russian program at Aix-la-Chapelle envisioned "the use of force by the Allies against the insurgent colonies of Spain."[33] There are no data to corroborate this view; moreover, references to the "Note on the conduct of talks," on which Robertson bases his argument, do not support the case.

Occasionally, confusing two different things, it is asserted that the Note proposes the application of economic sanctions against the insurgent Spanish colonies should they not accept the conditions of mediation proposed to them.[34] But we repeat, the "Note on the conduct of talks" in general gives no grounds for perceiving even a hint of any such sanctions. What, then, is the origin of the version about commercial sanctions? We assume that the stimulus was given by Webster, who, in his book *The Foreign Policy of Castlereagh,* wrote that following English objections to the Note, Capo d'Istria and Nesselrode supposedly advanced "the idea of using commercial boycott to overcome the resistance of the Colonies."[35] This is almost totally incorrect. We say almost, inasmuch as there is one piece of evidence according to which talks on commercial sanctions were held at Aix-la-Chapelle. But the picture was not as Webster has painted it.

This piece of evidence was the above-mentioned letter from Castlereagh to Bathurst. In this letter, Castlereagh, summarizing the ideas of Richelieu (stated by him after presentation of the Note, and not contained in it!), pointed out that they consisted in inviting the United States to participate in the mediation and in the intention of advising Spain that, were she to be liberal in her conditions for mediation and were the colonies to decline these conditions as proposed to them by the mediators, the mediating powers would sever all ties, "economic and other," with the insurgent colonies. The Russians supported Richelieu in his views, the English and the Austrians objected, and the Prussians shunned any

---

*In Slëzkin's introduction to the volume from which this selection is drawn, he dwells at some length on the relationship between the interests of current international politics, particularly as relates to Latin America, and the writing of the history of Latin America's relations with the major powers of the Western World. He notes that special interest has been shown in this area by U.S. historians and goes on to observe that "in considerable measure, this interest has been determined by the position which the United States occupies in the Western Hemisphere." And this, he concludes, "has largely determined an apologetic portrayal of the policies, past and present, of the American government." (*Rossiia i voina za rezavisimost' v Ispanskoi* Amerike, p. 25.)

argument. So wrote Castlereagh, yet this does not correspond to Webster's version.

There being no basis to question the veracity of Castlereagh's words, we should note that they are the only evidence of projects to apply commercial sanctions. Neither in the papers of the Congress of Aix-la-Chapelle which we have at our disposal (published and unpublished) nor in the papers written by diplomats and members of the governments who participated in the congress (published and unpublished) do we find any hints of a French proposal for commercial sanctions. Thus it occurs that in Castlereagh's letter the question of commercial sanctions stems from unofficial and unrecorded talks of a private nature. In any case, for some reason these talks are not reflected even in the reports written by the representatives of the powers to their own monarchs and ministries. It may be that in the course of these conversations Richelieu really did come out in support of a break in trade and other ties with the former colonies (in the first instance, of course, having in mind England). It is entirely probable that Nesselrode and Pozzo di Borgo could have supported this idea. But, that it did not originate with the Russian representatives and that the latter were not about to defend it is indicated, first, by the lack of any mention of it in the Russian documents, and second, by the evidence of Castlereagh, which points directly to Richelieu. Moreover, during the English minister's meeting with Alexander I, Castlereagh, avoiding the subject of applying force, which, as he himself observed, "had been eliminated as worthy of discussion," stated what he considered to be the uselessness of trade sanctions (referring, moreover, to their unsoundness, and not to their illegality!). In reporting this meeting in the aforementioned letter to Bathurst, Castlereagh did not write of any objections from the Tsar. The results of this meeting are familiar to us. Castlereagh himself came away very satisfied, especially because under the influence of the Russian government (!) Richelieu had withdrawn his proposals. Therefore, the evidence of Castlereagh can in no way serve as the basis for arguing that the idea of economic sanctions came precisely from the Russian representatives. If it indicates that at some given moment these representatives supported Richelieu's idea, it also indicates that the Russian government helped to bury it, together with the rest of the ideas of the French prime minister relating to the matter of the Spanish colonies.

Having made these observations, let us return to the Congress of Aix-la-Chapelle.

During their meetings with Alexander I, the English and Austrian representatives complained of Tatishchev, whom the Tsar chose not to defend. Furthermore, he agreed with many of the accusations directed at his diplomat, recognizing the latter's vanity and bent for intrigue. On 9 (21) November 1818, a letter was sent to Tatishchev in which he was given a severe reprimand. It was pointed out to the envoy that, willingly or unwillingly, by his vaunted intimacy with Ferdinand VII he supported the ambitious plans of the Spanish king. He was again reminded that Russia did not desire any special relations with Spain. The letter ended with a threat to withdraw him from Madrid if he did not alter his behavior.[36] In a confidential dispatch to Tatishchev dated 13 (25) December 1818 (its contents were made known to Castlereagh through Liven), the talks on mediation were summarized, beginning in the spring of 1817. The dispatch expressed obvious displeasure with the policy of the Spanish government and with its lack of a sense of realism. It was pointed out to the envoy that, in the event Spain should again wish to request mediation, she would have to formulate with perfect clarity liberal principles for the resolution of her dispute with the colonies, to which it would be necessary to direct special attention, as circumstances were such that the desire of the King of Spain to secure an armed intervention in the affairs of the colonies contradicted the position of England and did not meet the position of the other powers: "This condition could not be accepted by England in *principle*. . . . In fact, it is impracticable for the other powers as well."[37] Spain, it is further stated, had two options: to effect the pacification of the colonies herself, without foreign intervention, or to agree to English mediation, in particular to the mediation of the Duke of Wellington envisioned by the congress. "England would play the primary role." The other powers would be mediators between England and Spain in working out a just basis for the talks.[38] This document demonstrates that the Russian government, through its envoy, gave Ferdinand VII to understand that it was essential for him to discard dreams of armed intervention by the powers on his behalf.* The most

---

*The interpretation of the tone and, above all, intention of such a document is indisputably an area of subjectivity in the writing of history. Whereas Slëzkin attributes an essentially nonconciliatory posture to Russia on the question of Spanish pretensions vis-à-vis the New World colonies, this based on the above-cited dispatches to Tatishchev, related correspondence perhaps unavailable to Slëzkin permits another appraisal of that posture. For example, in a personal letter to Ferdinand VII dated Vienna, 10 (22) December 1818, Tsar Alexander I expressed "deep regrets" that the discussions at Aix-la-Chapelle had not dealt "more directly and more efficaciously" with the pressing affairs of the Spanish empire. "All obstacles to an identity of views on collective intervention," the Tsar wrote, "can be reduced . . . to a single difficulty, namely opposition to *the principle of military cooperation* as an obligation of the intervening Powers." In much the same language as that which Slëzkin attributes to the Tatishchev dispatch of 13 (25) December (written three days after the letter cited here), the Tsar places the blame for the existing state of affairs on England, who equated the *principle* of military cooperation with actual use of armed force and thus held that principle to be inadmissible. "It is no less inadmissible in the eyes of the other Powers," the Tsar added, "because it is *in fact* impracticable." (See Archivo Histórico Nacional [Madrid], Estado, leg. 2849, Carpeta 16).

Clearly central to a correct interpretation of tsarist policy in this matter is the qualifier "impracticable." What these documents really seem to indicate is not a spontaneous adherence to the position of England and certain other of the allied powers, but rather a reluctant resignation to practical circumstances beyond Russian control. Had the principle of military cooperation indeed enjoyed British support and thus been practicable, there is little if any evidence to suggest that Russia would not have committed itself to precisely that course of action on behalf of the Spanish Crown.

sensible way out of the situation which had developed was to accept English mediation and English terms for this mediation.[39]

But, as on previous occasions, Madrid ignored this counsel. Having failed to gain admission to the Congress of Aix-la-Chapelle, the Spanish government pretentiously declared that as a sovereign state it would not recognize any decisions or recommendations pertaining to it adopted without its consent. This settled the matter of the proposed Wellington mission. The attempts of the Russian government and of Tatishchev to persuade Ferdinand VII to accept the mediation of the English duke were not crowned with success.[40]

NOTES

1 R. A. Humphreys, ed., *British Consular Reports on the Trade and Politics of Latin America, 1824–1826* (London, 1940), pp. 344–46, 350 ff.; Timothy Pitkin, *A Statistical View of the Commerce of the United States of America* (New Haven, 1835), p. 222.

2 Arkhiv vneshnei politiki Rossii [Russian Foreign Policy Archives—Moscow, cited hereafter as AVPR], Chancery, delo 7554, fol. 13. See, also, C. K. Webster, ed., *Britain and the Independence of Latin America, 1812–1830: Select Documents from the Foreign Office Archives,* 2 vols. (London, New York, and Toronto, 1938), II, no. 348.

3 AVPR, Chancery, delo 7554, fols. 14–15.

4 AVPR, Chancery, delo 12187, fols, 9–10.

5 Jerónimo Bécker, *Historia de las relaciones exteriores de España durante el siglo XIX,* 3 vols. (Madrid, 1924–1926), I, 490–94. (The text of the note is quoted.)

6 As we will recall, this was demanded of Spain by Castlereagh. The same advice was given by Richelieu. See William Spence Robertson, *France and Latin-American Independence* (Baltimore, 1939), p. 136.

7 AVPR, Chancery, delo 7554, fols. 21–22.

8 Not without intention the author of the above-mentioned instructions to the Russian envoy to the United States underlined the words *from their metropolis.* Also of interest, in this regard, is the meeting which occurred in May 1818 between Capo d'Istria and the English ambassador in St. Petersburg, Cathart. Capo d'Istria considered it appropriate to invite Spain to the congress of allies precisely because even in the event Russia and England (as well as the other participants in possible talks) were to agree on conditions of mediation without Spanish participation, this would, as in the event of direct talks with the colonies, place in doubt the sovereign rights of the King of Spain in his overseas possessions. In all cases, the initiative should proceed (in form) from Spain to the colonies. See AVPR, Chancery, delo 6875, fols. 375–78.

9 See, for example, Robertson, *France and Latin-American Independence,* pp. 258–63; Mario Belgrano, *La Francia y la monarquía en el Plata (1818–1820)* (Buenos Aires,

1933); idem, *Rivadavia y sus gestiones diplomáticas con España (1815–1820)*, 2nd ed. (Buenos Aires, 1934).

10 William R. Manning, comp., *Diplomatic Correspondence of the United States Concerning the Independence of the Latin-American Nations*, 3 vols. (New York, 1925), I, no. 49, pp. 57–58; see, also, nos. 50, 55, 64, 69–70.

11 Webster, *Britain and the Independence of Latin America*, II, no. 522. Without any basis and with no reference to the source, Webster asserts that it was precisely Pozzo di Borgo who inspired Spain to issue this note. (See Webster, I, pp. 14–15.) As for the contents of the note, they do not coincide with the proposals advanced by Russian diplomats. As for the general need for Spain to offer a plan of colonial pacification, this was not Pozzo di Borgo's or Russia's point of view, but rather, as we have seen, that of all the powers who participated in the talks on mediation, including England. One can agree with Bourquin, however, that the advice of the Russian government influenced Spain's tractability in relation to English demands. See Maurice Bourquin, *Histoire de la Sainte Alliance* (Geneva, 1954), p. 386.

12 Webster, *Britain and the Independence of Latin America*, II, no. 326.

13 AVPR, Chancery, delo 7553, fol. 260 (the memorandum is dated 28 August 1818).

14 In mid-August, the Russian representative in Vienna, Golovkin, informed St. Petersburg that "Austrian policy probably would adhere completely to English policy in all American and maritime matters and that this mutual tractability would make itself felt in continental affairs." (AVPR, Chancery, delo 11674, fol. 114.

15 A. A. Polovtsov, comp., *Correspondence diplomatique des ambassadeurs et ministres de Russie en France et de France en Russie avec leurs gouvernements de 1814 à 1830*, vols. cxii, cxix, cxxvii of *Sbornik Imperatorskogo Russkogo Istoricheskogo Obshchestva*, 148 vols. (St. Petersburg, 1867–1916) [hereafter *Sbornik*], CXXVII, 204; AVPR, Chancery, delo 6874, fols. 218–26, and delo 6875, fol. 305; Robertson, *France and Latin-American Independence*, p. 145; Manning, *Diplomatic Correspondence*, II, no. 726, p. 1392.

16 *Sbornik*, CXXVII, 204 (appraisal of the position of Russia and France contained in the instructions to the French ambassador in St. Petersburg, 14 October 1819).

17 Fearing a revolution in France, former opponents of the Revolution secretly renewed their allied commitment.

18 AVPR, Chancery, delo 127 ("Résumé of a discussion on the matter of mediation"), fols. 59–61, 63–71; delo 130, fol. 141.

19 The United States was not advised of the talks being conducted on the matter of the insurgent Spanish colonies. American representatives in the European countries learned of these talks by bits and pieces. The greatest amount of information, albeit far from complete, was received from the English.

20 *Sbornik*, CXXVII, 204–5; Webster, *Britain and the Independence of Latin America*, II, no. 328.

21 AVPR, Chancery, delo 130 (memorandum from Wellington); Webster, *Britain and the Independence of Latin America*, II, no. 328.

22 Webster, *Britain and the Independence of Latin America*, II, no. 327, p. 57.

23 On this question, see "Zapiska grafa Ioanna Kapodistriia o ego sluzhebnoi deiatel'nosti," *Sbornik*, III, 234, 237; Webster, *Britain and the Independence of Latin*

America, II, no. 328; and instructions to Liven dated 13 (25) December 1818, AVPR, Chancery, delo 6875, fols. 463–67.

In giving an account of the position of Alexander I at the Congress of Aix-la-Chapelle on the matter of the insurgent Spanish colonies, Perkins emphasized that this was a conciliatory, moderate position and that it indicated "in the most striking form his willingness to give full weight to the views of Great Britain." See Dexter Perkins, "Russian and the Spanish Colonies, 1817–1818," *AHR* 28, no. 4 (July 1923), 668, 670.

24 Robertson, *France and Latin-American Independence,* pp. 152–54.

25 Sir Charles Webster, *The Foreign Policy of Castlereagh, 1815–1822: Britain and the European Alliance* (London, 1947), p. 419.

26 William Penn Cresson, *The Holy Alliance: The European Background of the Monroe Doctrine* (New York, 1922), pp. 79–80.

27 Robertson, *France and Latin-American Independence,* p. 154.

28 William Spence Robertson, "Russia and the Emancipation of Spanish America, 1816–1826," *HAHR* 21, no. 2 (May 1941), 207.

29 Bourquin, *Histoire de la Sainte Alliance,* p. 389.

30 Webster, *The Foreign Policy of Castlereagh,* p. 419.

31 Sbornik, CXXVII, 204–5 (instructions to the French ambassador to Russia).

32 Webster, *Britain and the Independence of Latin America,* II, no. 328.

33 Robertson, "Russia and the Emancipation of Spanish America," p. 207.

34 Bourquin, *Histoire de la Sainte Alliance,* p. 389.

35 Webster, *The Foreign Policy of Castlereagh,* p. 420.

36 AVPR, Chancery, delo 7554, fols. 43–44.

37 Ibid., p. 63.

38 Ibid., p. 65.

39 In a "Memorandum of the Russian government after the conference at Aix-la-Chapelle," drafted in Vienna on 19 (31) December 1818, it is stated, "If the King of Spain will not accept European mediation in the affairs of the colonies and under the conditions noted by England, he will in the end lose those provinces in America which still remain in his possession, as well as all self-respect in the peninsula." See AVPR, Chancery, delo 126, fols. 7–8.

40 In January 1819, Tatishchev wrote: "I have employed all the means at my disposal to persuade the King to request the presence of the Duke of Wellington, and if his favor toward me was as is ascribed to me, His Highness would most likely grant my urgent requests; but, in spite of everything, my efforts have proved useless, and, no matter how I presented the matter, the King continued to consider it dangerous to Spain and degrading to his person." See AVPR, Chancery, delo 7554, fols. 5, 24–31, 32–52, 54–55, 87–88, 92; delo 9085, fol. 214; delo 9086, fols. 105–6; also Webster, *Britain and the Independence of Latin America,* II, nos. 525–26.

9 ON THE THREAT OF INTERVENTION IN LATIN AMERICA BY THE HOLY ALLIANCE

(From the Background of the Monroe Doctrine)

N. N. BOLKHOVITINOV

THE QUESTION of the threat of intervention in Latin America by the Holy Alliance is closely connected with the background and pronouncement of the Monroe Doctrine. A determination of the nature of the Monroe Doctrine depends in many respects on a correct appraisal of this question. If a threat to the Western Hemisphere had actually existed, as asserted by numerous American historians, the Monroe Doctrine would have been defensive in nature and the United States of America and its leaders would then have acted as saviors of the young Latin American republics. If, on the other hand, this threat was not real, then the action of the U.S. President could not and indeed did not constitute a defense of the Latin American countries, but rather served only the interests of the United States and was an expression of its aspiration to expand its influence in the Western Hemisphere.

Rumors of threatened intervention in Latin America by the Holy Alliance were widespread in Europe as well as America, circulating persistently in the pages of the press of the 1820s. Their spread was furthered by the reactionary policies of the Holy Alliance, which acted to suppress the revolutionary movement in Europe, and in particular by France's intervention in Spain, in 1823.

Subsequently, the opinion was firmly established in the literature that the threat of armed intervention was averted as a result of the actions of [George] Canning and the pronouncement of the Monroe Doctrine. It must be said that this view has proved exceptionally tenacious, despite the fact that it was long ago placed in doubt by scholars of various countries on the basis of a thorough examination of archival materials. Among the first historians to oppose the

Originally published as "K voprosu ob ugroze interventsii Sviashchennogo soiuza v Latinskuiu Ameriku (iz predystorii doktriny Monro)," *NNI*, no. 3 (May–June 1957), 46–66.

traditional point of view on this question were Carlos Villanueva and Dexter Perkins. In this connection, it is well to recall an almost completely forgotten address on the Monroe Doctrine delivered by Dexter Perkins at a meeting of the American Association of International Law, on 22–25 April 1914.

Also participating in the session were such well-known political figures and scholars as Elihu Root, Charles Francis Adams, William R. Manning, and John H. Latané. Many enthusiastic words were spoken about the Doctrine and its authors. Of greatest substance, however, was what was stated not in the papers of the venerable scholars but in the address of a young and at the time little-known Dexter Perkins, who had returned to the United States from a trip to Europe, where he had been studying archival materials bearing on the background of the Monroe Doctrine. "We have heard a good deal in this discussion," stated Perkins,

> of European aggressions against South America, and the statement has been made more than once that the original message, Monroe's famous message of December 2, 1823, did prevent such European aggression against South America.
>
> I have been engaged in the course of the last two years in seeking to find out just how true that statement was. I have come to the conclusion that it rests, after all, on no basis of fact. . . . I find neither in the dispatches of the Russian Foreign Office nor in the dispatches of the French Foreign Office any tangible signs of an intention to interfere against the independence of the South American states.[1]

Perkins subsequently developed a critical attitude in his own writings toward the reality of threatened intervention by the Holy Alliance, as did a number of other scholars.[2] The number of "doubters" gradually increased, among whom one can cite such names as Harold Temperley, Samuel E. Morison, C. K. Webster, William Spence Robertson, J. Fred Rippy, and Samuel Flagg Bemis.

Unfortunately, however, one must recognize that the position of some scholars who have questioned the existence of a threat of intervention by the Holy Alliance in Latin America is singularly contradictory and inconsistent. Here, the viewpoint of the well-known English historian of foreign policy Harold Temperley is indicative.[3] Having studied quite thoroughly the documents, Temperley was obliged to recognize the lack of evidence supporting the assertion that the Holy Alliance or any of its members gave serious consideration to military intervention in Spanish America between 1818 and 1824, although he personally was inclined to believe this. His personal opinion, however, is completely refuted by the arguments which he himself introduces in support of a critical attitude toward the threat of intervention:

1. By 1822, the Spanish colonies had already achieved *de facto* independence and assistance to Spain by the European countries could not be sufficiently effective to regain them through conquest;

2. The French government, while it intended to install Spanish Bourbons on the throne in Peru, Chile, and Mexico, was unwilling to do so by force;
3. The archives contains few or no traces of any serious projects of armed intervention.[4]

Serious contradictions are also to be found in the works of J. Fred Rippy, William Spence Robertson, and other American scholars. Rippy, for example, having made correct observations about the Anglo-American rivalries, goes on to note: "Of course, this was not the only motive which led Adams to advocate the message of Monroe—Russia and the other 'Holy Allies' were also feared."[5]

In another of his works, Rippy wrote that only Russia offered material aid to Spain, yet even she had abandoned this idea by May 1824.[6] True, the well-known American specialist on this question William Spence Robertson, who for more than ten years worked with materials in European archives, has held, on the contrary, that precisely in May 1824 Nesselrode made "the only serious proposal ever made for an agreement by the Holy Allies to restore the authority of Ferdinand VII over Spanish America by force of arms."[7]

This assertion by Robertson not only contradicts the general course of events given in his work but completely lacks adequate documentation. As his only evidence, Robertson cites a conversation of [Count Pierre F. de] la Ferronays, French Ambassador to Russia, with Count [Karl Robert von] Nesselrode. When La Ferronays expressed regret that the tragic situation of the Spanish monarchy represented a tremendous obstacle to the suppression of the colonies by Ferdinand VII, Count Nesselrode noted: "But why cannot his Allies aid him? And besides, what could England say, or rather what could she do, if an army composed of Spaniards, Frenchmen, Russians, Prussians, and Austrians should embark upon a fleet equipped and financed by all the Allies of the Spanish King and should proceed to America in order to regain his lost rights for that monarch?"[8]

La Ferronays, of course, could not view such a suggestion favorably, as it failed to take sufficient account of the position of England. It is known, moreover, that precisely at this time (13 May 1824) Nesselrode himself instructed the Russian Ambassador in Paris, [General Carlo Andrea] Pozzo di Borgo, to the effect that allied assistance to Spain would serve no useful purpose if the position of England remained unchanged. Based precisely on this, Rippy felt that Russia had abandoned the idea of offering assistance to Spain.[9] Nesselrode's question, therefore, was in essence merely a probe, common in diplomatic practice but without any real consequences. Attention should also be drawn to the fact that all this refers to the period following the pronouncement of the Monroe Doctrine.

The soundest and most consistent position on the question of threatened intervention by the Holy Alliance, judging from the materials at our disposal, is that of Charles Webster. Based on an exceedingly thorough study of the documents,

Webster reached the following conclusion: "It seems clear that at no time in the course of the struggle for independence was there ever any considered or definite scheme in any European country to interfere by force. Tentative ideas were put forward by individuals with an imperfect knowledge of the facts or with a view to advancing their personal ambition, but no Government ever adopted them."[10] Webster correctly went on to observe: " Neither the Monroe Doctrine nor the Polignac Memorandum, therefore, preserved the independence of the Spanish Colonies in the sense that they safeguarded them from immediate European attack."[11]

We can therefore with full reason assert that those foreign scholars most familiar with the question of threatened intervention in Latin America by the Holy Alliance long ago placed in doubt the reality of that threat, and in a number of cases essentially refuted it. At the same time, even the best works on this problem are not lacking in contradictions and faulty premises.

In our [Soviet] literature, the question of threatened intervention has not received special study, and therefore an erroneous point of view on the threat of intervention has been disseminated in some of the best known and most widely read publications, including *The History of Diplomacy,* the *Diplomatic Dictionary,* and the *Great Soviet Encyclopedia.*[12] William Z. Foster, too, overestimates the threat of intervention in his well-known work on the history of America.[13]

In studying this problem it is especially important to understand the position of Russia, which has so often been distorted. Alexander and Ferdinand VII have not infrequently been singled out (even by historians who tended toward a critical analysis of the present question) as the only monarchs of the Holy Alliance desirous of armed intervention.[14] The generally accepted opinion that Russia favored armed intervention in Latin America was also shared by Temperley.[15] He, however, recognized that Alexander I was too occupied with Greece and Spain to have time to deal with the colonial question.

In a recently published work by the German historian Erwin Hölzle, Alexander I is portrayed as an advocate of the forcible restoration of Spanish rule in South America through armed intervention by the Holy Alliance. The United States, however, having declared the Monroe Doctrine, acted in Hölzle's opinion, as the defender of the freedom, independence, and self-determination of the peoples of the American continent. It is no coincidence, therefore, that Hölzle refers to Secretary of State John Quincy Adams as a revolutionary and champion of liberty.[16]

Such assertions give a false notion of the nature of Russo-American relations at that time, as well as of the United States' position with regard to the Holy Alliance. It is essential to bear in mind that even in so delicate a question as the problem of the Spanish American colonies, the relations of the United States with the Holy Alliance were not as hostile as some historians maintain. Here is what President Monroe himself wrote about this matter on 23 November 1818 to two of his predecessors, Thomas Jefferson and James Madison: "Our attitude with the allied powers, in regard to So. Am:, is as favorable, as it well can be, Mr. Rush & Mr. Gallatin having had conferences, the former with Ld. C[astlereagh], & the latter with the Duke of R[ichelieu], & the Russian Minister at Paris, in which they were inform'd by those Ministers, that their govts. could not well move in that affr. without the U States, by which it was meant, as is inferr'd, against the U States."[17]

Of great interest in this connection is an examination of the negotiations between Russia and the United States on official U.S. entry into the Holy Alliance. The possibility of the United States adhering to the Act of 14 (26) September 1815 was raised in detailed instructions of 7 (19) July 1817 to the new Russian envoy to the United States.[18] The envoy was authorized to clarify the viewpoint of the American government; it was noted [in the instructions] that the Emperor, Alexander I, favored U.S. adherence to this Act.[19]

The Russian proposals were preliminary and unofficial in nature, since the position of the United States was unclear. Understandably, an attempt was made to conduct these talks in strict confidence. In a conversation with Secretary of State Adams on 17 June 1819, [Pëtr Ivanovich] Poletica reported that the Emperor would like the United States to become a member of the Holy Alliance. In that case, should discords arise between the United States and European powers, for example Great Britain, the Emperor could exert his influence in favor of the former.[20]

Early in December 1819, it was agreed that Secretary of State Adams would advise Poletica of the American government's decision after Congress had convened. As observed by Poletica, this interval was set in order to give the government (executive branch) time to learn the attitude of the members of Congress toward this important Act. Subsequently, Poletica reported that, as seen from Adams' reply, the American government, having given serious consideration to the communication conveyed privately by Poletica, was persuaded that it would be impossible for the government of the United States to join the Holy Alliance. In closing, Adams stated that it might be advisable to postpone this question indefinitely.[21]

The attitude of the United States toward membership in the Holy Alliance is discussed most extensively and consistently in Adams' instructions of 5 July 1820 to the American envoy in St. Petersburg, Henry Middleton. These instructions warrant most careful study.[22] In them the Secretary of State wrote that the President, "approving the general principles of the Holy Alliance," at the same time believed that "the United States will more effectually contribute to the great and sublime objects for which it was concluded by abstaining from a formal participation in it than they could as stipulated members of it." Adams observed that "the United States not only give their hearty assent to the articles of the Holy

Alliance, but will be among the most earnest and conscientious in observing them."[23]

What, then, was the reason for the United States' refusal to participate in the Holy Alliance? Was it perhaps fear of public opinion, to which Adams had referred in his talks with the Russian Minister? This could hardly have been the main reason. For in the instructions to Henry Middleton, it was directly noted that the government of the United States was "free [sic] of the prejudices which have been excited against the Holy Alliance in the public opinion."*

The issue, apparently, was that the United States found it more advantageous to have the world divided into two parts. They could then pretend to leadership and influence in the Western Hemisphere. It is no coincidence, therefore, that Adams pointed out in these instructions that "for the repose of Europe as well as of America, the European and American political system should be kept as separate and distinct from each other as possible." Precisely this principle of two systems (the European and the American) found its way later into the Monroe Doctrine, and subsequently found expression in the establishment of a pan-American organization.

Despite the refusal of the United States to join officially the Holy Alliance, relations between Russia and the United States remained friendly. This is attested to, for example, by the permission granted the Russian envoy to take home with him and copy the original of the Spanish-American treaty of 22 February 1819, a highly uncommon occurrence in diplomatic practice. In giving this most "unusual sign of trust," Adams sought to influence not so much Poletica as the Emperor, Alexander I.[24] Poletica, for his part, familiarized the Secretary of State with the contents of the instructions issued by the Russian government. "In the most positive and solemn manner Poletica declared that Russia had no special treaty obligations with Spain and that the Emperor was utterly adverse to such obligations.[25]

Alexander I likewise showed himself favorably disposed toward the American envoy to Russia. In a conversation with the envoy in the summer of 1820, the Tsar asked him to assure the government of the United States that it would always find in him a "sincere and loyal friend."[26]

Friendly relations between the United States and Russia were preserved even after the Russian government's edict of 4 (16) September 1821, prohibiting foreign subjects from trading or conducting any business in the area of operations

---

*This rendering of the English original is imprecise. It should read: "But independent of the prejudices which have been excited against this instrument [i.e. the Holy Alliance] in the public opinion, which time and experience of its good effects will gradually wear away, it may be observed that for the repose of Europe as well as America, the European and American political system should be kept as separate and distinct from each other as possible." See John Bassett Moore, *A Digest of International Law*, 8 vols. (Washington, 1906), VI, 379.

of the Russian-American Company, and foreign vessels from sailing in the territorial waters of Russian possessions in the Pacific Northwest. The differences which arose between the United States and Russia in this regard were resolved through peaceful diplomatic negotiations between the two governments in 1822–24.

William Spence Robertson characterized Russian policy toward Spanish America as opportunistic and legitimist, asserting, moreover, that at one time Russian statesmen supported armed intervention.[27] Russian policy of the day did indeed take into account the "doctrine of legitimacy," although it is more exact, perhaps, to speak of a policy based on the principles of reactionary monarchy. While adhering to a reactionary monarchist system, however, the tsarist government could at the same time hardly ignore real power relationships and the prospects for the future development of the Spanish colonies and therefore did not prepare an armed invasion of South America to the glory of Ferdinand VII.

After meeting with Count Nesselrode in the spring of 1817, Zea Bermúdez, Spanish Minister in St. Petersburg, wrote Madrid that the Russian government's instructions to Tatishchev (Russia's Minister to Spain) "favor the adoption of means of conciliation and peace in preference to the use of force to re-establish tranquility in those colonies."[28] The Russian Ambassador in Paris, General Pozzo di Borgo, whom many scholars consider to be the initiator of interventionist plans[29] with respect to South America, wrote Nesselrode on 2 (14) June 1817: "Instead of being stubborn in her fruitless attacks, Spain ought to submit to Europe a plan for the pacification of the colonies based on improved local administration, an extension of privileges to the provinces, and greater facilities for trade. Should this system be recognized as just the great powers would become intermediaries."[30]

It must be noted that in the first place, plans for mediation could not be identified with plans for armed intervention, and in the second place, they remained by and large "good intentions" whose realization was exceedingly doubtful. Of great importance for an understanding of Russian policy are the instructions of second *Staatssekretär* [Ionnes Antonios] Capo d'Istria to Poletica, dated 18 (30) April 1818.[31] Capo d'Istria noted, in particular, that

while participating in the mediation (if mediation takes place) the Emperor is very far from wishing to contribute through His influence to the subjugation of the colonies by the metropolis. . . .

On the other hand, wishing to secure for these vast and rich countries a civil and political order such that it will promote the progress of civilization there, His Imperial Majesty does not feel competent to pursue these ends by means of direct or indirect intervention, undertaken independently of the Spanish government, or with intentions alien to the real and lawful interests of this state.

As a friend and ally of His Catholic Majesty, the Emperor *will not cease to insist that the colonies be granted by their metropolis an administration based on the principles of national representation and the liberties dependent thereon.*[32]

One must not, of course, give excessive credence to Alexander I's words about "the advancement of civilization," "principles of national representation," and so forth. Nevertheless, these instructions attest on the whole to a rather sober appraisal by the tsarist government of the outcome of the struggle of the insurgent colonies. Ferdinand VII could, of course, persist obstinately in the hope of bringing his former possessions in America once again under the authority of the Spanish crown. However, even to Alexander I, whom it would be difficult to suspect of sympathy toward the insurgent colonies, this seemed exceedingly doubtful. It became increasingly apparent that to return to the old situation was utterly hopeless. It was only possible to attempt to preserve what had not yet been lost, but this required firm measures and drastic reforms of which the Spanish monarchy was incapable.

In these circumstances, it was difficult to reach a decision acceptable to everyone. One can, perhaps, consider more or less serious a proposal made frequently between 1816 and 1823 to resolve the Spanish American question by establishing independent Bourbon monarchies in Spain's former colonies in America. To a certain extent this proposal was a compromise between the trading interests of France (the French bourgeoisie wished to expand trade with South America) and the "doctrine of legitimacy."[33] In 1819, the Count d'Oseri was sent to St. Petersburg on a special mission by the French government to hold talks with Alexander I on the matter of the Spanish American colonies, and, in particular, on the possibiltiy of a joint recommendation to Ferdinand VII regarding the establishment there of monarchical governments. As seen from the dispatches from D'Oseri to his government, Alexander I, recognizing the existence of a republican threat to Europe, felt that the best way to settle the Spanish colonial question was "to leave [the colonies] to their own devices, rejecting any offers they might make and denying them assistance."[34]

Although Alexander I thought that refusal to interfere in the Spanish American question would strenghten the influence of Spain, in reality, "left to themselves," the colonies could not possibly fall again under Spanish rule. The revolution of 1820 in Spain and the decisive successes achieved by the insurgent colonies during the early 1820s made their separation an indisputable fact.

This, as is known, resulted in recognition of the independence of a number of the new states by the government of the United States. In his message to Congress on 8 March 1822, President Monroe wrote that the insurgent provinces "are not only in the full enjoyment of their independence, but, considering the state of the war and other circumstances, . . . there is not the most remote prospect of their being deprived of it." The long period of time since the outbreak of hostilities, the complete victory of the insurgent provinces, "the actual disposition of the sides and the total inability of Spain to change it compels us to conclude that their future has been decided and that the provinces which have proclaimed their independence and in fact enjoy it ought to be recognized.''[35]

The view sometimes expressed that the tsarist government was irreconcilably opposed to U.S. recognition of the independence of the new states is far from adequately substantiated. To be sure, the reactionary nature of the tsarist government, which held sacred the rights of monarchy, precluded at that time any official endorsement of recognition of the insurgent colonies. The legitimacy of Ferdinand VII's ''rights'' with regard to the insurgent colonies was not questioned in the slightest by Alexander I. The tsarist government, however, could not ignore the realities of the situation and had no intention of prejudicing its traditionally friendly relations with the United States. This can be seen in the reaction of the tsarist government when the American envoy in St. Petersburg, Henry Middleton, broached the reasons for the U.S. decision to recognize the independence of the former Spanish colonies. The reply of the Russian Minister, Middleton reported to Washington on 8 (20) July 1822, ''was made in a tone which impressed me with the belief that he in some degree assented to the justness of my observations. His manner & language taken together encouraged me to think that the policy we had pursued in relation to the So. American question had as yet in no degree impaired our good standing with the Emperor.''[36] In the instructions of 2 (14) December 1822 to the Russian envoy to the United States, Baron Tuyll, Nesselrode wrote: ''We do not pretend to stop the march of the future; the emancipation of South America is probable, it may even be imminent. . . .''[37] (The word *imminent* can also mean ''inevitable.'') Thus, despite the tsarist government's adherence to a reactionary monarchist system, both in 1817–18 and 1822–23 it appraised quite soberly the prospects for a separation of the insurgent colonies from the metropolis, although, of course, it was far from wishing to recognize the new states.

The position of France is even more complex. The problem is that essentially France was the only country at that time which, generally speaking, was capable of planning an intervention in the affairs of the insurgent colonies. Having studied the position of France in relation to Latin America, Robertson reached the conclusion that 1823 was the year ''when European interposition in Spanish America seemed most imminent.''[38]

Rumors about a possible intervention appeared repeatedly in the European press, especially in connection with the French invasion of Spain in the spring of 1823 to restore the absolutist regime of Ferdinand VII. Already on 13 December 1822 an article appeared in the *Journal des Débats* proposing the transfer of Spanish *infantes* to Mexico and Peru under military escort.[39]

In principle, the idea of sending Spanish princes to the Western Hemisphere to head the various parts of Spain's former colonial empire seemed exceedingly attractive to France. This question, in particular, was discussed repeatedly in July

1823 in letters from French Prime Minister [Count Joseph de] Villèle to the Duke of Angoulême, commander of the French troops in Spain.[40] Villèle counted on the support which the conservative forces of the former Spanish colonies would accord the infantes.

At the same time, a letter dated 18 July 1823 reveals Villèle's belief that it would have been useless to attempt by force to bring the former Spanish colonies on the American continent again under the yoke of the metropolis and to oblige them to abolish the trade relations they had established with other countries.[41] As revealed in instructions sent early in 1823 to French warships in the Latin American area, the French government scarcely sought to aggravate relations with the new states, but rather, to the contrary, was preparing the way for a future expansion of trade with these countries. On 1 February 1823, Clermont-Tonnerre, French Minister of Marine, wrote to the commander of a naval station on the coast of Brazil, [Admiral A. M.] Grivel, of the need to seize warships flying the Spanish flag. At the same time, Grivel was ordered "to treat in a friendly fashion ships of the insurgent Spanish colonies and to maintain the relations that have been established with the new governments of southern America in such a manner as to prepare for us, whatever may be their future, relations which will be favorable to our commerce."[42] French Admiral [Jacques] Bergeret, who commanded a naval base in the Antilles, even planned to use French vessels, together with vessels from the insurgent colonies, against the Spanish royalists in the West Indies.

Nor did the French government give its approval to isolated proposals for intervention advanced by overly zealous individuals. In the fall of 1823, a French banker and speculator by the name of Ouvrard proposed that an expedition be sent to restore Spanish rule in the colonies. In a conversation with the English Ambassador, Charles Stuart, Villèle reported that in Spain plans were in motion to form a company under Ouvrard's direction which would finance an expedition to South America with a view, in the event of success, to obtaining territorial possessions, trade privileges, and the like. For the realization of his project, Ouvrard counted on securing the resources of other countries. "His views were defeated by the refusal of the French Government to acquiesce in the project."[43]

In November 1823, General McGregor presented to the French Minister of Foreign Affairs [Viscount François René de] Chateaubriand, one of the curious projects for the establishment of Bourbon monarchies in Spanish America. On this project, a skeptical official at the Quai d'Orsay made the following notation: "The plan is certainly very good, but its execution is difficult."[44]

For proper understanding of the international situation on the eve of the declaration of the Monroe Doctrine in 1823, it is important to examine the position of England. The attitude of Great Britain toward the insurgent Spanish colonies in America is on the whole fairly well known from the works of Harold Temperley, Charles Webster, and other historians.[45] The English government took into account the presence of extensive trade ties with the former Hispano-Portuguese colonies in America, where English merchants were essentially the heirs and virtual masters. Moreover, the separation of the colonies had the effect of altering the balance of power in England's favor.

True, in 1823 the English government had not yet recognized *de jure* the new states, but this was only a question of time. In a memorandum presented to the members of the cabinet on 15 November 1822, George Canning observed that, considering the interests of expanding trade, "no man will say that under such circumstances our Recognition of these States can be indefinitely postponed. The question is, therefore, one entirely of time and degree."[46]

The leaders of the national liberation movement in Latin America, too, were perfectly well informed of England's interest in the separation of the Spanish colonies from the metropolis. The president of Gran Colombia, [Simón] Bolívar, observed that England knew she ought to recognize Spanish America, particularly "if she is to provide herself with an immense new market for her industry and manufactures."[47]

Of particular interest are England's frequent warnings that she opposed interference by Europe, and particularly France, in the affairs of Spanish America. As early as the spring of 1823, Canning, through the English ambassador in Paris, Charles Stuart, positively warned the French government against possible intervention. "Disclaiming in the most solemn manner any intention of appropriating to himself the smallest portion of the late Spanish possessions in America," wrote Canning on 31 March 1823, "His Majesty is satisfied that no attempt will be made by France to bring under her dominion any of those possessions, either by conquest or by cession from Spain."[48]

It is characteristic that Canning did not simply warn France through Charles Stuart but also published the instructions of 31 March 1823 in the press, thus amply informing the other powers of England's position on the Spanish American question. The English Minister, however, remained uneasy. In August 1823, he shared his fears about the intentions of the Holy Alliance with the American envoy in London, Richard Rush, to whom he proposed joint actions by England and the United States, while on 9–12 October 1823, in conversations with French Prince Polignac, he issued a new warning to France known in the literature as the Polignac Memorandum.[49] The "Memorandum of a Conference between the Prince de Polignac and Mr. Canning," dated 9–12 October, represents one of the most interesting diplomatic documents of the fall of 1823.[50] Setting forth Great Britain's position on the Spanish American question, Canning declared "that the British Government were of the opinion that any attempt to bring Spanish America again under its ancient submission to Spain must be utterly hopeless; that all negotiation for that purpose would be unsuccessful; and that the prolongation or renewal of war for the same object would be only a waste of human life and an infliction of calamity upon both parties to no end."[51] In accord with his instructions, Prince Polignac, in turn, declared "that his Government believed it to be utterly hopeless to reduce Spanish America to the state of its former relation to Spain; that France disclaimed, on her part, any intention or desire to avail herself of the present state of the Colonies, or of the present situation of France towards Spain, to appropriate to herself any part of the Spanish possessions in America, or to obtain for herself any exclusive advantages."[52]

Canning's insistent warnings concealed a definite aim. For in point of fact, France had no workable interventionist plans which in 1823 might have received government approval. As pointed out by Harold Temperley, Canning was inclined to exaggerate the French threat. In Temperley's graphic expression, "Canning's stroke" was a unique "masterpiece" of diplomatic "bluff" that discredited France and exalted England.[53]

This well-staged performance unquestionably heightened the prestige of its producer, and, what is central, England's influence in Latin America. Canning's blows, although actually directed against an imaginary adversary (inasmuch as no real plans for armed intervention existed), because of this appeared to contemporaries all the more successful. On 29 November 1823, the U.S. Chargé d'Affaires in France, Daniel Sheldon, wrote the Secretary of State: "The decision and firmness which England has shown on the question of the Spanish American colonies have produced their effect. . . . [It] became obvious that the attempt to subdue those colonies for Spain by a foreign force, would certainly be unsuccessful, and would probably involve Europe in a general war. The project, therefore, is abandoned: a congress to consider the subject will not be called together."[54]

The reactionary monarchist principles held at that time by the French government served poorly the interests of France, while Canning took every advantage of his own situation. The leaders of the French government, however, did understand the danger of their situation, which stemmed from their "legitimist" attachment to the Spanish monarchy. Villèle himself quite pointedly called Spain the corpse to which France was wedded.[55]

Even so outspoken a reactionary as Prince Metternich was convinced of the hopelessness of Spain's efforts to restore her dominion in the Western Hemisphere. In a conversation with [Sir Henry] Wellesley, English Ambassador to Vienna, the Austrian Chancellor stated in the summer of 1823 that, in his opinion, it would be futile for Spain to attempt to reunite her colonies and that the Spanish government would be wise to limit its efforts to preserving the island of Cuba, maintaining through this island contact between Cádiz and Mexico, which would at least assure her a major portion of trade with this latter kingdom.[56]

It is interesting to note that on 19 August 1823 (which coincided with the start of Canning's August talks with Richard Rush concerning a possible threat to Latin America by the Holy Alliance), the English Minister of Foreign Affairs wrote Vienna: "We agree with the Austrian Minister (i.e., Prince Metternich–

NNB) in considering any attempt by Spain, either singly or aided by whatever Power, to reduce those Colonies to their former state of subordination as not less vain than the like attempt on the part of Portugal with respect to Brazil."[57]

Plans to discuss the Spanish American question, proposed by the members of the Holy Alliance, particularly France and Russia, can best be viewed in the light of the deepening conflict between the coalition of continental powers and England. The French government sought to strengthen its position by drawing on the support of the other members of the Holy Alliance. According to a plan proposed by French Foreign Minister Chateaubriand, however, talks should not deal at all with armed intervention but rather an entirely different range of matters. The French diplomatic representatives to the allied courts (La Ferronnays, Rayneval, and Caraman) were instructed to propose to the respective European governments that their ambassadors in Paris be authorized to conduct talks with the government of France and with the Spanish Minister on the matter of Spain's colonies. Chateaubriand sounded out the position of the powers on the following questions:

1. Should England recognize the independence of the Spanish colonies without the approval of His Catholic Majesty, would any of the allied governments also recognize their independence?
2. Would any of the allied governments join France should the latter feel obliged to side with Spain, declining to recognize the independence of those Spanish colonies recognized by England?
3. Would a government which had no colonies consider itself nonpartisan in this matter, leaving France and England to adopt the position which the powers might deem appropriate?
4. Should the Spanish government refuse to reach an accord with its colonies and insist on dominion over them, while in fact lacking all means to do so, would any of the allied governments consider each state free to act with regard to the Spanish colonies as dictated by its own interests?[58]

The French government thus took into account the fact of the colonies' separation from the metropolis, and, fearing in particular recognition of the new states by England, sought to prepare the way in the event of independence to follow her example.

At the end of 1823, the tsarist government turned its attention to the proceedings of the negotiations between England and France and to the proposals of Chateaubriand. As a result, on 25 November (7 December) 1823 instructions were sent to the Russian envoy in Paris, Pozzo di Borgo, in which the views of Alexander I on the matter of the Spanish American colonies were discussed in detail.[59] From the contents of these instructions it is seen that Alexander I approved of the "fully dignified and noble" position taken by the cabinet of the Tuileries in its negotiations with England. As for the position of Russia with regard to the matters which the French envoy, La Ferronnays, had laid before the Tsarist government for consideration, it can be summed up as follows:

1. The Tsarist government declared that it would not recognize the independence of the Spanish colonies.[60]
2. It was pointed out that Russia had colonies in the American Northwest and that she could not consider herself a disinterested power in the matter of the Spanish American colonies.
3. The wish was expressed that the matter of the Spanish colonies be settled through the coordinated actions of the allied powers, to which end appropriate negotiations could be undertaken. In particular, Pozzo di Borgo was authorized to conduct negotiations on this matter at a conference in Paris.

In the diplomatic documents of late 1823 and early 1824, greatest attention is given to the position of Great Britain (the position of the United States was at that time of little concern). The tsarist government realized that the colonial question could be resolved only as a result of an accord with Great Britain. Moreover, one must consider the fact that the proposed talks on the matter of the Spanish American colonies, in which states with the most varied interests would participate, could not, of course, be equated with a real threat of armed intervention, allegedly averted by Monroe's message of 2 December 1823.[61]

Once the final separation of the Spanish American colonies from the metropolis became a fact and decisive victories against Spain had been achieved by the new states, it is doubtful that the Holy Alliance actually planned to intervene if such plans were indeed discussed). At that time, the colonial question took on a radically distinct aspect. One had to consider that new states had been established, and above all, that it was necessary to trade with those states. For precisely this reason, the French government was obliged to study, not fanciful plans of intervention, but rather the possibility of recognizing the new states. It is known, in particular, that just at the time of the declaration of the Monroe Doctrine, the French government was preparing to send agents to Latin America with instructions to dispel the impression that France had at any time promised military aid to Spain in her struggle against the colonies.[62]

That the Holy Alliance, and in particular France, had no plans in the fall of 1823 to intervene in Latin America is seen in the business activities of English merchants. They, with their vested material interests, more than anyone else in Europe were interested in an accurate appraisal of the reality of threatened intervention.

As reported by The Times, on 22 November 1823 representatives of the merchants engaged in trade with the former Spanish colonies met for over two hours with English Ministers Canning and [William] Huskisson. They requested information about France's real intentions, advising the Ministers that thirteen or fourteen vessels were ready to depart English ports with valuable cargoes for

South America. The merchants did not wish to risk their goods if there was a threat of a concerted attack on the new states. As noted in the paper, Canning and Huskisson listened attentively to the merchants' representations. The Ministers declared that, judging from recent intelligence received by the British cabinet, France had no such intentions. Reported concentrations of armed forces in French West Indian ports were unfounded. Warships which in April and May were in the vicinity of the islands of Martinique and Guadeloupe had subsequently returned to France. The only French ship of the line in the West Indies was the *Jean Bart,* and it had been ordered home. As for preparations then in progress in Brest, the English Ministers thought them to be very limited in scope, their motive being the transfer of not more than five hundred men to relieve the regular garrisons in Martinique and Guadeloupe. And when the merchants insisted on a direct answer as to whether or not it would be advisable to postpone or reduce the shipment of goods to the former Spanish colonies, the Ministers stated, according to the report, that they saw no danger.[63]

The question frequently arises, however, whether or not, despite the absence of a real threat of intervention by the Holy Alliance, such a threat was indeed feared in America; whether the government of the United States was totally ignorant of the actual state of affairs and seriously expected an attack. The facts indicate, however, that in America, and particularly in the United States, it was known that there were no prospects of an armed intervention by the Holy Alliance and no possibility of a restoration of Spanish dominion in the Western Hemisphere.

Leaving aside the fact that England's warning of 31 March 1823 to France had been published, the United States had at its disposal numerous dispatches from its diplomatic representatives which indisputably attest to the absence of a real threat of intervention. Thus, upon returning to New York, U.S. envoy to France Albert Gallatin wrote the Secretary of State on 24 June 1823 about his conversation with French Foreign Minister Chateaubriand, in which the matter of possible intervention in South America had been specifically broached. In this connection, "Mr. de Chateaubriand answered in the most explicit manner that France would not make any attempt whatever of that kind or in any manner interfere in the American questions."[64] In this same letter, Gallatin reported an analogous conversation in Paris with the Russian Ambassador, Pozzo di Borgo, indicating that Pozzo apparently shared his views on this matter.[65]

The opposition of England to any interference by the Holy Alliance in Latin America was well known in Washington from the dispatches of the American envoy Richard Rush concerning Canning's confidential proposals in August 1823 for joint actions by England and the United States.[66] And thereafter, American representatives in Europe continued to inform their government accurately on the position of England and continental Europe regarding the Spanish American question. On 30 October 1823, Sheldon reported from Paris:

... I was informed by the British Ambassador that he had conferred with the French Ministers (M. de Chateaubriand and M. de Villèle) on the subject of the Spanish American Colonies. He told me that his object had been to prevent them from engaging hastily in any measures relating to those Colonies. ... The French Ministers assured him that they would undertake nothing by themselves, and that the subject would be brought forward for mutual consideration. In the Journal des Débats, the Ministerial paper, of today, will be found an article, confirming entirely this principle. ... [It] is difficult to conceive that England would consent to any plan which would again place the Colonies under the dominion of Spain. At all events, no steps are likely to be taken hastily or immediately in relation to those countries; and, indeed, the affairs of the mother Country will yet require for some time all the cares of [the French] Government.[67]

A number of contemporary American historians (e.g., Samuel Flagg Bemis, William Cresson, and Edward Howland Tatum) assert that the government of the United States had no information about the memorandum of the conference of 9–12 October 1823 at the time when preparations were being made to issue the Monroe Doctrine, and that it would not therefore have exerted any influence on the position adopted by the American government.[68] Indeed, Canning communicated the contents of the memorandum to the American envoy in London, Richard Rush, only on 24 November 1823, and Rush did not send the corresponding dispatch to Washington until 26 November.[69] Clearly, this report could not have reached the United States in time. Monroe sent his message to Congress on 2 December 1823.

It must be kept in mind, however, that one cannot entirely exclude the possibility that the United States was informed of the memorandum's contents before receiving the complete text from Rush, inasmuch as the talks between England and France were well known in European diplomatic circles already in late October 1823, specifically as a result of information provided by the English and French governments to the other European countries.[70] The important thing, however, is not whether the exact text of this document was known to the government of the United States, but whether the government had been informed of the essence of the matter, that is, of the absence of a real prospect of intervention by France, and the corresponding position of England. And precisely on this point there can be no doubt.

An exceedingly interesting argument against unjustly minimizing the significance of Monroe's message has been advanced by Dexter Perkins, who asserts that it was the result, if not of "unmitigated audacity," then at least of "calculated courage." Pointing out the need to view the Doctrine not in the light of contemporary data but on the basis of the information available to the United States in the fall of 1823, Perkins stresses that regardless of whether or not there existed a threat of intervention, President Monroe believed it to exist. With the exception of John Quincy Adams, his advisers thought so, too.[71] In fact, at special meetings of the American government held in November 1823 to draft the presidential message to Congress, President Monroe, and especially the Secretary of War, John Calhoun, expressed serious fears that with the fall of Cádiz the Holy Alliance would send an expedition to suppress Mexico and South America.

"Perfectly moon-struck" was how Secretary of State Adams referred to John Calhoun. From the very beginning, Adams was himself well aware of the lack of a real threat of intervention and did not believe it possible to reestablish Spanish dominion on the American continent. "I no more believe that the Holy Alliance will restore the Spanish dominion upon the American continent," he told a meeting of the American government on 15 November 1823, "than that the Chimborazo will sink beneath the ocean."[72]

Further developing his view of the unreality of intervention by the Holy Alliance and of a restoration of Spanish rule in the Western Hemisphere, Adams rightly observed that it was difficult to offer reasons which might lead the allied powers to restore the Spanish colonial regime. In his view, it was absurd to imagine that the allied powers "would waste their blood and treasure to prohibit their own subjects upon pain of death to set foot upon those territories."[73]

The position of Adams is especially important, because it was precisely his point of view which finally prevailed. The original text of Monroe's message was revised in accordance with Adam's views and agreed completely with the "political system" which he recommended.

Among those who did not believe in the reality of the threat and who knew the negative attitude toward such intervention of the English government were the best-informed political leaders of Latin America: Simón Bolívar, the Minister of Foreign Affairs of Buenos Aires, Bernardino Rivadavia, and the Minister of Foreign Affairs of Mexico, Lucas Alamán. As shown by a letter from Bolívar to the Vice President of Gran Colombia, Francisco Paulo de Santander, dated 20 September 1823, the "Liberator" knew of England's intention to recognize the independence of Spanish America.[74] From another letter (dated 16 March 1824) it is clear that Bolívar did not believe in the possibility of intervention and was well informed as to the position of Great Britain.[75] In mid-December 1823, Rivadavia termed improbable any intervention in Latin America on the part of the Holy Alliance.[76] Likewise, Alamán, who attached great significance to the position of England, did not believe in the reality of threatened intervention by the Holy Alliance. Characteristically, he later wrote of the friendly intentions of France, which were expressed simultaneously with the Monroe Doctrine.[77]

There remains one final question to be resolved. Why did the myth of a threat of armed intervention by the Holy Alliance spread so widely and how did it come into the historical literature?

In our view, those most interested in propagating the myth of armed intervention by the Holy Alliance in 1823 were the countries who stood to benefit therefrom, namely Great Britain and the United States. By spreading such a myth, the political leaders of these countries tried to appear as the "saviors" and "protectors" of Latin America and thus secure political capital, together with economic positions, in the fledgling republics of the New World. It seems indisputable that George Canning, in particular, was interested in exaggerating rumors about the threat of intervention. A major role in spreading these rumors was played by the press of England and the United States, particularly such publications as the *Edinburgh Review* and the *Morning Chronicle*. In February 1823, the *Edinburgh Review* carried an article entitled "The Holy Alliance Versus Spain, or Notes and Declarations of the Allied Powers," which was sharply critical of the policies pursued by the member powers of the Holy Alliance.[78] Rumors of a threat to the Western Hemisphere on the part of the Holy Alliance spread rapidly. In the fall of 1823, all manner of misgivings about European intervention were expressed repeatedly in the pages of the American press. Especially typical, in this respect, were a statement in the *North American Review*[79] and an article entitled "South America" in the Philadelphia paper *National Advocate,* which Tuyll transmitted to Nesselrode on 15 (27) November 1823. In the opinion of the author of this latter article, one could not doubt (?!) that a close union would be established between Spain and France and it was therefore necessary to consider the possibility of attempts to reconquer the colonies, at least in the case of Mexico. Further, the author of the article pointed out that the United States had an interest in the liberty and independence of North and South America and observed that if a decision of the English government on any question affecting the independence of South America were a matter of calculation, the United States would be in sympathy with it.[80]

Rumors of an impending intervention also found their way into the newspapers of continental Europe. In a report from London, the *Sankt-Peterburgskie vedomosti* of 29 January (10 February) 1824 observed: "The questions which now occupy the public here almost exclusively are the following: (1) Will Spain attempt to bring back under her dominion her former colonies in America? (2) In the event she should make such an attempt, will France and the other allied powers of Europe give her any armed assistance? (3) Can the former Spanish colonies repel such an attack with their own forces alone? (4) Will England participate openly in such a struggle? And (5) In this case, what will the United States of North America do?"[81]

Common fraud played an important role in propagating the myth of a real threat of intervention, allegedly averted by the declaration of the Monroe Doctrine. We refer here to the so-called Secret Treaty of Verona, allegedly concluded on 22 November 1822 between Russia, Austria, Prussia, and France. This "treaty" declared the intention of its participants "to put an end to the system of representative government" (?), to suppress by any means freedom of the press, etc. Although a number of points in this "document" do correspond to the actual policy of the powers of the Holy Alliance, it was nevertheless an obvious fraud, fabricated initially by an obscure correspondent of the London *Morning Chronicle* and published in the paper of 11 June 1823. After this, the fraudulent document began to circulate throughout the newspapers of Europe and America.[82] Perhaps this "document" would have been destined to remain in the pages of the press of the day had it not been for Jonathan Elliot, who in 1834 immortalized it by including it in a two-volume collection of treaties.*

In the mid-nineteenth century, however, after categorical denials by Chateaubriand (one of the alleged authors of the treaty), the fraud was almost forgotten. Its revival dates from the end of the nineteenth century, when, in 1894, Freeman Snow again published the ill-starred "document."‡ It was precisely this publication, which fundamentally distorted the early history of the Monroe Doctrine, that proved most pernicious to American historiography. In the American literature, especially for the first quarter of the twentieth century, one can find many works, including those penned by the most prominent scholars, in which the treaty is accepted as genuine. Among them are Frederic Jackson Turner, John Bassett Moore, Albert B. Hart, and John Latané.[83] Only in the past twenty or thirty years has the situation improved, especially as a result of the writings of Dexter Perkins, T. R. Schellenberg, and William Spence Robertson.[84] Today, the falsity of the "document" is beyond all doubt.

The above permits us to formulate the following basic conclusions:

1. No real threat of intervention in Latin America by the Holy Alliance existed in 1823. The Monroe Doctrine, therefore, was directed against an imaginary threat. Not one of the member governments of the Holy Alliance ever promoted or approved any real plan of armed intervention. This is not to say, of course, that the Holy Alliance was in principle opposed to intervention. It is generally known that the members of the Holy Alliance adhered in greater or lesser degree to reactionary monarchist principles and held sacred the sovereign "rights" of the Spanish King. In general, they were also favorably disposed toward the idea of joint discussion of the Spanish American question. The entire affair, however, was fraught with difficulties and a lack of necessary means to carry out any plan of actual intervention. (And, of course, there was no particular enthusiasm to wage a war for the glory of Ferdinand VII in his distant overseas possessions.)

2. The government of the United States was well informed about the international situation toward the end of 1823; it was aware of Great Britain's negative position on the possibility of interference by the Holy Alliance in the struggle against the insurgent colonies, and it did not believe in the possibility of restoring Spanish dominion in the Western Hemisphere. It must be kept in mind that,

---

*Johathan Elliot, comp., *The American Diplomatic Code Embracing a Collection of Treaties and Conventions between the United States and Foreign Powers: From 1778 to 1834*, 2 vols. (Washington, 1834).

‡Freeman Snow, *Treaties and Topics in American Diplomacy* (Boston, 1894).

although many political leaders, including James Monroe and John Calhoun, expressed fears of threatened intervention, it was the well-informed viewpoint of John Quincy Adams that prevailed in the discussions of the American government on this matter. As a result, the draft of the annual message to Congress of 2 December 1823 was adopted.

3. The governments most interested in creating and spreading the myth of a real threat of intervention in Latin America by the Holy Alliance were those of England and the United States. Acting as the "protectors" of the Latin American countries and supposedly preventing their enslavement by the Holy Alliance, the United States and England sought in this way to make political capital, strengthen their positions, and expand their influence in these countries. This aspiration found especially vivid expression in the Monroe Doctrine. The tendency to expand and strengthen U.S. positions in the Latin American countries, embodied in the Doctrine already at the time of its pronouncement, developed fully in the subsequent practice of American foreign policy, the main objective of which became the establishment of monopoly rule in the Western Hemisphere. As a result, the real threat to the independence of the Latin American countries would come from a completely different quarter, namely the United States of America.

NOTES

1 *Proceedings of the American Society of International Law at its Eighth Annual Meeting Held at Washington, D.C.,* April 22–25, 1914 (Washington, D.C., 1914), pp. 197–98.

2 Thus, for example, in 1922 Perkins published an article entitled "Europe, Spanish America and the Monroe Doctrine," while a few years later (in 1927) the first part of Perkin's large three-volume study on the Monroe Doctrine appeared, representing the result of archival research in Europe and the United States. Without examining here Perkin's general conception of the Monroe Doctrine, it must be noted that the factual material which he collected is very interesting, although his conclusions are not lacking in contradictions. Noting, for example, that no real threat of intervention in Latin America by the Holy Alliance existed, Perkins at the same time asserts that Monroe's message was designed to avert any such intervention. Here he makes the reservation that although the message pursued this end, this does not mean, however, that it really averted intervention. See Dexter Perkins, *The Monroe Doctrine, 1823–1826* (Cambridge, Mass., 1927), pp. 104 ff.

The further development of Perkin's views can be followed in his general work first published in 1941 and recently reissued in a revised edition, *Hands Off: A History of the Monroe Doctrine* (Boston, 1941); idem, *A History of the Monroe Doctrine* (Boston and Toronto, 1955), pp. 53–54, 59–60 ff.

3 Harold Temperley, "French Designs on Spanish America in 1820–1825," *EHR* 40 no. 157 (January 1925), 34 ff.

4 Ibid., p. 34.

5 J. Fred Rippy, *Rivalry of the United States and Great Britain over Latin America (1808–1830)* (Baltimore, 1929), p. 118.

6 J. Fred Rippy, *Latin America in World Politics* (New York, 1942), p. 51.

7 William Spence Robertson, "Russia and the Emancipation of Spanish America, 1816–1826," *HAHR* 21, no. 2 (May 1941), 217–18.

8 La Ferronnays to Chateaubriand, 14 May 1824, ibid., p. 217.

9 Rippy, *Latin America in World Politics*, p. 51.

10 C. K. Webster, ed., *Britain and the Independence of Latin America, 1812–1830: Select Documents from the Foreign Office Archives*, 2 vols. (London, New York and Toronto, 1938), I, 71.

11 Ibid., p. 73.

12 *Istoriia diplomatii* (Moscow, 1941), I, 392; *Diplomaticheskii slovar'* (Moscow, 1950), II, 165; *Bol'shaia sovetskaia entsiklopedia* (Moscow, 1954), XXVIII, 251–52.

13 William Z. Foster, *Ocherk politicheskoi istorii Ameriki* (Moscow, 1953), p. 196.

14 William Spence Robertson, "The Monroe Doctrine Abroad in 1823–24," *APSR* 6 (1912), 561; Samuel Eliot Morison, "The Origin of the Monroe Doctrine, 1775–1823," *Economica*, no. 10 (February 1924), 41.

15 Temperley, "French Designs," p. 34.

16 Erwin Hölzle, *Russland und Amerika: Aufbruch und Begegnung zweier Weltmächte* (Munich, 1953), pp. 108, 111, 125 ff.

17 James Monroe to Thomas Jefferson, 23 November 1818, in Stanislaus Murray Hamilton, ed., *The Writings of James Monroe, Including a Collection of His Public and Private Papers and Correspondence . . .* , 7 vols. (New York and London, 1898–1903), VI, 85. An analogous letter to James Madison is found in the same volume, p. 84.

The view found in the literature that right down to the early 1820s the reactionary nature of the Holy Alliance was not appreciated in the United States warrants critical examination. A letter from John Quincy Adams to his close friend Alexander Everett, dated 29 December 1817, attests to the fact that already at that time the Secretary of State realized the counterrevolutionary plans pursued by the Holy Alliance, disguised though they were by hypocritical phraseology. Adams noted that peace on the tongue of the strong always means submission of the weak to the will of the strong. See Adams to Everett, 29 December 1817, *AHR* 11, no. 1 (October 1905), 112–13.

18 The instructions were intended for Baron Tuyll. His appointment at that time, however, was not confirmed, and P. I. Poletica was sent as the new envoy to Washington.

19 Arkhiv vneshnei politiki Rossii (hereafter AVPR), Chancery, delo 12182, fols. 13–15. Apparently, the republican form of government of the United States was not considered an obstacle to joining the Holy Alliance. Alexander I pursued his old line of seeking in the United States a kind of rival to England.

20 Charles Francis Adams, ed., *Memoirs of John Quincy Adams Comprising Portions of His Diary from 1795 to 1848*, 12 vols. (Philadelphia, 1874–1877), IV, 394–95 (hereafter J. Q. Adams, *Memoirs*).

21 Poletica to Nesselrode, 13 (25) January 1820, AVPR, Chancery, delo 12195, fols, 109-12.
22 Adams to Middleton, 5 July 1820. These instructions have been published in many documentary collections, including John Bassett Moore, *A Digest of International Law . . .* , 8 vols. (Washington, 1906). VI, 376-79 (hereafter Moore, *Digest*).
23 The words "hearty assent to the articles of the Holy Alliance" and the like should not, perhaps, be taken too literally. One cannot exclude the possibility that they signified a polite rejection of participation in the Holy Alliance.
24 J. Q. Adams, *Memoirs,* IV, 376-77.
25 Ibid., pp. 380-81.
26 Cambell to Adams, 25 June (7 July) 1820, in J. Hildt, *Early Diplomatic Negotiations of the United States with Russia* (Baltimore, 1906), p. 142.

   Later on, following the death of Alexander I, Adams, having become President, wrote in his annual message to Congress at the end of 1826 that "a candid and confidential interchange of sentiments between him (Alexander I–NNB) and the Government of the United States upon the affairs of Southern America took place at a period not long preceding his demise, and contributed to fix that course of policy which left to the other Governments of Europe no alternative but that of sooner or later recognizing the independence of our southern neighbors, of which the example had by the United States already been set." See James D. Richardson, ed., *A Compilation of the Messages and Papers of the Presidents,* 20 vols. (New York, 1897-1917), II, 917.
27 Robertson, "Russia and the Emancipation of Spanish America," pp. 220-21.
28 Zea Bermúdez to Pizarro, 25 April (7 May) 1817, ibid., p. 197.
29 Charles Webster rightly notes that Pozzo di Borgo's projects could not be carried out without the support of England. Castlereagh's opposition was decisive and doomed them to failure. Pozzo di Borgo's projects, moreover, never received the support of Alexander I. See Webster, *Britain and the Independence of Latin America,* I, 14, 71-72. For the text of Castlereagh's memorandum of 20 August 1817, see Webster, II, pp. 352-58.
30 Pozzo di Borgo to Nesselrode, 2 (14) June 1817, in A. A. Polovtsov, comp., *Correspondence diplomatique des ambassadeurs et ministres de Russie en France et de France en Russie avec leurs gouvernements de 1814 à 1830,* vols. CXII, CXIX, and CXXVII of *Sbornik Imperatorskogo Russkogo Istoricheskogo Obshchestva,* 148 vols. (St. Petersburg, 1867-1916), CXIX, 230.
31 Capo d'Istria to Poletica (the draft of the instructions was approved by Alexander I on 12 (24) April and signed by Capo d'Istria on 18 (30) April 1818) AVPR, Chancery, delo 12187, fols. 4-13.
32 Capo d'Istria to Poletica, AVPR, Chancery, delo 12187, fols. 9-10. In underscoring the final words, we wish to call attention to the fact that Professor William Robertson completely changed the thought of this sentence. As a result, the meaning is precisely the opposite of the original. The words "Un ami et allié de Sa Majesté Catholique, l'Empereur *ne cessera point d'insister* pour que les Colonies obtiennent de *leur Mère Patrie* une administration fondé sur les principes d'une représéntation nationale, et des libertés qui en dépendent" Robertson translated in the following manner: "As a friend and ally of His Catholic Majesty, the Emperor *will not insist* that the Spanish colonies

should obtain from their mother country an administration founded upon the principles of a national representation.'' Thus it turns out in Robertson's translation that, as a friend and ally of the Spanish King, Alexander I *would not insist* that the colonies receive from the metropolis an administration based on the principles of national representation. This is all the more striking, for in the French text the negation is very strong—''ne cessera point d'insister''—that is, in essence, ''under no circumstances will he stop insisting,'' or ''he will continue to insist.'' See Robertson, ''Russia and the Emancipation of Spanish America,'' p. 204. (The words ''Leur Mère Patrie'' were underscored in the text of the instructions; the remainder was underlined by the author.-NNB)

33 Perkins, *The Monroe Doctrine, 1823-1826,* pp. 105 ff.

34 Dispatch from D'Oseri to the Marquis Dessolú, in Mario Belgrano, *La Francia y la monarquía en el Plata (1818-1820)* (Buenos Aires, 1933), pp. 146 ff.

35 William R. Manning, ed., *Diplomatic Correspondence of the United States Concerning the Independence of the Latin-American Nations,* 3 vols. (New York, 1925), I, 147-48.

36 Middleton to Adams 8 (20) July 1822, ibid., III, 1867.

37 Nesselrode to Tuyll, 2 (14) December 1822, ''Correspondence of the Russian Ministers in Washington, 1818-1825,'' *AHR* 18, no. 2 (January 1913), 540.

38 William Spence Robertson, *France and Latin-American Independence* (Baltimore, 1939), p. 255.

39 Temperley, ''French Designs,'' p. 40.

40 Joseph de Villèle, *Mémoires et correspondance,* 5 vols. (Paris, 1888-1890), IV, 188, 200-201.

41 Villèle to the Duke of Angoulême, 18 July 1823, in Villèle, *Mémoires,* IV, 239. French projects for sending the infantes were unrealistic, primarily because Spain itself was not in agreement with them. When the French Ambassador in Madrid, Talarou, proposed in early 1824 that one of the infantes be sent to Mexico, Ferdinand VII did not delay in expressing in this regard his decided disapproval, for he considered that in reality this would be tantamount to recognition of Spanish American autonomy.

42 Clermont-Tonnerre to Grivel, 1 February 1823, in Robertson, *France and Latin-American Independence,* p. 256.

43 Stuart to Canning, 18 November 1823, in Webster, *Britain and the Independence of Latin America,* II, 128; Court to Canning, 8 November 1823, ibid., p. 405.

44 Robertson, *France and Latin-American Independence,* p. 283.

45 C. K. Webster, *The Foreign Policy of Castlereagh (1813-1822)* (London, 1934); Harold Temperley, *The Foreign Policy of Canning (1822-1827)* (London, 1925); William W. Kaufmann, *British Policy and the Independence of Latin America, 1804-1828* (New Haven, 1951).

46 See Canning's memorandum to the cabinet of 15 November 1822, in Webster, *Britain and the Independence of Latin America,* II, 393-98.

47 Simón Bolívar, *Selected Writings,* comp. Vicente Lecuna, 2 vols. (New York, 1951), II, 379.

48 Canning to Stuart, 31 March 1823, in Webster, *Britain and the Independence of Latin America,* II, 112.

49 The proposal that the warning to the French government be made in the form of talks

with Prince Polignac was first suggested by the Duke of Wellington. (See Webster, *Britain and the Independence of Latin America,* I, 19–20.) Canning himself first proposed to send a special note to France, in which it would be pointed out that England could not look with indifference upon the transfer of any part of the former Spanish colonies to a foreign power, nor upon intervention by any foreign power for the purpose of suppressing these colonies. See the draft of Canning's note to Polignac of 22 September 1823 (ibid., II, 114). In the end, Canning decided to leave the choice to Polignac himself.

Declaring his wish to have a full and open exchange of views on the matter of South America, the English Minister proposed the following options to the Prince: (1) address an official note to him [Polignac]; (2) address an official note to the English Ambassador in Paris, Stuart, who in turn would make it known to Chateaubriand, allowing him to make a copy; and (3) hold a conference between Canning and Polignac, the contents of which would then be stated by one party and confirmed by the other. Polignac preferred this latter course (see Canning to Wellesley, 28 November 1823, ibid., II, 16). Subsequently, Polignac made an attempt not to attach official importance to the record, but he was forced to yield in light of Canning's firm stand on this question. Villèle and Chateaubriand, too, acknowledged the official nature of the memorandum (ibid., II, 121, 124–25, 127.)

50 At first the text of the memorandum was not published in the press. Its contents were communicated to other governments only through diplomatic channels. Apparently, this was Canning's mistake. In any event, following the pronouncement of the Monroe Doctrine, Canning hastened to publish the Polignac Memorandum, making available to the English Parliament in March 1824 correspondence with France and Spain in relation to the provinces of South America, so as to show the importance of England's position in averting European intervention in the affairs of the former Spanish colonies. See *Hansard's Parliamentary Debates,* new series, X (London, 1824), pp. 707 ff.

We should note, however, that the text of the memorandum was not published in its entirety. Those parts which dealt with other countries were omitted. If in October 1823, for example, Canning cited the need for the United States to participate in the discussions of the Spanish American question (the other European powers, of course, would not), in March 1824 he sought to play down the significance of the position taken in the Spanish American question by his dangerous rival and to show that precisely the action of England had had a decisive role in avoiding the convening of a congress on this matter.

The complete document was first published by Harold Temperley. Subsequently, the full text of the memorandum was included in Charles Webster's well-known publication (Webster, *Britain and the Independence of Latin America,* II, 115–20) and in many other documentary collections.

51 Webster, *Britain and the Independence of Latin America,* II, 115.
52 Ibid., p. 117.
53 Temperley, "French Designs," p. 53.
54 Sheldon to Adams, 29 November 1823, in Manning, *Diplomatic Correspondence,* II, 1400.
55 Villèle to Polignac, 10 February 1824, in Villèle, *Mémoires,* IV, 531.

56 Wellesley to Canning, 23 July 1823, in Webster, *Britain and the Independence of Latin America*, II, 12. (By "kingdom" is meant Mexico, although at that time the latter was already a republic).

57 Canning to Wellesley, 19 August 1823, ibid., p. 14.

58 Draft dispatch to La Ferronnays, Rayneval, and Caraman, together with a copy of the Memorandum of the conference between Prince Polignac and Mr. Canning, Paris 1 November 1823, in François Auguste Réne de Chateaubriand, *Le Congrès de Verone, Guerre d'Espagne. Négociations. Colonies espagnoles,* 2 vols. (Paris and Leipzig, 1838), II, 307–8.

59 Nesselrode to Pozzo di Borgo (draft instructions approved by Alexander I 24 November/6 December and signed by Nesselrode 25 November/7 December 1823), AVPR, Chancery, delo 9124, fols. 693–703.

60 The tsarist government's reluctance to recognize the new states was nothing new or unusual. Earlier, on 26 July (7 August) 1823, Nesselrode had informed Pozzo di Borgo of the refusal of Alexander I to receive as a representative from Colombia General d'Evreuz, in connection with which Pozzo di Borgo was instructed to reject all petitions from such persons for passports to travel to Russia with this objective. See Nesselrode to Pozzo di Borgo, 26 July (7 August) 1823, AVPR, Chancery, delo 9124, fol. 422.

61 One must also keep in mind the fact that, practically, the question of convening a congress of the allied powers on the matter of the insurgent colonies was raised by Spain at the end of December 1823, i.e., already after the pronouncement of the Monroe Doctrine. As a result of England's refusal to participate in the discussion of this matter, the idea of convening the congress was doomed to failure. The conference of allied ambassadors in Paris in 1824–1825 likewise produced no results. The records of these conferences have been published. See "Protocols of Conferences of Representatives of the Allied Powers Respecting Spanish America, 1824–1825," *AHR* 22, no. 3 (April 1917), 595–616.

62 Perkins, *A History of the Monroe Doctrine,* pp. 52–53.

63 *The Times,* London, 25 November 1823.

64 Gallatin to Adams, 24 July 1823, in Manning, *Diplomatic Correspondence,* II, 1398.

65 Ibid.

66 Richard Rush, *Memoranda of a Residence at the Court of London* (Philadelphia, 1845), p. 399.

67 Sheldon to Adams, 30 October 1823, in Hamilton, *The Writings of James Monroe,* VI, 398.

68 William P. Cresson, *James Monroe* (Chapel Hill, 1946), p. 436; Samuel Flagg Bemis, *John Quincy Adams and the Foundations of American Foreign Policy* (New York, 1949). As observed by Edward Tatum, the government of the United States knew absolutely nothing about the Canning-Polignac conference until February 1824. See Edward H. Tatum, *The United States and Europe, 1815–1823* (Berkeley, 1936), p. 286.

69 Rush, *Memoranda of a Residence,* pp. 448–54.

70 We should note, in particular, that the Russian Ambassador in London, Count Liven, reported the contents of the talks between Canning and Polignac in a dispatch to Nesselrode dated 17 (29) October 1823. Subsequently, on 18 (30) November, Liven

transmitted the text of the memorandum itself. See Liven to Nesselrode, 17 (29) October, 18 (30) November 1823, AVPR, Chancery, delo 6921, fols. 17 ff. For the text of the "memorandum," see *loc. cit.*, fols. 244 ff.
71 Perkins, *A History of the Monroe Doctrine*, p. 60.
72 J. Q. Adams, *Memoirs*, VI, 186 (underlining added–NNB)
73 Ibid., p. 207.
74 Simón Bolívar, *Obras completas*, I (La Habana, 1947), p. 813.
75 Ibid., pp. 933, 941, 944.
76 Perkins, *The Monroe Doctrine, 1823–1826*, p. 150.
77 *Obras completas de Lucas Alamán*, vol. IX of *Documentos diversos* (México, 1945), p. 120.
78 *Edinburgh Review or Critical Journal* 38, no. 75 (February 1823), pp. 241–64. Subsequently, the journal continued to defend this point of view. See, for example, "The Holy Alliance Versus Spain; Containing the Notes and Declarations of the Allied Powers, with the Replies of the Spanish Courtes. By a Constitutionalist," *ibid.*, vol. 39, no. 78 (January 1824), 467–88.
79 "The Principles of the Holy Alliance or Notes and Manifestations of the Allied Powers," *North American Review* 17 (October 1823), 340–75. (Microfilm copy sent by the University of California.)
80 AVPR, Chancery, *delo* 12213, fol. 31.
81 *Sankt-Peterburgskie vedomosti*, no. 9 (29 January 1824 o.s.), p. 109.
82 Four days later it was published in Paris. To be sure, the editor of the paper in which it was published, *Pilote*, was obliged to spend a month in jail and pay a fine. The paper itself was closed down for fifteen days. In the United States, the false document was published in the most diverse periodicals, first in New York (24 July 1823), then in Philadelphia (*Aurora*), Washington (*Washington City Gazette*), and elsewhere. It is true that some well-informed newspapers did not carry the report of the treaty. For example, the *New York Spectator*, and more important, the *National Intelligencer*. For more on this, see T. R. Schellenberg, "The Secrety Treaty of Verona: A Newspaper Forgery," *JMH* 7, no. 3 (September 1935), pp. 280–91.
83 Albert B. Hart, ed., *The American Nation: A History*, vol. XIV; Frederick Jackson Turner, *Rise of the West, 1819–1829* (New York and London, 1906). Chapter 12 (pp. 199–223) is devoted to the Monroe Doctrine. Reference to the treaty is found on page 211. John Bassett Moore, *A Digest of International Law*, vol. VI, p. 375; Albert B. Hart, *The Monroe Doctrine: An Interpretation* (Boston, 1916), p. 46; John H. Latané, *From Isolation to Leadership* (New York, 1920), pp. 21–24.
   To the credit of European scholars, it should be noted that they have not been inclined to use this "document." They have, it seems, been far more familiar with the archival materials on the history of the Holy Alliance and have not doubted the spuriousness of this "accord."
84 Perkins, *The Monroe Doctrine, 1823–1826*, pp. 52–53; T. R. Schellenberg, "The Secret Treaty of Verona," pp. 280–91; Robertson, *France and Latin-American Independence*, pp. 248–50.

10 NEW WORLD ARCADIA
(Unknown Materials on Paraguay in the 1820s)

M. S. AL'PEROVICH

ON THE night of 8 December 1821, four hundred armed men who had arrived that evening at the Paraguayan port of Itapúa (modern-day Encarnación) under the cover of darkness crossed the wide, deep Paraná, which separates Paraguay from the territory of Misiones,[1] and disappeared into the dense thickets along the southern bank of the river. Proceeding on for several kilometers through the forest, they approached the small settlement of Santa Ana, silently surrounding it from all sides. At daybreak, the intruders suddenly attacked the settlement. They killed a number of the Indians who were there and took the remainder prisoner. They destroyed and burned dwellings, broke utensils and other belongings, and trampled crops. Awakened by the cries of the Indians, a half-dressed middle-aged man, obviously European, rushed from one of the huts. Before he could offer resistence or even grasp what was happening, he was knocked senseless by a saber blow to the head. Unconscious, bound hand and foot, he was dragged to the river bank, thrown into a boat, and carried across to Itapúa. When he regained consciousness, he found himself already inside Paraguay.

So it was that the famous French botanist Aimé Bonpland (close friend and companion of Alexander von Humboldt during the latter's celebrated journey to America from 1799 to 1804), who had been studying the cultivation and processing of *yerba mate* (Paraguayan tea) in these regions, unexpectedly found himself in a country where he was to spend nine long years, far from his homeland, friends,and the customary benefits of civilization. Inasmuch as his abduction was witnessed by a French merchant from Montevideo, news of the incident quickly

Originally published as "'Arkadiia Novogo Sveta' (Neizvestnye materialy o Paragvae 20-kh godov XIX veka)," *NNI*, no. 3 (May–June 1969), 112–24.

spread throughout the provinces of the Río de la Plata and remaining regions of America, and a short time later reached Europe. In October 1823, the president of Colombia, [Simón] Bolívar, addressed a note to the Paraguayan government requesting the release of Bonpland. It was followed by analogous petitions from other statesmen, diplomats, and scholars. But all of these efforts were in vain.

Bonpland was by no means the only foreigner in Paraguay against his will. At different times and in varying circumstances the Uruguayan patriot leader [José Gervasio] Artigas, the Swiss physicians Rengger and Longchamp, English merchants, Frenchmen, Italians, Portuguese—in all, several dozen individuals— came here. But they were not allowed to leave, for free entry to and exit from the country were prohibited. This exceptional measure was taken for pressing reasons.

Situated in the heart of the South American continent, Paraguay was bounded on the east by the Portuguese colony of Brazil, on the north by Upper Peru, on the south and west by Corrientes and other provinces of the River Plate. For some three hundred years Paraguay had been a Spanish colony. It was part of the viceroyalty of the Río de la Plata, but at the same time depended economically on Buenos Aires. After the May revolution of 1810, the Paraguayan patriots opposed efforts by the junta of Buenos Aires to establish control over all the territory of the viceroyalty. In 1811, Spanish rule in Paraguay was overthrown and the country declared independent, with a republican system being established in 1813. Supreme state power was exercised by two consuls. A year later, a national congress elected one of them, doctor José Gaspar Rodríguez de Francia (1766–1840), "Supreme Dictator of the Republic" for a five-year term, declaring him dictator for life in 1816.

The continued threat to Paraguay's independence on the part of the Spanish and Portuguese colonialists[2] and ruling circles in Buenos Aires, external attempts at intervention in the internal affairs of the country, and also the wish of the Paraguayan government not to become involved in the armed conflict between the neighboring governments and provinces prompted Francia to close the republic's borders and to restrict severely contacts with the outside world. Only in exceptional cases and with the special permission of the dictator was it possible to enter or leave Paraguay. Correspondence abroad was subject to the strictest censorship and was constantly interrupted. No newspapers or journals or books were published in the country.

At the beginning of 1821, Francia learned that the participants in an antigovernment conspiracy discovered in Asunción a short time before had colluded while in prison with [Francisco] Ramírez, *caudillo* of the Platine province of Entre Ríos, who was preparing for war with Paraguay. (Francia ordered the seizure of Bonpland primarily because he considered him an agent of Ramírez, with whom the scholar maintained friendly relations.) Having dealt with the conspirators (their leaders were shot beneath an orange tree on the plaza in front of the supreme ruler's residence), the dictator decided to terminate trade completely, and subsequently severed all ties abroad.

Introducing a regime of self-isolation, Francia quickly understood the serious difficulties which the severence of economic ties with other countries held for the republic. And no sooner did neighboring Brazil become an independent state (September 1822), than the Paraguayan government decided (in April 1823) to trade with it, designating for this purpose the port of Itapúa. However, trade with Brazil was strictly regulated and in volume was exceedingly limited. In essence, this was the only channel linking Paraguay to the outside world. But even through this channel, almost no information flowed. The "realm of doctor Francia" remained a country of mystery, about which nothing was known for many years. The first eye-witness evidence, according to the historical literature, appeared in print only in 1826–27.

Meanwhile, in the spring of 1825, a rather detailed description of Paraguay under Francia was published in the pages of a journal which came out in far-off Russia.[3] It is entirely possible that this publication would have gone unnoticed by researchers had it not been signed with the initials of one of the most radical members of the Decembrist Northern Society, the writer and historian N. A. Bestuzhev. Since it has been primarily historians of the Decembrist movement who have taken notice of this description and discussed it in the scholarly literature, it has attracted interest mainly as a source for characterizing the views of Bestuzhev.

Works published in recent decades have examined this publication as a reflection of Bestuzhev's position on certain problems which in the first half of the 1820s evoked heated debates among the participants of the secret societies. Commenting on this text as early as 1933, the historian I. M. Trotskii expressed the view that the social structure and the actions of Francia seemed to Bestuzhev, who idealized them, an example worthy of imitation. The researcher saw this publication as evidence of an attempt by Bestuzhev to establish a republican order and a revolutionary dictatorship in Russia. "It is difficult to conceive," he wrote, "that Bestuzhev, in publishing such articles, could belong to those who accused Pestel of dictatorial projects or who supported the constitution of Nikita Muravëv."[4]

An analogous point of view was formulated in other works which appeared during the 1940s and '50s.[5] In some it is expressed even more categorically. Thus, E. E. Boborykina holds that "with this article Bestuzhev established a special position in the Northern Society on a question which at the time was most critical for the Decembrists." Siding with Pestel, he "defended the idea of dictatorship and established its necessity."[6] Agreeing with this formulation of the question, R. Kh. Yakhin emphasized that "N. Bestuzhev, expressing in this article his views on a republic and revolutionary dictatorship, stated his wish to establish in Russia the very same order as that in Paraguay.''[7] The article on Paraguay comes into the scholarly literature as an important argument for the thesis that Bestuzhev was ''the strongest theoretician and political thinker of the Ryleev tendency,'' that he ''subjected to criticism not only serfdom, but also capitalist relations,'' and so on.[8]

The overwhelming majority of authors who in one connection or another have shown an interest in the aforementioned publication[9] hold that it belongs to the pen of Bestuzhev himself. True, some historians note that it was a compilation, but emphasize, as noted above, that it nonetheless reflects Bestuzhev's views.[10] According to E. E. Boborykina, ''N. Bestuzhev's article on Paraguay,'' a compilation in terms of its contents, ''represents a truly original article given the position taken by the author and his appraisal of events and facts.''[11]

The only exception of which I am aware is the opinion expressed by S. S. Volk, according to whom Bestuzhev published not an original essay, but only ''his translation of an article of Paraguay that greatly interested him.'' Subsequently, however, even Volk writes of Bestuzhev not as a translator, but as the author, who ''with an example from contemporary history . . . substantiated and supported . . . Pestel's idea of a provisional revolutionary government.''[12]

Of course, the question as to just what it was that Bestuzhev published in the pages of *Syn Otechestva*—whether a translation or an article written by him, even if compiled—is fairly significant. And to answer it is a rather simple matter, inasmuch as the source is given at the end of the text: ''From Hamb. pol. Jour.''[13] Indeed, an unsigned article entitled ''Paraguay (from American papers)'' was printed in the February issue of the Hamburg *Politisches Journal* for 1825.[14] A comparison with Bestuzhev's publication shows that the latter was not a compilation, rather a literal, somewhat abbreviated translation of the article from the German periodical with the title expanded to read ''On the Contemporary History and Present State of South America.'' As for the cuts, they were, with one exception, immaterial: the translator omitted a few lines which referred to the supposed election in Paraguay of popular representatives, who, the article contended, formed a council of state.[15]

Far more complex is another question, which, very likely, does not greatly concern the scholar investigating Decembrist views, but which is of extraordinary interest to the historian of the Latin American independence movement of the nineteenth century: how, given the severe isolation of Paraguay and the lack of any information about this country, did such a detailed report reach the Hamburg periodical? With whom did it originate and is the information which it contains accurate?

To begin with, where was this material obtained? On this the *Politisches Journal* is vague: from American papers. But at that time there were over five hundred such papers. To search out the required material in this limitless sea of periodicals would be a very difficult, almost impossible task even in the United States. And in our libraries, the North American press of the first quarter of the past century is hardly represented at all. At best, one can find odd issues of this or that paper. No, this is a hopeless affair. It was necessary to abandon any further search.

Having made such a judicious decision, in all likelihood I would have held to it, if one rainy fall day, specifically 14 October 1966, N. N. Bolkhovitinov had not given me his new monograph, *The Establishment of Russo-American Relations, 1775–1815.** On pages 39–40 of this interesting book, the author, who is well informed on nineteenth-century U.S. periodical holdings in the USSR, notes that in the Leningrad library of the Academy of Sciences a complete run had been uncovered of the most famous and influential periodical publication of its time—*Nile's Weekly Register,* which had appeared in Baltimore since 1811.

Securing a microfilm for the necessary period represented no special problem, and in the issue of 18 December 1824 a brief notice was discovered which began, "An account of Paraguay has recently been published in Paris, containing, as the English newspapers say, the following facts."‡ The text went on, conforming essentially to the contents of the article in *Politisches Journal.* But this material was greatly summarized and therefore could not possibly have been the source of the article in question.

Its source was possibly that cited at the end of the notice in *Nile's Weekly Register,* given as "Phil. pap." What does this abbreviation stand for? Most likely, Philadelphia Paper. Apparently, it refers to a newspaper by this name. However, in [Winifred] Gregory's very complete catalog of newspapers appearing in the United States from 1821 to 1936§ there is no such title. Perhaps the mysterious "Phil. pap." is not the abbreviated title of a specific newspaper, but rather should be understood simply as indicating that the material was adopted from a newspaper published in Philadelphia (in the sense of "from Philadelphia newspapers"). If this was so, then precisely from what paper? At that time, some two dozen papers were published in Philadelphia. Most likely, perhaps, this was the most prominent and well-informed *Philadelphia Gazette and Daily Advertiser,* although other possibilities, of course, were not excluded.

Indeed, even if such an assumption were true, judging by the notice in *Nile's Weekly Register* the Philadelphia publication was not the original at all, but merely a reprint of material from the English press, which in turn came from the

---

*N. N. Bolkhovitinov, *Stanovlenie russko-amerikanskikh otnoshenii, 1775–1815* (Moscow, 1966).

‡*Nile's Weekly Register* (Baltimore), 18 December 1824, p. 245. This notice actually began with the interesting observation that "The important political events that have taken place in South America, have given a new impulse to inquiries into its resources and history."

§Winifred Gregory ed., *American Newspapers, 1821–1936: A Union List of Files Available in the United States and Canada* (New York, 1937).

pages of the Parisian press. The circle, it seems, has been closed: a Hamburg journal published an article taken from an American publication, which, it turns out, reprinted it from European papers. In any event, it was necessary, albeit approximately, to establish the article's date of publication.

Considering the short distance between Baltimore and Philadelphia, there is every reason to assume that the notice in the Baltimore weekly, even with the means of communication of the day, could have appeared a few days after the article in the Philadelphia paper. The average duration of the transatlantic crossing from Europe to America at that time was from thirty to forty days. Consequently, one could with every certainty expect to find the sought-after item in the European press for October–November 1824. To be certain, it would seem well to include also September and August.

An examination of the principal English and French newspapers available in our libraries for these months (there are at least a dozen) took a great deal of time, but failed to produce the desired results. True, the search proved not entirely fruitless: it permitted me to elucidate certain material circumstances which are mentioned below. However, not a trace was uncovered of the article in question.

Now it remained only to await the microfilm of the *Philadelphia Gazette* for the second half of 1824, which had been ordered from the United States, and, maintaining a cautious optimism, hope for success. Almost half a year passed before the arrival of the long-awaited microfilm. In the paper of 5 November was an article entitled "Paraguay," more extensive than the notice in *Nile's Weekly Register,* but still considerably shorter than the text published in *Politisches Journal.* This meant that it, too, could not have served as the source for the Hamburg paper. However, beneath the title of this article was written something, which, perhaps, would provide the key to the solution: "From the London *Morning Chronicle.*" And there was no mention of the report in the Parisian press cited by the Baltimore weekly.

But neither the Lenin State Library, nor the Saltykov-Shchedrin Public Library, nor the library of the Institute of Marxism-Leninism, nor the Fundamental Library of Social Sciences, nor any other book repositories in Moscow or Leningrad had the *Morning Chronicle* for the period in question. Was it really necessary to order a microfilm copy from England? In despair, I consulted with specialists in nineteenth-century English history, but they could tell me nothing encouraging. All the same, E. B. Cherniak advised me, just to be sure, to try my luck in one more place.

Excitedly, I climbed the stairs of a two-story building on Bol'shaia Pirogovskaia Street, which houses the foreign periodicals collection of the former Russian Ministry of Foreign Affairs. At long last luck was with me: among the various foreign papers here was found a complete run of the *Morning Chronicle* for 1824. Impatiently I turned the yellowing pages. October... September... 23 August.... There it was: a lengthy, unsigned article about

Paraguay. Yes, this was undoubtedly the same one which was published in translation in *Politisches Journal*. It coincided completely, including even editorial comments.

And thus, the original source was found. It turns out that the text which Bestuzhev translated was itself not the original, but rather a German translation of material from the *Morning Chronicle*. But who was the author of this article and how did it get into the London press?

To find the answer, might it not prove helpful to consult another, likewise anonymous work with the very long title of *A Narrative of Facts Connected with the Change Effected in the Political Condition and Relations of Paraguay under the Direction of Dr. Thomas Francia . . .*, published in London a short time later, in November 1826?[16] It figures in the bibliographies of several works on the history of Paraguay (by English historian P. H. Box, Paraguayans Julio César Chaves and Efraím Cardozo, etc.), although for some reason none of the authors cite it in their texts.

To run this small pamphlet down, however, proved to be exceedingly difficult. As was to be expected, it could not be found in the holdings of our libraries. Moreover, it did not appear even in the catalogs of the principal book repositories of England, including the London Library and the British Museum. No wonder that the majority of historians who have studied the Francia dictatorship have failed altogether to mention this pamphlet! Subsequently, I discovered that this publication, now a bibliographic rarity, was among the holdings of the Library of Congress, in Washington, where, on my request, an order was placed for a microfilm copy.

Months passed, an entire year went by, and still the film was not sent. There is no way of knowing how long this might have dragged on had it not again been for a fortuitous circumstance. On 3 September 1968, the director of the Hispanic Foundation of the Library of Congress and prominent American historian, Professor Howard F. Cline, visited the Institute of History, having come to the USSR on an invitation from the Presidium of the Academy of Sciences. When in conversation with him I related how I had been unable to secure a microfilm copy of the pamphlet in which I was interested, he promised to help. In less than a month, a Xerox copy of the pamphlet was on my desk.[17]

An examination of the pamphlet showed that the author was certainly familiar with the article in the *Morning Chronicle* and that he had made extensive use of that article: the first part of the pamphlet (pp. 7–20) was based on specific data contained in the newspaper account. However, the subsequent text and general tone of this piece reveals that the authors of the two compositions were different individuals. Whereas the newspaper article gave a most favorable account of Francia and his policies and praised the order which he had instituted, there was none of this in the pamphlet. The latter described Francia as a disciple and faithful follower of the Jesuits, seeking to restore the situation which existed in the Jesuit *reducciones* of the seventeenth and eighteenth centuries.

The second half of the pamphlet represents a compilation of wild and preposterous fabrications concerning Francia (to whom was imputed an attempted secret accord with the Spanish monarchy and Portuguese court, and even a willingness to help restore Spanish rule on the American continent), and also the internal political situation in the Paraguayan republic. The appearance in the press of these truly fantastic reports was in all likelihood connected with the activities and declarations of a certain Spanish adventurer and imposter, who in the mid-1820s presented himself at various European courts as the Marquis of Guaraní, special emissary of Francia.[18]

Although this pamphlet was published anonymously, the copy held by the Library of Congress has an autograph which would appear to establish the author's identity. On the title page, in a clear calligraphic hand in Spanish, is written: "From the author to Mr. Berry. Ch. B. Mansfield, London, 1853, 24 April." This signature led Professor Cline to conclude that the author of the pamphlet was Ch. B. Mansfield, and he so wrote in his letter accompanying the Xerox copy of the pamphlet.

Just who was Ch. B. Mansfield? This would be most important to determine. In the multivolume Oxford Biographical Dictionary (vol. XII)* it states that Charles Blackford Mansfield, a chemist and author, visited Paraguay and that his travel notes were published posthumously in 1856. He was not born, however, until 1819, and he made his trip to Paraguay in 1852–53, while the pamphlet appeared in 1826. A reading of Mansfield's book *Paraguay, Brazil and the Plate*[19] clarified nothing. It contains only a description of Paraguay in the early 1850s. In the text there is no mention of the 1826 pamphlet. Moreover, the title of the pamphlet does not even figure in a letter by Mansfield of 15 April 1854 which is quoted in the foreword to his book and wherein existing publications on Paraguayan history are listed. This confirms once again that Mansfield had nothing to do with the pamphlet.

How, then, does one explain the autographed dedication? Apparently it was merely a joke or prank. On 17 April 1853, only a week before the date of the signature, Mansfield returned from a prolonged trip to Paraguay, a country theretofore rarely visited by Englishmen. On encountering some friend or acquaintance soon after, he gave him as a souvenir the pamphlet printed a quarter-century before, and, inasmuch as it had been published anonymously, signed it in jest as if he himself were the author.

But if the author was not Mansfield (and clearly it was not), then who was it? Might not some clue be found in *El Repertorio Americano,* a Spanish-language

Dictionary of National Biography, 22 vols. (London: Oxford University Press, 1921–22).

journal published in London from October 1826 through August 1827 (precisely the period in which the pamphlet appeared) by the renowned Venezuelan states-man and writer, Andrés Bello? Since the journal treated the widest range of subjects relating to South America, it was not inconceivable that its pages might contain comments on this publication. We in fact were able to determine that in April 1827, *El Repertorio Americano* published a review by Bello which briefly discussed the contents of the pamphlet. As for its authorship, the reviewer wrote, "Although the author presents himself incognito, it is not difficult to recognize him from the particulars which he provides about himself in the first pages."[20]

Turning back to the text, we find mention that the author spent his childhood near the majestic Illimani (the Cordillera Real of the central Andes, thirty-two kilometers distant from La Paz); that the vicissitudes of life and the love of liberty which he was unable to enjoy in his homeland took him to various South Ameri-can countries enveloped by the revolutionary movement; and that he had lived in Cuzco, the River Plate, Brazil, France, Spain, Portugal, the United States and England. The author declares that the fates of peoples ought not to rest with individuals, yet in various regions of America small groups of people usurped power and abused it with impunity. He underscores the fact that little had yet been done to improve the lot of the native population. As seen from the text, the author knew Aymará and Quechua.

Based on this information, it follows that the anonymous author of the pam-phlet was apparently of Indian origin and a native of La Paz (Upper Peru until 1825, thereafter the Republic of Bolivia) or the immediate area, that he spent time in several American and European countries, that he took part in the wars of independence in several of Spain's South American colonies, and that he was of democratic persuasions.

These particulars fit in every respect the biography of a prominent figure of the independence movement in South America, the Bolivian publicist and diplomat Vicente Pazos Kanki, who in 1825 settled in London. He was a pure-blooded Aymará Indian born in a village near La Paz. (In his *Historico-Political Memoirs*, published in 1834, he mentions Illimani specifically.) Pazos Kanki received his schooling in Cuzco, and on the eve of the wars of independence set out on a trip through the Platine provinces. The "May Revolution" of 1810 found him in Buenos Aires, where he joined the radical wing of patriots headed by [Mariano] Moreno.

The conservative victory obliged Pazos Kanki to emigrate in 1812, but in 1816 he again returned to Buenos Aires, where he published a republican newspaper in whose pages he resolutely opposed the supporters of monarchy. At the same time, he advocated the idea of unifying the entire territory of the former viceroyalty of the River Plate, including Paraguay, into a single state. An inten-sification of the political struggle forced him to quit Buenos Aires a second time in 1819. Pazos Kanki went to the United States, and then to Europe. He spent time in Spain, Portugal, and France, finally settling in England.

Thus, there is every reason to consider Vicente Pazos Kanki the author of the pamphlet *A Narrative of Facts*. This is the view, in particular, of the contemporary Paraguayan historians Julio César Chaves and Efraím Cardozo, although they offer no arguments in support of their view.[21]

A determination of the name of the author of the anonymous pamphlet is, of course, important in itself, but unfortunately, it brings us no closer to the object of our search, namely a clarification of who wrote the article in the *Morning Chronicle*. Could the key to the solution lie in a careful analysis of the article itself?

A close examination of the article shows that the unknown author was well informed about the situation in Paraguay, drawing either on personal observations or on the testimony of eyewitnesses. He presents a number of facts not to be found in the available literature. The article not only gives a most positive appraisal of Francia and his regime, but the author is obviously inclined to speak on behalf of both. Judging by all the evidence, this was a man who in the period of the Francia dictatorship (at least until late 1823 or early 1824) lived in Paraguay or in any event had contact with the country through someone there.

Given Paraguay's strict isolation from the outside world, those with some possibility of sending or receiving information were literally few. The number of foreigners in the country was not more than forty, all of whom were under the watchful eye of the Paraguayan authorities. Moreover, from 1819, when the Frenchman Pierre Saguier was expelled from the country, until May 1825, Francia did not allow a single foreigner to leave Paraguay. One might, of course, suppose that somebody managed secretly to send out information on the situation in the republic, but it is difficult to imagine that those whom the dictator held in Paraguay by force would be sympathetic to Francia and his regime. Even Rengger and Longchamp, who did note positive aspects of Francia's rule, were generally rather critical.

Of the foreign diplomats who during these years had occasional contact with the Paraguayan government must be mentioned, above all, the British Consul General in Buenos Aires, Woodbine Parish. On his initiative, a special committee was formed (including the leading English merchants of Buenos Aires), which in July 1824 prepared a report on the state of trade in the River Plate. A special section of this document was devoted to Paraguay. That same month, Parish petitioned Francia to allow Englishmen to leave Paraguay. But the consul's attitude toward Francia was exceedingly hostile. On 30 July 1824, he wrote the British Minister of Foreign Affairs [George] Canning that he fully concurred with the opinions expressed in the aforementioned report, which spoke of Francia's despotism. Parish went on to describe Francia as a tyrant who was establishing a reign of brutality and arbitrary rule without equal in history.[22] An article extolling Francia, therefore, could not possibly have originated with him.

The only diplomatic representative to visit Paraguay in the mid-1820s was Antônio Manoel Correia da Câmara, who, on 31 May 1824, was named Brazilian consul and commercial agent in Asunción. But he arrived in Itapúa only in June of the following year and was not officially received by Francia in the Paraguayan capital until 27 August. Thus, his arrival in the country belongs to a period later than that in which the article in question was published.

From December 1823 through March 1824, in the city of Corrientes, near the Paraguayan border, Juan García Cossío, a representative of the government of Buenos Aires, awaited permission to go to Asunción. His repeated requests to Francia produced no results, however, and, having received no reply to any of his messages, he was obliged to return to Buenos Aires.

In connection with the captivity of Bonpland, the Institut de France, supported by Foreign Minister Viscount Chateaubriand, sent the naturalist Richard de Grandsir to South America to try to persuade Francia to release the prominent French scholar. He arrived in Itapúa in August 1824, and from there wrote to Francia requesting permission to go to Asunción. Receiving the normal refusal, he left Paraguay in mid-September without even seeing Bonpland. Thus this brief visit, too, occurred after the article had been published.

Perhaps the only foreigner who, because of his familiarity with the area and his personal relations with Francia, could in principle be the author of this article was Bonpland himself. Placed by the Paraguayans in the village of Santa María, sixty leagues to the southeast of Asunción (the Paraguayan league is over four kilometers), he soon settled on a nearby hill called Cerrito. Here he farmed, studied the local vegetation, and treated the Indian sick, with medicines he himself prepared. Later he ran a distillery, a woodworking shop, and a sawmill, producing goods which once a week he took to Itapúa to sell.

Though Bonpland was a victim of Francia's arbitrary rule, by his will cut off for many years from the outside world, it is nonetheless not strange that he felt no hatred toward the dictator, later speaking of him and his own stay in Paraguay with moderation. Recalling a meeting with the scholar in May 1832, slightly more than a year after Bonpland's departure from Paraguay, W. P. Robertson, who was exceedingly ill-disposed toward Francia, wrote, "Mr. Bonpland left Paraguay without any ill feelings toward Francia, which quite naturally might have been aroused by the latter's actions, and spoke of him with philosophical detachment, only lamenting again and again the fact that there was no chance of receiving the dictator's permission to return to Paraguay."[23] Writing about his stay in Paraguay in a letter to the botanist [Alire Raffeneau-] Delile, Bonpland noted, "I am as happy and full of life as when you knew me in Navarre and Malmaison."[24] With satisfaction he wrote Humboldt that he had had the opportunity to study personally over a long period of time the splendid flora of Paraguay.[25]

It would seem that for a man of his constitution, totally absorbed in science and far removed from politics, a forced stay in a country where he could occupy himself with interesting scientific research while enjoying the universal respect of those around him did not represent a great hardship. As for his separation from loved ones, it must not be forgotten that Bonpland's family life had been a failure, and that he was divorced from his wife in 1820. Upon leaving Paraguay, the scholar had no desire to return to Europe and lived to the end of his days in South America, which for him had become a second homeland.

Nonetheless, the suggestion that Bonpland wrote the article raises serious objections. First, the article contains details and statistical data which, in the absence of newspapers and books, could hardly be known to someone living in the backwoods, far from urban centers and without freedom of movement. Second, how could Bonpland have sent this information abroad if the first person to leave Paraguay during his stay in the country was Grandsir, who, as already pointed out, left three weeks after the article was published?

The latter question is crucial in the event there was possibly some other author, for it is clear that the article was written either by an eyewitness or on the basis of information received directly from Paraguay. Meanwhile, there is a curious fact in the article which may possibly explain how this material reached the English press. It is stated that two Paraguayan vessels were dispatched to England with a cargo of goods and a special emissary for the purpose of establishing political and trade relations. If this report is true, and the ships indeed reached their destination, it sheds light on the circumstances in which information on Paraguay appeared in the London paper.

It must be said that revolutionary developments in Latin America were discussed widely and in great detail in the European press of the 1820s. They attracted special interest in England, where, in conjunction with the changing tide of events in favor of the American patriots, the urge to recognize the independence of the newly-established states of the Western Hemisphere was growing noticeably. British consuls were sent to Buenos Aires, Montevideo, Bogotá, Mexico, and other cities in late 1823 and early 1824. One after another Latin American representatives began to arrive in London. During the year 1824, England prepared to recognize Mexico, Colombia, and Buenos Aires, which it did on 31 December. In these circumstances, the English press paid great attention to the situation in Latin America. Reports of the latest news from the area were published daily by almost all of the leading papers. Their pages regularly carried extensive reports from correspondents in Buenos Aires, Montevideo, Rio de Janeiro, Pernambuco, Lima, Quito, Caracas, Bogotá, Mexico, Havana, and elsewhere.

Against this background, the absence over several years of any newspaper accounts about Paraguay is particularly striking, although interest in this distant country was substantial in Europe and grew still more (albeit considerably later) when the arrest of Bonpland became known. But suddenly the prolonged silence was broken. On 21 August 1824, the *Morning Chronicle* carried a brief editorial note which reported that "Mr. Bonpland, the illustrious botanist and companion of Humboldt, still remains a prisoner in Paraguay, where he was detained over two years ago." This notice was reprinted by many London, Parisian, and other European papers.

On 23 August, the *Morning Chronicle* published the above-mentioned article on Paraguay[26] with a note which indicated specifically that the material from which this information had been taken was in the possession of the editors, in consequence of which the latter vouched for its authenticity. The following day, the London correspondent of the Augsburg *Allgemeine Zeitung* reported the arrival of the two Paraguayan vessels and the emissary mentioned above.[27] True, on 27 August he stated that this report had not been confirmed, for no information had been made available on the arrival of the vessels from Paraguay, nor did they even figure in the famous *Lloyd's Register*.[28] But before a month had passed, the Parisian *Journal de Débats* printed a report from London dated 18 September on the arrival there of two ships loaded with goods direct from the Paraguayan capital of Asunción. A week later, this report was published in the *Allgemeine Zeitung* as well.

From the foregoing it follows that in August 1824 the Paraguayan merchant vessels arrived in London, and with them the representative of the Francia government for talks on the establishment of economic and other relations with England. Publication of the article in the *Morning Chronicle* undoubtedly was connected with the arrival of these vessels: apparently, some passenger either brought a prepared text or gave an interview to one of the paper's correspondents. The latter is unlikely, since the article does not impress one as an extemporaneous composition, but rather a carefully prepared piece written out beforehand.

Such an impression is created not only by the fact that the text contains figures and other factual data which would be difficult to commit to memory, but also by the very nature of the account, which has a clear, definite objective: to convince the reader that Paraguay is a "marvellous garden" and a "New World Arcadia." Describing its natural riches, the fertility of its soil, its splendid climate, and the industriousness and honesty of the population, the author characterizes the order established in the Paraguayan republic under its ruler as a model of just and rational social organization that guarantees universal equality and well-being, political stability, and the economic prosperity of the country. He stresses that trade with Paraguay promised extensive profits.

Who, precisely, could have written such a panegyrical article? Neither Bonpland nor any other foreigner in Paraguay could have done so. In the first place, they did not know about the dispatch of ships to Europe. Even Rengger and Longchamp, who enjoyed far more freedom of movement than Bonpland and who had access to the "supreme dictator," failed to mention this fact in their memoirs.

In all probability, the author was either Francia himself, or someone in his confidence, or a person acting on behalf of the Paraguayan government (perhaps the emissary sent to England, whose name is not known to us). In this regard, on publishing an abbreviated text of the article, the *Philadelphia Gazette* observed that "the preceding report undoubtedly originated with a representative from Paraguay."[29] Considering that Francia encountered no manifestations of independence even on the part of higher functionaries, who merely did his bidding, it is most likely that he personally wrote or dictated, or at the very least, went through and edited this text.

To what degree is the factual material contained in the article accurate? It is rather difficult to answer this question, since in essence the only direct evidence from eyewitnesses which could be used for comparison and verification is the essay by Rengger and Longchamp, who remained in Paraguay from July 1819 through May 1825. Written considerably later, in the 1860s, and based primarily on the oral accounts and recollections of several surviving contemporaries of Francia, the books by [Charles A.] Washburn, U.S. envoy to Asunción, and [Francisco] Wisner, a Paraguayan army engineer (who also had access to pertinent archival documents), add very little to the information reported by the Swiss physicians.[30] It is true that Grandsir mentioned several details in his letters and in an interview upon his return from Paraguay, but this data is very scanty and fragmentary.

A number of facts contained in this article are confirmed, either directly or indirectly, by other sources. Moreover, Rengger and Longchamp, as well as Grandsir, note certain positive features of the Francia regime which are not discussed in the article. But several statements made by the author of the article obviously do not correspond to reality. Thus, the indication that the territory of Paraguay was divided into six departments contradicts the data of Rengger and Longchamp, according to which the country was divided into twenty administrative districts. In addition, Concepción and Villarreal are cited as departments, although they were one and the same city, known at that time as Villa Real de la Concepción (this mistake may have been made by the translator). Also incorrect is the assertion that Francia had freed the slaves, for the law abolishing slavery and prohibiting the slave trade was not proclaimed in Paraguay until after the dictator's death, in 1842. The estimates of population and of the Paraguayan armed forces differ substantially from figures now available.

At the same time, the article contains highly important information for an understanding of the Francia regime; information generally lacking in other sources. In particular, it discusses the existence of a popularly elected state council and the conduct of the elections, the complete legal equality of the citizenry, Francia's publication of a provisional code of laws, the elected nature of all officials from top to bottom and the lack of remuneration for their services, the efforts of the Paraguayan government to initiate political and economic relations with the countries of Europe, the creation of state trading companies in the provinces for the purpose of stimulating foreign trade, the conversion of former Jesuit property into farms, the accumulation of large sums of money in the Paraguayan treasury, and so on.

Of course, other authors, too, might well have known these facts, yet chosen, for one reason or another, to keep them quiet. It must not be forgotten, however, that in sending a trade mission to Europe, Francia was extremely interested in creating a more favorable image of Paraguay overseas. The attempt made in the article to depict the country's situation in the most glowing terms, obviously embellishing reality, compels one to admit the possibiltiy of direct deviations from the truth dictated by a desire to play on the tastes and political sympathies of the European public. To what degree the factual material contained in the article is accurate, therefore, remains an open question.

Despite the widespread view, however, that from the early 1820s on Francia pursued a consistent and unswerving policy of complete isolation, it is undeniable that the "supreme dictator" realized the negative consequences of such a course. He understood perfectly that trade with Brazil alone was insufficient to satisfy even the minimal needs of Paraguay. In seeking a way out of this difficult situation, Francia decided to attempt to secure trade and also diplomatic relations with the most developed state of that time—England. It might be mentioned that this idea had first occurred to him considerably earlier. Back in 1814, while serving as consul of the Paraguayan republic, Francia had asked the Scottish merchant [John Parish] Robertson, who at the time was preparing to leave for England, to convey to the British parliament in his name a proposal for establishing trade ties and exchanging diplomatic representatives between the two countries, and also various samples of Paraguayan products.[31] But circumstances obliged Robertson to postpone his departure until 1817. He never carried out the commission which Francia had given him.

In 1824–25, in conditions of Paraguay's forced isolation from the neighboring states, Francia urgently sought "to cut open a window to Europe." A major step in this direction was the dispatch of the special mission to England in the first half (presumably in April or May) of 1824. The products it took were intended to demonstrate clearly the possible assortment of Paraguayan exports, while the article on the situation in Paraguay aimed at propagandistic ends. This mission was by no means accidental. It was part of a preconceived political campaign, as evidenced by several other actions of the Francia government in pursuit of analogous objectives.

Thus, in response to the petition of the British consul in Buenos Aires, Parish, that all Englishmen held in Paraguay be permitted to leave the country, on 26 January 1825 the Paraguayan Secretary of State, [Bernardino] Villamayor, promised that such permission would be granted. At the same time, he declared his government's desire to establish trade and consular relations with England.[32] On 25 May of that year, sixteen English merchants, together with the Swiss Rengger and Longchamp, and a French captain by the name of Hervaud, sailed from Asunción for Buenos Aires. This was an obvious gesture of good will toward England.

We are unaware of the concrete results of the mission that Francia sent to London, but the efforts to establish ties with England were not crowned with success. The only channel which permitted the Paraguayans to associate, albeit minimally, with the outside world continued to be through Brazil. Having spent several months in Asunción, Correia da Câmara left for Rio de Janeiro at the end of 1825 to obtain instructions, but his return was delayed. War had broken out between Brazil and the United Provinces of the River Plate (Argentina). In conjunction with a Brazilian proposal for a joint invasion of Corrientes in 1827, Francia began to fear additional attempts by Brazil to draw Paraguay into its sphere of influence. Therefore, when Correia da Câmara again arrived in Itapúa in September 1827, this time as chargé d'affaires, he did not receive permission to travel to Asunción.

Violation of the Paraguayan border by the Brazilians in the course of the war with Argentina (1828) further aggravated relations between the two states and soon led to a complete break: in June 1829, the Brazilian representative was expelled from Itapúa. The country's isolation was thus total.

It may be, in this regard, that Francia, who previously had failed to respond to the numerous petitions to free Bonpland, decided to release him in order to deny those who manifested concern for the scholar's fate grounds for holding talks with the Paraguayan authorities. In May 1829, Bonpland was ordered to go to Itapúa, and in mid-January 1831, was allowed to leave the country. No sooner had he set foot on the territory of the province of Corrientes than his horses were stolen. "It was immediately apparent," Bonpland wrote in his diary, "that we were no longer in Paraguay."[33]

The body of material on the history of Paraguay in the years of the Francia dictatorship is extremely limited. For this reason, the article published almost a century and a half ago in a London newspaper and which all this time has gone unnoticed by scholars concerned with this problem unquestionably warrants serious attention. All the evidence, of course, indicates that this document is extremely subjective in nature and accordingly requires careful verification and critical analysis. But it undoubtedly contains valuable and previously unknown information, which, together with the very fact and circumstances of its appearance in the press, make it possible to introduce essential correctives into the interpretation of an important period of Paraguayan history.

NOTES

1 A part of this territory lying to the northeast of the region between the Paraná and Uruguay rivers belonged nominally at the time to Paraguay, but in reality the authority of the Paraguayan government did not extend that far. In practice, the southern and southeastern borders of the Paraguayan republic ran along the Paraná.

2 Due to Napoleon's invasion of Portugal, the Portuguese court resided in the capital of Brazil, Rio de Janeiro, from 1808 to 1821.

3 "O noveishei istorii i nyneshnem sostoianii Yuzhnoi Ameriki. I. Paragvai," *Syn Otechestva* 100, no. 7 (1825), 264–79.

4 I. M. Trotskii, "Debkabrist N. A. Bestuzhev i Severnoe obshchestvo," in N. A. Bestuzhev, *Stat'i i pis'ma* (Moscow and Leningrad, 1933), p. 43.

5 L. A. Lebedeva, "Literaturnaia deiatel'nost' dekabrista N. A. Bestuzheva" (candidates's thesis, Leningrad, 1948), pp. 63–64; M. K. Azadovskii, "Memuary Bestuzhevykh kak istoricheskii i literaturnyi pamiatnik," in *Vospominaniia Bestuzhevykh* (Moscow and Leningrad, 1951), p. 607; S. S. Volk, "Dekabristy o burzhuaznom Zapade," *IAN* (Seriia istorii i filosofii) 8, no. 1 (1951), 79; idem, *Istoricheskie vzgliady dekabristov* (Moscow and Leningrad, 1958), pp. 279–80; M. Yu. Baranovskaia, *Dekabrist Nikolai Bestuzhev* (Moscow, 1954), pp. 30–32; N. M. Lebedev, "Otrasl' Ryleeva v Severnom obshchestve dekabristov," in *Ocherki iz istorii dvizheniia dekabristov* (Moscow, 1954), pp. 337, 350 ff.

6 E. E. Boborykina, "Dekabrist N. Bestuzhev" (candidate's thesis, Leningrad, 1955), pp. 226, 234, 240.

7 R. Kh. Yakhin, *Politicheskie i pravovye vzgliady dekabristov Severnogo obshchestva* (Kazan, 1964), p. 276.

8 Boborykina, "Dekabrist N. Bestuzhev," pp. 238–40.

9 It has also attracted the attention of Soviet historians of Latin America. See V. Miroshevskii, "Khose-Gaspar Fransia—vozhd' paragvaiskoi revoliutsionnoi demokratii (1814–1840)" [José Gaspar Francia—leader of Paraguayan revolutionary democracy (1814–1840)], *Vop. Ist.*, no. 4 (1946), 76, 81; N. R. Matveeva, "Paragvai i Paragvaiskaia voina 1864–1870 godov i politika inostrannykh derzhav na La-Plate" [Paraguay and the Paraguayan War of 1864–1870 and the policies of foreign powers in the River Plate] (candidate's thesis, Moscow, 1951), pp. xiii, 27, 33–34, 39, 42, 46; L. Yu. Slëzkin, *Rossiia i voina za nezavisimost' v Ispanskoi Amerike,†* pp. 344–46; L. A. Shur, *Rossiia i Latinskaia Amerika,†* pp. 58–60.

10 See I. M. Trotskii, "Dekabrist N. A. Bestuzhev: Severnoe obshchestvo," pp. 42, 303; G. E. Pavlova, "Dekabrist N. A. Bestuzhev" (candidate's thesis, Leningrad, 1952), pp. 216–20.

11 Boborykina, "Dekabrist N. Bestuzhev," p. 225.

12 Volk, "Dekabristy o burzhuaznom Zapade," pp. 279–80.

13 Syn Otechestva 100, no. 7 (1825), 279.

14 "Paraguay (Aus Amerikanischen Blattern)," Politisches Journal, no. 2 (1825), 108–21.

15 Ibid., p. 118.

16 A Narrative of Facts Connected with the Change Effected in the Political Condition and Relations of Paraguay, under the Direction of Dr. Thomas Francia, by an Individual Who Witnessed Many of Them and Obtained Authentic Information Respecting the Rest (London, 1826).

17 I wish to take this occasion to express by sincere gratitude to Dr. Howard F. Cline for his kind assistance.

18 See [Johann Rudolph] Rengger and [Marcelin] Longchamps, Essai historique sur la révolution du Paraguay, et le gouvernement dictatorial du docteur Francia (Paris, 1827), pp. xvii–xxi; Julio César Chaves, El Supremo Dictador (Buenos Aires, 1958), pp. 298–302; Efraím Cardozo, Paraguay independiente (Barcelona, 1949), p. 76; Peter Adolf Schmitt, Paraguay und Europa: Die diplomatischen Beziehungen unter Carlos Antonio López und Francisco Solano López (Berlin, 1963), pp. 16–17.

19 Charles B. Mansfield, Paraguay, Brazil and the Plate (Cambridge, 1856).

20 Andrés Bello, Obras completas, vol. XIX (Caracas, 1957), p. 487.

21 Chaves, El Supremo Dictador, pp. 301, 454; Cardozo, Paraguay independiente, p. 78.

22 Woodbine Parish, Buenos Aires and the Provinces of the Río de la Plata, 2nd ed. (London 1852), pp. 264–65. (The first edition appeared in 1839.)

23 J. P. and W. P. Robertson, Letters on Paraguay: Comprising an Account of a Four Years' Residence in that Republic, under the Government of the Dictator Francia, 3 vols. (London, 1838–39), III, 289.

24 Cited in W. Schulz, "Aimé Bonpland," Akademie der Wissenschaften und der Literatur: Abhandlungen der Mathematisch-Naturwissenshaftlichen Klasse, no. 9 (1960), 610–11.

25 René Bouvier and Édouard Maynail, Aimé Bonpland: Explorateur de l'Amazonie, botaniste de la Malmaison, planteur en Argentine, 1773–1858 (Paris, 1950), p. 156.

26 It aroused interest in other European countries and overseas, as evidenced by its publication in German translation in Politisches Journal (February 1825) and Allgemeine Zeitung (14–15 December 1825), in Russian translation in Syn Otechestva, and in an abbreviated form in the U.S. press.

27 Allgemeine Zeitung, 4 September 1824.

28 Ibid., 8 September 1824.

29 Philadelphia Gazette and Daily Advertiser, 5 November 1824.

30 Charles A. Washburn, The History of Paraguay, with Notes of Personal Observations, and Reminiscences of Diplomacy under Difficulties, 2 vols. (Boston and New York, 1871); Francisco Wisner, El dictador del Paraguay, José Gaspar de Francia, 2nd ed. (Buenos Aires, 1957).

31 Robertson, *Letters on Paraguay,* II, 279–85.
32 Chaves, *El Supremo Dictador,* pp. 294–95.
33 Atilio García Mellid, *Proceso a los falsificadores de la historia del Paraguay,* 2 vols. (Buenos Aires, 1963–64), I, 203.

11 THE ARCHIVE OF THE G. I. LANGSDORF EXPEDITION TO BRAZIL (1821–29)

B. N. KOMISSAROV

IN AUGUST 1811, Alexander I issued a decree establishing, "for the benefit of trade," a consulate general in Rio de Janeiro.[1] The first Russian consul in the Brazilian capital was M. I. Labenskii, who previously had occupied an analogous post in Paris. By the fall of 1812, however, academician Grigorii Ivanovich Langsdorf [Georg Heinrich von Langsdorff] had already been named to replace him. The interests of the new consul, a well-known naturalist and traveler, extended far beyond the limits of his official duties, and on 13 June 1821, while in St. Petersburg, he proposed to the Russian Minister of Foreign Affairs, K. V. Nesselrode [Count Karl Robert von Nesselrode], the organization of a major Russian expedition to the interior regions of Brazil. At that time, this little-studied country was attracting the attention of numerous European researchers. In the early nineteenth century alone it was visited by Maximilian von Wied Neuwied, Johann Baptist von Spix and Karl Friedrich von Martius, Johann Pohl and Johann Natterer, Auguste de Saint-Hilaire, Henry Koster, and others. Langsdorf's project received the approval of the tsarist government and funds were authorized for the journey.

The expedition's organizer led an unusual life. He was born in April 1774 in the small town of Wöllstein, in southwestern Germany. In 1797, he received the degree of doctor of medicine from the University of Göttingen, then lived in Portugal, and, in 1803–05, took part in the round-the-world expedition of I. F. Kruzenshtern and Yu. F. Lisianskii. During the voyage, Lansdorf visited the Brazilian island of Santa Catarina. This visit made a great impression on the young scholar and to a large extent determined his future interests. In March

Originally published as "Arkhiv ekspeditsii G. I. Langsdorfa v Braziliiu †(1821–1829)," in Grigulevich et al., eds., *Ot Aliaski do Ognennoi Zemli,*† pp. 275–85.

1808, he returned to St. Petersburg overland across Siberia and for several years lived in Russia, studying the natural sciences and preparing for publication the description of his travels, which appeared in 1812.[2] That same year, only a few months before being named to the post in Rio de Janeiro, Langsdorf was elected a member of the St. Petersburg Academy of Sciences.

In the years 1813–21, Langsdorf traveled a great deal in Brazil, established ties with European researchers working there[3] and with representatives of the Brazilian administration,* and reported regularly to the Conference of the Academy of Sciences in St. Petersburg on his findings and observations. The scholar's name soon became well known in Brazil.[4] Once placed in charge of the Russian expedition, Langsdorf began actively to implement the plans which had already formed in his mind for a comprehensive study of Brazil's natural history, population, and economy.

In its breadth of conception, its participants, and its extensive provisioning, this scientific enterprise was unusual for its time. Langsdorf's companions were the botanist Lüdwig Riedel; the zoologists E. P. Ménétrie and, later, Christian Hasse; the astronomer and Russian naval officer N. G. Rubtsov; an assistant, Georg Wilhelm Freyreiss; and the artists Johann M. Rugendas and, after 1825, Hercules Florence and Amado Adrien Taunay.

From 1821 through the first half of 1825, the participants in this expedition worked primarily in the provinces of Rio de Janeiro and Minas Gerais, turning next to the exploration of the country's central regions. In the years 1825–28, they followed rivers and undertook long overland marches, investigating the provinces of São Paulo, Mato Grosso, Pará, and adjoining territories. In the spring of 1828, while moving down the Arinos and Juruena rivers, many of the travelers fell ill with a tropical fever. Langsdorf's illness soon took the form of mental disorder and the expedition was terminated. In 1829–30, Rubtsov and Riedel brought the collections gathered by the expedition to Russia. They were distributed among various museums and reading rooms of the Academy of Sciences. In 1831, Langsdorf retired, settling in the great duchy of Baden, in Freiburg (Breisgau).

The scholar's grave ailment prevented him from organizing the materials collected during the trip and from writing up the results of his many years of observations in Brazil. The expedition's archive, which reached St. Petersburg along with the other collections, soon disappeared without a trace and for almost a hundred years was thought to have been lost. The detailed accounts which throughout the expedition Langsdorf sent to the Ministry of Foreign Affairs and the St. Petersburg Academy of Sciences likewise failed to become widely known. The accounts addressed to Nesselrode, in the Ministry of Foreign Affairs, were never published, while of the letters to the Academy of Sciences only

*Most notably, with Dom Pedro's minister of state, José Bonifácio de Andrade.

one ever appeared in print; it was dated April 1827 and related the trip from Pôrto Feliz, on the Tietê River, to Cuiabá.[5] It might be noted, too, that in 1825 an extract of a letter from Langsdorf to his father in which the scholar tells of his plans to explore Brazil was published in *Severnyi arkhiv*.[6] Additional scattered materials on the expedition and Langsdorf's activities in South America published in the pages of *Sank-Peterburgskie Vedomosti, Moskovskii Telegraf,* and other periodicals are little more than empty chronological notices.[7] Thus, Russian readers who followed the course of the expedition in that distant and exotic country received rather scanty news about it.

Of works by expedition participants, Freyreiss' Brazilian notes and an album of Rugendas' drawings were published in Germany and France in the 1820s and '30s. Freyreiss began working under Langsdorf's direction in 1813, and in 1815–17 explored the central regions of Brazil together with Maximilian von Wied Neuwied. His participation in the Russian expedition of 1821–29 was quite brief, however, and therefore the above-mentioned notes relate only indirectly to that expedition.[8] The masterfully executed drawings of Rugendas depicted the Brazilian landscape and the daily life and customs of the Indians, Negroes, and descendants of the Portuguese conquerors. The artist's album stimulated great interest in Europe and was reprinted a number of times.[9]

Langsdorf died in Freiburg, in June 1852. Although the scholar had lived in extreme seclusion after returning from Brazil, his death did not pass unnoticed. Obituaries recounting his life and travels were published in Russia, Germany, and France.[10] In Russia, there was one further passing mention of the expedition in *Morskoi Sbornik,* published in connection with the death of Rugendas in 1858.[11]

In the 1870s, A. V. Freigang, a vice-admiral and writer, became interested in the history of foreigners who had rendered service in Russia. It is interesting to note that, while the admiral was of German origin, he was an ardent Slavophile,[12] and looked upon the activities of foreigners precisely in these terms. Turning to Langsdorf's biography, he thought to include it in a series of essays devoted to exposing "the innumerable foreign vampires who . . . unceremoniously had exploited the fatherland in the good old days,"[13] to which end he began to collect materials. Freigang's work was based on a few dispatches he found from Langsdorf to Nesselrode, in which the scholar, rendering account of work accomplished, requests funds needed to continue his travels. Unaware of the expedition's archive and not having familiarized himself with the collections it contained, Freigang wrote an article depicting Langsdorf as a swindler who for years had cheated the Russian government. This article never came out, although apparently it reached the hands of the typesetter, for its edges are soiled with typographic ink.

In Freigang's view, the biography of G. I. Langsdorf ought to be followed by an essay about the well-known adventurist Georg Scheffer, who in 1815–17 attempted to extend the influence of the Russian-American Company to the Hawaiian Islands. After Freigang's death in 1880, his papers were acquired by N. Ya. Voskoboinikov,[14] who began to write an article entitled, "Scheffer and Langsdorf."[15] Voskoboinikov probably did not finish this article, and it was never published.

Following the 1858 mention in *Morskoi Sbornik* down to the beginning of the twentieth century, rarely if ever did Langsdorf's name appear in the Russian press as leader of the expedition to Brazil. At the end of the nineteenth century, meanwhile, research and publications on the history and materials of the Langsdorf expedition were undertaken in Brazil and Germany. In 1875–76, Brazilian historian Alfredo Taunay, nephew of Afonso Taunay, published a Portuguese translation from the French of the diary of Hercules Florence.[16] To the diary's text he added an introductory article, which, despite a number of serious inaccuracies, nonetheless summarized a variety of data on the course of the expedition and its participants. Since then, this diary has been used repeatedly in works on the ethnography of Brazil. In Germany, a short article on Langsdorf by F. Ratzel appeared in 1886, another by K. Gödeke in 1898, and the following year the journal *Globus* carried an interesting study by the well-known German traveler and ethnographer K. von den Steinen on the drawings of Florence, a portion of which had come into the scholar's possession.[17] In 1911, the Swiss researcher H. Ten Kate published an interesting article on artists who had traveled in South America and left sketches of an ethnographic nature.[18] In this study, much space was devoted to Rugendas and Florence. In 1912, Ten Kate's article was included in the proceedings of the Seventeenth International Congress of Americanists, published in Buenos Aires.[19]

An article on Langsdorf was included in volume ten of the *Russian Biographical Dictionary* [Russkii biograficheskii slovar'], which came out in 1914. Not a word is said in the article about the expedition to Brazil, however. By the second decade of the twentieth century, it seems, the very fact had been completely forgotten.

The history of this journey attracted attention unexpectedly. K. K. Gil'zen, head of the Central and South American department of the Academy's Anthropological and Ethnographic Museum, discovered a large number of objects—some totally unidentified, some marked with the name "Langsdorff"—unknown to him. He related the discovery of the mysterious objects to G. G. Manizer, a young ethnographer closely tied to the museum, who was studying there under the direction of Professor L. Ya. Shternberg, but at the time, he, too, found them a riddle.

In April 1914, Manizer went to South America as part of a Russian scientific expedition, and, in February of the following year, had occasion to work in the Museu Nacional in Rio de Janeiro. Here the scholar noticed that objects collected among the Indians of the Mundurucu tribe were very similar to the exhibits shown him by Gil'zen, and for the first time he heard of Langsdorf's journey.

Immediately following his return home, Manizer began an intensive search for materials relating to the forgotten expedition. Gil'zen, who had undertaken an ethnographic study of some of the Indian tribes visited by Langsdorf and his companions, also became interested in the history of the expedition.[20] But at the beginning of 1917 he abandoned his intention of writing a biography of Langsdorf and turned his materials over to Manizer, who received a proposal from academician V. V. Radlov, director of the Museum of Anthropology and Ethnography, to begin work on a book about the first Russian expedition to Brazil.[21]

Manizer based his study on the Brazilian edition of Florence's diary. He also used N. G. Rubtsov's manuscript "Astronomical Observations," part of Langsdorf's correspondence, drawings by the expedition's artists, and the collections gathered by the travelers. He completed the envisioned book in the spring of 1917. Later that year he died of typhus on the Rumanian front, at age twenty-eight. The work of this talented scholar on the Langsdorf expedition was not published at the time and was consigned to the archives of the Academy of Sciences.[22] It was not forgotten, however. Papers were read and articles written based on the materials which it contained.

In the 1920s, the Soviet ethnographer and linguist V. G. Bogoraz-Tan undertook to study the drawings of Florence, Taunay, and Rugendas.[23] In 1926, he read a paper at the Twenty-Second International Congress of Americanists in Rome on Russian expeditions to South America, in which he also recounted the Langsdorf expedition.[24] In 1928, I. D. Strel'nikov, a companion of Manizer's on the journey to South America, reported on the Langsdorf expedition at the Twenty-Third International Congress of Americanists.[25]

In 1930, the archives of the USSR Academy of Sciences began to take stock of its holdings and to centralize archival materials located in various academic institutions. That same year, in one of the cabinets of the Botanical Museum, among pasteboard containers of dried plant specimens, L. B. Modzalevskii, an archival assistant, discovered the large, splendidly preserved archive of the Langsdorf expedition, which immediately attracted the attention of the scientific community.[26]

In the early 1930s, this archive was studied by N. G. Shprintsin, who began her scientific career under the direction of V. G. Bogoraz-Tan and L. Ya. Shternberg. She undertook the complicated and laborious task of systematizing and describing the newly discovered materials, which constituted an entire collection. Included in this collection were Langsdorf's extensive diaries for the years 1824–1828, an unknown copy of Florence's diary, and the completed works of the expedition's participants, as well as various of their notes, outlines, and bibliographic annotations. The collection contains ample materials bearing on history, ethnography, economics, statistics, economic geography, and Indian languages. There are copies which Langsdorf made in Brazilian archives of documents relating to the mining of useful minerals, the construction of the first factories, economic policy, and the status of the Indians; there are statistical tables that give an idea of the numerical strength and the social and racial composition of the populace in various cities and provinces, and also of foreign commerce; there are notes on trade and agriculture, documents on Brazil's struggle for independence, dictionaries of Indian languages, records on folklore, and many other materials. Also of interest is Langsdorf's vast correspondence for the years 1824–28.

In 1935, Shprintsin read a paper on the Langsdorf expedition at the Institute of the History of Sciences and Technology of the USSR Academy of Sciences.[27] At the same time, she began to ready G. G. Manizer's work for publication. The scholar related the results of her work in an article entitled ''The expedition of G. I. Langsdorf to Brazil in the first quarter of the nineteenth century.''[28] This article not only set forth briefly the contents of the Manizer manuscript and provided information on the study of the expedition, but also showed the place of the expedition in the history of research on the life and ways of the Indian tribes of Brazil. Publication of Manizer's book, however, was not realized until 1948.[29] With its appearance, information about the expedition became available to a wide circle of scholars—ethnographers, historians, geographers. In addition to a biography of Langsdorf and an essay on the history of his expedition, Manizer's book contained an introductory article and detailed commentary by Shprintsin.

In studying the archive of the Langsdorf expedition, and also the materials collected by Manizer and his companions in 1914–15, Shprintsin raised for the first time (1947) the question of the importance of using Russian sources for the study of the ethnography and history of the Latin American countries,[30] while two years later, in an article entitled ''The status of the Indians and Negroes of Brazil (as recorded by Russian expeditions),'' she demonstrated the value of such sources, which were based on concrete material.[31] Shprintsin also initiated the scholarly publication of materials from the expedition's archive. In 1936, she published one of Florence's manuscripts, and in succeeding years excerpts from Langsdorf's diaries concerning the Guato and Apiaka Indians.[32] Even a cursory acquaintance with these diaries in German makes clear that much work is required to render them intelligible. Langsdorf's handwriting is extraordinarily illegible. He wrote with the most varied inks, both in quality and color; he used Gothic script, abbreviated words, ran letters together, and inserted words in Portuguese, Latin, and French. Credit for initially organizing the deciphering of Langsdorf's manuscripts belongs to Shprintsin. This work was begun in 1936 by V. A. Egorov, and at the present time is being continued by M. V. Krutikova.

In 1952, in connection with the one-hundredth anniversary of Langsdorf's death, Shprintsin presented a paper on the expedition at a meeting of the Department of the History of Geographical Knowledge of the Geographic Society of the USSR,[33] following which she published a new article about the expedition.[34] In her paper, she gave a breakdown of expedition materials; in the article, she related their significance for the study of the history and ethnography of Brazil.

In 1953, Shprintsin discovered in the Leningrad section of the Archives of the USSR Academy of Sciences an anonymous manuscript entitled, "Langsdorf's Journey to South America in the 1820s," and suggested that this was the diary of N. G. Rubtsov.[35] A more detailed investigation of the manuscript confirmed Shprintsin's hypothesis about the author, but this proved not to be a diary, but rather an account written in the early 1830s following the traveler's return to Russia, apparently on the basis of travel notes.[36]

In the late fifties and early sixties, Shprintsin turned her attention to the study of linguistic materials collected by the expedition.[37] Several of her works remain unpublished and are currently housed in the Leningrad section of the Archives of the USSR Academy of Sciences.[38]

V. F. Gnucheva, O. K. Vasil'eva-Shvede, V. L. Nekrasova and A. V. Prusak have also written about the expedition's archive and its history.[39] The Langsdorf expedition is mentioned in works on the history of Brazil, the history of geographic exploration, and Russo-Latin American relations.[40]

A major effort has been undertaken in recent years to uncover new materials bearing on the history of the Langsdorf expedition. Unknown documents have been found in the Russian Foreign Policy Archives, the Central State Historical Archives of the USSR, and other archival repositories. Not long ago, the geographer A. I. Alekseev ascertained that the Central State Archives of the Navy of the USSR has among its holdings twenty-eight maps of the expedition's routes and eight colored plans of Brazilian cities, ports, and manufactories compiled and drawn by N. G. Rubtsov.[41] Also uncovered there were documents on the life and work of this traveler. Finds have sometimes been made in the most unexpected places. Thus, in the mid-forties the natural historian A. E. Gaisinovich purchased a manuscript in one of Moscow's antiquarian bookshops, which turned out to be the travel diary of E. P. Ménétrie.[42]

Since the Second World War, and even before, the materials of the Langsdorf expedition have attracted the attention of researchers from various countries, especially Brazil.[43] They have had an opportunity to familiarize themselves with the contents of the expedition's archive through translations of Shprintsin's articles.[44] In addition, in 1956 the well-known Soviet geographer S. V. Kalesnik gave Brazilian scholars photocopies of individual pages from Langsdorf's diary at the Eithteenth International Geographical Congress in Rio de Janeiro. Through the collaboration of Afonso Taunay, Florence's journal record, first published in 1875–76, has been reprinted several times in São Paulo. These editions have been illustrated with many of the artist's famous drawings.[45] A whole series of writings on Rugendas' artwork has come out in Brazil, Mexico, and the Federal Republic of Germany.[46] The primary source for these writings has been the artist's more than three thousand works, purchased in 1848 by the King of Bavaria, Lüdwig I, most of which are today housed in libraries and museums of the FRG. Among them are many drawings made by Rugendas during the Langsdorf expedition.

Recently, there has been growing Brazilian interest in the archives of this Russian expedition. During a visit to Leningrad in 1963 Professor Clemente Maria da Silva-Nigra, the well-known Brazilian ethnographer and historian, was able to familiarize himself with this archive. He noted the great value of the materials of the Langsdorf expedition for the study of his country's past. In the Brazilian press, an article has appeared on "the discovery of Brazil in Russian archives."[47]

At the present time, the USSR Academy of Sciences is preparing a complete edition of the materials of the Langsdorf expedition, which will make it possible for specialists in various fields of knowledge to subject them to full investigation. This is an undertaking of major scientific significance. An important aspect of this undertaking is the study of the materials of the Langsdorf expedition as a source for the socio-economic history of Brazil in the first third of the nineteenth century.* Also worthy of further study—initially begun by Shprintsin—are the ethnographic materials collected by the travelers, which provide abundant information on the life and ways of the Brazilian populace in towns large and small, on the *fazenda* estates, and in the gold and diamond fields, and on the status and culture of a number of Indian tribes, many of which have now either been annihilated or assimilated. Worthy of the attention of linguists are numerous dictionaries of Indian languages. In our view, the expedition's archive is also of considerable interest from the viewpoint of the history of geography, for the travels of Langsdorf and his companions represent one of the stages of the continuing process of man's opening up of the Brazilian Highlands and the Amazon Lowlands. Finally, the expedition's archive is of primary significance for treating the history of Latin American studies in Russia. The study and publication of the results of the years-long activity of the first Russian expedition to Brazil is an important task of Soviet Latin Americanists.

---

*A suggestive step in this direction was taken recently by Komissarov and a colleague. See B. N. Komissarov and S. L. Tret'iakov, "Materialy po statistike naseleniia Brazilii pervoi chetverti XIX v. v arkhive ekspeditsii G. I. Langsdorfa" [Statistical materials on the population of early nineteenth-century Brazil in the archive of the G. I. Langsdorf expedition], in V. K. Furaev, B. N. Komissarov, and K. B. Vinogradov, eds., *Issledovaniia po novoi i noveishei istorii* [Research in modern and contemporary history], festschrift in honor of V. G. Revunenkov (Leningrad, 1972), pp. 17–30. See also, in this vein, B. N. Komissarov, "Brazil'skaia fazenda pervoi treti XIX veka v dnevnikakh G. I. Langsdorfa i na kartakh N. G. Rubtsova" [The Brazilian *fazenda* of the first third of the nineteenth century in the journals of G. I. Langsdorf and the maps of N. G. Rubstov], *VLU*, vyp. 2, no. 8 (1969), 62–70.

NOTES

1 Tsentral'nyi gosudarstvennyi istoricheskii arkhiv SSSR [Central State Historical Archives of the USSR, hereafter cited as TsGIA SSSR], fond 1329, opis' 3, delo 310, fol. 78.

2 Georg Heinrich von Langsdorff, *Bemerkungen auf einer Reise um die Welt in den Jahren 1803 bis 1807*, 2 vols. (Frankfurt-am-Main, 1812).

3 J. B. von Spix and C. F. P. von Martius, *Reise in Brasilien in den Jahren 1817 bis 1820*, 3 vols. (Munich, 1823–31), I, 150, 158, 176; Auguste de Saint-Hilaire, *Voyages dans l'intérieur du Brésil*, 8 vols. Paris, 1830–51), I, 51, 129, 137, 225.

4 L. Bourdon, *Lettres familières et fragment du journal intime de Ferdinand Denis à Bahia (1816–1819)* (Coimbra, 1957), pp. 73, 80.

5 "Noveishie otkrytiia v Brazilii: Izvlechenie iz pis'ma G. Langsdorfa: Kuiba, glavnyi gorod provintsii Matto-Grosso, 7 aprelia 1827 g.," *Severnyi arkhiv* 31 (1828), 371–77; *St. Petersburgische Zeitung*, 29 June 1828.

6 Excerpt from a letter by Langsdorf to his father, in *Severnyi Arkhiv* 18 (1825), 405–7.

7 *Sankt-Peterburgskie vedomosti*, 11 June 1818, 29 November 1818; *Moskovskii telegraf*, pt. 4, no. 14 (1825), 178. See also *Revue encyclopédique* (Paris) 16 (1822), 199.

8 G. W. Freyreiss, *Beiträge zur naheren Kenntnis des Kaiserthus Brasilien, nebst einer Schilderung der neuen Kolonie Lepoldina* (Frankfurt, 1824).

9 Moritz Rugendas, *Die malerische Reise in Brasilien und Voyage pittoresque dans le Brésil* (Paris and Muhlhausen, 1827–35); idem, *Das Merkwurdigste aus der malerischen Reise in Brasilien von Moritz Rugendas* (Schaffhausen, 1836).

10 *Morskoi sbornik* 8, no. 9 (1852), 254–55; "Notice necrologique sur le baron George-Henri de Langsdorff . . . ," *Extrait de écrologe universel du XIX siècle* (Paris, 1853), etc.

11 *Morskoi sbornik* 37, no. 9 (1858), 89–90.

12 See, for example, letters to him from I. S. Aksakov, P. I. Bartenev, and A. F. Gil'ferding, Leningrad Branch of the Archives of the USSR Academy of Sciences (hereafter cited as LOAAN), fond 220, opis' 5, nos. 12, 13, 16.

13 A. V. Freigang, "Georg Heinrich von Langsdorff," LOAAN, razriad IV, *opis'* 1, no. 1012, fol. 15.

14 *Novoe vremia*, no. 6794 (1895).

15 N. Ya. Voskoboinikov, "Scheffer and Langsdorff," LOAAN, razriad IV, *opis'* 1, no. 1012, fols. 1–14.

16 "Esboço da viagem feita pelo Sr. do Langsdorff no interior do Brasil, desde Setembro de 1825 até Março de 1829 escripto em original francez pelo 2⁰ desenhista de Commissão científica Hercules Florence, traduzido por Alfredo d'Escragnolle Taunay," *Revista Trimestral do Instituto Histórico, Geográphico e Ethnográphico do Brasil*, vol. 38 pt. 1 (1875), pp. 355–469; pt. 2, pp. 231–301; pt. 3, vol. 39 (1876), pp. 157–82.

17 *Allgemeine Deutsche Bibliographie*, vol. 17 (Leipzig, 1886), pp. 689–90; *Grundriss zur Geschichte der deutschen Dichtung*, no. 6, vol. 7, bk. I (Leipzig, Dresden, and Berlin, 1898); K. von den Steinen, "Indianertypen von Hercules Florence," *Globus* 75 (1899), 5–9, 30–35.

18 H. Ten Kate, "Sur quelques peintures-ethnographes dans l'Amérique du Sud," *L'Antropologie* 22 (1911), 15–35.

19 *Actas del XVII Congreso Internacional de Americanistas* (Buenos Aires, 1912), pp. 568–95.

20 K. K. Gil'zen, "Chelovecheskaia golova, kak voennyi trofei u indeitsev plemeni munduruku," *SMAE* (Petrograd) 5 (1919); LOAAN, fond 46, opis' 1, no. 83.

21 LOAAN, fond 142, opis' 1 (to 1918), no. 71, fols, 37–38; fond 46, opis' 1, no. 84, fols, 1–2.

22 LOAAN, razriad IV, opis' 1, no. 645.

23 W. Bogoras, "Langsdorff expedition to Brazil: A series of drawings by Florence, Taunay and Rugendas," LOAAN, fond 250, opis' 1, no. 109.

24 Idem, "Le Centième Anniversaire des expéditions russes a l'Amérique du Sud," in *Atti del XXII Congresso Internazionale degli Americanisti*, vol. II (Rome, 1928), pp. 607–17.

25 I. D. Strel'nikov, "Russkaia ekspeditsiia v Braziliiu akademika Langsdorfa (1821–1829)," *Priroda*, no. 1 (1929), 43–54; idem, "The Expedition of G. I. Langsdorff to Brazil in 1821–1829," in *Proceedings of the Twenty-Third International Congress of Americanists* (New York, 1930), pp. 751–59.

26 *Vestnik AN SSSR*, no. 2 (1931), 52–53; "Arkhiv Akademii nauk SSSR: Obozrenie arkhivnykh materialov," *Trudy Arkhiva Akademii nauk SSSR* (Leningrad), vyp. 1 (1933), 94.

27 LOAAN, razriad V, opis' L-6, no. 8.

28 N. G. Shprintsin, "Ekspeditsiia akademika G. I. Langsdorfa v Braziliiu v pervoi chetverti XIX veka," *SE*, no. 1 (1936), 109–20.

29 G. G. Manizer, *Ekspeditsiia akademika G. I. Langsdorfa v Braziliiu (1821–1828)* (Moscow, 1948).

30 N. G. Shprintsin, "Materialy russkikh ekspeditsii v Yuzhniuiu Ameriku, khraniashchiesia v Arkhive AN SSSR i Institute etnografii," *SE*, no. 2 (1947), 187–94.

31 Idem, "Polozhenie indeitsev i negrov v Brazilii," *Kratkie soobshcheniia Insituta etnografii AN SSSR*, vyp. 7 (1949), 62–69.

32 Idem, "Zhivopisnoe opisanie puteshestviia iz Portu Felis v Kuiaba G. Floransa," *SE*, no. 6 (1936), 104–10; N. G. Shprintsin and M. V. Krutikova, "Indeitsy guato," *IVGO* 75, vyp. 5 (1948), 500–506; N. G. Shprintsin, "Indeitsy apiaka (Iz materialov pervoi russkoi ekspeditsii v Yuzhnuiu Ameriku)," *Kratkie soobscheniia Instituta etnografii AN SSSR*, vyp. 10 (1950), 84–96.

33 LOAAN, razriad IV, opis' 69, no. 8. See also *IVGO* 85, vyp. 5 (1952), 526–27.

34 N. G. Shprintsin, "Pervaia russkaia ekspeditsiia v Braziliiu," in I. P. Gerasimov et al., eds., *Voprosy geografii* (Moscow and Leningrad, 1956), pp. 344–49.

35 Ibid., p. 346.

36 B. N. Komissarov, "Novyi istochnik po istorii i etnografii Brazilii 20-kh XIX veka (Zapiski N. G. Rubtsova)," *SE*, no. 3 (1963), 172–76.

37 N. G. Shprintsin, "Iz arkhivnykh materialov po iazykam indeitsev Brazilii," *SE*, no. 3 (1964), 139–40.

38 LOAAN, razriad opis' 69, nos. 3, 7, 10.

39 V. F. Gnucheva, comp., "Materialy dlia istorii ekspeditsii Akademii nauk v XVIII i XIX vv.," *Trudy Arkhiva AN SSSR* (Moscow and Leningrad), vyp. 4 (1940), 167–71; O. K. Vasil'eva-Shvede, "Lingvisticheskie materialy russkoi ekspeditsii v

Braziliiu 1821–1829 gg.," *Nauchnyi biulleten' LGU*, nos. 14–15 (1947), 36–42; V. L. Nekrasova and A. V. Prussak, "K istorii brazil'skogo filiala S.-Peterburgskogo botanicheskogo sada (1831–1836 gg.) i brazil'skikh kollektsii Langsdorfa i Ridelia," *Botanicheskii zhurnàl*, no. 5 (1957), 804–13.

40 V. I. Ermolaev et al., eds., *Ocherki istorii Braziliï*†; I. P. Magidovich, *Istoriia otkrytiia i issledovaniia Tsentral'noi i Yuzhoi Ameriki*†; L. A. Shur, *Rossiia i Latinskaia Amerika*†; etc.

41 A. I. Alekseev and B. N. Komissarov, "N. G. Rubtsov i ego rol' v issledovanii Brazilii," *IVGO* 97, vyp. 6 (1966), 500–506.

42 At the present time, this manuscript is in the private archive of A. E. Gaisinovich, in Moscow.

43 Pedro Calmon, "Do Tietê ao Amazonas," *O Cruzeiro* (25 August 1962), 86; Boris Schnaiderman, "Caminhos de compreensão," *O Estado do São Paulo* (7 July 1962).

44 N. G. Chprintsine, "A primeira expedição russa ao Brasil," *Boletim Paulista de Geografia*, no. 28 (1958), 70–77.

45 See, for example, Hercules Florence, *Viagem fluvial do Tietê ao Amazonas de 1825 a 1829* (São Paulo, 1941). On the materials of H. Florence housed in foreign repositories and the study of these materials, see foreword to this volume by Afonso Taunay and Atalib Florence.

46 F. Hernández Serrano, "Juan Moritz Rugendas y su colección de pinturas costumbristas," *AINAH* (Mexico) 2 (1947), 463–72; G. Richert, *Johann Moritz Rugendas: Ein Deutscher Maler in Ibero-Amerika* (Munich, 1952); D. James, "Rugendas no Brasil: Obras inéditas," *Revista do patrimonio histórico e artístico nacional* (Rio De Janeiro), no. 3 (1956), 9–16; E. Núñez, "America in Paint and Charcoal: German Artist Rugendas' Record of His Travels," *Américas* 12, no. 11 (November 1960), 10–15.

47 O. Tavares, "Redescoberta nos arquivos da Rússia do Brasil," published in *Diario de Notícias* (Salvador, 16 May 1965) and *O Cruzeiro* (19 December 1964), 95–102.

12 ROMANTICISM AND POSITIVISM IN LATIN AMERICA: A RESPONSE TO LEOPOLDO ZEA

A. F. SHUL'GOVSKII

THE PATRIOTIC vanguard of Latin America is struggling tenaciously to defend the national culture and the economic, political, and spiritual independence of its peoples. Much space in the works of progressive scholars is given over to the study of the origins and development of national self-consciousness, of culture, and of progressive, freedom-loving traditions. In this regard, one's attention is drawn to the works of the prominent Mexican philosopher Leopoldo Zea. The principal works of this Mexican philosopher are dedicated to a study of the history of social and philosophical thought in Latin America and to problems of Latin American culture. In recent years, Zea has written works on the philosophy of history and on Latin America's place in the general development of world culture. Worthy of special note are the following: *The Rise and Fall of Positivism in Mexico*,[1] *Two Stages in the Development of Thought in Hispanic America*,[2] *America as Conscience*,[3] *From Liberalism to Revolution in Mexican Education*,[4] and *America in History*.[5] The works of Leopoldo Zea attract attention and interest for their broad, well-selected sources and extensive factual content. Zea's books are permeated with a spirit of democracy, love, and esteem for the progressive thinkers and representatives of national culture. The Mexican philosopher consistently speaks out as a confirmed partisan of an independent Latin American culture and a heightened national consciousness for the countries of Latin America. This explains Leopoldo Zea's great respect for the cultures and spiritual make-up of the peoples of other countries, including Russia. In one of his latest works, *America in History*, Zea resolutely dissociates himself from the currently popular theory of the existence of isolated and supposedly antagonistic Eastern and Western cultures. The equality of all cultures, the enrichment and

Originally published as "Romantizm i pozitivizm v Latinskoi Amerike: Otvet na stat'iu Leopol'do Sea," *VIMK*, no. 4 (July–August 1960), 3–19.

development of world culture with the appearance of new states in Asia, Africa, and Latin America—this is the basic idea in Zea's works.

The general outlines of Leopoldo Zea's views were clearly expressed in an article of his published recently in the Soviet Union.* The reader of this article will note that Leopoldo Zea's views differ widely from Marxism, for they rest on different ideological and methodological principles. For Leopoldo Zea, the key to the study of the history of ideological currents is the history of ideas themselves, their self-generation and filiation. Zea explains all the peculiarities of the development of philosophical ideas in Latin America in terms of the Hegelian dialectic, of the nature of solving dialectical contradictions in the sphere of self-generating ideas. It is precisely ideas, in Zea's view, that determine the particular approach of given social forces to the problems of Latin American reality. In other words, ideas are the principal moving force for or obstacle to (depending on the circumstances) the development of the Latin American countries. True, Leopoldo Zea speaks—and this is seen in the above-mentioned article—of the struggle of different social forces and of their differing economic interests, but for him these forces are important above all as bearers of certain ideological principles, for once again ideas act as the initial cause. In the present article, we wish to express our view on the questions raised by Leopoldo Zea, namely, the role of progressive ideas in the Spanish colonies' war of independence, the essence of the view of the romantics, and the reasons for the spread of positivist ideology in Latin America.

Let us begin with the causes and nature of the war of independence. In the war of emancipation of the peoples of the Spanish American colonies, a major role was played by progressive democratic ideas, ideas of the great French Revolution and of those who fought for the liberation of the English colonies in North America. Yet, however great the role played by these ideas, the necessity of independence lay not in them but in the very socio-economic conditions of Latin American reality. The development of local forces of production, attempts by various social groups to secure independence, the growth of a national consciousness—all these led to a clash with the oppression of the Spanish colonialists and represented the principal and decisive cause of the war of independence.[6] A prominent Latin American Marxist, the Peruvian José Carlos Mariátegui, characterized the causes of the war of independence with great perception:

> The ideas of the French Revolution and the North American Constitution encountered a climate favorable to their dissemination in South America, for in South America there already existed, albeit in embryo, a bourgeoisie which, because of its needs and economic interests, could not but embrace the revolutionary mood of the European bourgeoisie. . . . Viewed from the perspective of world history, South American inde-

*Leopoldo Zea, "Ot romantizma k pozitivizmu v Latinskoi Amerike" [From romanticism to positivism in Latin America], *VIMK*, no. 3 (May–June 1960), 12–26.

pendence is seen to have been produced by the developmental needs of Western or, more precisely, capitalist civilization. The function of the capitalist impulse in the elaboration of independence was less apparent and ostensible, but without a doubt more decisive and profound than the echo of philosophy and the literature of the encyclopedists.[7]

The struggle for independence was at bottom popular in nature. Simón Bolívar (1783–1830) and José de San Martín (1778–1850), the leading figures of emancipation, understood well that a successful struggle must rest on mass support. Bolívar promulgated laws abolishing Negro slavery and providing land to the peasants of the Llanos, and took some steps to improve the lot of the Indian population. San Martín built his army on democratic principles, introducing into its ranks Negro slaves and Indians. It was precisely these popular patriotic armies who, through great feats of heroism, proved decisive in defeating the professional troops of the Spanish empire. The war of independence was of a national and progressive character and in its course partially achieved the objectives of a bourgeois revolution. At the same time, one must remember that the privileged classes of Latin America (the large landholders and the upper echelons of the Catholic clergy, who also possessed vast landed wealth), while they began increasingly to seek separation from Spain, nonetheless endeavored by every means possible to narrow the aims of the struggle and not infrequently colluded with the colonialists in fear of popular actions. Such was the case, for example, at the time of the popular anti-Spanish uprising headed by the national hero of Mexico, the parish priest Miguel Hidalgo y Costilla (1753–1811).

In Argentina, conservative forces greatly hindered the activities of the first patriotic junta, formed in May 1810 in Buenos Aires. A prominent role in the first junta was played by Mariano Moreno (1778–1811), an attorney, a representative of the radical democratic wing of the independence movement, and an advocate of the most progressive ideas of his time. The reactionaries attacked him, calling him a Jacobin and an iconoclast. But despite all attempts by the reactionaries to divest the May revolution in Argentina of its progressive content, the traditions of May inspired the following generation of Argentines to struggle for democracy and progress.

In 1826, after bloody and bitter fighting, Latin America gained its independence. Somewhat apart is the case of Brazil, where independence was achieved peacefully and where, in contrast to the other countries, a monarchy was declared. But even here independence was the result of irreconcilable contradictions between the mother country (Portugal) and the colony. The trials of the young Latin American states, however, did not end here. The new republics were torn by internal conflicts, civil strife, and the struggles of various factions. The internal conflicts led to the collapse of state formations—for example, Gran Colombia, founded by Bolívar—the emergence of smaller states, and the self-isolation of the new countries. Thus in Paraguay power was for many years held by the dictator José Gaspar Francia, who closed the country off from the outside world with a blank wall. Whatever "progress" the country made was enjoyed by a small minority of whites, while the great bulk of the population, non-white Indians, lived in ignorance and without civil rights. The example of Paraguay is indicative of the distorted ways in which Latin American countries occasionally developed.

At the same time, in the Argentina of the 1820s there came to power the progressive government of [Bernardino] Rivadavia, which, proclaiming "the need to accelerate the passage of time, to feel the pulse of the future in our time," sought to implement bourgeois-democratic reforms in the country, through collaboration with the progressive forces of Europe. But Rivadavia's reforms failed to embrace the entire country, and in point of fact were restricted to Buenos Aires, while the remainder of Argentina responded to the reformers with hostility. The main reason for this lay in the fact that in Argentina, as in the other countries of Latin America, the socio-economic structure did not undergo radical changes. On the whole, large landholdings remained untouched and the position of the Catholic Church and the *latifundistas* was not undermined. Precisely these social forces sought to retard the development of the Latin American countries, to maintain the status quo. These same forces were the main obstacle to the realization of Bolívar's plans, endeavoring by every means to bring to naught Bolívar's progressive undertakings. All the subsequent history of Latin America takes place under the banner of struggle between the forces of progress and reaction. In the aforementioned article by Zea this struggle is treated as a clash of differing principles and differing forms of government. This is apparent from [Zea's] evaluation of Bolívar and Rivadavia, among others. This approach appears especially clear from [his] appraisal of the historical period immediately following the war of independence.

Soon after the conclusion of the war of independence, feudal-clerical reaction raised its head anew. In Argentina, the cattle rancher Juan Manuel de Rosas, supported by disgruntled rural cowhands (*gauchos*) and declassed elements from Buenos Aires, seized power in the city in the early 1830s and established a bloody dictatorship. The feudal elements who came to power destroyed the democratic institutions created by Rivadavia, throwing the country back to the times of the colonial regime. At the same time (1834), in Mexico a coalition of landowners, clerics, and militarists overthrew the liberal government of Gómez Farías and established the dictatorship of general Santa Ana. All progressive anticlerical reforms promulgated by the liberals were abrogated. In Chile, conservative forces came to power under the leadership of Diego Portales, who sought to "freeze" the democratic development of the country. Ecuador was ruled tyrannically by the clerical dictatorship of Gabriel García Moreno. The struggle of the liberals of Central America for the unification of the Central

American countries ended tragically. The leader of this struggle, general Francisco Morazán, was shot down in 1842 by order of the *latifundistas* and the clergy. The dictators of the Central American countries celebrated splendiferously this "glorious victory." And so it was in many other countries. Latin America was passing through terribly difficult years. It seemed that the forces of restoration and feudalism had completely destroyed the budding young democracy, wiping from the face of the earth all progressive reforms of government. The victors triumphantly declared that the "exotic plant" of democracy had been torn from the soil of Latin America by the roots, and that an era had begun of return to the traditional way of life, to true "Americanism."

The progressive forces of Latin America, however, continued the struggle. Precisely at this time a whole pleiad of prominent thinkers, statesmen, publicists, and writers openly opposed to the forces of restoration initiated their multifaceted, truly titanic activities. The Argentineans Domingo Faustino Sarmiento (1811–88), Juan Bautista Alberdi (1810–84), and Esteban Echeverría (1805–51), the Mexican José María Luis Mora (1794–1850), the Chileans José Victoriano Lastarria (1817–88) and Francisco Bilbao (1823–65), the Venezuelan Andrés Bello (1781–1865), and the Ecuadorian Juan Montalvo (1833–89) left an indelible mark on the history of Latin American social thought and literature. Closely tied to the progressive forces of the Latin American countries of the day, they devoted all their activity to the struggle for the progressive, democratic development of Latin America. These people can in no way be called abstract thinkers or creators of abstract, impractical solutions. It is sufficient to say that Sarmiento, that indefatigable, selfless toiler who spent many years in exile, was the creator of the progressive secular school in Argentina, for which he actively fought during his term as president of the republic. Mora was one of the guiding lights behind the progressive reforms instituted by the government of Gómez Farías. Andrés Bello, who for many years lived in Chile, contributed enormously to the creation of a [Chilean] national university and to the development of a national culture. Victoriano Lastarria is known not only as a prominent writer and thinker but also as a statesman (he more than once held ministerial posts) who sought to put into practice his ideas. Juan Montalvo employed all his talent as a writer and publicist in the struggle against the Moreno and Veintemilla dictatorships and for the triumph in his country of democracy. This generation of thinkers, looking to the future, inspired by the idea of rebuilding society, has been called the "romantic generation."

These progressive thinkers did not always hold identical views, and often there occurred heated arguments and debates among them (for example, Sarmiento's polemic with Bello and Alberdi). This was explained by the fact that among the forces for progress there existed various tendencies (more radical or more moderate), whence there occurred a struggle of ideas. But for us it is important in the present article to stress what in the overall historical perspective unites these leaders and reveals the common threads of their views. And what united them was above all the search for truth, for the way to the democratic development of the Latin American countries. How to surmount the backwardness of Latin America? What were the causes of chaos, anarchy, and backwardness? How to end this evil? These and other questions were raised by the generation of romantics, who passionately and honestly searched for their answers.

Emphasizing their faith in the transient nature of the triumph of reaction and polemicizing with the "Americanists," the "romantics" decisively and openly declared their fidelity to the traditions of those who fought for independence, whom they viewed as their predecessors and whose struggle had to be continued and promoted. "For us the only legitimate tradition, the only one which we should adopt, is the tradition of May"[8]—thus Esteban Echeverría formulated the position of the progressive forces of his time. Echeverría, Sarmiento, Alberdi, and others associated this tradition with the struggle between the forces of progress and reaction on a worldwide scale, with "Americanism" opposed to "Europeanism." In the words of Echeverría, the tradition of May "is nothing less than a remote result of the movement for human liberation which began in the fifteenth century and still continues."[9] Expressing these ideas in his own distinctive way, Sarmiento wrote of the struggle between civilization and barbarity, between Europe and America. This explains the popular expression "the struggle of civilization and barbarity" which was generally used to characterize the essential conflict of that period. Stressing this same idea in a paradoxical way, Alberdi declared: "The Republics of South America are the product and living testimony of Europe's action in America. What we call independent America is nothing more than Europe established in America."[10] Whatever form the concept of Europeanism took, it was above all a reflection of the position of the progressive forces of Latin American society, who identified their struggle with the movement for democratic reforms in Europe and fought against the reactionary theories of "American exclusiveness" propagated by feudal-clerical circles. The representatives of progressive thought concentrated all the inspiration of the struggle against feudal barbarism on the interpretation of Latin American reality so as to demonstrate that reactionary regimes were doomed. "With one eye," said Echeverría, "we shall follow the progress of other nations, and with the other we shall look inward at our society."[11] In the unique book *Facundo* (first published in 1845 under the title *Civilization and Barbarity in the Argentine Pampa*), another Argentinian, Sarmiento, offered a broad picture of Argentine society of that time in an effort to uncover the roots and causes of barbarism in the country and to substantiate the inevitability of the triumph of civilization. An analogous attempt to analyze Mexican reality was made by Mora, who compiled the fundamental three-volume work *Méjico y sus revoluciones* (the first edition appeared in 1836).[12]

In Sarmiento's book, much space is allotted to an explanation of the causes of the Rosas dictatorship. For Sarmiento, Rosas was not an isolated, accidental phenomenon, a monstrous aberration, and the dictatorship could not be terminated by curses and denunciations. Rosas was the result of the social conditions in which people lived, of the "barbarism" of the rural areas, which enveloped the cities and there destroyed democracy. Rosas' triumph is explained by the fact that the forces for progress, concentrated in the cities (Sarmiento looked with great respect upon the endeavors of Rivadavia, and openly acknowledged the historic significance of his progressive reforms), were unable to stand against the rest of the country, where barbarism ruled.[13] And for Sarmiento, as is seen from his book, barbarism was synonymous with feudal conditions of life, a legacy of the colonial era.[14] In order to end the dictatorship, it was necessary to combat backward forms of life, to destroy barbarism. And speaking of the growing popular discontent in the country, Sarmiento emphasized that the forces for this struggle indeed existed. He emphatically attacked the fatalistic view that opposition to Rosas was impossible, underscoring in every way possible the inevitability of the fall of tyranny and the triumph of democracy:[15] "Simply because the task is arduous, is it therefore absurd? Simply because an evil principle triumphs, must one resignedly relinquish one's position to it? Are civilization and liberty today weak in the world simply because Italy suffers all manner of despotisms and Poland wanders the earth begging a little bread and a little liberty?"[16] This was the answer Sarmiento gave the fatalists and the sceptics.

The idea of the necessity of progressive development is strikingly apparent in the works of Mora. Mora's great interest in the economic history of Mexico is characteristic. The book *Méjico y sus revoluciones* is based on extensive economic material which reconstructs a comprehensive picture of Mexican society in the colonial period and the first years of the country's independent existence. Mora disagrees with those who argue that social shocks are engendered by the acts of individual personalities. He emphasizes that the causes [of such shocks] must be sought not in the souls of people, not in special properties of the Mexican character, and not in the supposed natural disposition of Mexicans to anarchism, but rather in the objective state of things.[17] Revealing the causes of conflict between the partisans of progress and the representatives of the old order (in Mexico these corresponded to centralists and federalists), Mora stresses the economic and social basis of their struggle: the attempt to confiscate real estate from the clergy, abolishing their privileges and redistributing landed property, the dissemination of education among the populace, and the achievement of complete independence of education from control of the clergy, etc.[18] Mora is a firm believer in the inevitable triumph of progress and considers the state of social disorder and chaos to be transient. The conservative, regressive forces can only delay or retard the consolidation of a new order of things "which ultimately must come into being and which, in the light of the evolution of all known human societies, must always represent progress."[19]

This faith in the progressive development of the Latin American countries links Mora with another prominent representative of Latin American social thought, Andrés Bello. Polemicizing with the Spaniard [Martín Fernandez de] Navarrete, a representative of the traditionalist school who urged the countries of Latin America to repudiate "the false ideas of the French Revolution" and to return to "the bosom of Mother Spain," Bello emphatically rejected the assertion that the war of independence was a chance phenomenon introduced from abroad. Bello underscored that by no means did European ideas constitute the decisive cause of the Latin Americans' struggle. The cause of that struggle was "the inherent desire of every great society to govern its own affairs and not be subject to the laws of another society; a desire which, in the circumstances of America, had become an urgent necessity."[20]

For an understanding of Bello's views, his polemic with Victoriano Lastarria is characteristic. Combatting the "Spanish colonial legacy," the Chilean philosopher accused Spain of having followed an obscurantist policy which reduced the inhabitants of the colonies "to a pitiful state of insignificance." In essence, he renounced the study of the past and adopted a purely Enlightenment attitude of opposing one society to another as spokesmen of different ideas. Lastarria saw nothing instructive in the history of the colonial period. While in much he agreed with Lastarria and shared his progressive, democratic views, Bello at the same time noted that Lastarria's nihilistic view of history rendered meaningless all the heroism and self-sacrifice shown by the patriots in the struggle against Spanish rule.[21] Moreover, felt Bello, the study of history would help to discard various kinds of traditionalist conceptions of the well-being of the people under Spanish rule. Bello refuted such views by pointing out that repeatedly in the colonial period there occurred popular uprisings and rebellions among the Indian population.[22]

Of course, these Latin American thinkers remained idealists, seeing in the liberation of thought from the old reactionary concepts and ideas the moving force for the development of society. But Echeverría, Sarmiento, Mora, Bello, and others expressed profound, often brilliant conjectures about the governing laws of development in the Latin American countries and about the nature of the struggle between the forces of progress and reaction. One simply cannot agree with Leopoldo Zea's assertion that these thinkers viewed their principal goal as the "spiritual liberation" of the peoples of Latin America, as the "enlightenment" of these peoples. Their entire struggle shows rather convincingly that they understood their objectives much more broadly and deeply than one might think from a formal analysis of their conceptions. A struggle to transform reality—this was the principal goal of the generation of romantics.

Confidence in the progressive development of society united the generation of Echeverría, Sarmiento, Mora, and Bello in the faith that a democratic form of government was the only effective form for the Latin American countries, one capable of providing greatness and prosperity. No temporary failures could shake or weaken their faith. For the romantics, democracy was in no way a collection of abstract formulas, but rather an effective means of restructuring the entire life of the Latin American countries.[23] This trait of the romantics once again persuades us that Zea errs when he narrowly characterizes them as partisans of "enlightenment." Leopoldo Zea's point of view complicates efforts to expose and combat present-day falsifiers of the ideological legacy of the progressive figures of the past. The representatives of democratic thought have struggled to make the Latin American countries as strong and developed as the United States of America and the advanced countries of Europe, but in these countries they saw no models worthy of blind imitation, and, moreover, opposed bowing down to their strength and power.[24] The romantics attached great significance to the development of a national culture, which, absorbing all the best that other peoples had to offer, at the same time would draw its own force and vitality from Latin American reality. Speaking out against slavish submission to the culture of other countries, Andrés Bello noted that national problems ought to find expression in literature.[25]

Such an apparently passionate partisan of "European progress" as Alberdi emphasized in every way possible that the development of Latin America would be assured only if the Latin American countries addressed themselves to their own problems, refusing to submit to foreign powers and to copy their constitutions. It was time to put an end to fruitless scholastic debates, it was essential to work for the economic transformation of the Latin American countries—such was Alberdi's fundamental thought.[26]

It should be pointed out that it would be incorrect to consider as representatives of this generation the supporters of the Manchester school of liberalism, with their unrestrained utilitariansim and aspiration to wealth and profit. To a greater or lesser degree, all of the romantics thought in terms of the participation of the people in the development of the Latin American countries.[27] Some of them, above all Esteban Echeverría, openly expressed their sympathy for the workers. "Industry which does not tend to emancipate the masses and to elevate them to a state of equality, but rather concentrates wealth in a few hands, is to us repugnant."[28] Speaking of the grievous situation of the native Indian population of Ecuador, Juan Montalvo wrote: "If my pen were able to shed tears, I would write a book entitled 'The Indian' and cause the whole world to weep."[29] Victoriano Lastarria noted that a society occupied only with the accumulation of wealth has a weak foundation, and can easily degenerate into a despotism supported by bayonets. Addressing himself to the progressive intelligentsia, Lastarria asked that they sacrifice all for the good of the fatherland and the people, that they carry enlightenment to the masses. "Let us serve the people, let us illuminate their social development so that one day our children may see them happy, free, and strong."[30] A profound faith in the people and in their intelligence permeates the works of Mora; he considers that only the people, and not the privileged classes (the clergy, military, and *latifundistas*), constitute the repository of that intelligence which will bring progress to Mexico. For this reason Mora sought with such insistence the destruction of the monopoly held by the Catholic Church in education and the broadening by all means available of popular enlightenment.[31]

It would of course be a mistake not to see that, in the final analysis, the people did not represent for the romantics the decisive, moving force of social progress. Enlightenment, reforms from above—for them this was the answer. But the very fact that they sincerely endeavored to carry out reforms in the interests of all the people, and not for the mercenary interests of some particular social group, imparted to the ideas of the romantics a progressive, democratic character. The fact that frequently (for example, in Mexico) the objective result of the reforms did not correspond to the subjective wishes of the reformers is another matter, but this is explained above all by the correlation of social forces and the peculiarities of Latin America's historical development.

While fighting for the democratic, progressive development of their countries, these forward-looking people also showed themselves to be staunch patriots, giving worthy rebuke to the slanderous attempts to represent the peoples of Latin America as incapable of determining their own destiny. This was the time when the aggressive slave-holding interests of the United States of America unleashed a predatory war (1846–48) against Mexico, while later (1861–67) Mexico suffered an intervention by troops of the French emperor Napoleon III. And other European powers were not opposed to using the internal difficulties of the Latin American countries in order to establish their own domination. In 1847, that is, during the Mexican-American War, Mexican patriot Mora sharply criticized the predatory policy of the United States. He wrote that the United States represented a constant threat to Mexico and would seek to continue its expansion.[32] The indignation and apprehension aroused in the patriotic circles of Latin America by the aggressive acts of the United States is reflected in a statement of Francisco Bilbao, who declared that the United States was endeavoring to establish its dominion in Latin America, "swooping to the south." Addressing himself to a United States that was expanding into Latin America under the banner of "struggle against creole barbarity," Bilbao wrote that despite all difficulties, the Latin American countries had "eliminated slavery from all the republics of the south, and this we did—we, a poor people—while you, a happy and rich people, have not done so."[33] At about the same time, Lastarria attacked a treaty between Chile and the United States which he considered inequitable and an infringement on the national dignity of the country.[34] Lastarria subjected the aggressive policy of the empire of Napoleon III to savage criticism.[35] Speaking in the name of Latin American democracy, Lastarria declared that authoritarian, monarchist Europe threatened the freedom and independence of Latin America, seeking under the banner of struggle against "anarchy and chaos" to enslave it. Responding to the ideologues of aggression, Lastarria said that the struggle of the Latin American peoples was not "a fruitless struggle of passion, but rather represented the battle of right and justice against force and falsehood. The battle which today unfolds in independent America—its sufferings, all its sacrifices—points to the advent of a new form of life, to the triumph of light over darkness."[36] And this historical optimism, it seemed, found growing confirmation in the successful struggle of the progressive forces against feudal barbarism and tyranny.

In 1852, the Rosas dictatorship was overthrown in Argentina. The constitution adopted in 1853 carried the stamp of Alberdi's ideas, discussed in his book *Bases*. People came to power in the country who to a large extent shared liberal, progressive views. And, finally, in 1868, Sarmiento was elected to the post of president (he remained in power until 1874), and began a vast effort to reform popular education and to promote the economic development of the country. In Mexico in the 1850s the liberal party, headed by Benito Juárez and supported by the popular masses, carried on a revolutionary struggle against the reactionary forces headed by the clergy. The "Reform Laws" published at the end of the 1850s and beginning of the 1860s undermined the economic and political power of the Catholic Church—the principal stronghold of reaction in the country. The ideas of Mora and other ideologists of Mexican liberalism determined the basic direction of this legislation. The new Mexican constitution adopted on 5 February 1857 was one of the most progressive in the world. The Mexican people, rallying around Juárez, crushed the foreign intervention of 1861–67, expelled the soldiers of Napoleon III from the country, and destroyed the puppet empire of Maximilian. The popular masses, worn out with suffering, linked the coming of peace with a continuation and deepening of social reforms and of a decisive struggle against reaction. Social battles occurred also in Venezuela, Guatemala, and other countries of Latin America. The period of revolutionary shocks and popular actions was followed by a period of reconstruction, a period of peaceful development of the Latin American countries. Also characteristic of this period was a "reexamination of values," the appearance of new ideas, and the spread in Latin America of positivism. What interests us in the present case is the role played by the ideas of the generation of Echeverría, Sarmiento, and Mora in this historical stage of the development of Latin American society. Leopoldo Zea argues that the new positivist world view came to life with the appearance of a new generation of people, people with a practical cast of mind, who fought for the establishment of order and for the material progress of their nations. These people called on their countrymen to desist from "sterile discussions about freedom" and to occupy themselves with the establishment of order and the development of industry. According to the logic of Leopoldo Zea's conception, the ideas of Sarmiento, Alberdi, and Lastarria coincide organically with the ideas of positivism, since independently they developed ideas on Latin American soil akin to positivist ideas. But one cannot agree with this assertion of Zea, as one cannot agree that Sarmiento, Alberdi, and others were positivists *sui generis*. A formal search for points of contiguity between two ideological tendencies based on the common character of the words "progress," "order," and so on, cannot provide an answer to problems rooted in the peculiarities of the development of Latin American social thought in the late nineteenth and early twentieth centuries. Moreover, Leopoldo Zea's viewpoint hinders an understanding of the significant socio-economic changes which gave rise to the spread of positivism.[37]

The key question to be answered is whether or not the struggle of the progressive forces against the reaction of feudal landowners was successful and continued to develop, and whether or not the popular masses, who are the principal participants in social movements, reaped the benefits of this success. One can only answer in the negative.

The expropriation of real estate held by the Catholic Church in Mexico served the interests, in the first instance, of secular landholders, whose properties remained untouched, and of many representatives of the victorious liberal party, who themselves became landholders. On grounds of "freedom to hold private property," they seized peasant communal lands. In promulgating legislation to "emancipate" the land and provide for its free purchase and sale, the representatives of the liberal party's left wing (Juárez, Ocampo) sought to create a class of small landed property owners who would support them in the countryside. But however sincere the intentions of the left liberals, the fact that feudal land tenure rights were not abolished in all of their manifestations proved decisive for the subsequent economic and political development of the country. In the final analysis, large landownership in Mexico was strengthened due to the compromise and alliance of reactionary bourgeois groups, satisfied by the results of the reforms, with feudal landholding elements. The expression of this compromise and the triumph of the conservative forces was the dictatorship of General Porfirio Díaz, who in the course of many years tyrannized the country (1877–1911).

In Argentina, the land also fell into the hands of large landholders and representatives of the government bureaucracy, and ties were strengthened between landholders and the commercial circles of Buenos Aires. These groups began to set the tone of the political and economic life of the country. This occurred just at the time when the countries of Latin America were being drawn increasingly into the orbit of the world capitalist economy, when foreign capital (English and American) began to penetrate the Latin American countries on a wide scale. The ruling circles of Mexico, Argentina, and other countries opened their doors wide to foreign capital, thus facilitating the enslavement of their countries. To a greater or lesser degree, analogous processes occurred in the other Latin American countries. There emerged in Latin America a new social force, the oligarchy, which opposed any radical social transformations, yet at the same time was interested in an expansion of world trade and the spread of "progress," albeit with the aid of foreign capital. As their primary goal, the ruling circles sought to maintain "order" in the interests of the oligarchy and foreign monopolies. This, then, is the basis for the spread of positivist ideas (the theory of Comte and Spencer), which the ruling circles converted into their own kind of official ideology, molding and changing them to suit their interests.[38]

In the conditions of Latin America, positivist ideology constituted an expression of compromise between the bourgeois sectors of the Latin American countries and the landholders, as well as a growing subjection of the ruling circles of Latin America to the interests of foreign capital.[39] For this reason, it would be a mistake to view it as the ideology of a triumphant bourgeoisie whose interests now lay in a more conservative, "protectionist" theory.[40]

The coming to power of the oligarchy marked a break with the democratic traditions of the generation of Sarmiento, Mora, and Lastarria. For the ruling circles, they represented an "out-dated," "alien" element. This process can be observed very clearly in Mexico, where there occurred an open break with the progressive democratic traditions of Gómez Farías, Mora, and Juárez. Thus, *La Libertad*, organ of the positivists, which supported the Díaz dictatorship, wrote that the liberals of Juárez' generation had attempted to give the people freedom, for which they were not prepared. It was imperative first to establish order, declared the paper. The Constitution of 1857 was declared the basic obstacle to the establishment of this order, since it had been drafted by individuals of a "utopian mentality" for a "nonexistent people." One of the paper's editors, Francisco Cosmes, wrote that "the most irritating thing is that there are still people with such an outdated mentality that they still believe in the ideas espoused by the legislators of 1857."[41] And in the name of an "order" directed against the popular masses, the ideologists of positivism were willing to sacrifice national sovereignty. "The day is not far off," wrote that same Cosmes, "when the nation will say: I want order and peace even at the cost of losing my independence."[42] This policy was actively put into practice by the so-called *científicos* (scientists) party. Representing a group of big-time operators, bureaucratic officials, and intellectual "elites," the *científicos,* under the positivist slogan "order and progress," wholesaled and retailed the country's national riches, declaring the Díaz dictatorship an indispensable element for the "organic development of the country."

The Argentine oligarchy, too, sought the destruction of the democratic spirit. The government of Julio Roca, which came to power in 1880 under the slogan "peace and administration," expressed the interests of the forces of oligarchy. Precisely at this time, it became "unfashionable" to speak of the traditions of May or the ideas of Sarmiento. In the final years of his life, Sarmiento fought against the governments of the oligarchy, against their policies and ideology. For Sarmiento, who had devoted his entire life to the struggle for a free, democratic, and independent Argentina, the political course of the oligarchy, which justified its subservience to foreign capital with Spencerian arguments about "progress" and the role of industry in the development of society, was unacceptable.

In defending the interests of the oligarchy, the ideologists of official positivism in Argentina distorted the country's history. They ignored the popular masses, whom they defamed, and falsified the nation's democratic, revolutionary traditions. As in Mexico, "enlightened dictatorship" was advanced as the ideal form of government, that which best "answered" Latin American needs. True, the necessity of dictatorship was no longer justified in terms of "Americanism," but rather with positivist arguments of development, the differentiation of functions in society, and so on. Such conceptions found expression in particular in the books of sociologist [Lucas] Ayarragaray.[43] Ayarragaray's views differed fundamentally from the democratic conceptions of the author of *Facundo*. For Ayarragaray, the causes of anarchy and disorder were rooted in the peculiarities of the Argentine character. To Ayarragaray's mind, "enlightened dictatorship" was the only possible and necessary form of state authority in Argentina; it alone could resolve all difficulties.[44] The possibility of achieving democracy was relegated to a nebulous future, and the culprit turned out to be—the people.

Disdain of the popular masses runs like a red thread through all the works of those who represent oligarchic positivism. This withdrawal from the people likewise entailed a break with Latin American reality and led to a cosmopolitanization of spiritual life. A striking example of this can be seen in the prominent representative of Peruvian positivism, [Francisco] García Calderón, who was closely tied to the local oligarchy and its *civilista* party. In his writings on Peru and Latin America as a whole,[45] García Calderón treats all issues from the position of an "enlightened oligarchy." Feudal anarchy is condemned, but only to contrast it with "progress," which García Calderón equates with slow evolutionary development achieved under *civilista* rule.[46]

García Calderón also sheds light on the question of aristocratic, elitist attitudes toward the people, toward its mass base of Indians, the country's native population. The Indians were not yet ready for freedom, nor did they understand democracy. It was therefore necessary to "civilize" them, a task which was to be fulfilled by the "select few" who were called on to exercise a "beneficient wardship" over the Indians—such was the solution to the Indian question proposed by García Calderón.

The positivist ideology of the ruling oligarchy, however, did not hold unlimited sway. Yet from Leopoldo Zea's article one can reach precisely this conclusion, for, according to Zea's conception, positivism represented the determinant stage successive to romanticism in the intellectual development of Latin American society. The late nineteenth and early twentieth centuries are also a time of growing national-liberation, social, and class struggle in the Latin American countries. In Cuba, under the leadership of that great son of the Cuban people and revolutionary democrat José Martí (1853–1895), there unfolds a popular war of liberation against Spanish rule. At the same time, the Cuban patriots led by Martí opposed U.S. attempts to establish control over Cuba. "We must secure the independence of Cuba," wrote Martí; "otherwise the United States will seize the Antilles and from there will assault the lands of our America."[47] In 1910, the Mexican people, the oppressed peasantry, rose up and overthrew the dictatorship of Porfirio Díaz. The struggle of the popular masses against internal reaction began to fuse with the anti-imperialist struggle. Democratic elements among Latin American intellectuals raised their voices in defense of national culture; they sought a revival of the progressive democratic traditions, and addressed themselves to the vital needs of the people. But the major event of that period was the appearance in the political arena of the Latin American working class. Stating its rights ever more forcefully, the working class undermined the "social order" which had been established in the interests of the oligarchy. All of these phenomena had a decisive influence on the development of social thought. One senses this, in particular, in the writings of the founder and ideologist of the Socialist Party of Argentina, Juan Justo (1865–1928), and of the sociologist and psychologist José Ingenieros (1877–1925). To Juan Justo belongs the distinction of having translated Karl Marx's *Das Kapital* from German into Spanish. Justo played no small role in the struggle of the working class for its immediate needs and for the improvement of its social rights and living conditions. However, Justo was not an advocate of scientific socialism. In his writings, and particularly in his fundamental theoretical work, *Teoría y práctica de las historia,*[48] the basic problems of Marxist theory are discussed from the perspective of biologism, while the question of class struggle is replaced by the positivist conception of societal development. Accordingly, in practical politics Justo adopted reformist positions and was an advocate of class cooperation.

A prominent place in the history of Argentine social thought is occupied by José Ingenieros. Positivism had a decisive influence on his views; this was especially so in the first period of Ingenieros' activity. Ingenieros applied the laws of biology to the development of human society, and at one time was fascinated by social Darwinism, endeavoring with its help to "amplify" and "expand" Marxism. But at the same time, Ingenieros was a passionate champion of human happiness, believing in mankind and in its future felicity. It is hardly a coincidence that Ingenieros turned to the study and propagation of Argentina's democratic traditions, the traditions of May, and to an analysis of Argentine reality. Under the patent influence of Marxism, Ingenieros, in his study of the history of Argentine social thought, stressed the need to take into account the economic factor, the economic development of Argentina. This approach is particularly apparent in Ingenieros' polemic with Ayarragaray on the causes of dictatorship in the country. It is interesting to note that here Ingenieros shares Sarmiento's views, speaking of the latter's "ingenious conjecture" regarding the economic causes of anarchy in the country.[49] The views of José Ingenieros did not remain static. He persistently and selflessly sought the way to unity with the people and in a short time evolved remarkably in his world view. José Ingenieros ardently welcomed the Great October Socialist Revolution [Russian October Revolution of 1917], and with all his energy spread the ideas of the October Revolution in Latin America.

Another champion of freedom and critic of oligarchic rule was the remarkable representative of Peruvian democratic thought Manuel González Prada (1848–1918). A continuer of the best traditions of Latin American progressive thinkers, González Prada opposed the petty positivism of the ideologists of oligarchy,[50] and fought for the interests of the people and the rights of the Indian population. Denouncing the positivist theories of "progress" and "democracy," he angrily exclaimed: "Our form of government amounts to a great lie, for a State in which two or three million individuals live outside the law does not deserve to be called a democratic republic."[51] "The groupings of creoles and foreigners who inhabit the strip of land situated between the Pacific and the Andes," he wrote elsewhere, "do not form the real Peru; the nation is formed by the masses of Indians spread over the eastern slopes of the *cordillera*."[52] González Prada understood the necessity of social reforms and of the redistribution of land for the true emancipation of the popular Indian masses. He ridiculed the positivists, who held that the social question was above all a question of enlightenment, a cultural-pedagogical and administrative matter. Will the people really be free and happy if they know the tributaries of the Amazon and the average temperature of Berlin?—such was the question which, with his uniquely penetrating irony, González Prada put to the positivist *Kulturträger*. And in answer to his question, he wrote: "Where the coastal *haciendas* occupy four or five thousand *fanegadas*, where the *latifundia* of the *sierra* measure thirty and even fifty leagues, the nation has to be divided into masters and slaves."[53] González Prada believed deeply in the popular masses and their struggle. It is no coincidence that in the proletariat he saw a revolutionary force destined to replace the old order.

The political ideals of González Prada were unclear and had an anarcho-romantic, dream-like quality. Many of his views now belong to history. But his revolutionary optimism, abhorrence of the old order, and impatience to reach the future were adopted by a new generation of Peruvian revolutionaries.

At the beginning of the twentieth century, broad segments of the intelligentsia, especially university students, read the works of Uruguayan philosopher, sociologist, and literary critic José Enrique Rodó (1871–1917), whose views represented a unique expression of protest against the predominance of positivist ideology and the abandonment by a part of the intelligentsia of national culture. Rodó was a popularizer of the heroic, romantic pages of Latin American history. The very themes of his writings are indicative: "Bolívar," "Montalvo," "Juan

María Gutiérrez and his epoch'' (dedicated to one of the outstanding Argentines of the generation of Echeverría, Sarmiento, and Alberdi).[54] Reviving the images of the romantics, Rodó, upon whom the progressive youth looked as their teacher, called on his disciples to follow the example of these figures who fought heroically for the interests of Latin America and for the progressive ideals of the time. In his celebrated book *Ariel,* Rodó attacked the banality, the mercenary positivist morality of contemporary society, where the strong devoured the weak, and autocratic government rested on the Nietzschean superman concept. In this book, Rodó at the same time criticized the expansion of the United States; he defended a national Latin American culture and opposed its absorption by Anglo-Saxon culture.[55] Rodó's views were idealist in nature, and his criticism of the policies of the United States took the form of contrasting the crass materialism of the Anglo-Saxon race with the idealsim of the Latin race. But his role in the struggle to develop a national culture and to prevent its cosmopolitanization, his role in the unification of the patriotic forces of the intelligentsia was considerable, and the vivid memory of this Uruguayan thinker lives on in the hearts of the Latin American peoples.

A strenuous ideological struggle unfolded also in the largest country of Latin America—Brazil. The abolition of slavery in 1888 and the elimination of the monarchy in 1889 are indicators of the serious changes which were occurring in the socio-economic life of the country. Scientific and technical know-how and the exact sciences were being rapidly disseminated in Brazil. As in other Latin American countries, positivist ideology, whose greatest representatives were Miguel de Lemos and [Raimundo] Teixeira Mendes, attracted the interest of the ruling classes, who sought to limit the transformation of the country by abolishing slavery and declaring the republic. At the same time, as it developed in Brazil, a number of features of positivism changed. Here, positivist ideology developed in the most orthodox form, adopting even the religious side of Comte's philosophy. Suffice it to say that a positivist church was created in Rio de Janeiro, and the ideologists of positivism were declared its apostles. The positivist movement gradually degenerated into a sect,[56] ceasing to meet the interests even of the country's ruling circles. An attempt by the positivists to label the country a ''republican dictatorship'' was rejected by the leaders of the republic, who sought to govern the country by more versatile, camouflaged methods. But the principal blow to positivist ideology was delivered by representatives of progressive, democratic social thought, who, in one form or another, expressed the awakening of the popular masses. The effort to break out of the narrow, dogmatic limits of positivism and move into the realm of progressive philosophic thought is forcefully manifested in the writings of the eminent Brazilian materialist philosopher and sociologist Tobias Barreto (1839–89). The materialist philosophical school of Recife founded by Barreto played a major role in the cultural and spiritual development of the country and in the education of the progressive intelligentsia. Barreto firmly believed in the progress of humanity, in mankind's bright future. He ridiculed the flat evolutionism of the positivists, who held that the people were not prepared for freedom. Tobias Barreto manifested a profound interest in economic matters. He wrote that "the cardinal question of our time is not politics or religion, it is above all social and economic in nature."[57] His interest in the works of Karl Marx, particularly *Das Kapital,* was not accidental. Barreto wrote that "Karl Marx was a formidable critic of capital and the most audacious thinker of the nineteenth century in the field of economics."[58] Tobias Barreto considered Karl Marx's great merit to lie in the discovery of the laws of the historical development of human society. However, in the conditions of backward Brazil, Barreto could not adopt a position of dialectical materialism. In his views, Barreto approached a democratic-revolutionary orientation.[59]

With tremendous force rang out the accusing voice of another prominent progressive writer and thinker of Brazil, Euclides da Cunha (1866–1909).[60] In his book *Os Sertões,* published in 1902, Da Cunha depicted with great sympathy the revolt of the poor peasantry against the planters, known in history as the peasant war of Canudos. For the first time in the history of Brazilian literature a book appeared which offered a broad picture of the life and struggle of the peasant masses, written with obvious love for them. This book is significant, moreover, because with great depth it illuminates Brazilian reality, showing the reverse side of that "progress" proclaimed by the ideologues of the ruling classes, showing the true situation of the country from a popular, progressive position. Euclides de Cunha also showed deep and constant interest in scientific socialism. Da Cunha's statements in defense of socialism at a time when in Brazil the labor and socialist movement had only begun to come into being, while not always consistent, acquired outstanding significance.

Thus progressive Latin Americans selflessly and passionately searched for the truth. Indeed, they suffered every step of the way. Vast new changes in the world and in Latin America itself gave a new character, a different direction to this search for the truth. The Great October Socialist Revolution exercised a profound influence on the ideological struggle in the Latin American countries. Under its influence, a growing number of progressive intellectuals manifested interest in the ideas of Marxism-Leninism. Marxist theory offered the progressive forces of Latin America an effective instrument for the comprehension of Latin American reality and for the solution of its vital and pressing problems.

NOTES

1 Leopoldo Zea, *Apogeo y decadencia del positivismo en México* (Mexico, 1944).
2 Idem, *Dos Etapas del pensamiento en Hispanoamérica* (Mexico, 1949).

206 | A. F. SHUL'GOVSKII

3 Idem, *América como conciencia* (Mexico, 1953).
4 Idem, *Del liberalismo a la revolución en la educación mexicana* (Mexico, 1956).
5 Idem, *América en la historia* (Mexico, 1956).
6 For a more detailed acquaintance with the views of Soviet historians on the causes of the war of independence, see L. Yu Slëzkin, "Obrazovanie nezavisimykh gosudarstv v Latinskoi Amerike," in *Vsemirnaia istoriia*, ed. E. M. Zhukov et al., 10 vols. (Moscow, 1955–65), VI, 174–84; M. S. Al'perovich, V. I. Ermolaev, I. R. Lavretskii, and S. I. Semënov, "Ob osvoboditel'noi bor'be ispanskikh kolonii v Amerike (1810–1826),"† pp. 52–71.
7 José Carlos Mariátegui, *Siete ensayos de interpretación de la realidad peruana* (Santiago de Chile, 1955), pp. 7–8.
8 Juan Antonio Salceda, *Aníbal Ponce y el pensamiento de Mayo* (Buenos Aires, 1957), p. 10.
9 Ibid.
10 Juan Bautista Alberdi, *Bases y puntos de partida para la organización política de la República Argentina* (Santa Fe, 1957), p. 64.
11 Salceda, *Aníbal Ponce*, p. 13.
12 José María Luis Mora, *Méjico y sus revoluciones*, 3 vols. (Mexico, 1950).
13 Domingo Faustino Sarmiento, *Facundo* (Mexico, 1957), pp. 37, 75, 79, 86, 122–23 ff.
14 Ibid., p. 47.
15 Ibid., p. 250.
16 Ibid., p. 31.
17 Mora, *Méjico y sus revoluciones*, I, 471.
18 Ibid., pp. 279, 451, 453 ff,; Eli de Gortari, *La ciencia en la Reforma* (Mexico, 1957), pp. 21, 27–28.
19 Mora, *Méjico y sus revoluciones*, I, 470.
20 Andrés Bello, *Bello: Prólogo del doctor Gabriel Méndez Plancarte* (Mexico, 1943), p. 79.
21 Ibid., p. 71.
22 Ibid., p. 77.
23 It is worthy of note that in our own time the progressives, in their struggle against reaction, repeatedly turn to the traditions of those who fought for democracy in the nineteenth century. In Venezuela, for example, the progressive forces denounced the *false assertions of the ideologues of the dictatorial regime of Perez Jim*énez concerning the incapacity of the popular masses for democracy by citing the ideas of Andrés Bello and his profound faith in democracy.
24 It is especially important that this be noted, for in recent times, particularly in such countries as Mexico, Argentina, and Chile, reaction has sought by all the means at its disposal to distort the views of progressive thinkers, to represent them as supporters of the "Anglo-Saxonization" of Latin America and opponents of national culture. This conception has found particularly brilliant expression in the work *Breve historia de México* (Mexico, 1956), by the leading exponent of conservative ideology in the country, José Vasconcelos.
25 Bello, *Bello*, pp. 22, 26 ff.
26 Alberdi, *Bases*, pp. 17, 32–33, 53.

27 It is no accident that in the works of several thinkers, and especially Echeverría, one senses the ideas of utopian socialism, with its dream of equality and work as the basis of life. This was not simply a vogue, a submission to European models. In the conditions of backwardness in Latin America and the underdevelopment of class relations, there existed fertile soil for the germination of utopian socialist ideas of building a new society founded on equality and brotherhood and respect for work.

28 Salceda, *Aníbal Ponce*, p. 11.

29 Juan Montalvo, *Montalvo: Prólogo y selección de Manuel Moreno Sánchez* (Mexico, 1942), p. 12.

30 José Victoriano Lastarria, *Lastarria: Prólogo y selección de Lius Enrique Délano* (Mexico, 1944), p. 6.

31 Mora, *Méjico y sus revoluciones*, I, 279; Gortari, *La ciencia en la Reforma*, p. 27.

32 José María Luis Mora, *Ensayos, ideas y retratos* (Mexico, 1941), p. 162.

33 Zea, *Dos etapas del pensamiento en Hispanoamérica*, p. 132.

34 Lastarria, *Lastarria*, p. xxv.

35 In 1864, on a motion by Lastarria, the Chilean chamber of deputies refused to recognize the puppet Franco-Austrian monarchy in Mexico.

36 Lastarria, *Lastarria*, p. 183.

37 The influence of Leopoldo Zea's conception is particularly felt in the interesting and pithy book by Argentine scholar Berta Perelstein, *Positivismo y antipositivismo en la Argentina* (Buenos Aires, 1952), pp. 111–12.

38 In a more general sense, of course, the period of spreading positivist views coincided with a growing interest in the countries of Latin America in the natural and exact sciences and in technology, but in the present article we are not examining these questions, focusing our attention instead on an elucidation of the peculiarities of positivism's influence on Latin American political and social thought, in other words, on the characteristics of positivist ideology.

39 Perelstein, *Positivismo y antipositivismo*, pp. 133, 181 ff.

40 In this connection, it must be pointed out that among progressive Latin American scholars there is a fairly widespread view of positivism as an expression of the interests of the Latin American bourgeoisie. In particular, in the interesting book by the Mexican philosopher Eli de Gortari, *La ciencia en la Reforma*, the author argues—in our view, erroneously—that the Díaz dictatorship was a dictatorship of the national bourgeoisie, acting in unity with foreign capital. All the positivist philosophical categories of "freedom," "order," and "progress" are treated accordingly. This point of view greatly weakens Gortari's criticism of Leopoldo Zea's conception of the development of Mexican positivism.

41 Zea, *Dos etapas del pensamiento en Hispanoamérica*, p. 352.

42 Ibid., p. 354.

43 Lucas Ayarragaray, *Cuestiones y problemas argentinos contemporáneos* (Buenos Aires, 1937).

44 These conceptions later found their "classic" development in the book *Cesarismo democrático: Estudios sobre las bases sociológicas de la constitución efectiva de Venezuela* (Caracas, 1952), written by Laureano Vallenilla Lanz, Venezuelan Minister of Internal Affairs under the dictatorship of [Juan Vicente] Gómez. The system of positivist views whereby the most reactionary regimes were justified is especially

clear in this book. It should be noted that the concept of "democratic Caesarism," of "enlightened dictatorship," was widely used by the dictatorial regimes which came to power in Latin America following the Second World War. The "ideology" of the Pérez Jiménez dictatorhip in Venezuela was based on this concept. It is also characteristic that the peculiar revival of the positivist views of the *científicos* is explained by the efforts of dictators to "justify" the domination of Latin America's economy by American monopolies.

45 Francisco García Calderón, *Le Pérou contemporain* (Paris, 1907); idem, *Latin America: Its Rise and Progress* (London, 1913).

46 Describing the social basis of *civilismo,* García Calderón speaks of a union of the old creole aristocratic families with the new commercial and financial plutocracy.

47 José Martí, *Izbrannoe* (Moscow, 1956), p. 280.

48 Juan B. Justo, *Teoría y práctica de la historia* (Buenos Aires, 1915).

49 José Ingenieros, *La Evolución sociológica argentina de la barbarie al imperialismo* (Buenos Aires, 1910), pp. 142, 145.

50 With devastating accuracy and irony, González Prada described the ideologues of positivism as "a generation of pitiful pedants, who, having filled their heads with the half-baked ideas of Spencer and Le Tourneau, preached the constitution of a national spirit, the creation of an elite, the rule of a categorical imperative, peaceful evolution, and other such nonsense." See Manuel González Prada, *Bajo el oprobio* (Paris, 1933), p. 102.

51 Manuel González Prada, *Manuel González Prada: Selección y prólogo de L. S. Sánchez* (Mexico, 1945), p. 85.

52 Mariátegui, *Siete ensayos,* p. 190.

53 González Prada, *Manuel González Prada,* p. 90.

54 José Enrique Rodó, *Obras completas* (Madrid, 1957), pp. 708–9 ff.

55 Ibid., p. 225.

56 João Curz Costa, *Esbozo de una historia de las ideas en el Brasil* (Mexico and Buenos Aires, 1957).

57 Zh. Bazarian, "Tobias Barreto—ilustre pensador brazileiro," *Novos Rumos,* no. 17 (19–25 June 1959), p. 9.

58 Ibid.

59 For a more detailed treatment of the views of Tobias Barreto, see *Istoriia filosofii,* vol. 4 (Moscow, 1959).

60 In 1959, through the initiative of the World Council of Peace, the fiftieth anniversary of his death was observed throughout the world.

13 THE CLAYTON-BULWER TREATY OF 1850 AND RUSSIAN DIPLOMACY

A. M. ZORINA

THE PROBLEM of building a canal linking the Atlantic and Pacific oceans was of interest to American ruling circles and occupied a prominent place in the foreign policy of the United States as early as the first quarter of the nineteenth century. It became especially acute at mid-century, in connection with mounting Anglo-American rivalry in Central America, and remained a fundamental problem right down to the beginning of the twentieth century.[1]

As the economic and political development of the United States progressed, so, too, grew the appetites and aggressiveness of American ruling circles. Already in the first quarter of the nineteenth century, the United States, hiding behind the notorious Monroe Doctrine, pursued an actively expansionist policy in the Western Hemisphere. As noted by Marx, the basic objective of U.S. foreign policy in the mid-nineteenth century "was to seize new territories for the expansion of slavery and the rule of the slaveholders."[2] The slaveholding bloc was actively supported by the bourgeoisie of the northern states. As a result of the predatory war with Mexico in 1846–1848, the United States seized vast territory on the Pacific coast—almost half of Mexico—including Upper California, where, in search of recently discovered gold, came a rush of goldminers, adventurers, and entrepreneurs. This circumstance significantly heightened U.S. interest in building inexpensive and convenient routes to the Pacific coast.

The predatory war against Mexico and entry into the Pacific Ocean were only the beginnings of a policy that sought to establish U.S. supremacy in the Pacific and to dominate China and other Asian countries. This policy was pursued not only by the slaveholders, who held power in the United States, but was the dream

Originally published as "Dogovor Kleiton-Bul'vera (1850 g.) i russkaia diplomatiia," in I. R. Grigulevich et al., eds., *Ot Aliaski do Ognennoi Zemli,*† pp. 58–70.

as well of broad segments of the American bourgeoisie. The intervention of William Walker's band in Central America—especially in Nicaragua—the meeting of diplomats at Ostend on the Cuban question, the imposition on China of an inequitable treaty and the participation of Americans in the suppression of the Taiping rebellion, the Perry mission to Japan, the growth of a merchant marine and strengthening of trade with the countries of the Far East—these and many other facts revealed the true objectives pursued by the United States, the need to build an interoceanic canal being part of the order of the day.

The link with California was thus important, but far from the only reason for United States interest in a canal. A shorter route to Asia (and also to the west coast of South America) to promote its expansion in these areas—this is what the United States sought.

The significance of Cuba and the entire Caribbean basin was viewed in a different light. The United States ceased to regard this region solely in terms of its own commercial interests, taking into account its strategic role in [American] offensive policy, and began to seek political control over the area.

The struggle for an interoceanic canal in the nineteenth century, therefore, occupied a most important place in the expansionist policy of North American capitalism. But in order to obtain the possibility of constructing a large canal of international significance, the United States had to eliminate, or at least neutralize, the opposition of so powerful a rival as England. By pursuing an active, offensive policy, the English bourgeoisie managed to secure (and to maintain throughout most of the nineteenth century) a predominant position in a majority of the young states of the American continent, who in the aftermath of the war of independence had not yet become consolidated.

Toward the middle of the nineteenth century, the mounting rivalry between England and the United States in Latin America in general and Central America in particular became exceedingly sharp. One of the centers of British influence in Central America was Belize, which, as a result of having been seized from Guatemala, received the name British Honduras.[3] The first British settlements were founded there as early as 1662. Belize served as a bridgehead for England's expansion into Honduras, Nicaragua, and the Mosquito Coast. In 1848, England seized the town of San Juan del Norte, which was renamed Greytown.[4] This small port on the Atlantic coast was of important strategic significance. With its seizure, one of the outlets of the proposed canal, together with the San Juan river all the way to lake Nicaragua, fell into British hands. In fact, controlling the northeastern coast of Central America and having so strong a base as Jamaica, with its excellently equipped port of Kingston, and possessing in addition a powerful navy, England held almost unrestricted sway in the Caribbean basin. Although she was not directly interested in building a canal, it was important to [England] to secure for herself the key positions around the approaches to [a future canal] and to check the growing influence of the United States in Central America.

Not surprisingly, the English ambassador to the United States, [Sir Henry Lytton] Bulwer, wrote in one of his dispatches: "Central America is no longer what it was and is daily becoming the most important spot of earth in ye whole world: to us especially. . . . We cannot, we must not see it American, I mean belonging to the U.S."[5]

Despite the fact that in the mid-nineteenth century the United States was not yet noted for its economic or political power and did not yet occupy a favorable position in the alignment of forces, it already had significant commercial and political interests in the countries of Central America and, through pillage, armed force, or diplomatic intrigue, persistently sought to expand its influence there. Following the successful conclusion of the war with Mexico, the United States adopted a firmer stance in this matter. Noting this situation in one of his dispatches to St. Petersburg, the first secretary of the Russian embassy in Washington, Baron [Eduard de] Stekl, underscored the fact that United States agents had become unusually active in Central America, but everywhere were confronted with the activity of representatives of Great Britain.[6]

The relentless efforts of England to seize and expand strategic positions in the area of the future canal created such a complicated and strained situation in Central America, and so hampered the aggressive policy of the United States, that American diplomacy considered it essential to instigate a special agreement with England. In the mid-nineteenth century, however, the United States could not yet hope for exclusive rights to build, fortify, and exercise unrestricted political control over an interoceanic canal. Taking into account the potential significance of a future canal for ruling-class interests in the United States, and as yet lacking any concrete possibility of attaining their objectives, American diplomacy struggled to prevent any other power, and especially England, from establishing control over the future canal zone.

It was also important to United States ruling circles to conceal the aggressive nature of their policy in Central America and to assure the execution of that policy under cover of a compromise accord with England. As a result, consideration was given to the necessity of concluding an accord whereby England and the United States would jointly guarantee the neutrality and international character of the canal, without receiving any exclusive advantages. Direct negotiations were conducted between U.S. Secretary of State [John Middleton] Clayton and the English ambassador in Washington, Bulwer.

The compromise Anglo-American Clayton-Bulwer Treaty was signed on 19 April 1850.[7] Its basic contents were as follows: (1) neither Great Britain nor the United States would endeavor to secure exclusive control over the canal; (2) neither side had the right to erect fortifications in the canal zone or territory adjacent thereto; (3) neither side had the right to occupy, fortify, colonize, annex, or impose its rule on any part of Central America; and (4) both powers promised to guarantee the security and neutrality of the canal, and invited other foreign powers to subscribe to this treaty. They both promised, in addition, to assist capitalists wishing to undertake construction of this canal. Both powers were granted on an equal basis the right to use any railroad or canal built in isthmian territory.

At this point, the accord completely satisfied the interests of United States ruling circles. Despite the unfavorable alignment of forces, American diplomacy succeeded in blocking England's establishment of exclusive control over the future canal and was able, if not entirely to exclude, then at least to limit the possibilities of future [English] expansion in Central America. Distrusting England, and fearing that the bilateral guarantee of the Clayton-Bulwer Treaty might prove insufficient, the United States, in accordance with Article VI, attempted to bring Tsarist Russia into the agreement. Article six read: "Both contracting parties to the present agreement pledge to invite any state with whom both or one of the parties individually have friendly relations to conclude an analogous accord so that all states might share both the honor and benefits of contributing to such an important and generally useful undertaking as the proposed canal."[8]

Precisely because the position of the United States was weaker than that of England, which likewise pursued an aggressive policy, the United States sought to use other countries, and especially Russia, in its own mercenary interests. Naturally, the United States was not about to secure any benefits for other countries. In a conversation with Stekl, U.S. Secretary of State Clayton declared that the American government wished to ascertain whether Russia might approve of the principle of neutrality, which formed the basis of the treaty, and whether it would agree to support with "its mighty name an act meant to guarantee to the entire world the advantages of this great means of communication," that is, an interoceanic canal.[9]

U.S. Ambassador D. P. Brown, in St. Petersburg, was instructed to stress the significance which the United States attached to Russia's endorsement of the Clayton-Bulwer Treaty.[10] A study of the diplomatic correspondence for the years 1850–1852 between the Russian ambassadors in London and Washington and [Count Karl Robert von] Nesselrode, State Chancellor and Minister of Foreign Affairs, permits us to ascertain how tsarist diplomacy and the official financial and business circles of Russia responded to the signing of the Clayton-Bulwer Treaty, as well as to the matter of building an interoceanic canal.

Based on a study of archival materials, one can conclude that the government of the United States sought to entice Russia with an optimistic picture of the construction of an interoceanic canal and to persuade it to endorse the accord of 19 April 1850. Taking into account the tension in Anglo-Russian relations (on the eve of the Crimean War) and Russia's strained relations with Turkey, American diplomacy clearly tried to pressure Russia to serve [American] interests in the struggle with England. In the event of a clash between England and the United States, Russia was to play the role of arbiter in the conflict, which the ruling circles of tsarist Russia in no way desired.

On the other hand, the invitation to Russia to adhere to the accord of 1850 entailed an element of diplomatic maneuvering, which, in playing on Anglo-Russian conflicts, was calculated to force England to be more tractable. This apparently was understood in London, and, due precisely to this fact, British diplomacy regarded the proposal to invite endorsement of the treaty by other powers without particular enthusiasm.

One cannot but note the perceptive and sober appraisal of current events in Stekl's dispatches. Taking into account the increasing role of the Isthmus of Panama as a transport route between the United States and its possessions on the Pacific coast, as well as the rapidly growing might and power of the United States, Stekl made a prediction which in large measure proved prophetic. "It is possible that the day is not far off," Stekl wrote, "when these American adventurers who are flooding over the isthmus in connection with the discovery of gold in California, imitating their predecessors in Texas, will raise the flag of the United States and easily find a suitable pretext to declare the annexation of the Isthmus of Panama to the confederation."[11] Stekl recognized the tremendous international significance of building an interoceanic canal that would spare ships the dangerous voyage around the Cape of Good Hope and Cape Horn. "Russia," wrote Stekl, "also will derive great benefits from the construction of this canal, which will bring her American colonies two thousand miles closer."[12] He considered very unlikely, however, the realization of this gigantic project at that time, given the severity of Anglo-American rivalry in Central America and the relative economic and political weakness of the United States at this stage.

Stekl kept Nesselrode apprised of all developments in the matter of the interoceanic canal and in Anglo-American relations as they pertained to it. He elucidated in considerable detail the events leading up to the conclusion of the treaty, and pointed out the tension in relations between England and the United States stemming from the question of a [British] protectorate over the Mosquito Coast and the struggle for other bridgeheads in the countries of Central America. Stekl's dispatches testify to the fact that he understood perfectly that the alignment of forces at that moment in no way favored the United States. "As they are weaker," Stekl wrote, "the Americans can act in no other way, and will be obliged strictly to support the principles of the canal's neutrality."[13]

At the end of April 1850, there arrived in Washington an ambassador extraordinary and plenipotentiary of the tsarist government, Aleksandr [Andreevich] Bodisko. He, for his part, considered it indisputable that the construction of an interoceanic canal, albeit in the distant future, would have great advantages for the trade relations of Russia.[14] As for the Russian ambassador in London, [Count Filipp Ivanovich] Brunnov, in his dispatches at the beginning of 1850 he shed very little light on matters pertaining to the Clayton-Bulwer Treaty, in fact limiting himself to a summary of [the treaty's] contents.[15]

Before reaching a final decision on a matter of such import, the Russian Ministry of Foreign Affairs felt it necessary in the interests of Russian landowners and merchants to seek the views of several official organizations, particularly the Finance Ministry. To this end, on 28 August 1850 the State Councillor for Foreign Affairs, [Lev Grigorevich] Seniavin, addressed a memorandum to the Minister of Finance, [Count Fëdor Pavlovich] Vronchenko.[16] Recalling the treaty of 19 April 1850, and citing Article VI of that accord, which called on other powers to adhere to the treaty "in order to facilitate such an important and universally useful enterprise," Seniavin reported that U.S. Ambassador Brown, recently arrived in St. Petersburg, had addressed a note to him in which he proposed that the Russian government conclude with the United States an accord analogous to the Clayton-Bulwer Treaty. Seniavin summed up his own point of view in the following manner: "For Russian trade, the proposed canal will represent undoubted benefits, because the voyage to our North American colonies will be shortened by two thousand English miles."[17]

The Chancery of the Minister of Finance forwarded Seniavin's note to the Department of Foreign Trade. The latter, however, proceeding from the fact that the Clayton-Bulwer Treaty obliged the interested parties to guarantee the neutrality of the canal and freedom of movement through it, concluded that such an arrangement must unavoidably entail monetary expenditures for the maintenance of national or foreign troops to protect the canal. Considering the insignificant amount of Russian maritime trade along the west coast of America, the Department of Foreign Trade could not assume "that the building of a canal between the Atlantic and Pacific Oceans would in the not-distant future favor [Russian] maritime traffic, with the exception of Russian-American Company ships, whose route to our North American colonies would be shortened via the canal by two thousand English miles," and, consequently, [concluded] that only "the importance or insignificance of this benefit in comparison with government contributions to the canal's defense can serve as the primary basis for discussing whether or not in the matter of trade relations it is advantageous for the government to adhere to the aforementioned treaty."[18]

Inasmuch as matters pertaining to the Russian-American Company were within the purview of the Department of Manufactures and Domestic Trade, on 2 September 1850 the Department of Foreign Trade sent Seniavin's memorandum there, along with a statement of its own views. From there, Seniavin's memorandum was forwarded to the Central Board of Administration of the Russian-American Company, with a request to make its views promptly known. Two days later, on 6 September, the Central Board of Administration of the Russian-American Company gave its reply: "The conclusion of a treaty between Russia and the aforesaid powers on the subject of the construction of a canal between the Atlantic and Pacific Oceans would be of indisputable benefit to our American colonies, as much because of the shortened voyage to the colonies as of the guaranteed movement of our ships in case of a break in diplomatic relations, which, given our present growing trade with those countries, constitutes a subject of fundamental importance."[19] In a report based on the information collected and presented on 25 September 1850 to [Baron Aleksandr Fëdorovich] Grevnits, director of the Chancery of the Minister of Finance, the Department of Manufactures and Domestic Trade made the following observations:

> One can assume with certainty that the commercial operations of this company will not remain within the narrow limits to which they are presently restricted, and that its board of directors will open new trade routes and sources to its ships along the west coast of America, where the rapidly growing population of California serves as a great stimulus to such trade, as well as along the coast of China, where in accord with Article VI of the company's imperially approved charter of 10 October 1844 its ships have been authorized to visit all ports. . . .
>
> There is no doubt that the shortening of the voyage for our ships sent to the North American colonies by two thousand English miles will greatly promote the development of our trade in that area, and therefore, if in time monetary contributions are required for the maintenance of warships to defend the neutrality of the proposed canal, then, in the view of the Department of Manufactures and Domestic Trade, such an obligation ought not to stop the government from taking part in an enterprise that promises such important benefits. . . . For all of these reasons, the Department of Manufactures and Domestic Trade cannot but recognize that conclusion of the accord with the North-American United States which has been proposed to the Russian government represents major benefits in the area of trade. The Department of Manufactures and Domestic Trade has the honor to submit this conclusion to the Council of the Minister of Finance for its consideration.[20]

Exactly one month later, on 25 October 1850, the Department of Manufactures and Domestic Trade was informed of the Finance Minister's agreement. In the journal (protocol) of the Council of the Minister of Finance for 2 October is recorded the following: "The council of the Minister of Finance, taking into consideration that the construction of a canal between the Atlantic and Pacific Oceans will, by shortening the voyage of ships, be of considerable value to the Russian-American Company, and in general promote the growth of our commerce, finds that Russian sponsorship of such an important and universally useful enterprise would be exceedingly desirable, which it presumes to communicate to the director of the Ministry of Foreign Affairs."[21] In all probability the original of this document was transmitted to Seniavin at the Ministry of

Foreign Affairs. In addition, Vronchenko felt it necessary to underscore his personal approval in a special memorandum to the State Chancellor, Count Nesselrode, dated 2 November 1850.[22]

This interdepartmental correspondence shows that such state institutions as the Department of Manufactures and Domestic Trade, the Central Board of Directors of the Russian-American Company, the Council of the Minister of Finance, and, finally, the Minister of Finance himself, Vronchenko, were favorably disposed toward the proposed conclusion of a treaty with the United States on the construction of an interoceanic canal. At bottom, they all were persuaded that the creation of a new maritime communications link would promote the further development of Russian trade relations with the west coast of America and the coast of China, the growth of Russian-American Company commercial operations, and also the supply of the Russian colonies in North America.[23]

Naturally, the Minister of Foreign Affairs could not ignore the views of the interested departments, but this was by no means sufficient for the tsarist government to place its signature on a document of international import and, in so doing, to allow itself to be drawn into an enterprise fraught with "dangerous" consequences. In particular, Nesselrode wrote on this matter: "The construction of a canal joining the Pacific and Atlantic oceans promises too many advantages for the Russian imperial cabinet to remain indifferent to such an enterprise. But can these benefits compensate Russia for difficulties which may arise as a result of the obligations entailed by our adherence to the accord of 19 April? This is the question."[24] This was still unclear and required more precise definition.

On 12 January 1851, the Chancery of the Ministry of Foreign Affairs sent special instructions to its ambassadors—Bodisko in Washington, and Brunnov in London—to gather all pertinent information and set forth their views on this matter from the viewpoint of Russia's commercial and political interests. These instructions comprised a whole complex of questions requiring clarification. Most delicate, in the opinion of those who wrote the instructions, was the matter of each signatory's obligation to uphold strictly the conditions of the treaty. Consequently, it was important that the significance of these obligations be made as clear as possible.

In the instructions mention was also made of the rivalry between the two Anglo-Saxon powers who had concluded the Clayton-Bulwer Treaty, in view of which fear was expressed that this rivalry had all the makings of future deterioration and even threatened to lead to conflict. The other guarantor powers of the treaty could find themselves in a difficult situation should an "injured" party turn to them for aid or mediation. Tsarist diplomacy sought to avoid this at all costs, and herein lay the instructions' central idea.

In the instructions it was further pointed out that, inasmuch as the American government intended to make an analogous proposal to France and other powers, it was necessary to clarify, albeit indirectly, how they would respond to such a proposal and what their views on the matter might be. And finally, the ambassadors were invited to submit their own thoughts on "what form our adherence to the treaty ought to take should it prove beneficial, and what reservations ought to be attached to this adherence. On the basis of all these data the government of His Imperial Highness will be able to judge how well adherence to the treaty of 19 April 1850 suits it."[25]

Although Bodisko's reply was far from covering all the questions raised in [his] instructions,[26] we learn from it that the United States government addressed a formal invitation of adherence to the treaty of 19 April 1850 to France and Holland, and, in a less clearly articulated form, to Spain, Austria, Prussia, Belgium, and others. In Paris, the U.S. proposal at first received a most favorable response, but subsequent correspondence which the French ambassador in Washington (Bois le Comte) made known to Bodisko shows that it remained without consequences. France, it seems, wished to obtain in return for its endorsement of the treaty more practical and direct benefits than the United States was able or willing to assure, and therefore no final answer to the U.S. proposal issued from Paris.

In general, the other powers did not regard seriously something which still seemed so remote. They failed to respond to the U.S. proposal, moreover, because they did not, perhaps, wish to upset relations with the great powers, and feared to meddle in arguments between them. The matter of an interoceanic canal was largely unrelated to their immediate interests. Most curious is Bodisko's observation that he was unable to report any efforts on the part of the British government to draw other powers [into the accord]. This observation is typical, in that it demonstrates that England was not interested in the adherence of other powers to the treaty, and apparently did not feel obligated to observe Article VI of the treaty.

Concerning himself with the practical side of the matter, Bodisko determined that already in 1849 two influential Americans[27] had secured from the government of Nicaragua a concession for the construction of an interoceanic canal. Possessing, however, patently insufficient capital for its construction, but having secured rights to the proposed canal zone, they were able to cover the costs of organizing and building a rail and steamship link (via lakes Nicaragua and Managua) between the Atlantic and Pacific oceans, which they in fact did. In addition, Bodisko decided to sound out the new United States Secretary of State, [Daniel] Webster, who replaced Clayton in this post. In a talk with Bodisko, Webster stated that as soon as the matter of the canal was finally settled, he would propose to the imperial [Russian] government "that it negotiate the proper form of Russia's adherence" to the Clayton-Bulwer Treaty.[28]

Outlining all the complexities of the situation created in Central America as a result of conflicting Anglo-American interests, Bodisko reached the conclusion that there was no need for Russia precipitously to adhere to the Clayton-Bulwer Treaty, and that it would be wisest to adopt a wait-and-see position.

The reply of the Russian ambassador in London was far more thorough. In seeking to elucidate the questions raised by the Minister of Foreign Affairs in his instructions of 12 January 1851, Brunnov broke the problem down into three parts, around which he wrote his report. In the first part, he responded to the basic questions of principle, having ascertained in a special conversation with Lord Palmerston the latter's attitude toward these questions.[29] In the second part, he provided detailed information on the canal project itself. And finally, in the third part, he expounded his own views on the Clayton-Bulwer Treaty and his thoughts on the matter of Russia's adherence to it.

Brunnov's report shows that Palmerston, playing on Brunnov's Anglophilic tendencies, tried to prompt a reply useful to England. Palmerston sought to persuade Brunnov that powers endorsing the treaty of 1850 were in no way obliged to intervene in conflicts which might arise between the principal contracting parties. He "readily" approved the tsarist government's wish to maintain its own freedom of action and not to play the role of arbiter in Anglo-American disputes. Palmerston was not at all interested in the adherence of other powers, especially Russia, to the treaty, since he understood that Russia's adherence would strengthen the hand of American diplomacy in its opposition to British policy.

Not wishing to limit himself to his own account of this conversation, Brunnov requested that Palmerston answer the questions raised in writing. On 21 February 1851, Palmerston handed Brunnov a written reply.[30] In this exceedingly brief document is stated the following: (1) The canal should be open to the trade and ships of all nations on an equal basis, independently of whether or not the governments of other states adhere to the treaty; (2) no monetary guarantees were envisioned; (3) no additional decisions had been taken in regard to political guarantees; (4) all obligations assumed by the contracting parties were stipulated in the treaty.

In a detailed report to the Minister of Foreign Affairs, Brunnov made several observations worthy of attention. He noted that of the two powers the United States was particularly interested in the prompt implementation of the conditions of the Washington accord, which the British government by no means considered a diplomatic success. Also important is Brunnov's observation that American entrepreneurs sought by every means to avoid the intervention of foreign firms in the construction of an interoceanic canal. Brunnov foresaw that in the future there would be a heightened struggle for Japanese and Chinese markets, and that following construction of the canal, U.S. expansion westward would increase significantly. He saw the Clayton-Bulwer Treaty itself as a diplomatic action designed to neutralize, if only for a time, Anglo-American conflicts in Central America.

Brunnov further discussed his view of Russia's endorsement of the Clayton-Bulwer Treaty. Russia, to his mind, could take such a step, but only with certain stipulations spelled out in a special declaration to precede the act of endorsement. The essence of these stipulations was to be that for Russia it was essential to maintain complete freedom of action and not to become involved in possible clashes between Great Britain and the United States. He wrote: "Russia certainly can affirm for its own part that it seeks no dominion whatsoever in the states of Central America, as stipulated in Article I of the treaty, and the fact of its adherence to the treaty decidedly should not mean that Russia obligates itself to fulfill conditions assumed by the English and American governments in relation to each other."[31] The tsarist government, in Brunnov's view, should seek to derive from its adherence to the treaty only benefits of a trading or commercial nature, avoiding any kind of political obligation.

The archival documents show that the prospect of constructing an interoceanic canal was not without interest for the ruling circles of the Russian state. The creation of a new maritime route would promote the development of Russian trade relations with the west coast of America and China, the growth of Russian-American Company commercial operations, and also the supply of the Russian colonies in the American Northwest. Not until significantly later than the 1850s did tsarism take into account the great strategic significance of an interoceanic canal, which made possible the transfer of the U.S. navy from the Atlantic Ocean to the Pacific. In 1910, influential bourgeois-landholding circles in Russia became exceedingly interested in how the opening of the Panama Canal might affect bread exports and prices on the world market, what prospects this would open up for Russian trade and navigation in the Far East, and so on.

However, those who directed tsarist foreign policy in the mid-nineteenth century did not consider all these interests sufficiently "vital" to risk signing the Anglo-American accord of 1850. The tsarist government, proceeding in accordance with the alignment of forces in the world, decided to refrain from adhering to the Washington treaty [of 19 April 1850].

NOTES

1 This problem was resolved to the satisfaction of the United States only after the latter engineered the Panamanian "revolution" of 1903 and imposed on the Republic of Panama a unilateral and exceedingly self-serving treaty for an interoceanic canal.

2 Karl Marx and Friedrich Engels, *Sochineniia*, XV, 342.
3 Lindley M. Keasbey, *The Nicaragua Canal and the Monroe Doctrine* (New York, 1896), p. 171.
4 Ibid., p. 181.
5 "Documents, Anglo-American Relations, 1853–1857: British Statesmen on the Clayton-Bulwer Treaty and American Expansion," *AHR* 42, no. 3 (April, 1937), 495.
6 Arkhiv vneshnei politiki Rossii (Russian Foreign Policy Archives, hereafter AVPR), Chancery (1850): Washington, delo 1034, dispatch from Stekl. 2 (14) April.
7 Keasbey, *The Nicaragua Canal*, pp. 600–604.
8 Ibid., pp. 602–3.
9 AVPR, Chancery (1850): Washington, delo 138, dispatch from Stekl, 5 (17) February.
10 Tsentral'nyi gosudarstvennyi istoricheskii arkhiv v Leningrade (Central State Historical Archives—Leningrad, hereafter TsGIAL). Department of Manufactures and Domestic Trade (1850), delo 1798, fols. 4–5.
11 AVPR, Chancery (1850): Washington, delo 138, dispatch from Stekl, 2 (14) April.
12 Ibid., dispatch from Stekl, 24 December (5 January 1851).
13 Ibid., dispatch from Stekl, 5 (17) February 1850.
14 AVPR, Chancery (1851): Washington, delo 147, dispatch from Bodisko, 7 (19) January 1851.
15 AVPR, Chancery (1850): London, delo 1311, dispatch from Brunnov, 31 May (12 June).
16 TsGIAL, Department of Manufactures and Domestic Trade (1850), 2nd section, stol II, delo 1789, fols. 4–5.
17 Ibid.
18 Ibid., fols. 1–3.
19 Ibid., fol. 17.
20 Ibid., fol. 24.
21 Ibid., fol. 28.
22 Ibid., fol. 29.
23 AVPR, Chancery (1851): delo 17.
24 AVPR, Ministry of Foreign Affairs: Instructions, 12 January 1851.
25 Ibid.
26 AVPR, Chancery (1851), delo 147, reply from Bodisko, 10 (22) June.
27 The individuals in question were [Joseph L.] White and Cornelius Vanderbilt, organizers of the so-called Accessory Transit Company, which existed from 1850 to 1856.
28 AVPR, Chancery (1851): Washington, delo 147, dispatch from Bodisko, 10 (22) June.
29 In one of his dispatches, Brunnov drew a fairly detailed and most uncomplimentary picture of Palmerston. See AVPR, Chancery (1852): London, delo 76, fols, 55–69.
30 AVPR, Chancery (1851): London, delo 71, Appendix no. 40 to Brunnov's dispatch of 19 February (3 March), fol. 244.
31 Ibid., delo 81, fol. 268.

14 RUSSIAN VOLUNTEERS IN THE CUBAN WAR OF NATIONAL LIBERATION, 1895-98

L. A. SHUR

THE CUBAN war of national liberation at the close of the nineteenth century has received rather detailed study in Soviet historiography. Not a single work, however, has drawn on materials pertaining to the participation of Russian volunteers in the Cuban revolutionary movement in 1896, uncovered in 1960 by B. F. Fedotov in the Central State Historical Archives of the USSR, in Moscow (TsGIAM).[1]

An article was published about these documents in *Komsomol'skaia Pravda*. Journalists Yu. Zerchaninov and V. Mashkin conducted a search for relatives of the Russian volunteers who fought in Cuba during the years 1895-98.[2] Zerchaninov tells of this search in an essay entitled "That Night at Montezuelo."[3] Documents from Soviet archives and from the Archivo Nacional de Cuba (Havana) make it possible to expand considerably and to complete the story of the participation of Russian volunteers in the Cuban war of national liberation at the end of the nineteenth century, and to correct the inevitable shortcomings and factual errors of previous research.[4]

In May 1896, D. E. Shevich, Russian ambassador in Madrid, informed St. Petersburg that the French government had demanded of Spain that French citizens be tried "by ordinary, rather than extraordinary military courts when captured with arms in hand during an uprising in Spanish territory. I told the [Spanish] Minister of Foreign Affairs that, while one could hardly foresee a similar occurrence with regard to Russian subjects, nonetheless I must stipulate these same privileges for them as well. . . ."[5] But Shevich was deeply mistaken

Originally published as "Ob uchastii russkikh dobrovol'tsev v natsional'no-osvoboditel'noi voine kubinskogo naroda 1895-1898 godov," *Vop. Ist.*, no. 1 (January 1963), 200-207.

in believing that Russians would not participate in the liberation movement in Cuba.

Colonel I. Zhilinskii, sent in 1898 by the Russian general staff as an observer with the Spanish troops, wrote from Havana on 29 August 1898 that among the rebels there had been many foreigners, including "several Russians: Nikolai Melent'ev, Efstafii Konstantinov [ich], and Pëtr Strel'tsov—all three very young. . . . A fourth, the nobleman Panenkov, is still with the insurgents."[6] Thanks to this document, we have learned for the first time the name of a fourth Russian volunteer.[7]

The revolutionary war initiated by the Cuban people in February 1895 evoked a wide response in Russia. The Russian periodical press reported in detail on the course of the war and the mass heroism of the Cuban patriots, condemning the terror of Spanish colonial authorities.[8] The uprising in Cuba, which, according to Zhilinskii, "constituted a movement of a social nature as well as a struggle against Spanish rule,"[9] could not but attract the revolutionary youth of Russia.

In April 1896, three Russian youths—Pëtr Platonovich Strel'tsov, Evstafii Iosifovich Konstantinovich, and Nikolai Gerasimovich Melent'ev—left Russia for New York, whence they intended to go to Cuba. All three had been brought up in the Gatchina Institute for Orphans and were tied "by bonds of friendship."[10] Arriving in New York in May 1896, the three friends went directly to the Cuban revolutionary junta in that city, which was headed by Tomás Estrada Palma,and asked to be sent to Cuba.

A very interesting document was recently uncovered among the papers of the New York Cuban revolutionary junta, housed in the Archivo Nacional de Cuba. It is a page on which are noted in the careful hand of E. Konstantinovich the names of the three Russians: Eustache Konstantynovich, Architect; Nicolas Coecus, le Chemicien; Peter Strelzov, Officer de l'armé Russe. Their address in New York is given as 153 Fulton Street. In a different hand, in Spanish, is written: "Los 3 tienen una sola dirección."[11] This document corroborates information from Strel'tsov's diary, that arriving in New York in May 1896, he and his comrades immediately contacted the Cuban revolutionaries and volunteered to participate in the Cuban people's fight for independence. From this document we also learn for the first time that Nikolai Melent'ev was in Cuba under the name "Tsekus." He used this pseudonym in later years while taking part in the revolutionary struggle in Russia.

In his diary, P. P. Strel'tsov noted that the junta "agreed to our request not without some hesitation, and only after getting to know us better, for which purpose we took up residence with a Cuban family."[12] In New York, Strel'tsov and his friends met Carlos Roloff, a Polish émigré who devoted all of his intelligence and energy to the cause of Cuban independence. The three friends studied Spanish intensively. At the beginning of July 1896, they were assigned to one of the expeditions which the Cuban revolutionaries were getting ready to send to Cuba. This was the expedition commanded by Colonel Rafael Cabrera, the dispatch of which was under the direction of General Emilio Núñez. The names of the three friends were on the list of expedition members.[13] The Cabrera expedition was to have met on Navassa Island (south of Santiago de Cuba) with other rebel groups under the command of General Carlos Roloff.[14] Thus one can presume that the young Russians formed part of this force on Roloff's recommendation. The Cabrera expedition left Charleston on 12 August 1896 aboard the ship *Dauntless*. But, as Strel'tsov wrote in his diary, our three friends arrived late at the place of assembly and missed the boat.[15]

In the middle of August, the Russian volunteers traveled from Charleston to Jacksonville, sailing for Cuba on 3 September aboard the steamship *Three Friends*.[16] At the head of this group of rebels was General Juan Ruiz Rivera. Members of the group included Captain Francisco Gómez (son of Máximo Gómez, commander-in-chief of the Cuban Liberation Army), Captains César Salas and Donato Soto, engineer José Ramón Villalón, and several North American artillerymen. The list of members of the Ruiz Rivera expedition contains the names "Eustache Constantinovich, Nicolás Conceus, Peter Strelzew."[17] The Ruiz Rivera expedition took with it about a thousand rifles, a half-million rounds of ammunition, two thousand pounds of dynamite, a pneumatic field piece, and other supplies. The ship reached the Cuban coast on 8 September and the landing began in Corrientes Bay in the province of Pinar del Río, at a place known as María de la Gorda.[18]

In the company of a detachment sent by Antonio Maceo, the members of the Ruiz Rivera expedition set out for Maceo's encampment. This initial, relatively short march allowed the Russian volunteers to know at first hand heroes of the Cuban revolution. With enthusiasm and admiration Strel'tsov wrote:

> They [the insurgents–L. Sh.] were lame from walking barefoot over the rocks; their backs were worn raw from carrying heavy, cumbersome cases. Some came down with yellow fever: they fell on the bare rocks groaning forlornly as the healthy ones marched past them and moved ever forward, literally carrying on their shoulders the success of the liberation of their fatherland. Throughout the entire march, i.e. in the course of four or five days, many ate almost nothing. . . . Yet despite this, I heard not a single complaint, nor a single rebuke, so great was the spirit of patriotism among the insurgents. This march, these "unseen heroes," made a greater impression on me than anything that I was to see in Cuba subsequently.[19]

On 18 September, General Ruiz Rivera's detachment, of which the three Russians formed part, reached the area of Rematas, where Antonio Maceo had set up camp.[20] Meeting Maceo left a deep impression on Strel'tsov and his comrades. "Maceo's intelligent appearance involuntarily caught one's attention," wrote Strel'tsov.

This was a tall, heavy-set man with a face of large, energetic features, whose dark complexion seemed more the result of sunburn than the fact that its possessor was a mulatto. Wrinkles and streaks of grey hair notwithstanding, Maceo looked much younger than his forty-eight years. In conversation, his whole face seemed to smile, glowing with purely Cuban good nature. In contrast to some of his aides, he addressed everybody as an equal and never raised his voice. This attitude earned him popularity among the Cubans, characteristically expressed in the fact that a majority of Negro rebels joined precisely his detachment. Had he survived to see Cuba free, he would have been a second Spartacus. Even in uniform, Maceo avoided all distinction, limiting himself only to the Cuban colors, which were faded beyond recognition from the sun and bad weather. Not once did I hear a negative remark among the insurgents about Maceo: they all spoke wonders of his bravery and resourcefulness, and somehow one found it difficult to believe that such an apparently healthy man had been wounded twenty-four times. . . . Maceo received us most amicably, and, in addition, said he was very pleased to see in his ranks people from so distant and great a nation as Russia. Each new foreigner, he noted, gives me new hope for the prompt liberation of our unfortunate fatherland, since with the sympathies of the entire world we cannot lose.[21]

Strel'tsov and his comrades immediately understood "how much the insurgents owed their success to this good-natured and outwardly simple mulatto."[22]

The Russian volunteers found themselves in the army of Antonio Maceo, which not long before had undertaken the "campaign of invasion," one of the most brilliant and glorious pages in the history of the Cuban liberation movement. For three months (from 22 October 1895 to 22 January 1896), the Cuban Liberation Army had fought battles over the entire island—from Baragua, in Oriente province in eastern Cuba, to Mantua, in the western province of Pinar del Río, covering a distance of 1,700 kilometers. "The campaign of invasion played a decisive role in the war of liberation of 1895–98. Embracing all of the island's territory and bringing into the struggle the western provinces of Cuba, which had been the stronghold of Spanish rule, it helped give the struggle a broad national character."[23]

In order to confine Maceo's troops to Cuba's westernmost province, Pinar del Río, on the order to the Spanish governor-general of Cuba, Valeriano Weyler, a *trocha* was built in 1896 from Mariel to Majana at the western end of the island—that is, a series of forts connected by trenches, to which other fortifications were added. Weyler's *trocha,* supported by forts on its ocean flanks, severed the island at its narrowest point, and was twenty-four miles in length. "In such a small space," observed Strel'tsov, "were concentrated sixty thousand troops for the purpose of preventing Maceo's force of four thousand from leaving this barren province."[24] "General Weyler has taken personal command of the military operations against Maceo in the province of Pinar del Río," wrote the Russian ambassador to Madrid in a dispatch in October 1896.[25]

With the arrival of General Ruiz Rivera's expedition, which brought quantities of arms and ammunition, Antonio Maceo decided to turn east, cross Weyler's *trocha,* and join forces with Máximo Gómez in the province of La Habana. Maceo's plan consisted in staging battles across the provinces of La Habana and Matanzas so as to demonstrate the falsity of Weyler's assertion that these two provinces had finally been "suppressed."

In order to do this, Maceo had to get from the Rematas area (northwest of the city of Pinar del Río) past the Spanish forts of Mantua, Arroyos, and Levante, and cross the fortified line that ran from Viñales to Levante. This *trocha,* less well known, to be sure, than the Mariel-Majana *trocha,* constituted nonetheless a serious military obstacle. Here were based several Spanish columns (not less than a brigade), which had been operating against the rebel soldiers in this part of Pinar del Río province. It was impossible, therefore, for the rebel army to cross the *trocha* without engaging in bloody battle.[26]

Skirmishes with the Spanish troops began in the very first days of the eastward march. Strel'tsov and his comrades took part in battles at Montezuelo and Tumbas de Estorino, where, in all probability, they served as artillerymen.

The battle of Montezuelo began early on the morning of 24 September. Maceo sent a detachment under the command of Lieutenant-Colonel Pedro Delgado against the Spaniards and ordered artillery fire on the hill which the Spaniards occupied.[27] Strel'tsov described the beginning of the battle as follows:

> Many crowded around the field piece awaiting an opportunity to try out their one and only cannon. They selected a target at random, roughly calculated the distance, and the air resounded with the first cannon shot. . . . It was followed by a second. . . . For a time both sides ceased firing, as if to evaluate the effectiveness and shortcomings of the weapon. The insurgents remained quite satisfied, but for the Spaniards this was a very unpleasant surprise: another two or three such weapons, and the impregnability of the log, tile-roofed forts would be more than doubtful.[28]

The firing began again at dawn. The Cuban positions were situated very near the positions of the Spanish forces. A fierce battle broke out. Under cover of artillery and small arms fire, the Spaniards attacked Maceo's right flank. The insurgents were forced to withdraw and take up new positions. But the Spanish forces, having suffered heavy losses, also withdrew to a nearby hill. "The battle of Montezuelo, which the Spaniards called the battle of Jagua, caused us serious losses," observed José Miró in his book. "Sixty-eight men were put out of action—a fifth of those who took part in the battle."[29]

Following the battle of Montezuelo, Maceo, not wishing to linger in this area, headed for Naranjal and Rubí, where his troops were joined by a detachment of General Pedro Díaz. Strel'tsov recorded in his diary:

> The farther east we moved, the more animated the countryside became, and not so ravaged by war. This was offset by the fact that Spanish forts were more numerous. Each extra day spent by the insurgents in one place or another threatened to end in an engagement with the Spaniards. Maceo never stayed anywhere longer than twenty-four

hours, seeking to preserve his forces for that fatal moment when they would have to force their way across the *trocha*. For nocturnal encampments they usually selected a ravine or valley protected from surprise attack from the mountains or forest.[30]

On 26 September, Maceo approached Tumbas de Estorino, an area situated in the Sierra de los Órganos between Francisco and Majana. The following day, the lead rebel units joined battle with the Spaniards, who attempted to keep Maceo from moving into the mountainous area of Levante. Simultaneously, a battle broke out in the vicinity of Majana, in which Maceo himself took part. There was hand-to-hand combat, and the Spaniards were forced to withdraw.[31] Strel'tsov noted in his diary:[32]

> In the morning the insurgent vanguard entered battle, and in the afternoon the main forces began to move. Suddenly, ahead of us, there was a volley of small arms fire, which echoed several times through the mountains. It was followed by a second, and a third. . . . The insurgents quickly took up positions and began to return the fire. Several officers from Maceo's staff hurried off in search of a position for the field piece. We were forced to climb a high hill. The trunks of fallen trees so impeded our movement that it took us an hour to reach the top. Bullets whined over our heads. We were separated from the line of skirmish by a pine forest that spread over the sides of the mountains and part of the valley. Showing yellow in the distance was the road held by the Spaniards. The crack of gunfire subsided and stopped, then began again with renewed force.[33]

In the course of these battles, fourteen rebels were killed and forty-seven wounded.[34] One of the wounded was Russian volunteer E. I. Konstantinovich.[35]

The following day, Maceo led his troops over a mountain trail to Francisco, there to give the rebels rest, especially those who had carried on their shoulders the ammunition and supplies brought to the expedition by the steamship *Three Friends*.[36] "Due to the continuous rain, the ground became so soft that we were obliged to proceed very slowly," recorded Strel'tsov.

> The unshod horses stumbled and went lame. On top of that, the countryside became mountainous: you no sooner managed to climb one mountain than another, higher and steeper, appeared beyond. On reaching a ravine, the entire detachment came to a halt: people and horses skidded down the embankment, piling up in a filthy yellow, soggy heap. The other side was taken by assault—on all fours. They lowered the field gun with ropes or carried it across in pieces. There was no fear of running into the Spaniards, for they did not use such out-of-the-way paths. By evening we reached the prefecture of Francisco.[37]

Maceo's soldiers spent 29 and 30 September resting in Francisco. The gravely wounded and the ill who could continue no further were left here in the care of local peasants.[38] The three Russians stayed behind in Francisco. E. Konstantinovich had been wounded, and N. Melent'ev "had fallen sick with two illnesses at once—yellow fever and dysentery," wrote Strel'tsov in his diary. "It was impossible to secure horses, as they were in great scarcity. I stayed with [Konstantinovich and Melent'ev] pending their recovery."[39]

Strel'tsov, Konstantinovich, and Melent'ev spent about two weeks in Francisco. "We took up residence in the prefecture, overcrowded with wounded, sick, and even persons in perfect health seeking refuge."[40] There were no doctors, and one of the Russians (apparently Strel'tsov himself) dressed wounds and cared for the sick. "One would like to leave this hole as quickly as possible," Strel'tsov wrote, "and return to Maceo. . . ."[41] But in mid-October the three Russians fell into the hands of the Spaniards and were sent under escort to the city of Pinar del Río, and from there to Havana, where they were at the disposal of Captain-General Weyler. In Havana, the Russian volunteers were placed in the Morro fortress, where, as Strel'tsov noted in his diary, "almost all the prisoners were held either on suspicion or for sympathizing [with the rebels]. . . . During our entire stay in the fortress, [the prisoners] treated us most kindly."[42] In late October 1896, the Havana newspapers wrote of the imprisoned Russian volunteers.

On 1 November, the Spanish authorities informed the Russian consul supernumerary in Havana, Repère de Truffin, of the three Russians who had fought in the rebel army.[43] After several days, Strel'tsov and his comrades were turned over to the consul, who on 5 November placed them on an American steamship bound for New York, providing them with clothing and money for the trip, since "they had shown up at the consulate not only without any monetary means, but literally in rags."[44]

In New York, Strel'tsov, Konstantinovich, and Melent'ev "were placed in quarantine, after which the Bureau of Immigration refused to admit them, since they did not have the established amount of money required of immigrants for entry into the country." The three friends turned, not to the Russian consulate general in New York, but to revolutionary émigrés who "sponsored them and thereby made it possible for them to disembark in New York." The participation of Strel'tsov and his comrades in the rebel movement in Cuba and their ties with Russian émigrés in the United States attracted the attention of the Russian consul general in New York, A. E. Olarovskii, who, on 13 November 1896, sent a special letter to the St. Petersburg police department reporting that Strel'tsov, Konstantinovich, and Melent'ev "are present in a group of our revolutionaries, and I have placed them under surveillance through Liubin."[45] Attached to Olarovskii's dispatch was a copy of a letter from Truffin and also two reports from Liubin, who from this moment forth attentively followed the three young men.[46]

Thus, on 23 November, Liubin reported to Olarovskii that Strel'tsov, Konstantinovich and Melent'ev "have fallen into the hands of the local socialists."[47] And at the end of December, Strel'tsov "gave a lecture in Valhalla Hall on the revolutionary movement in Cuba. . . . Proceeds from the lecture went to Konstantinovich, Melent'ev, and Strel'tsov."[48] Beyond this brief record of a police informant, we have at our disposal no other materials pertaining to Strel'tsov's lecture. But, judging by the fact that someone who spoke after Strel'tsov, according to Liubin's record, "advised the young people from Russia to defend Russia and not Cuba," one can presume that Strel'tsov not only related his impressions of the revolutionary island, but also called on the Russian émigrés to assist the Cuban people in their struggle for national liberation. The three young men, reported Liubin, attended meetings of various Russian exile groups in New York and took part in discussions of the Russian Social-Democratic Society, where on this very occasion one of the speakers declared that "solely on the outcome of social revolution, in whatever country it might be carried out, depends the liberation of Russia."[49]

Participation in the revolutionary struggle in Cuba was not lost on the Russian volunteers. To a greater or lesser degree, they fought in the ranks of the Russian revolutionary movement against tsarist autocracy.

Following his return home in 1898, E. I. Konstantinovich graduated in 1907 from the Superior Art College of the Academy of Arts and became an architect.[50] He took part in the revolution of 1905–7. In his police record it is mentioned that in 1896 Konstantinovich "during a stay on the island of Cuba took part in a rebellion which occurred there. . . ."[51]

After returning home in 1897, N. G. Melent'ev immediately established ties with the Social Democrats and became a professional revolutionary. Already in New York, police informant Liubin had observed that Melent'ev "was of greater importance to the revolutionaries than his comrades."[52] In 1897, Melent'ev was "detained for questioning by the St. Petersburg provincial police administration about a criminal association called 'the Union of Struggle for the Liberation of the Working Class.' "[53] In August of that year he was arrested in the matter of a secret printing press in Novgorod. Melent'ev was "convicted of possessing revolutionary publications," and, in 1898, after a preliminary detention, was sent under police escort to Tambov.[54] It is interesting to note that the police file on Melent'ev mentions that "in 1896 he was expelled from the island of Cuba for having participated in the revolutionary uprising against the Spanish government."[55] In January 1900, Melent'ev was again arrested, this time for involvement in the Tambov Social-Democratic Circle and in a secret printing press in Tambov, and was exiled for three years to Viatskaia *guberniia*. He was accused of "helping to guard and conceal a printing press, together with its appurtenances."[56]

On his return home in 1897, P. P. Strel'tsov took up residence in Gorodok (Vitebskaia *guberniia*), but after a short while moved to Vitebsk. From the beginning of 1898, he worked as a reporter for the *Vitebskie gubernskie vedomosti;*[57] in 1901 he became assistant editor of the paper, and in 1906 served as editor and managed the provincial press.[58] Like his comrades, Strel'tsov, too, found his way to the revolution. In December 1906, very likely in connection with his involvement in the revolutionary movement, Strel'tsov was removed from his position as editor of the *Vitebskie gubernskie vedomosti,* and in February 1907 he was forced to resign from the paper.[59] In March and April 1907, Strel'tsov came under secret police surveillance as a result of his membership in the Social-Democratic Workers Party.[60]

Following his return to Russia, Strel'tsov worked extensively on his notes on the trip to Cuba, having already sent the first part of these notes to the editors of *Vestnik Evropy* from New York in late February or early March 1897.[61] In September 1897, Strel'tsov sent M. M. Stasiulevich, publisher and editor of *Vestnik Evropy,* the second part of his notes,[62] which were published in the May issue of *Vestnik Evropy* for 1898 under the title "Two Months on the Island of Cuba." Strel'tsov's notes were signed "P. S-ov."[63] Until very recently they have scarcely been used by Soviet researchers. This piece represents an extraordinarily valuable source for the history of the Cuban national-liberation movement at the end of the nineteenth century. Researchers, however, have doubted the accuracy of the notes, since Strel'tsov "ciphered" his diary as much as possible so as to conceal from tsarist authorities the participation of Russian volunteers in the armed struggle of the Cuban people. Comparing Strel'tsov's notes, based, in all likelihood, on his diary, with Cuban sources and the memoirs of José Miró y Argenter, the notes of Maceo's adjutant Manuel Piedra-Martel, and others, we are persuaded that Strel'tsov's article is accurate.[64]

Materials on the participation of Russian volunteers in the Cuban War of national liberation in the years of 1895-1898 are evidence of the deep attention and sympathy of progressive groups in Russia toward this distant island of the Caribbean.

NOTES

1 See Z. Peregudova and B. Fedotov, "Russkie vmeste s kubintsami: Stranichka istorii," *Nedelia* (supplement to the newspaper *Izvestiia*), no. 22 (24-30 July 1960), 11; and "Khronikal'nye zametki," *Vop. Ist.,* no. 10 (1960), 149.

2 See Yu. Zerchaninov and V. Mashkin, "Troe russkikh na Kube," *Komsomol'skaia Pravda,* 7 August 1960; also idem, "Tres rusos que combatieron en Cuba en la guerra del 95," *URSS* (Havana), no. 2 (March, 1961).

3 Yu. Zerchaninov, "V tu noch' pod Montesuelo," *Yunost',* no. 3 (1962), 96-106.

4 Thus, not having checked Strel'tsov's notes on his sojourn in Cuba in 1896 against Cuban sources, Yu. Zerchaninov entitles his essay "That Night at Montezuelo," when in fact he should have called it "That Night at Tumbas de Estorino," since in his notes Strel'tsov mistakenly called the battle of Tumbas de Estorino the battle of Montezuelo (see below).

5 Arkhiv vneshnei politiki Rossii (Russian Foreign Policy Archives, hereafter AVPR). Chancellery (1896), delo 132, fol. 36.

6 Tsentral'nyi gosudarstvennyi voenno-istoricheskii arkhiv (Central State Military History Archives, hereafter TsGVIA), fond 401, opis' 5 (1898), delo 39, pt. II, fol. 236. Lieutenant D. B. Pokhvisnev, who was sent at the same time as I. Zhilinskii by the Russian naval ministry in the capacity of an observer with the Spanish fleet, also reported from Havana on 20 July 1898 on the participation of Russians in the rebel movement in Cuba. See A. A. Guver, comp., "Agressiia SShA na Kube," *IA*, no. 3 (1961), 38.

7 A search for papers on Panenkov has as yet produced no results.

8 See L. A. Shur, "Russkie puteshestvenniki na Kube v XVIII–XIX vv.," in A. V. Efimov and I. R. Grigulevich, eds., *Kuba: Istoriko-etnograficheskie ocherki* (Moscow, 1961), pp. 288–89.

9 TsGVIA, fond 401, opis' 5 (1898), delo 39, pt. II, fol. 236. Zhilinskii recorded that the insurgents "destroyed sugar, coffee and other plantations . . . belonging not only to Spaniards, but to Cubans and foreigners as well, acting in general against the wealthy classes of the population." (See loc. cit., fols. 236–37.)

10 Tsentral'nyi gosudarstvennyi istoricheskii arkhiv v Moskve (Central State Historical Archives—Moscow, hereafter TsGIAM), fond DP, 00 (1898), delo 648, fol. 6.

P. P. Strel'tsov was born of an impoverished noble family on 1 January 1875 in the town of Gorodok, in Vitebskaia *guberniia*. In 1885, he was turned over to the Gatchina Institute for Orphans as a "welfare pupil," graduating from the Institute's sixth class in April 1893. In June 1893, "he was nominated to serve in the 163rd Lenkoransko-Nasheburgskii infantry regiment as a private with volunteer status." In October 1894, he entered the reserves at the rank of ensign. He served as a "clerk" in the offices of the provincial government (Tsentral'nyi gosudarstvennyi istoricheskii arkhiv Belorusskoi Sovetskoi Sotsialisticheskoi Respubliki [Central State Historical Archives of the Byelorussian Soviet Socialist Republic, hereafter TsGIA BSSR], fond 1416, opis' 1, delo 19385, fols. 6, 8, 10–11, 57, 81), and then as a traffic agent on the St. Petersburg-Warsaw railroad. In January 1896, Strel'tsov arrived in St. Petersburg and became an accountant with the railroad, where he worked until his departure for America (TsGIAM, loc, cit., fols. 6, 29).

E. I. Konstantinovich was born on 29 June 1874 to the family of a major in the border patrol on Dagö Island. He early became an orphan and was turned over to the Gatchina Institute for Orphans, whence following his graduation he entered in 1894 the department of architecture of the Superior Art College of the Academy of Arts. His material situation appears to have been serious, since in his second year of studies he applied for a monthly allowance. See Tsentral'nyi gosudarstvennyi istoricheskii arkhiv v Leningrade (Central State Historical Archives—Leningrad, hereafter TsGIAL), fond 789, opis' 12 (1894), delo 14–I, fols. 2, 4–5, 15, 17.

N. G. Melent'ev, the son of a college registrar, was born on 5 December 1874 in St. Petersburg (TsGIAM, fond DP, 3 d-vo [1897], delo 671, fol. 32). Upon graduation from the Gatchina Institute, he worked in the offices of state control (TsGIAM, fond DP, 00 [1898], delo 648, fol. 6).

11 Archivo Nacional de Cuba (hereafter ANC). Delegación cubana en Neuva York, 1892–1898, leg. 3-22-4. The author expresses his profound gratitude to the director of

the Cuban National Archives, Professor Julio Le Riverand, who provided photocopies of documents pertaining to the sojourn in Cuba of the Russian volunteers.

12 P. S[trel']tsov, "Dva mesiatsa na ostrove Kuba," *Vestnik Evropy*, no. 5 (1898), 131.

13 ANC, Delegación cubana en Nueva York, 1892-1898, leg. 3-22-4.

14 Justo Carrillo Morales, *Expediciones cubanas*, 2 vols. (Havana, 1930-36), I, 61.

15 In a letter dated 14 August 1896 to Estrada Palma in New York, Rafael Cabrera expressed regret that the three Russian volunteers had not arrived in time to board the ship and called them "splendid fellows." See Partido Revolucionario Cubano, *La Revolución del 95, según la correspondencia de la Delegación cubana en Neuva York*, 5 vols. (Havana, 1932-1937), V, 223.

16 José Miró y Argenter, *Cuba: Crónicas de la guerra* (Havana, 1943), p. 89. In some sources a different date is given for the departure of this expedition to Cuba: 31 August. See Ramiro Guerra y Sánchez et al., *Historia de la nación cubana*, 10 vols. (Havana, 1952), VI, 315. Strel'tsov records in his notes that the expedition put to sea on 3 September 1896.

17 Carrillo Morales, *Expediciones cubanas*, I, 69.

18 Guerra y Sánchez et al., *Historia de la nación cubana*, VI, 315; Miguel Varona Guerrero, *La Guerra de independencia de Cuba, 1895-1898*, 3 vols. (Havana, 1946), II, 1308; Miró y Argenter, *Cuba: Crónicas de la guerra*, pp. 89-90.

19 Strel'tsov, "Dva mesiatsa na ostrove Kuba," p. 135.

20 See memoirs of Antonio Maceo's chief-of-staff, José Miró y Argenter, *Cuba: Crónicas de la guerra*, p. 90.

21 Strel'tsov, "Dva mesiatsa na ostrove Kuba," p. 138.

22 Ibid., pp. 138-39.

23 A. M. Zorina, *Iz geroicheskogo proshlogo kubinskogo naroda* (Moscow, 1961), p. 195.

24 Strel'tsov, "Dva mesiatsa na ostrove Kuba," p. 137.

25 AVPR, fond II, department 1-5, razriad III (1896), delo 1/5, fol. 52.

26 Miró y Argenter, *Cuba: Crónicas de la guerra*, p. 91; Guerra y Sánchez et al., *Historia de la nación cubana*, p. 240; Manuel Piedra-Martel, *Campañas de Maceo en la última Guerra de Independencia* (Havana, 1946), p. 199.

27 Miró y Argenter, *Cuba: Crónicas de la guerra*, pp. 92-93; Piedra-Martel, *Campañas de Maceo*, pp. 199-201.

28 Strel'tsov, "Dva mesiatsa na ostrove Kuba," p. 140.

29 Miró y Argenter, *Cuba: Crónicas de la guerra*, p. 95. Strel'tsov wrote in his diary that forty-five men were killed or wounded; see "Dva mesiatsa na ostrove Kuba," p. 142.

30 Strel'tsov, "Dva mesiatsa na ostrove Kuba," p. 142.

31 Miró y Argenter, *Cuba: Crónicas de la guerra*, pp. 97-98; Manuel Piedra-Martel, *Mis primeros treinta años: Memorias* (Havana, 1945), p. 261.

32 Strel'tsov incorrectly called the battle of Tumbas de Estorino the battle of Montezuelo.

33 Strel'tsov, "Dva mesiatsa na ostrove Kuba," p. 144.

34 Miró y Argenter, *Cuba: Crónicas de las guerra*, pp. 98, 100.

35 He is not named in Strel'tsov's diary. But in February 1897 (having already returned from Cuba to New York), Konstantinovich himself wrote in an official statement to the [St. Petersburg] Academy of Arts that he had been forced to tarry in America "due to a serious leg injury, which had occurred in September." See TsGIAL, fond 789, opis' 12 (1894), delo 14-I, fol. 54.

36 Miró y Argenter, *Cuba: Crónicas de la guerra*, p. 100.
37 Strel'tsov, "Dva mesiatsa na ostrove Kuba," p. 146.
38 Miró y Argenter, *Cuba: Crónicas de la guerra*, p. 100.
39 Strel'tsov, "Dva mesiatsa na ostrove Kuba," p. 146.
40 Ibid., p. 148.
41 Ibid., p. 151.
42 Ibid., p. 164.
43 François du Repère de Truffin was the Russian consul in Havana. According to P. Sipiagin, Russian consul general in Barcelona, he wrote "valuable reports of a political nature" on the situation in Cuba. See AVPR, Chancery (1896), delo 132, fol. 25. In 1898, Truffin rendered assistance to the Russian observers attached to the Spanish army and navy, Colonel Zhilinskii and Lieutenant Pokhvisnev, as a result of which Shevich felt moved to propose Truffin for a decoration. See AVPR, Departament lichnogo sostava i khoziaistvennykh del, opis' 740/1 (1898), delo 1258, fols. 131–32.
44 TsGIAM, fond DP, 00 (1898), delo 648, fols. 9, 11–12.
45 Ibid., fol. 1.
46 Ibid., fols. 3–4.
47 Ibid., fol. 4.
48 TsGIAM, fond DP, 3 d-vo (1897), delo 671, fol. 3.
49 TsGIAM, fond DP, 00 (1898), delo 648, fol. 4.
50 See S. N. Kondakov, *Yubileinyi spravochnik imperatorskoi Akademii khudozhestv, 1764–1914*, 2 pts. (St. Petersburg, 1914), II (Biograficheskaia), p. 344; TsGIAL, fond, 789, opis' 12 (1894), delo 14-I.
51 TsGIAM, fond DP, 00 (1913), delo 9, pt. 1, 3 gr., fol. 167.
52 TsGIAM, fond DP, 3 d-vo (1897), delo 671, fol. 4.
53 Ibid., fol. 48.
54 Ibid., fols. 11, 13, 15–16.
55 Ibid., fol. 15.
56 Ibid., fols. 26, 41–42.
57 TsGIA, BSSR, loc, cit., fols, 1–3. See also V. Pokhvalov and A. Liudina, "Russkie na Kube," in *Mogilevskaia Pravda*, 11 September 1960.
58 TsGIA BSSR, fond 1416, opis' 1, delo 19385, fol. 81.
59 Ibid., fols. 64, 69–70, 81–82.
60 TsGIAM, fond DP, 00 (1907), delo 9, pt. 7, fol. 61.
61 The manuscript was received by the editors on 20 March 1897. See Manuscript Department, Institute of Russian Literature of the USSR Academy of Sciences (Pushkinskii Dom), fond 293, opis' 3, fol. 33.
62 Ibid., fol. 43.
63 Strel'tsov's authorship was established on the basis of the "Katalog rukopisei postupivshikh v redaktsiiu 'Vestnika Evropy' (1896–1899)" [Catalog of manuscripts received by the editors of *Vestnik Evropy* (1896–1899)], housed in the manuscript department of Pushkinskii Dom (fond 293, opis' 3 delo 6, fols. 33, 43), and also of the "Kniga vydachi gonorara po zhurnalu 'Vestnik Evropy'" [Record of fees paid by the journal *Vestnik Evropy*], fond 293, delo 11, fol. 65.
64 In addition to the notes on his sojourn in Cuba which appeared in *Vestnik Evropy*, Strel'tsov wrote a lengthy article entitled "The Island of Cuba," which was published

in three issues of the *Vitebskie gubernskie vedomosti* (no. 49 [25 April 1898], 5–6; no. 50 [28 April 1898], 5–6; no. 51 [30 April 1898], 7) under the signature "Sinus." Strel'tsov's authorship was established on the basis of textual coincidences with his article in *Vestnik Evropy,* as well as individual details pointing to the author's having been on the island of Cuba.

15 | THE EMERGENCE OF THE FIRST LABOR ORGANIZATIONS AND MARXIST GROUPS IN THE COUNTRIES OF LATIN AMERICA, 1870–1900

V. I. ERMOLAEV

As A rule, contemporary Latin American bourgeois historians ignore the history of the revolutionary labor movement, or if they do write about it, more often than not they paint a distorted picture.[1] In like fashion they also misinterpret the history of the spread of Marxist thought in Latin America. In this regard, Latin American bourgeois authors frequently repeat the fundamental tenets of reactionary U.S. historiography.

In the United States, Professor Robert Alexander of Rutgers University, who published the voluminous book *Communism in Latin America*,[2] defends a "conception" typical of American bourgeois historiography. In essence, it comes down to the erroneous thesis that Marxism and communism are somehow alien to Latin America, and, for that matter, to the entire Western Hemisphere. According to Alexander, the ideas of Marxism began to circulate in Latin America only after the October Revolution, and solely through the influence of Soviet Russia.[3] By falsifying the history of the Latin American labor movement, Alexander and other apologists for the aggressive policies of U.S. monopolies seek to impose on the peoples of Latin America the ideas of colonialism and Pan-Americanism.

Latin American socialist leaders (Juan B. Justo, Emilio Frugoni, Nicolás Repetto, Américo Ghioldi, and others) hold that the dissemination of the ideas of scientific socialism in the Latin American countries was tied exclusively to the emergence of socialist parties at the end of the 1890s and the beginning of the present century. The first to express this view was Juan B. Justo.[4] Such an interpretation is clearly designed to exalt the socialist leaders and to exaggerate

Originally published as "Vozniknovenie pervykh rabochikh organizatsii i marksistskikh kruzhkov v stranakh Latinskoi Ameriki (1870–1900 gg.)," *Vop. Ist.*, no. 1 (January 1959), 81–97.

their significance in the development of the labor movement in Latin America. Without negating the positive role of the socialist parties in disseminating Marxism during the first years of their existence, one cannot fail to state that after the late 1890s the socialists propagated revisionist Bernsteinian* views. It was not by chance that Justo and his followers responded with hostility to the October Revolution, fighting for class peace as if that were the means of delivering the working class from poverty and exploitation.[5]

The reformist followers of Justo (e.g. Repetto, Ghioldi, Haya de la Torre) held even more rightest views, and became ardent accomplices of the bourgeoisie. In the 1930s one of Justo's closest disciples, the rightest socialist [Jacinto] Oddone, duly recognized the activity of Argentina's first Marxist revolutionaries in his book *The History of Argentine Socialism*.[6] But fifteen years later, in the volume *The Argentine Trade Union Movement*,[7] he espoused revisionism, while slandering Marxism and the October Revolution.

In Latin American Marxist historiography, only a few articles and books touch on the history of the spread of Marxism in nineteenth-century Latin America.[8] In Soviet historical literature, neither this problem, nor the question of the emergence in Latin America of the first labor organizations, has yet been treated. The present article seeks to examine several aspects of the history of the emergence of labor organizations and the spread of Marxism in this area of the world during the final three decades of the last century.

At the beginning of the 1870s, the countries of Latin America were still in the initial stage of capitalist development. Capitalist relations developed here at a time when the major European powers and the United States were experiencing the rapid formation of trusts and monopolies. By taking advantage of difficulties in the fledgling, as yet unconsolidated Latin American states, the Anglo-American monopolists gradually entangled them in chains of financial and economic dependence, converting them into suppliers of agricultural goods and raw materials, a source of enrichment and plunder. In a number of places the growth of capitalism was hindered by slavery, semifeudal agriculture, and an artisan-based form of production. The progress of society was also hampered by the Catholic Church, which in a majority of the Latin American countries exercised economic and political power. But to stop the growth of new productive relations in these countries was no longer possible.

Latin America had embarked on the road to capitalist development already in the first half of the nineteenth century. This was facilitated by its independence from the Hispano-Portuguese yoke and resultant inclusion in the sphere of world trade, and also by the influx of foreign capital and the intensive construction of

*Eduard Bernstein (1850–1932)—German socialist theoretician of gradualist views.

railroads and ports. At the same time, there sprang up textile, food, and mining industries. Agriculture in the Latin American countries became increasingly commercial, export-oriented.

In the 1880s and '90s Argentina, Brazil, Chile, Mexico, Uruguay, and Cuba experienced some industrial development, but because of feudal vestiges and the dependency of these states on the imperialist powers, the growth of capitalist production dragged on for decades. With the development of new productive relations in the countries of Latin America, working-class cadres were gradually formed. The uneven economic development of the Latin American countries is seen in the peculiarities of the formation of the proletariat and in the degree of maturity of the labor movement. It is a characteristic fact that the Latin American proletariat was formed mainly from European immigrants. The Europeans who went to Latin America became an organic part of the bourgeois nations which were being formed in these countries, together with the old Indian-Negro and Creole-Mestizo population.[9]

The situation of the fledgling proletariat in the Latin American countries was extremely difficult. According to the testimony of contemporaries, workers had "no rights or guarantees" and their economic situation was one of "hopeless poverty."[10] A working day in the factories and mines lasted from twelve to sixteen hours, and, due to a lack of technology and sanitary facilities, working conditions were horrible. Mutilation on the job was a usual and systematic phenomenon. Workers did not have Sundays off; they had no holidays, nor accident insurance. Jobs were subject to a system of fines and the arbitrary rule of bosses and overseers. As a rule, the employer and his assistants were armed. In the mines of Mexico, Brazil, Colombia, Chile, and Peru, where a significant part of the workers was comprised of Indians and Negroes, a system of corporal punishments for the least negligence on the job was in force down to the end of the nineteenth century.

From the very beginning, the Latin American proletariat conducted a struggle for more humane working and living conditions. A large role in this struggle belongs to the immigrant workers. Until the late 1860s, emigration from Europe to South America was insignificant, but following the bloody repression of the Paris Commune there came a great wave of refugees. The Communards were the first propagandists of Marxist ideas among the workers of Latin America. Before that time, there had been some dissemination of the utopian-socialist ideas of Fourier, Saint-Simon, and Owen, and of the petty-bourgeois socialism of Proudhon and Louis Blanc. Before the 1870s, the writings of the founders of scientific communism appeared in Latin America only rarely. As early as the sixties, Luis M. Olea in Chile, Carlos Baliño in Cuba, and Santiago Villanueva in Mexico, progressive representatives of the Latin American intelligentsia, who were connected with labor organizations, read the *Manifesto of the Communist Party* and other works by Marx and Engels. But the widespread dissemination of the ideas of scientific communism and also the creation of class organizations of the proletariat date from the early seventies, and are tied to the activities of the General Council of the First International.

The first relatively important trade unions and labor papers appeared in the 1860s and '70s in Argentina, Mexico, Chile, and Uruguay. These proletarian organizations sought persistently to establish ties with the European labor movement and with the First International.

The formation of proletarian-class organizations in the countries of Latin America became possible due to the growth of the working class, and the latter's gradual realization of their class interests and of the necessity of carrying on an organized struggle for their rights and improved living conditions. Naturally, the organizational and ideological level of the labor movement in one Latin American country or another was determined in large measure by the degree of economic development in that country. Thus in Argentina, which embarked on the capitalist path earlier than other countries in Latin America, the labor movement was distinguished by a relative maturity; here the ground was relatively fertile for the ideas of Marxism, cultivated by revolutionaries who emigrated from Europe. In other countries, where there were still vestiges of feudalism and even slavery (for example, Brazil) and where industry developed slowly, there were fewer possibilities for a class organization of workers and for propagandizing among them the ideas of scientific socialism. There revolutionary Marxists were obliged to carry on a more difficult struggle against petty-bourgeois and anarchosyndicalist ideas.[11] Without pretending to offer an exhaustive discussion of all aspects of the topic (owing to a lack of sufficient materials), the present article seeks to show, based primarily on the examples of Argentina, Mexico, and Brazil, that the spread of Marxist ideas and the creation of labor organizations in Latin America were the result of internal historical processes and constitute a phenomenon inherent in all the countries of the world where there has emerged that new, most progressive and revolutionary class of contemporary society, the proletariat.

By the close of the last century, the population of Argentina had grown from 1.8 million (in 1869) to 4 million people. There already existed in the country a railroad network of 16,500 kilometers of track; light industry and agriculture were being developed. Buenos Aires had become a major city, with 500,000 inhabitants and a splendid port.[12] According to the census of 1895, there were 22,000 enterprises in Argentina, employing a total of 176,000 workers.[13]

The first trade unions and workers' societies appeared here in the 1850s and '60s. Labor papers and leaflets began to be published in the late sixties and early seventies. In 1870 there already existed unions of masons, bakers, construction workers, and printers. The printers union of Buenos Aires (Sociedad Tipográfica Bonaerense) was founded in 1857. It issued the paper *Anales de la Sociedad Tipográfica Bonaerense*. In 1870, this union began to establish international ties.

From archival sources it is known that in that year the first numbers of the paper were sent to Spain, to the Federal Council of the Spanish section of the First International. The secretary of the Federal Council, Francisco Mora, recalled this fact in a letter to the General Council of the International in London, dated 14 December 1870.[14] He noted that the *Anales de la Sociedad Tipográfica Bonaerense* shed light on the social problems of the South American cities of Montevideo, Rio de Janeiro, Córdoba, and Valparaíso. "Judging from the press," wrote Mora, "this organization [the printers union of Buenos Aires-V. E.] is international in nature." Mora recommended that the General Council associate itself with the printers union of Buenos Aires, "inasmuch as through it, it will be possible to establish sections of the International throughout South America." For his part, he promised to assist in establishing contact with Latin America, and assured [the General Council] that the Spaniards could "do something in this vast Spanish-speaking area."[15] On 12 August 1871, in an ordinary letter, Mora tersely informed the General Council: "We are doing everything possible to establish a section of the International Workingmen's Association in South America. You should work toward the same end. Success will then be assured."[16]

Two weeks before this, on 31 July, Friedrich Engels sent a letter to Buenos Aires in the name of the General Council, the subject of which was the all-important General Council meeting of 30 May 1871 devoted to discussion of the lessons of the Paris Commune.[17] At this meeting the celebrated proclamation *Civil War in France,* written by Marx, was adopted.[18]

The above-cited materials permit us to conclude that already in the 1870s labor organizations which studied Marxist literature were formed in Argentina. These organizations endeavored to establish ties with the first international proletarian organization, founded by Marx and Engels, which exercised international leadership of the labor movement and actively brought socialist ideas into that movement. By this time, the proletarian organizations of Argentina already exercised some influence on the labor movement and were gravitating toward the First International. It is known that in 1871 the General Council adopted a resolution which obliged local organizations affiliating with the First International to change their names and call themselves sections of the First International.[19]

In the 1870s several proletarian organizations in Argentina called themselves sections of the International Workingmen's Association. They were formed by proletarians from Europe, based on language. The first section of the International in Argentina was the French section, organized on 28 January 1872.[20] Its membership included not only Frenchmen but also representatives of other nationalities who had become naturalized in Argentina.[21] In a letter to the General Council dated 10 February 1872, the section asked to join "the great family and to be honored with reciprocal correspondence." It communicated its need of support and advice. The letter also spoke of the growth of the section's ranks.

This letter was signed by twenty-six members, including a former member of the Paris Normal School section, Auguste Monnot.[22] A second letter to the General Council dated 14 April 1872 related that the section numbered eighty-nine members (on the fifteenth of March there had been seventy). "Everywhere," the letter noted, "people are talking about the International." The section saw as its most important task the organization of a socialist newspaper.[23]

As seen from a letter to the General Council of 16 July 1872, by this time the French section of the International Workingmen's Association in Buenos Aires numbered 273 members. Émile Flèche wrote, "We will not stay at this figure." In his letter he reported the formation of an Italian section, the nucleus of which had detached itself from the French section. The Italian section, in Flèche's view, "will acquire tremendous significance, since the Italians comprise the most significant part of foreign residents in Buenos Aires."[24]

Soon there appeared a Spanish section as well. In a letter to Engels dated 25 March 1873,[25] Larocque-Latrac, one of the leaders of the Buenos Aires section of the First International, wrote: "At present in Buenos Aires there exist three International sections based on various languages: the French section, founded first, and the Italian and Spanish sections, established a short time later. In each section there is a governing Central Committee. General matters are discussed in a Federal Council comprised of six members (two from each section)."[26] The author of the letter also reported growing difficulties in the activities of International sections, a strengthening of reaction in Argentina, and the isolation of sections from the European labor movement.[27]

On receiving news from Buenos Aires about the establishment of the French section, the General Council of the First International immediately recognized its existence. The secretary of the General Council, [Benjamin] Le Moussu, sent official notification of this from London to Buenos Aires on 1 July 1872. "The General Council," read the letter, "recognizes your section and takes cognizance of your initiative in spreading the ideas of the International in South America."[28] Together with this letter, Le Moussu sent to Buenos Aires twelve copies of the Charter of the International Workingmen's Association, adopted in September 1861 at the IWA's London Conference.

The number of supporters of the International in Buenos Aires grew. In September 1872 they began to publish a newspaper, El Trabajador.[29] At the International's Hague Congress, mention was made of the activity of the Buenos Aires associations in the summary report of the General Council.[30] The sections' representative at the congress was Raymond Vilmar, a prominent member of the International and one of [Paul] Lafargue's closest friends. At the beginning of May 1873, Vilmar was in Buenos Aires. On 13 May he wrote to Marx acknowledging the receipt of a letter and thanked Marx for his attention and assistance.[31] Along with Marx's letter, Vilmar apparently received a package of literature. "I regret," he wrote, "that you did not add to this Civil War in France, the

Manifesto of the Communist Party, and other writings.'' Especially significant in Vilmar's letter is the following: ''In the future I shall advise you as to the possibility of disseminating *Das Kapital.*''[32]

Elsewhere, Vilmar informed Marx that the Federal Council of the International sections had discussed the matter of organizing a federation of artisans. In this regard, he points out that there existed in Buenos Aires associations of carpenters and tailors.[33] This reference indicates the active efforts of the International sections to organize the workers.

The leadership of the sections observed precautionary measures against conspiracy, in accordance with the Charter of the International. In order to join the Association, recommendations were required and an investigation was conducted. In July 1872 Émile Flèche informed the General Council about Alexandre Picard, a former member of the Paris Commune: ''This citizen is known to the Council, and we should like to have some information on him before finally allowing him to work in the Association. We would also like to have information on citizen Job Désiré,[34] who in turn was sent as a delegate to the militia of Marseilles, and also on citizen Bernaton Auguste, who was a member of the Commune in Marseilles.''[35]

Workers societies and groups were formed also in other cities of Argentina. In 1874, for example, labor organizations in Córdoba joined together to form an association of workers, calling themselves a section of the First International.[36] The association's membership included university students as well.

The growth of the labor movement in Argentina produced the violent reaction of clerical-landholding sectors. Revolutionary organizations were systematically crushed. Repressive measures against partisans of the International were most savage.

The associations of workers and students in Argentina ceased to exist in 1876, as did the International Workingmen's Association. Many revolutionaries— members of the sections of the First International—continued to work in proletarian organizations of other Latin American countries (Uruguay, etc.). In 1879, following a wave of strikes by unionized printers, stone masons, and bakers, former section members of the International in Argentina founded the revolutionary society Avantgard, which published a newspaper by the same name which propagandized the ideas of scientific socialism. The increased activity of the anarchists in Europe also had an influence on Argentina, where there existed an anarchist organization which published a newspaper, *La Idea.*

After 1878 the influx of emigrants from Germany into Argentina increased. Among others, the following socialists warrant mention: the engineer Hermann Lahlman, August Kühn, Friedrich Weber, Johann Schaffer, Heinrich Müller. The German socialists founded the Vorwärts Club[37] in Buenos Aires in January 1882, which through its published organ, the newspaper *Vorwärts,* propagandized the ideas of Marx and Engels.[38] They drew support for their activities from local workers societies and the progressive intelligentsia. For thirty years before the founding of the Argentine Socialist Party, the Vorwärts Club, which included not only European immigrants but also some progressive Argentine intellectuals and workers, played a major role in organizing the proletarian movement and actively directing the strike movement of the Argentine proletariat.[39] The club's directors—president Weber, Schaffer, and Lahlman—maintained correspondence with the European socialists. Many of these revolutionaries, Lahlman for example, spoke and wrote in Spanish. In 1889 the representative of the Vorwärts Club at the Paris Congress of the Second International was the prominent German revolutionary Wilhelm Liebknecht.[40] As seen from the accounts of the first congress, the meeting was attended also by a delegate from the socialist groups of Argentina, Alexandre Payret—the oldest activist of the Argentine socialist movement.[41]

In accordance with the decisions of the Paris Congress of the Second International, an organizing committee was formed in Argentina in January 1890 to run the May Day celebrations; committee members included José Winiger (editor of *Vorwärts*), Wilhelm Schultz, August Kühn, and Marcel Jakel.[42] The committee addressed a manifesto to the workers calling for a demonstration on May first in demand of an eight-hour workday.

On 30 March the committee held an enlarged meeting of representatives of proletarian organizations, which was attended by workers of all nationalities living in Argentina. It was decided to summon the workers of the capital to the May Day celebration, to form the Labor Federation of the Republic, to issue a newspaper defending the rights of workers, and to address a petition to the National Congress demanding legislation in defense of the working class.[43] Three thousand workers took part in this first labor demonstration in Buenos Aires on 1 May 1890.[44] In connection with the growth of the labor movement, the leadership of the Vorwärts Club created the Federación de los Trabajadores de la Región Argentina. In December 1890 the Federation's paper, *El Obrero*, began to appear; its editor was the indefatigable propagandist of Marxism Hermann Lahlman. The editorial offices of the paper were located in the home of August Kühn, one of the Federation's organizers, subsequently a member of the first Central Committee of the [Argentine] Communist Party. The federation's vice president was Carlos Mauli, also a preeminent Argentine Marxist. *El Obrero* actively propagandized the ideas of Marxism, while fighting against utopian socialism and anarchism. In one of its editorial articles in December 1890, *El Obrero* wrote: "We enter the political arena of Argentine life as the vanguard of the proletariat, which has separated itself from the exploited masses and become the nucleus of a new class, inspired by the great teachings of contemporary scientific socialism, whose bases are: a materialist understanding of history and exposure of the nature of capitalist production—surplus value—two great discoveries of our immortal teacher, Karl Marx."[45]

Argentine Marxists carried on a persistent struggle against anarchism, which after the late 1880s spread widely in the country. The Marxist paper, *El Obrero,* combatted the penetration of anarchism into the working masses, systematically publishing materials which exposed the Bakuninists. On 1 May 1891, *El Obrero* wrote that anarchism was the shame of the working class.[46]

Despite the dissident activities of the anarchists, the partisans of scientific socialism grew in number. In 1891 the Argentine Marxists sent an account of the socialist and labor movement in their country to the Brussels Congress of the Second International.[47] The report noted the disenfranchisement and wretched status of the Argentine working class; it spoke of the brutal suppression of the demonstrations on May Day, 1890, and of the harmful influence of the anarchists on the labor movement. The social democrats, the report stated, were holding closed meetings not only in Buenos Aires, but also in La Plata, Santa Fe, Mendoza, and other cities. The report was signed by all members of the Provisional Committee of the Capital of the Labor Party of the Argentine Republic, whose membership included, along with other revolutionaries, August Kühn and Carlos Mauli.[48]

From 1882 to 1894, *El Obrero* and *Vorwärts* were the only published organs to propagandize Marxism in Argentina. On 7 April 1894, the Marxists began to publish the weekly *Vanguardia,* subtitled "Gaceta del Socialismo Científico, Defensor de la Clase Obrera,"[49] which on 29 June 1896 became the official organ of the Socialist Party. By this period, revisionism had begun to spread among Argentine socialists, and in labor organizations and the trade unions the influence of anarchism and syndicalism grew quickly.

Not only Marxists (Kühn, Lahlman, Mauli), but reformists as well participated in the founding of *La Vanguardia,* and also in the creation of the Argentine Socialist Party. Despite the fierce opposition of opportunists of all shades, Argentine Marxists worked actively to rally the workers to revolutionary struggle.

The founding congress of the Socialist Party took place on 28–29 June 1896. The congress was attended by two hundred delegates from thirty-five socialist groups, labor organizations, and the trade unions of the printers, glaziers, mechanics, shoemakers, construction workers, and others. The work of the congress, as well as the basic document adopted by the congress, the "Declaration of Principles," reflects the militant political nature of the struggle of the Argentine proletariat, bearing witness to the successes of the Marxist current in the labor movement. The "Declaration of Principles" spoke of the need to overthrow the capitalist structure through revolution, which "can be realized with the force of an organized proletariat"; they also expressed certainty that the proletariat "was in condition to seize power in its own hands."[50]

During the first years of its existence, the Argentine Socialist Party actively defended the vital interests of the working class: the eight-hour workday, paid

vacations, Sundays off, and improved working conditions. The Argentine socialists made a major effort to disseminate Marxism in Argentina and other
countries of Latin America. The first volume of *Capital* was translated into
Spanish and published in Madrid in 1898, whence it was disseminated to Latin
America.[51] But already at that time many leaders of the Socialist Party were
propagating revisionist views and distracting the workers from political struggle.
Under the guise of combatting anarchism, the socialist leaders rejected revolutionary methods of struggle. At the second congress of the Socialist Party in
1898, the points which spoke of the necessity of establishing the political power
of the proletariat were removed from the Declaration of Principles. Within the
Socialist Party there appeared a left opposition headed by Kühn, Lahlman, and
Müller, which opposed the revisionist course of the socialist leaders. The strenuous and prolonged struggle of revolutionary elements against the opportunists
within the Argentine labor movement resulted in 1918 in the founding of the
Communist Party of Argentina.

In Mexico, the formation of a proletariat and the growth of a labor movement
occurred in more complex conditions than in Argentina. In contrast to Argentina,
where European immigrants comprised the basic cadres of the working class, in
Mexico the proletariat was formed primarily from the local population. The
principal branch of Mexican industry, gold and silver mining, employed Indians.
But these enterprises belong to Europeans. The economic and legal situation of
the miners was exceptionally difficult. They worked fourteen to sixteen hours a
day for miserly wages. Indians and some mestizos were also employed laying
track and performing other manual tasks connected with railroad construction,
which in the 1880s and '90s was intensively promoted in Mexico by English
capitalists. In 1877 total trackage amounted to only eight hundred kilometers; in
1890 there were about nine thousand kilometers of track, and by the end of the
century fifteen thousand kilometers.[52]

In light industry, whose basic branches were textiles and food processing,
composition of the proletariat was heterogeneous. The most strenuous jobs fell to
the Indians, while skilled laborers were immigrants, primarily Englishmen and
North Americans. Foreign capital held a dominant position. Seeking to derive
maximum profits, it mercilessly exploited the local population, preserving feudal
vestiges. The legal status and working conditions of the Mexican proletariat were
from the outset worse than those of Argentine workers.

The spread of socialist ideas in Mexico evolved from the utopian socialism of
the mutual labor organizations of the 1860s to the propagandizing of the ideas of
scientific socialism in associations affiliated with the First International. However, many workers and intellectuals, Mexican as well as immigrant, lacked a
consistent scientific world view, and more often than not their views represented
a confusion of the ideas of utopian socialism, anarchism, and Marxism.

In the words of Manuel Díaz Ramírez, a prominent Mexican revolutionary, news of the founding of the First International by Marx "raised the spirits of Mexican workers."[53] The workers associations and societies of textile workers, stone masons, shoemakers, tailors, and printers formed in the 1860s began to expand their ranks, but still remained small in numbers. Active in conducting propaganda among these societies were the utopian socialist Rodocanti, the Polish anarchist Goskowski, and the prominent Mexican supporters of the First International Santiago Villanueva[54] and Francisco Zalacosta. At the end of 1869, Villanueva and other socialists distributed a pamphlet among Mexican proletarians containing the text of the Charter of the International Workingman's Association, adopted at the Geneva Congress of 1866.[55]

On 10 January 1870, in consequence of a merger of associations, there was created under the leadership of Villanueva a Centro de Trabajadores Organizados, reconstituted in September of that same year as the so-called Gran Círculo de Obreros de México.*[56] This was the first proletarian organization created by Mexican Marxists "to begin to be socially meaningful," in the words of Ramos Pedrueza.[57]

On 9 July 1871 the first issue appeared of the weekly paper *El Socialista,* organ of the Gran Círculo de Obreros de México, whose goal was to defend "the rights and interests of the working class." The paper advocated the ideas of the First International and the Paris Commune, whose example encountered enthusiastic response in the hearts of Mexican proletarians. The Gran Círculo de Obreros de México and its paper, *El Socialista,* had ties with the leadership of the First International. This is revealed in many facts, both directly and indirectly. Thus, on 5 February 1872 a report was published in *El Socialista* which stated: "According to letters from London received in the latest mail from England, on 23 December [1871] a meeting was held in London of the General Council of members of the International under the chairmanship of Karl Marx. The Council meeting discussed the achievements of this great Association in France, Belgium, Austria, the United States, and Mexico."[58]

Mexican Marxists maintained ties with organizations of the First International in the United States. Evidence of this is seen, for example, in a letter to the chairman of the Gran Círculo de Obreros de México, dated New York, 12

---

*Carlos M. Rama gives a somewhat different account. Initially, he writes, "the Mexican labor movement was organized with the aid of the Círculo de Obreros de México, created in 1872 and rechartered as the Gran Círculo de Obreros in 1874. Two years later this society numbered some eight thousand members among its affiliates in the other Mexican states and convened the Primer Congreso Obrero Permanente, held in Mexico City on 6 March 1876. A second congress was convened in 1881." See C. Rama, "L'Amerique latine et la Première Internationale," in *La Première Internationale: L'Institution, l'implantation, le rayonnement,* Colloque International organisé à Paris du 16 au 18 novembre 1964 par le Centre National de la Recherche Scientifique et la Commission Internationale d'Histoire des Mouvements Sociaux et des Structures Sociales (Paris, 1968), p. 421.

September 1872, and signed by William Wast. The letter told of the adverse conditions in which the International was operating in Europe. Wast wrote that these difficulties "had been surmounted thanks to the instructions of Karl Marx and all his assistants, accepted and supported by all socialists: Germans, Englishmen, Belgians, Frenchmen, Italians, Americans, and Mexicans." Calling for close ties between Mexican socialists and the International, the author of the letter reported: "According to instructions which I have sent, Mexico should appoint one member to take part in the discussions and decisions of the Council in New York."[59] This representative, wrote Wast, "can be sent to New York as a permanent resident, but he may be nominated by the Mexicans from among the members of the International. . . ." At the end of the letter, Will Wast recommended that the materials which he had sent exposing the activities of the opponents of Marxism be published in El Socialista—"the official organ of the Mexican association."

The Mexican Marxist historian [Rafael] Ramos Pedrueza confirms the presence of a section of the International in Mexico and its ties with the General Council in New York during the years 1874-75. "A Mexican delegation," he wrote, "took part in the General Council in New York. The labor leader Juan de Matta Rivera was Karl Marx's representative in Mexico."[60]

In 1875 a severe struggle developed in the Mexican labor movement between Marxist and anarchist tendencies. Anarchist influence grew in workers organizations and in the labor press. In conditions of persecution and baiting, the Marxists, led by Villanueva, Francisco Zalacosta, and Alejandro Herrera, all comrades in the struggle, fought valiantly against the supporters of Bakunin, defending the ideas of scientific communism.

On 4 July 1878 Mexico's first socialist party was founded, which in 1879 had seventeen small "political centers." The socialists published their own paper, La Revolución Social, which advocated the principles of Marxism. In one number, for example, a distinction was drawn between genuine socialists and all those who merely imitate them. "Members of the party," the paper explained, "will be called communists, in contrast to those who do not recognize that the proletariat itself is the organizer of a class party."[61]

In 1888, Mexico's Socialist Party was smashed. One of its leaders, Zalacosta, was arrested. In Mexico the somber era of the bloody Díaz dictatorship (1876–1910) was beginning. The development of the labor movement was retarded for many years. The elimination of revolutionary organizations did not entail restrictions of the press, and in this regard several legal possibilities remained for propagandizing revolutionary ideas. El Socialista, for example, continued to appear. Despite the pernicious influence of anarchism, it often carried Marxist material. The Manifesto of the Communist Party was published in this paper on 10 July 1888. This was the first time the celebrated work of Marxism was published in Mexico in Spanish.[62]

At the end of the 1890s, the labor movement again began to revive in Mexico, and the proletariat resorted increasingly to strikes. The weavers, railroad workers, and metal workers actively actively defended their vital interests. In the state of Tlaxcala in 1898, there was a large strike by workers of the San Manuel iron foundry.[63] The strikers demanded improved working conditions and a shorter workday. Under the slogan "Workers of All Countries, Unite!" the proletarian papers *La Comuna* and *La Huelga* called on the workers to carry on a decisive struggle for a shorter workday, improved working and living conditions, the right to vote, and the elimination of poverty and tyrannical power. Unafraid of repression, the revolutionaries, in fierce battle with the anarchists and opportunists, carried Marxist ideas to the workers. The seeds sown in Mexico by the supporters of the First International did not disappear without a trace. At the beginning of the present century, Marxism found fertile soil in Mexico for a broader penetration of the labor milieu.

In Brazil, Negro slavery existed until 1888. African Negroes, imported in the course of three centuries, played an important role in the formation of the Brazilian nation. The country's plantation economy, based on the production of coffee and cotton and the cultivation of sugar cane, rested on slave labor. But in the second half of the nineteenth century, when Brazil was included in world trade, capitalism began to undermine slavery and the foundations of absolute monarchy. Manufacturing and machine production in the country increased. Slavery was quickly displaced by developing capitalist relations. On 13 May 1888 slavery was abolished in Brazil, and the following year the monarchy, too, collapsed. The way to capitalism was thus in large measure opened. Bourgeois relations developed especially rapidly in the state of São Paulo, where the use of slave labor had been curtailed long before abolition.

In 1872 there were in this state around 837,400 inhabitants, and by the end of the century about 1.8 million. The population grew primarily as a result of European immigration. From 1827 to 1902 more than 1,075,000 Europeans went to São Paulo: Italians, Portuguese, Spaniards, Germans, and Russians.[64] The Brazilian port of Santos became a major center of foreign trade. Through this port passed rapidly growing coffee exports. In 1867 Brazil exported 30 million kilograms of coffee, and in 1887 150 million kilograms. From 1890 to 1900 the number of coffee plantations in the state more than doubled.

A growing branch of the Brazilian economy was cotton production. From 1867 to 1876 Brazil exported annually 7 to 8 million bales of cotton. Textile production developed in the country: by 1903 there were already 143 textile mills. These enterprises were especially numerous in the states of Minas Gerais (37), Rio de Janeiro (29), and São Paulo (18).

Of the other branches of production, wine-making and the cultivation of tobacco developed rapidly. Railroad construction grew in the 1870s, '80s, and

'90s. In 1866 Brazil had a mere 513 kilometers of track; in 1880 about 3,500 kilometers, and in 1889 9,600 kilometers.[65]

The number of workers employed in the textile and other branches of industry grew. By the end of the 1890s there were over 120,000 industrial workers in the country, a significant number of whom joined various trade unions, mutual-aid societies, and circles. But this was only the first step in organizing the proletariat. The Brazilian working class was extremely retarded, in its overwhelming majority illiterate. For this reason, the ideas of socialism penetrated its midst exceedingly slowly. Socialist ideas in Brazil were the property of the revolutionary intelligentsia and the students, who, surmounting bans and repression, carried them to the workers through the press, leaflets, and oral propaganda. This activity prepared the soil in the early 1870s for the creation of the first secret workers' organizations ideologically affiliated with the First International.

In a letter to London dated 5 July 1871, the representative of the Federal Council of the Spanish section of the First International, Francisco Mora, reported to the General Council the formation of the nucleus of a section in Portugal. With the founding of a section of the International Workingmen's Association in Portugal, Mora felt "it will be possible to do the same in Brazil, which is closely tied to Portugal and shares with her a common language." Mora wrote: "Then, having in mind the probability in the near future of establishing sections of the International in Buenos Aires, Montevideo, and Valparaíso, it will be possible to organize a number of regional federations in South America, which, extending a hand to their International brothers in North America, will soon be able to effect a social revolution, discarding the decayed, putrid contemporary society and founding a new society of the sons of labor."[66]

The principal tasks facing the revolutionary movement in Brazil in the 1870s and '80s were the abolition of slavery and the liquidation of the monarchical regime. These demands, bourgeois-democratic in nature, brought together broad segments of the population.[67]

In the 1890s, when the numerical strength and organization of the proletariat grew, and the country freed itself of slavery and monarchy, the ideas of socialism began increasingly to penetrate to workers and progressive intellectuals. The first labor congress was held in Rio de Janeiro in 1892, at which an attempt was made to form a labor party. At almost the same time, the first Marxist group was founded in the port city of Santos—the Centro Socialista, which in 1895 organized the country's first May Day demonstrations in Santos and São Paulo.[68]

In 1896 there were already in Brazil several circles propagandizing the ideas of scientific socialism among the workers. The largest of them was the Centro Socialista in São Paulo, which in that same year published the labor paper *O Socialista*, with the subtitle "Proletarians of All Countries, Unite!"[69] This was the first newspaper in Brazil to disseminate the ideas of scientific socialism and the writings of Marx and Engels.

But the semiprimitive nature of Brazilian industry precluded the necessary conditions in the country for the acceptance of Marxism by the broad masses of workers. Anarchism and anarchosyndicalism became the basic current in the Brazilian labor movement. In this regard, at the end of the 1890s, the Second International failed to conduct a decisive struggle against anarchism, slipping more and more into positions of opportunism. This caused severe damage to the world proletarian movement, including the revolutionary labor movement in Brazil and other Latin American countries. In Argentina the labor movement began to develop under the salutary influence of the First International in the 1870s and quickly achieved major successes in propagandizing Marxism. In Brazil, the dissemination of Marxist ideas among the workers occurred later, at a time when the world bourgeoisie was strengthening its attacks on proletarian organizations, and the Second International in fact failed to play its role as an international center for the direction of the revolutionary struggle of the working class. Despite these difficulties, there was a Marxist tendency in the Brazilian labor movement.

The ideas of socialism began to penetrate Chile together with the European emigration that followed the revolution of 1848. In 1854 Marx's book *The Poverty of Philosophy* was freely sold by the Morella and Valdés bookshop in Santiago.[70] The first known Chilean socialists, Luis L. Olea and Francisco Bilbao, were already in the 1860s familiar with the *Manifesto of the Communist Party* and with several other works by Marx and Engles. Chile's contact with Europe was maintained through Buenos Aires; therefore the founding and activities of the sections of the First International in Argentina also influenced the Chilean labor movement.

In Chile the 1870s and '80s were characterized by a relatively rapid development of capitalism and the growth of a proletariat.[71] It must be noted that proletarian organizations of a socialist tendency appeared here in a later period. In 1896 the Centro Social Obrero was founded in Chile, which published the paper *El Grito del Pueblo*. In one article, entitled "Socialism in Chile," this paper noted: "After penetrating the midst of the Argentine proletariat, the liberating ideas of socialism reached Chile and began to have their salutary effect."[72]

In the 1890s, along with the Centro Social Obrero, there appeared the Agrupación Fraternal Obrera, whose director was Luis L. Olea. He was among the first Chilean Marxists to defend the ideas of socialism. In a letter to his friend David Acosta, he compared Marx's theory with an anvil used to forge the weapon of thought. Olea actively advocated Marxism among the Chilean workers. It is known, for example, that in 1897 he gave public lectures on "Socialism and Religion," "Socialism and Militarism," "Strikes," etc. In October 1897, Olea was among those who initiated a merger of the Centro Social Obrero and the

Agrupación Fraternal Obrera into a single organization, the Unión Socialista, which published the Marxist paper *El Proletario*. On 17 October of that year *El Proletario* wrote: "The Unión Socialista represents an organization whose basic goal consists in propagandizing and disseminating the theory of scientific socialism. In this way, the basis will be laid for the founding of a party."[73] The program of the Unión Socialista stated that it would fight for the establshment of socialism in Chile.

The founding congress of the Socialist Party was convened in December 1897 under Olea's chairmanship; it was attended by 148 persons and adopted the decision to build the party based on the Unión Socialista and to publish a new paper called *El Martillo*—"an organ of political propaganda."[74] Like the labor organizations that preceded it, the Socialist Party was a numerically small and unstable organization. It had to struggle with a large number of enemies, especially the anarchists, who split the labor movement and undermined the activity of the Marxists. This first socialist party in Chile did not last long. In July 1901 leftist elements of the socialist groups joined together, forming in Valparaíso a Democratic-Socialist Party. An active role in its organization and activity was played by the young worker-printer Luis Emilio Racabarren, who soon became one of the consistent advocates of scientific communism in South America.

In Uruguay, too, there existed in the last third of the past century labor organizations which supported the principles of the First International. According to the testimony of an agent of the Bakuninist Alianza, one A. Juánez, who was in Montevideo in April 1872, his attempts to find support among the workers ended in failure, since at that time the partisans of the First International enjoyed a predominant influence. From his trip, Juánez wrote a confederate in Mexico, "I have returned disappointed. Only among the small bakers did I encounter a favorable attitude. . . ."[75]

We have at our disposal very little material on the labor movement in Uruguay. What is available to us, however, confirms the unquestionable fact that in this country labor organizations adhering to Marxist principles did develop. The labor movement in Argentina had considerable influence on Uruguay, representing the primary center for the dissemination of Marxism in the Latin American countries during the period under consideration.

The formation of the first trade union in Uruguay dates from 1875, with the rise of the Federación Obrera, which quickly burned out. Only in 1885 did a strong labor organization appear in the country—the Federación Obrera Local Uruguaya. The first major strikes and May Day demonstrations are tied to the existence of the latter. In 1895 the labor paper *El Defensor del Obrero* began publishing in Uruguay, in conjunction with which was formed the so-called Centro de Investigaciones Sociales, which conducted fairly extensive propaganda of Marxism in Uruguay. This socialist circle was the forerunner of the important Centro de Carlos Marx, finally formed in 1904.[76]

The Cuban labor movement was considerably influenced by the U.S. labor movement. During the civil war of 1868–78, Cuban tobacco workers fled to the United States to escape the persecution of the reactionaries. They returned home only ten years later, after the end of the bloody war in the country.[77] In the 1880s and '90s, over thirty trade unions were formed in Havana: the tobacco workers, dockers, construction workers, etc.; in Cienfuegos there were sixteen trade unions with two thousand members, and in Matanzas there were ten unions.[78] In the 1880s hundreds of Cuban workers living in New York participated in a mass funeral meeting on the occasion of the death of Karl Marx. The Cuban revolutionary José Martí wrote of the meeting in a special dispatch [to La Nación of Buenos Aires]: "The International was Marx's creation: men from all nations come to honor him. . . . Karl Marx studied ways to reorder the world on new bases. He awakened the dormant and taught them how to tear down broken supports." In a resolution adopted at the New York meeting, continued Martí, Marx was called "the noblest hero and mightiest thinker of the working world."[79] The articles and correspondence of José Martí were widely disseminated in Cuba.

In January 1892 a regional labor congress was convened in Havana, attended by over a thousand delegates representing the trade unions of Cuba. Here were discussed questions of the struggle for independence and the task of liberating the working class from the yoke of exploitation. The fundamental political resolution of the congress stated: "The Congress considers that the working class will not achieve liberation until it adopts the ideas of revolutionary socialism. The Congress recommends that the workers of Cuba study and accept these ideas."[80] The congress was disbanded by the police, and its leaders—Máximo Fernández, Eduardo González, and Ramón Villamín—were arrested.

One of the brilliant representatives of Marxism in Cuba during this period was the ardent revolutionary Carlos Baliño (1848–1926). Under his leadership there appeared in Havana a Grupo Obrero.[81] This was a small socialist circle which advocated the ideas of scentific socialism and called the workers to a revolutionary struggle for the independence of Cuba. Its members fully supported the petty-bourgeois Partido Revolucionario de Cuba in the latter's struggle against Spanish colonial rule and the intervention of the U.S. imperialists, who sought to suppress the popular movement in Cuba and to turn the island into their own colony.

José Martí, leader of the Partido Revolucionario, and the propagandists of socialist ideas [Diego Vicente] Tejera and [Carlos] Baliño were close friends and comrades in the struggle against the expansionist plans of the United States. Baliño, a socialist like Martí, was an ardent fighter for the freedom of his homeland. Evaluating Baliño's revolutionary activity, the secretary general of the Partido Socialista Popular de Cuba, Blas Roca, wrote: "In Baliño's countenance we see a forerunner and fighter for Cuban independence, a precursor, propagandist, and founder of the revolutionary party of the proletariat."[82] In the 1890s, when the revisionists became active in the country, Baliño remained the most consistent Marxist in Cuba.[83] At that time he headed the socialist groups there, while a little more than two decades later he was one of the organizers of the Cuban Communist Party.

The indisputable facts of the existence and activity of proletarian Marxist organizations and revolutionary circles in Latin America in the past century, and also the dissemination of Marxism in the labor and socialist press of these countries already at the time of the First International, demonstrate the total lack of foundation in the views of the bourgeois falsifiers of history, which hold that communist ideas were carried to Latin America "by Bolsheviks and red agitators" only after the October Revolution in Russia. The historical truth is that the ideas of scientific socialism, spilling their unfading light on the world in the middle of the last century, reached Latin America in the early 1870s, where they found fertile soil among the most advanced workers and intellectuals.

Marxism was first spread in the Latin American countries by selfless activists and supporters of the First International, Europeans and Latin Americans. The founders of scientific communism themselves, Marx and Engels, had ties with the leading representatives of the Latin American proletariat—Vilmar, Flèche, and others—whom they aided with counsel and literature. Engel's words that Marx "represented for the proletariat of the Old World and the New a counsellor to whom they constantly turned and who never refused his help," are filled with a most profound and vital sense.[84] The great ideas of Marxism awakened the workers of Latin America, rallying them together, instilling in them the feeling of proletarian solidarity, and calling them to struggle against their exploiters.

In light of the study of the history of the spread of Marxism and the first steps in the organization and struggles of the Latin American proletariat, it becomes easier to understand the appearance in Latin America already at the beginning of the twentieth century of the prominent organizers of working-class political struggle, the ardent advocates of Marxism-Leninism, Luis Emilio Recabbaren in Chile; August Kühn, Rodolfo Ghioldi, and Victorio Codovilla in Argentina; Carlos Baliño in Cuba; Mariátegui in Peru; and many others. The appearance and spread of Marxism in Latin America is as regular a phenomenon as in other capitalist countries. As the ideology of the international proletariat, Marxism has its own history of many years' standing on Latin American soil as well. The beginning of this history is rooted in that time when in Latin America there appeared the first labor organizations, and in Europe Marx and Engels created an international organization of the proletariat—the First International, whose foundation was the eternal principle of proletarian internationalism, which, in the words of Marx, provided hope for a bright communist future for mankind.

NOTES

1 Américo J. Lacombe, *Brasil, período nacional* (Mexico, 1956); Luis Galdames, *Historia de Chile* (Santiago de Chile, 1943); Felix Luna, *Irigoyen* (Buenos Aires, 1954); Pedro Calmon, *História social do Brasil*, III (São Paulo, 1943).

2 Robert J. Alexander, *Communism in Latin America* (New Brunswick, N.J., 1957).

3 Ibid., pp. 18–31; see also Harry Bernstein, "Marxismo en México," *HM*, no. 4 (1958), 497.

4 Juan B. Justo, *El Socialismo argentino* (Buenos Aires, 1915); idem, *Teoría y práctica de la historia* (Buenos Aires, 1909).

5 Idem, *La Internacional socialista: Informes de los delegados argentinos* (Buenos Aires, 1919), p. 3.

6 Jacinto Oddone, *Historia del socialismo argentino* (Buenos Aires, 1934).

7 Idem, *Gremialismo proletario argentino* (Buenos Aires, 1949).

8 *Esbozo de historia del Partido Comunista de la Argentina* (Buenos Aires, 1947), p. 8; Rafael Ramos Pedrueza, *La lucha de clases a través de la historia de México* (Mexico, 1941), pp. 410–12; Manual Díaz Ramírez, *Apuntes históricos del movimiento obrero y campesino de México* (Mexico, 1938), pp. 32–63; R. Iscaro, *Origen y desarrollo del movimiento sindical argentino* (Buenos Aires, 1958), pp. 45–59.

9 During the 1880s, the aborigines—Indians of various tribes—were almost entirely annihilated in Argentina, Uruguay, Costa Rica, and Cuba. Only in Peru, Ecuador, Bolivia, Guatemala, and Mexico did they comprise a majority of the population. In the vast territory of Brazil, and also in Venezuela, Colombia, Haiti, and Santo Domingo, the number of Indians was insignificant, and they took refuge primarily in the mountains and forest areas far from the basic economic centers. In the seventeenth and eighteenth centuries, Negroes were brought to these countries from Africa. Haiti, for example, became a country with a predominantly black population. Negroes comprised a large share of the populace in Brazil, Cuba, and the Dominican Republic. By 1870, the broad mass of Latin America's inhabitants was comprised of mestizos and so-called creoles (the descendants of the Hispano-Portuguese conquerors and colonizers).

10 See Congrès International Ouvrier Socialiste, *Rapport* (Brussels, 1893), pp. 103–4.

11 It must be kept in mind that anarchism began to make rapid inroads into the Latin American labor movement only in the 1890s, almost at the same time as the spread of revisionism and anarchosyndicalism. But while anarchism acquired a dominant influence in the working class in the first years of the twentieth century, revisionism and syndicalism spread significantly only on the eve of the First World War, especially in

Argentina, Mexico, and Uruguay. In the 1870s and '80s, when bourgeois ideology on the whole exercised great influence over the proletariat, the progressive part of the working class was guided by Marxist ideology, and not the revisionist or anarchist current.

12 Richardo M. Ortiz, *Historia económica de la Argentina* (Buenos Aires, 1955), pp. 206, 208, 243.

13 Gino Germani, *Estructura social de la Argentina* (Buenos Aires, 1955), p. 225 (chapter notes).

14 Tsentral'nyi partiinyi arkhiv Instituta marksizma-leninizma pri TsK KPSS [Central Party Archives of the Institute of Marxism-Leninism attached to the Central Committee of the CPSU—cited hereafter as TsPA IML], fond 21, opis' 1, delo 200, fol. 1.

15 Ibid.

16 Ibid., fol. 5.

17 Ibid., delo 151, fol. 6. From 30 May through 31 July 1871 there were no further meetings of the General Council.

18 This was a period of reaction and mounting repression against the labor movement in Europe. Many prominent revolutionaries underwent arrest and exile. Communications among the revolutionaries were greatly complicated. A letter which Engels sent to Buenos Aires on 31 July 1871 did not arrive until 5 January 1873. See ibid., fols. 3, 6.

19 G. Iekk, *Internatsional* (Moscow, 1923), p. 200.

20 TsPA IML, fond 21, delo 151, fol. 1.

21 Oddone, *Historia del socialismo argentino,* p. 118.

22 TsPA IML, fond 21, delo 151, fols. 1–2.

23 The letter was signed by the secretary general of the section, Émile Flèche, who officially called himself "the founder of the International in Buenos Aires." See ibid., fol. 2.

24 Ibid.

25 This is the only letter from which Jacinto Oddone published an excerpt in his book, *Historia del socialismo argentino,* pp. 119–20. The letter is quoted from the original.

26 TsPA IML, fond 21, delo 151, fols. 3–6.

27 The letter carried the triangular seal of the Buenos Aires section of the International Workingmen's Association. In the center of the triangle were the words "International Workingmen's Association," and around the edges the inscription "There are no rights without responsibilities, no responsibilities without rights."

28 TsPA IML, fond 21, delo 82, fol. 15.

29 Oddone, *Historia del socialismo argentino,* p. 119.

30 Ibid.

31 TsPA IML, fond 21, delo 151, fols 4–5.

32 Ibid., fol. 4 Reference was to the French edition of *Capital*.

33 Ibid., fol. 5.

34 The Frenchman Job Désiré was arrested in 1875 by the Argentine authorities, together with active members of the International. See Oddone, *Historia del socialismo argentino,* p. 120.

35 TsPA IML, fond 21, delo 151, fol. 2.

36 Oddone, *Historia del socialismo argentino,* p. 120.

37 Ibid., p. 121.
38 Justo, *El socialismo argentino*, p. 25; *Esbozo de historia del Partido Comunista de la Argentina*, pp. 9–10.
39 Justo, *El socialismo argentino*, p. 25.
40 *RH* (Buenos Aires), no. 1 (1957), 61.
41 Congrès International Ouvrier Socialiste de Paris, *Appel de la Commission d'organisation: Liste des délégués et des Associations ouvriers; Resolutions* (Paris, 1889), pp. 2, 5.
42 Oddone, *Historia del socialismo argentino*, p. 123.
43 Ibid., pp. 124–25.
44 Justo, *El Socialismo argentino*, p. 25.
45 See *RH*, no. 1 (1957), 69.
46 Ibid., 72.
47 Congrès International Ouvrier Socialiste, *Rapports* (Brussels, 1893), pp. 103–5.
48 Ibid., p. 105. There was no workers' party in Argentina, but representatives of the socialist groups, not taking into account the difficulties, believed the party would be formed that very year of 1891.
49 Oddone, *Historia del socialismo argentino*, p. 221. Facsimile.
50 "Declaración de principios," quoted ibid., p. 269.
51 *Esbozo de historia del Partido Comunista de la Argentina*, p. 10.
52 M. Romero, *Coffee and India Rubber Culture in Mexico* (New York, 1898), pp. 220–24.
53 Dìaz Ramìrez, *Apuntes históricos*, pp. 30–32.
54 The editor of *El socialista* died at the end of 1872.
55 Díaz Ramírez, *Apuntes históricos*, p. 37.
56 Ibid.
57 Ramos Pedrueza, *La lucha de clases*, p. 410.
58 Díaz Ramírez, *Apuntes históricos*, p. 49.
59 Ibid., p. 50.
60 Ramos Pedrueza, *La lucha de clases*, p. 410.
61 Ibid., p. 411.
62 A. L. Aparicio, *El Movimiento obrero en México* (Mexico, 1952), pp. 118–20.
63 Víctor Alba, *Le Mouvement ouvrier en Amérique Latine* (Paris, 1953), p. 110.
64 *The State of São Paulo: Statistics and General Information* (São Paulo, 1904), p. 6.
65 João Pandiá Calógeras, *Formação histórica do Brasil* (São Paulo, 1938), pp. 325, 358.
66 TsPA IML, fond 21, delo 200, fol. 3.
67 Joaquim Nabuco, *O abolicionismo* (São Paulo, 1938).
68 *A Classe Operária* (Rio de Janeiro), 5 April 1952.
69 Ibid.
70 Hernán Ramírez Necochea, *Historia del movimiento obrero en Chile* (Santiago, 1956), p. 146.
71 See Luis Emilio Recabarren, *Ricos y pobres* (Santiago, 1910), p. 5.
72 Cited in Ramírez Necochea, *Historia del movimiento obrero*, p. 228.
73 Cited ibid., pp. 228–29.
74 Ibid., pp. 234–35.

75 See Díaz Ramírez, *Apuntes históricos,* pp. 50–51.
76 Carlos M. Rama, *Ensayo de sociología urugauya* (Montevideo, 1957), pp. 126–28.
77 See R. Calderio, "Inicios del movimiento obrero en Cuba," in *Primer Congreso Nacional de Historia,* vol. II (Havana, 1953), pp. 190–93.
78 Justo, *Teoría y práctica de la historia,* pp. 365–66.
79 José Martí, *Obras Completas,* vol. I (Havana, 1953), pp. 1517–18.
80 Calderio, "Inicios del movimiento obrero," p. 190.
81 Carlos Baliño, *Verdades del socialismo* (Havana, 1941), p. 4.
82 Ibid., p. 3.
83 Ibid., p. 14.
84 K. Marx and F. Engels, *Izbrannye proizvedeniia,* vol. II (Moscow, 1952), p. 338.

16 THE SUPREME REVOLUTIONARY CONVENTION

(From the History of the Mexican Revolution, 1910–17)

N. M. LAVROV

THE SUPREME Revolutionary Convention is an exceedingly interesting phenomenon in the history of the Mexican Revolution. Rare is the monograph that fails to mention it, although the subject is still little studied. This can be explained in part by the fact that many records perished when, in the conditions of civil war which obtained in Mexico during the years 1914–16, the convention was transferred from one city to another.[1] In the Archivo General de la Nación (Mexico City), the convention documents used by the author of the present article have not yet been sorted out, described, or even numbered. In the unique collection of newspapers, journals, and pamphlets from the revolutionary period 1910–17 housed here are the stenographic records of the sessions of the convention assembly for the years 1914–15.

In Soviet literature there are no specialized works on the history of the Revolutionary Convention. Of the books by non-Soviet authors, two monographs dealing specifically with this topic warrant note. In 1960 Robert E. Quirk (United States) published a volume tracing the genesis, evolution, and fall of the convention.[2] In 1966, a book was published on the history of the convention by the Mexican scholar Luis F. Amaya.[3]

Beginning in November 1910, the Mexican Revolution evolved through several stages. The first spans the period from November 1910 to May 1911, that is, from the start of the Revolution to the fall of the Díaz dictatorship. The second runs from May 1911 through February 1913, or from the fall of the Díaz dictatorship to the counterrevolutionary uprising of Porfirian general Victoriano Huerta and the overthrow of the national bourgeois government of Francisco Madero.

Originally published as "Verkhovnyi revoliutsionnyi konvent (iz istorii meksikanskoi revoliutsii 1910–1917 gg.)," *Vop. Ist.*, no. 3 (March 1972), 94–106.

The third stage (February 1913–July 1914) is the period of the dictatorial rule of Huerta, whose fall initiates the fourth and final stage of the Revolution. Already in the third stage there begins to appear a united bloc of democratic and anti imperialist forces opposed to the reactionary Huerta dictatorship. The historical necessity of abolishing this dictatorship—as an attempt by the most dyed-in-the-wool reactionaries to reestablish the prerevolutionary order—united all classes and social sectors of Mexican society behind a single revolutionary platform. But as the Huerta dictatorship came to an end, this unity began to disintegrate, and the various interests of each class came to the surface ever more clearly.

On the eve of the Revolution and during its first stage, the principal slogans were Madero's demands for elections and for the resignation of Porfirio Díaz; all classes opposed to the dictatorship marched under the general banner of struggle for democracy. Yet subsequently, with the growth of mass participation and the development of class struggle, the abstract slogan "democracy" began to acquire specific content. Lenin noted the natural course of such an evolution of the concept of democracy in conditions wherein a bourgeois revolution becomes a bourgeois-democratic revolution. He wrote: "Before a bourgeois revolution and at its inception, all act in the name of democracy: both the proletariat and the peasantry together with elements of the urban petty bourgeoisie, and the liberal bourgeoisie together with liberal landowners. Only in the course of class struggle, only in the more or less prolonged historical development of the revolution does there come into being a different understanding of this "democracy" by different classes. Moreover, there comes into being a profound abyss between the interests of different classes, who demand *different* economic and political measures in the name of one and the same 'democracy.'"[4] In the third stage of the Mexican Revolution serious differences arose between the various classes participating in the Revolution. This was a manifestation of an objective process, for only in the course of struggle, only in the course of this process of the developing revolution "does it become clear that one 'democratic' class or sector does not wish or is unable to go as far as another; that in the pursuit of 'common' (allegedly common) aims there arise embittered clashes over *means,* for example, over the degree, extent, and sequence of freedom and popular democracy, distribution of land to the peasantry, and so on."[5]

This diverse approach of individual classes to the fundamental problems of the Revolution became ever more apparent with the approaching fall of the Huerta regime, when the choice lay between either a further development of the class struggle or its curtailment; an agrarian revolution or an end to the Revolution altogether. The forces for agrarian revolution were drawn from the broad masses of the peasantry, petty-bourgeois sectors, and the revolutionary intelligentsia. They had well-organized military units: Francisco Villa's Division of the North, and, at the gates of the capital, the Liberating Army of Emiliano Zapata. Like a battering ram, Villa's Division of the North shattered the main defenses of the

Federal Army and moved inexorably southward, with a real possibility of reaching the capital first. This did not enter into the plans of Venustiano Carranza, leader of the Mexican bourgeoisie and liberal landowners. In June 1914, on the eve of Huerta's fall, there arose a conflict between Villa and Carranza, "First Chief" of the Revolution, who sought to secure Villa's resignation as commander of the Division of the North. But into this conflict entered Felipe Angeles, Eugenio Aguirre Benavides, Monclovio Herrera, José Isabel Robles, Tomás Urbina, and other leading generals of the Division of the North, who, in a telegram to Carranza, wrote that "the resignation of Villa at the present moment would have undesirable and serious consequences not only within the country but beyond its borders as well."[6] Not wishing to enter into a conflict with all the generals of the Division of the North, Carranza was obliged to leave Villa in his post as division commander, but from this point on, Carranza's attitude toward Villa was one of hostility. Sooner or later there had to be a clash with this new force, inasmuch as Villa's political line was opposed to the aspirations of Carranza and inspired fear among the bourgeois Constitutionalist leaders. In one of his statements, Villa explained: "I have always been faithful to the fatherland and to the ideals of my people. I solemnly declare that I have no ambitions and seek only the triumph of our principles, namely, the establishment of a democratic and just government created by the will of the people, which will carry out the reforms necessary for the establishment of a new regime based on equality, truth, and justice for all; a regime which will deliver the deprived classes from poverty, humiliation, and persecution; and, finally, I call for the establishment of a strong government capable of eliminating any threat to the sovereignty and unity of the country."[7]

Villa's revolutionary activities and program not only frightened the *latifundistas*, the forces of the old regime, and the imperialists, but also inspired apprehensions among the liberal landowners and bourgeoisie of the revolutionary camp, whose interests were represented by Carranza. They were no less disturbed by the activities of Zapata as leader of the agrarian revolution in the country's south. From the different regions controlled by the Liberating Army came peasant demands, issued in Zapata's name, for the return, in fulfillment of the Plan de Ayala,[8] of lands seized by the landowners. Thus the peasants and peons of the Ahuacatitlán and Rivera haciendas wrote to Zapata: "The Plan de Ayala is the only document in which there is clearly formulated an agrarian program reflecting the demands of the Mexican people. We swear by our parents and our children to defend and fight for its total implementation."[9] Peasants and peons from many villages approached representatives of the Liberating Army's command with petitions for assistance in confiscating land from the landowners. Implementation of the Plan de Ayala was a difficult process, attended by sharp class conflicts. The landowners resisted it, and when conditions permitted, took the offensive. In the countryside there was a cruel, bloody peasant struggle for land. This struggle coincided with the movement of the broad masses of the Mexican people towards a radical solution to the aims of the bourgeois-democratic revolution. Development of the Revolution in this way did not correspond to the interests of the liberal landowners and the bourgeoisie. They were ready to join with the peasantry in the struggle against the Díaz and Huerta dictatorships, but they were afraid of the independence and radicalism of the masses—of the radicalism of such popular leaders as Zapata and Villa.

The more sharply the central question of the Revolution was raised, that is, the question of power (Should it be placed in the hands of Villa and Zapata, or should it remain in the hands of Carranza?), the more actively some individuals from the ranks of the "First Chief" worked on a plan to crush Villa and Zapata. Thus, for example, José Vasconcelos, representing the right wing of the Revolution, asked Carranza to form a central government and to enunciate a program capable of "reassuring the conservative classes, who will see that you and the Revolution guarantee them legal rights."[10] Carranza ordered generals Alvaro Obregón and Pablo González to block the advance of Villa's army southward and not to permit its union with the army of Zapata. Implementation of this plan commenced with the battle of Zacatecas. The Division of the North was unable to move south, since on Carranza's request its supply of coal was discontinued. Villa's troop trains came to a halt in the vicinity of Zacatecas. Annoyed, Villa telegraphed Obregón, proposing a meeting to exchange views on the strained relations with Carranza. Obregón replied, however, that he did not consider such talks necessary as long as the Federal Army was under attack.[11] Villa then turned to Pablo González, commander of the Northeastern Division. Among the generals of this division were some (Antonio Villarreal, for example) who were not blind tools of Carranza, and who proposed an accord with Villa. González did not object to talks, especially since the Northeastern Division faced no operations of particular importance. Delegates of the Northern and Northeastern Divisions met in Torreón on 4 July 1914. The delegation from the Division of the North demanded that Carranza continue to supply the Division of the North with ammunition, rations, and equipment.[12] It was precisely at this conference that the question of convening a revolutionary convention to resolve the matter of a constitutional government was settled. The convention was to be convened by the "First Chief of the Revolution" and commander-in-chief of the Constitutionalist Army, General Venustiano Carranza. It was envisioned that delegates to the convention (one per thousand men of the ranks) would be named by the commanders of the various units of the Constitutionalist Army. Thus it was to be a meeting solely of the military.

After the capitulation of Huerta's army in July 1914, the capital was occupied by the army of Alvaro Obregón. Carranza arrived there a short time later. On 4 September, he sent a telegram to all military leaders and state troop commanders, in which he pointed out that, insofar as the convening of a meeting of military leaders and statesmen had been envisioned already in the Plan de Guadalupe,[13] as soon as the capital was liberated, he, Carranza, would call such a meeting for 1 October. This meeting was given the name "Convention of Revolutionary Forces." At about this time, Carranza entertained the hope of delivering blows to the armies of Zapata and Villa. On 21 September he ordered formations of the Constitutionalist Army to attack units of the Division of the North.[14] With the first movements of Carranza's soldiers, Villa ordered the Division of the North to prepare for battle and decided to move south, proposing to Zapata that they join forces and take joint action against Carranza.

On 22 September Villa sent Zapata a letter, in which he wrote: "It is no longer possible to endure the anti-popular conduct of Venustiano Carranza, who has taken measures to cut us off and to discredit us in the eyes of foreign countries. All my generals and I myself consider it necessary to deliver the fatherland as soon as possible from the ambitious schemes of the so-called first chief of the Constitutionalist Army. As of today, we no longer recognize him as the leader of the nation and consider indispensable the transfer of supreme power into the hands of true representatives of the people." Advising Zapata of his preparations for a campaign against the capital, Villa emphasized that he knew him to be a steadfast defender of the interests of the people and therefore, he continued, "I hope with full reason that you, inspired by the same aspirations as I, will declare your non-recognition of Carranza and will ready your troops as necessary, so that we may simultaneously begin to move against the capital and, coordinating our actions, create an authority that will sustain the true glory of our fatherland."[15]

The Convention of Revolutionary Forces opened in Mexico City on 1 October 1914, but as it was dominated by anti-Carrancista sentiments, the delegates decided to move to Aguascalientes in order to be farther away from Carranza, who was then in the capital. Here there arrived a delegation from the Division of the North, headed by Villa's personal representative, General Felipe Angeles. The convention's anti-Carrancista majority attempted to use the convention to prevent a civil war, by resolving the fundamental questions of the Revolution in a peaceful way. At a session on 14 October, a number of delegates proposed that the convention be declared the supreme organ of authority in the country. However, a delegate from the Division of the North, Colonel Roque González Garza, raised the question, how was it possible to declare the Convention a supreme assembly if there were no representatives from Emiliano Zapata? General Angeles proposed that Zapata and his representatives be invited "to discuss jointly the principal problems of the country." On 15 October a delegation headed by Angeles was formed to contact Zapata. Upon his return on 26 October, Angeles advised the convention that "all along the way the delegation was received with exceptional courtesy and cordiality, and even, one could say, with enthusiasm."[16] He reported that Zapata had named his representatives, who already had arrived and were awaiting instructions from the convention.

The appearance in the convention's hall of sessions on the morning of 27 October of the delegation from the Liberating Army of the South was met with loud applause. The chairman of the convention, Antonio Villarreal, greeted the delegation and then gave the floor to its leader, Paulino Martínez, who announced the revolutionary program of the *zapatistas*, the Plan de Ayala, which reflected the efforts of the revolutionaries of the South "to guarantee economic freedom to the Mexican people, that is, the basis of political freedom." Expressing the negative attitude of the *zapatistas* toward Carranza and characterizing the Plan de Ayala as the basis of action for all of the country's revolutionaries, Martínez nonetheless failed to suggest how the ideals of the Revolution might be put into practice.[17] The *zapatistas* had no clear notion of how to institute revolutionary reforms. One member of the delegation, Antonio Díaz Soto y Gama, expressed anarchistic opinions about revolutionary power and the state.[18] He did not feel that a government could be formed capable of fulfilling the aspirations of the people. At the suggestion of González Garza and Angeles, leaders of the delegation of the Division of the North, the convention unanimously adopted the Plan de Ayala.[19] After this, the convention proceeded to discuss the question of supreme authority and the frictions between Villa and Carranza. In the interests of the Revolution, it was decided to ask Carranza to resign as plenipotentiary head of the executive and as supreme commander-in-chief. Since Carranza ignored this petition, the convention decreed that he be relieved of all of his posts. General Eulalio Gutiérrez was elected provisional president of the country.

Carranza, however, did not intend to leave power willingly. He did all that he could to weaken the position of revolutionary democracy and ordered that Zapata and Villa be prohibited from further political and military activities and that they be exiled from Mexico. Seeking to split the convention and to assure a decisive position in the Revolution for the bourgeois-landowner bloc, which was interested in crushing the forces of revolutionary democracy, Carranza ordered that all generals and officers of the Constitutionalist Army abandon the convention, remove their formations and units from its authority, and place them under his orders as supreme commander-in-chief.[20] To this end, Carranza played on the existence of two tendencies in the convention. The radical tendency of the delegations from the revolutionary armies of the South and North was watched closely by the Constitutionalist faction of the convention. Submitting to Carranza's order, Generals Villarreal, Obregón, and Eduardo Hay, together with Manuel Chao, a former general in the Division of the North, all left the convention, turning actively against it. It should be noted that Villarreal and Obregón had sought the post which the assembly conferred on Eulalio Gutiérrez. At the assembly session of 19 October, Obregón had stated that anyone who violated the oath taken by the convention should be declared a rebel. "Let them take my general's stripes from me," he said, "I shall fight as a sergeant against anyone who rebels against the convention." "I will accompany Sergeant Obregón," repeated Manuel Chao, "as a common soldier."[21] Yet a month later Obregón and Chao, preserving their general's stripes, initiated armed actions against the convention. In an appeal to Villa, Obregón demanded that the Division of the North halt its march to the south. At the same time, he advised Carranza of his readiness to initiate armed action against Villa.[22] At the beginning of December 1914, Obregón issued the "Manifesto to the Nation" which signalled the start of civil war. In this document, he called on "honorable revolutionaries" to oppose "the monstrous Villa" and the "nest of traitors" that was the Division of the North, so that the "just cause of Venustiano Carranza" might be victorious.[23]

Meanwhile, the convention did everything possible to avoid civil war. Its main aim was to return the country to peace and to resolve the problems raised by the Revolution, so that the situation of the popular masses might be changed and the country prosper. At the very beginning of its work, the convention elaborated a plan for an economic program. This plan reflected its authors' aspirations for a better future for their fatherland, although it was permeated with petty-bourgeois illusions about harmonizing class interests and with admiration for bourgeois legality. Fearing that "public opinion" might blame them and, of course, the convention for favoring some classes and political groups over others, the authors of the program made appropriate qualifications. In the plan it is pointed out that "the well-being of the nation is tied intimately to its economic development"; that there is no social peace where "there is not a just distribution of wealth, where the proletariat finds itself in unfavorable conditions vis-à-vis the property-owners. In order to achieve economic development, it is necessary to have reforms; industry must not be in the hands of a small group of the privileged. Up until now, everything has been controlled by monopolies, tied, as a rule, to Washington." Characterizing the role of foreign capital in Mexico, the authors of the plan explained that it "played an important role in the birth and early growth of Mexican industry," but expressed the wish that foreign capital already invested in the country's economy "not have an advantage over national capital" and "that the investment of Mexican capital be stimulated wherever possible. To do this it will be necessary in the course of the next few years to replace basically foreign technical and industrial personnel with Mexican nationals." It was pointed out in this document that one of the main goals of the convention, "in accord with the ideals of the Revolution, is to improve the situation of the working class." In this connection, legislation was envisioned which would guarantee wages to the proletariat, the payment of pensions for job-related disabilities, prohibition of wage freezes, and the elimination of *tiendas de raya*.[24] (*Tiendas de raya* were company stores where the laborer was obliged to purchase goods, as a rule, at exhorbitant prices.)

In discussion of the problem of economic development, there was heated debate on the question of what attitude to adopt toward foreign capital. Gutiérrez called for the liquidation of "shameful concessions offered foreign companies by the Díaz and Huerta governments.'' Supporting this proposal, David Berlanga emphasized that these concessions served only as a means of enriching foreign companies, the *porfiristas,* and the oppressors of the people, their goal being ''to deprive us of our land, our wealth, our national spirit, our fatherland. And if we recognize them, this will be the end of the Revolution.'' Opposed to the proposal to reexamine and annul contracts of concession concluded with foreign companies by the Díaz and Huerta governments was Díaz Soto y Gama, who declared that it was ''necessary to fulfill obligations concluded with foreign states prior to the Revolution of 1910.'' Otilio E. Montaño, a prominent figure in the *zapatista* movement, supported Díaz Soto y Gama, looking to the ''civilized countries,'' particularly the United States, for assistance in developing Mexican industry. Again taking the floor, Berlanga said that he was prepared to honor the commitments of which Díaz Soto y Gama spoke, but how, he asked, was it possible to honor these commitments ''if the concessions were obtained by bribes, and the companies did not meet their own obligations?'' noting by way of example that the Compañía de Fundición de Fierro had not paid taxes in forty years. ''We, as revolutionaries,'' Berlanga underscored, ''have the right to annul contracts with foreign companies; this right is based on revolutionary justice, and we must force these companies to pay taxes.'' In his address, Julio Madero emphasized that the concessions to foreign companies in question were illegal and unconstitutional, and he supported the proposal that they be reviewed. Expressing astonishment at the strange position of ''the leaders of socialism,'' Guillermo Castillo Tapia said that Díaz Soto y Gama and Montaño ''forget the enormous misfortunes occasioned Mexico by the United States, and that President Wilson has never recognized and will not recognize the Mexican Revolution.'' ''The Yankees only humiliate Mexico,'' he said, ''and exploit the Mexican people; the primary significance of the Revolution lies in the fact that it has taken an enormous step forward toward making the Mexican nation independent.''[25]

Disagreement over the role of imperialism in Mexico reflected the ideological immaturity of many of the convention's delegates. This ideological weakness caused their inability to understand, for example, the significance of the proletariat in the Revolution. The convention passed no labor law, nor did it adopt measures to combat hunger and the high cost of living. Instead of decisive revolutionary measures against speculators in foodstuffs who enriched themselves at the expense of the people, it appealed to the merchants, ''in light of the terrible situation arising from the misery and hunger enveloping the capital, to demonstrate in the name of philanthropy noble human sentiments and of their own good will place on sale goods of primary necessity, in order to lessen the people's want.''[26]

As early as 16 November 1914, the convention announced that a new revolutionary government would be formed which would ''carry out the ideals of the Revolution, establish democratic institutions to fulfill its solemn obligations to the nation, and replace tyranny with a government that will satisfy the urgent needs of the people."[27] But such a government was not formed.

The convention approved the Plan de Ayala but did not adopt an agrarian law. Letters reached the convention from peasants requesting aid in taking land from the landowners and returning it to the villages; there were many complaints about the arbitrariness of local authorities and military leaders who called themselves revolutionaries. (Any "general" who did not recognize Carranza called himself a "revolutionary.") Individual military leaders of this kind, like the *caciques* of the old order, were the cause of tyranny and lawlessness. Local landowners plied with liquor and bribed ambitious "generals," and, feigning great revolutionary spirit, managed to manipulate them at will. Such was the case, for example, with "General" Salas, who became the puppet of a landowner named Cortés, an ardent supporter of Huerta and commander of a punitive force of federal troops that set fire to villages engaging in revolutionary struggle against the landowners.[28] Degenerate "revolutionaries," taking advantage of the absence of a stable authority, became little dictators in outlying neighborhoods and districts and even in towns. One Colonel García, for example, commander of the garrison in the town of Tlalmanalco (state of Morelos), drove a farm laborer by the name of González out of town, together with his family, in order to give [González'] house and plot of land to his own henchman. González made a complaint to the convention.[29]

But as a rule, peasant complaints remained unanswered. The convention was torn by internal conflicts: it suffered from the absence of a revolutionary party with a precise and clear program. The convention's work was notable for its lack of decision and its constant doubts: Was the Convention sovereign or was it not? Did it possess the authority to decide matters of state? and so on. There were unending arguments over procedure and matters of secondary importance; weeks were spent creating and recreating all manner of commissions, reelecting the convention's governing organs, and endlessly investigating the unseemly behavior of delegates. One must also keep in mind that the convention was wholly comprised of soldiers, more accustomed to giving orders than taking them. There were 12 captains, 18 majors, 24 lieutenant-colonels, 41 colonels, and 142 generals. Only in the *zapatista* delegation were there "nonmilitary citizens," such as Díaz Soto y Gama, who correctly considered the absence of civilian representatives in the convention a serious shortcoming. At one of the sessions he said that "the convention ought to open its doors to civilians, to those who, lacking weapons, nonetheless fight for the great revolutionary cause; the doors must be opened to the proletariat, to the worker, so that his voice may be heard here."[30] On 26 June 1915, the delegate Alfonso de San Martín gave the secretariat of the assembly a memorandum entitled "On the Participation of Civilians in the Convention,"[31] in which the following was stated: "In the convention only the military is represented. The time has come for the participation of civilian representatives of the people. The people expect results from the convention—from the people who fought for the abolition of the recent dictatorship. But, unfortunately, months have already passed, and within the convention more and more passions flare which make it difficult to fulfill solemnly-made promises. As a result, the convention has not justified the hopes which the people placed in it. It is regrettable, but one must recognize that the convention is dominated by discord and chaos." San Martín called for an urgent rectification of the situation. To this end, he wrote, "the convention must be infused with civilian elements, so that it will be possible to form a durable, truly national government, in which all honest revolutionaries must be represented in order to put Mexico on the path of national revival."[32]

After endless arguments, the convention proceeded to discuss a program of political and economic reforms only in March 1915, when a split was already imminent between its two principal factions, the northerners and the southerners, the *villistas* and the *zapatistas*. At the same time, as the convention sank deeper and deeper into the abyss of dissention, Carranza and his supporters not only took the initiative militarily, but also sought by every means possible to convince the workers and peasants that only a Constitutionalist government could open the way to their prosperity and freedom. In this connection, at one of the convention's sessions the delegate Santiago Orozco stated: "The *carrancistas* are carrying out revolutionary acts that we are unable to undertake, for all we do is waste time in the most pitiful and imprudent way." Obregón, continued Orozco, "has done what we have not: he has compelled all the bourgeoisie, all the capitalists, to give bread to the poor, and has forced all the wealthy of the capital to donate money for these poor people; he has demanded this in order to win over those afflicted by hunger. This is a highly significant fact, and if we—today or tomorrow, we who act in the name of the people—do not do something similar, however insignificant, to assure the people in some measure what we promise, then, gentlemen, the Revolution certainly shall fail." On this same occasion, a delegate by the name of Cepeda stated: "The assembly platform has turned into a professorial chair from which they lecture to us about the rights of man and his future prosperity, while children cry from hunger and ask for a little bread; the people to whom we promise freedom, law, and justice in the future, live as before in hunger and poverty; they have neither shoes for their feet nor clothes for their backs. We dwell on the fact that the people are sovereign, while they find themselves as before in the fetters of oppression. The people have already become disillusioned with their liberators, who they no longer believe speak to them."[33]

The people demanded that the convention take decisive steps against speculation, exorbitant prices, hunger, and poverty; the people demanded bread. Here is how a correspondent of *La Convención* described the situation in the hall of sessions on 21 May 1915: "Hundreds of women who already for several days had come to complain about the shortage of maize furiously shouted 'Bread!' On the city streets, crowds of hungry people awaited maize promised by the authorities. Terribly emaciated infants in the arms of mothers wasting away from want, women with signs of severe deprivation on their faces, fainting, losing consciousness. . . . ''[34] The government of the convention knew that in the city's "cellars and stores there was a considerable amount of maize and goods of primary necessity,''[35] yet it failed to carry out the confiscation of foodstuffs. The convention's financial situation was exceedingly grave. Vast sums were spent to maintain the administrative apparatus and to pay the salaries of the convention's delegates, many of whom spent much of their time in restaurants and night clubs. The behavior of some delegates was scandalous. Thus, a General Mendoza shot the convention delegate General Valenzuela. The affair was discussed at a session of the convention's assembly, but Mendoza went unpunished, declaring that "Valenzuela had deserved to be killed.''[36] The number of examples of unworthy behavior on the part of convention delegates could be multiplied. Provisional president Eulalio Gutiérrez, who secretly left the capital on 15 January 1915 and fled to the Carranza camp, took ten million pesos with him. On 6 March *La Convención* published an article entitled "The Tragic Truth," which asserted "there is no money, and there is no revenue, but there is hunger." At a meeting of the convention on 20 May, the new provisional president, Roque González Garza, reported on the disastrous financial situation, stating that every ten days he turned over 200,000 pesos to Zapata's army. Today, he said, "I must transfer to the Army of the South 2,700,000 pesos. In the treasury their remain 234,000 gold pesos, which we must dearly save. Such is the bitter truth, despite the smiles of delegate Soto y Gama. The treasury is empty. It is possible, of course, to issue new money—for every one peso, one hundred—but this would only worsen the situation. It would be well to spend some fifteen million for the purchase of goods to alleviate the situation of the proletariat, but I do not know where to get this money.''[37]

The delegation from the Liberating Army of the South demanded that González Garza, a representative of the Division of the North, resign as president so that he might be replaced by Manuel Palafox, a representative of the South. One can judge the relations between the two delegations on the basis of the stenographic records of one of the sessions. On 25 May 1915, Orozco delivered a harsh speech attacking González Garza, in which he declared that González Garza had never sympathized with the *zapatista* southerners (applauded by the delegates from the South), that he "had become the bulwark of the rich, the bourgeois, and those who stole from the people, and that for this reason the delegates of the South did not place their trust in him." Refuting these charges, José Castellanos, delegate from the North, described González Garza as the unifying link between Villa and Zapata (applauded by the *villista* delegates from the North). Immediately the southern delegate Luis Méndez declared, "If need be, we shall dissolve the union with the North." Seizing the floor, Federico Cervantes, delegate from the Division of the North, called for a strengthening of the union between North and South, but he was not allowed to speak by the *zapatista* delegates, who shouted "Out with González Garza!" As a sign of protest, the delegates of the Division of the North abandoned the hall of sessions.[38] The following day, *zapatista* soldiers were drawn up in front of the convention building.

As shown by the documents, the delegation of the Division of the North treated the revolutionaries of the South with respect. It was precisely the delegates of the Division of the North who proposed that representatives of Emiliano Zapata be invited to the convention, and when the delegation of southerners proposed acceptance of the Plan de Ayala, the first to offer their support were the esteemed and nationally known representatives of the Division of the North, Villa's associates Roque González Garza and Felipe Angeles. They were supported by the remaining delegates of the Division of the North. The delegation of the Division of the North did all in its power to bring Zapata and Villa together. On 4 December 1914, Zapata and Villa met at Zapata's headquarters in Xochimilco. A stenographic record of these talks has been preserved, which makes it possible to reconstruct them in detail. Present from the Liberating Army were General Emiliano Zapata, his brother, General Eufemio Zapata, Paulino Martínez, and Manuel Palafox. Accompanying Villa at the meeting were Generals Roque González Garza and Amador Salazar.

During the talks, discussion centered on land. Addressing Zapata, Villa said, "All my thoughts are of dividing up the lands of the rich," to which Zapata answered, "The people thirst for land, this is their dream." Villa continued: "Our people have known neither justice nor freedom. All the lands are in the hands of the rich, while the landless poor must work from morning to night. I think that in the future there must come a different life, but until then we shall not lay down our arms." Zapata assured Villa that as long as he and his companions in arms lived they would carry on the struggle for this better life. Villa then addressed those present as follows: "We have long experienced the oppression of tyranny. I am the son of plain people, and we who represent these people must make them happy. You can be certain that Francisco Villa will never betray the people.... And I declare that I shall not seek, nor do I wish to hold any government posts; for me the happiness of my fatherland stands above all else. As for these large landholders, I am ready to support the idea of the Plan de Ayala to take away their lands and to redistribute them to the people." Paulino Martínez, in turn, emphasized the importance of the meeting of these two selfless fighters for the happiness of the people and expressed his confidence in the triumph of the Revolution and the liberation of the Mexican people. González Garza, addressing himself to the two distinguished leaders of the Revolution, said: "Generals Zapata and Villa! The destiny of the fatherland is in your hands;

consider some disinterested advice. . . . General Zapata must assure the triumph of the Revolution in the South, and you, General Villa, must assure the triumph of the Revolution in the North.'' Subsequently, he recalled the tasks facing the convention in the matter of resolving economic and social problems and asked Zapata and Villa to support the convention's efforts in this area, adding, ''you will be even greater and more highly esteemed not only in our country, but all over the world.'' There in Xochimilco a pact was signed which stipulated the following: (1) a military alliance between the Division of the North and the Liberating Army of the South; (2) recognition of the Plan de Ayala by Villa and the Division of the North; (3) the supply of arms and ammunition by Villa to Zapata's army; and (4) the mutual commitment of both leaders, following the triumph of the Revolution, to fight for the election of a civilian as president.[39]

This very same alliance between North and South now fell apart in the convention. The delegation of the Division of the North, on leaving the hall of sessions, presented the assembly with a document in which it was pointed out that ''the position adopted by the group of delegates from the South under the direction of Díaz Soto y Gama threatens the Villa-Zapata alliance, the alliance of North and South, at such a crucial time for the country and the Revolution.''[40] But this document remained without effect. The *zapatista* delegates moved to Jojutla (Morelos), remaining there as a faction of the convention until 1916. The *villista* delegates moved northward from Toluca, first to Ixtlahuaca, and then to Río Verde (San Luis Potosí), where, on 29 November 1915 at the hacienda ''La Gruñidora,'' the remains of the *villista* faction of the convention were defeated by *carrancista* Colonel Encarnación Aguilar Frías.[41] Such was the sad end of the convention.

The convention was an attempt by Mexico's petty-bourgeois democracy to find a way to resolve the most burning issues of the Revolution. It formulated a program of sociopolitical reforms. On the agrarian question, this program called for the elimination of the latifundia, their subdivision into parcels for distribution among the peasants—each of sufficient size to meet the needs of a single family—the return to the villages of *ejidos* (common pastures, grazing lands, public domain), land, and water usurped from them previously, the development of agriculture through improvements in agrotechnical methods, and the development of agronomy. On the labor question, it declared essential the elaboration of legislation to extenuate (but not eliminate) exploitation, and the elimination of poverty by means of appropriate social and economic reforms—specifically, educational opportunities for workers, enactment of laws providing pensions and job insurance, a standard work day, observance of health regulations in factories and plants, recognition of unions and labor groups as juridical entities so that employers would be obliged to deal with unionized, rather than individual, defenseless workers, recognition of the right to strike and boycott, and the elimination of *tiendas de raya*.[42]

Under the heading "Social Reforms," it was proposed to promote the emancipation of women. Under the heading "Administrative Reforms," it was declared essential to introduce secular instruction, expand the system of public education, liquidate monopolies, and review legislation pertaining to joint stock companies "in order to prevent abuses on the part of management and to guarantee the rights of small shareholders." The program provided for a reform of the mining laws so as to expand the rights of the government and protect the lives and health of the miners. It also stipulated that "foreign companies wishing to conduct business in Mexico" be obliged to establish local representation authorized to distribute dividends, to provide information to stockholders, and to make available for inspection all books and documents. It was proposed that Mexican courts be given the right to review claims arising in connection with foreign companies. Further on in the program, mention is made of the need to revise the tax system, eliminate the privileges of large capitalists, and do away with indirect taxes. Under the heading "Political Reforms," the program calls for the abolition of the Senate as an aristocratic, conservative institution; guaranteed independence of judicial organs; introduction of a system of direct elections; confiscation of the property of enemies of the Revolution and prosecution of the same.[43] As we can see, this program was exceedingly moderate, yet it represented a decisive contribution to the bourgeois-democratic program as a whole.

The convention did in fact adopt some measures. Thus, a decree was issued annulling all juridical acts of the Huerta government. The possessions and property of former ministers in the Díaz and Huerta governments were confiscated, including such prominent representatives of Porfirian reaction as José Yves Limantour, Emilio Rabasa, Manuel Romero Rubio, Enrique Creel, Pablo Macedo, and Vera Estañol.[44] Rising above the erroneous position of Otilio Montaño and Díaz Soto y Gama, the convention took a patriotic stand on the matter of U.S. intervention, and resolutely demanded that the Wilson government withdraw American troops from Mexican territory.[45] When in late May, 1915, Wilson again threatened Mexico, González Garza issued (1 June) an order to all unit commanders of the army of the convention to be prepared for armed intervention by the United States. In an article entitled "Intervention?" published on 2 June, La Convención wrote: "Only unity can prevent the intervention which threatens the future of Mexico."

On 14 June the convention sent a telegram to Carranza proposing a truce. Without waiting for an answer, the assembly declared a truce throughout the country in order that "all revolutionary forces might send their representatives to Mexico City" to elect a provisional president and to form a government comprising representatives of the three factions (three from each faction)—the Constitutionalist Army, the Liberating Army of the South, and the Division of the North.[46] The assembly decided that the program of the future government should be based on the principles set forth in the program of socio-political reforms, the

Plan de Guadalupe and the Plan de Ayala. But this attempt at compromise also failed: in the convention itself there was no unity, a fact which played into the hands of the leaders of the bourgeois-landowning bloc. The proposed formation of a coalition government was rejected by Carranza. *Carrancista* general Pablo González demanded that the convention recognize unconditionally the Carranza government and that it renew the offensive against the capital.[47] The convention's attempt to resolve pacifically the issue of power failed. Now began the final stage of the civil war, in which the bourgeois-landowning bloc proved victorious.

Carranza struck first at Villa's Division of the North, which was routed in April 1915. Then, in the course of 1915–16, Carranza's troops delivered a series of major defeats to the Liberating Army of Zapata, isolating its remnants in the mountains of Morelos. Given the anarchosyndicalist leadership of the government, Carranza was able to use a part of the capital's proletariat in the struggle against the armies of Zapata and Villa, forming the "Red Battalions" which fought on the side of the *carrancista* army. When the workers realized that they were being deceived and made demands for a radical improvement of their situation, Carranza, in 1916, brutally crushed these demonstrations and even introduced the death penalty for participation in strikes.

Thus, having come to power with the aid of labor, the fledgling Mexican bourgeoisie turned on its former allies. This was possible because the peasants and workers of Mexico were disunited and the Mexican proletariat was not yet capable of dominating the Revolution, while spokesmen for the petty bourgeoisie were unable to satisfy labor's aspirations for freedom, democracy, and a better life.

NOTES

1 Having initiated its work in the capital in October 1914, the convention moved to Aguascalientes, then returned to the capital, whence it moved to Cuernavaca, returning once again to the capital, and, finally, moving to Toluca.

2 Robert E. Quirk, *The Mexican Revolution, 1914–1915: The Convention of Aguascalientes* (Bloomington, 1960).

3 Luis Fernando Amaya C., *La soberana convención revolucionaria, 1914–1916,* (Mexico, 1966).

4 V. I. Lenin, *Polnoe sobranie sochinenii*, XV, 277.

5 Ibid., pp. 277–78.

6 Isidro Fabela, ed., *Documentos históricos de la Revolución Mexicana: Revolución y régimen constitucionalista*, 5 vols. (Mexico, 1960–64), I, 275. (Cited hereafter as *DHRM*.)

7 Ibid., p. 287.

8 Revolutionary agrarian program proclaimed by Emiliano Zapata on 28 November 1911.

9 Archivo General de la Nación Mexicana (hereafter AGNM). Convención Revolucionaria: Secretaría de Gobernación, Asuntos agrarios, leg. 3.

10 *DHRM*, I, 121.

11 Alvaro Obregón, *Ocho mil kilómetros en campaña* (Mexico, 1960), pp. 127, 132–33.

12 *Planes políticos y otros documentos* (Mexico, 1954), pp. 152–53.

13 On 26 March 1913, right after Huerta's counterrevolutionary uprising, representatives of various volunteer units which had started an armed struggle to restore constitutional rule met at the hacienda "Guadalupe," in the state of Coahuila, where they adopted a program to carry out the Revolution.

14 Florencio Barrera Fuentes, ed., *Crónicas y debates de las sesiones de la soberana convención revolucionaria*, 3 vols (Mexico, 1964–1965), I, 10–11.

15 AGNM. División del Norte: General en Jefe, Correspondencia particular, Documento No. 36 (482).

16 *La Convención* (23 December 1914); "Debates de las sesiones... ," 14 and 26 October 1914.

17 Ibid.

18 *La Convención* (1 June 1915); "Debates de las sesiones..."

19 *La Convención* (16 January 1915).

20 *La Convención* (17 November 1914); *Vida Nueva* (25 November 1914).

21 *La Convención* (5 January 1915).

22 Archivo General de la Secretaría Exterior. L-E-841, R, leg. 2, f. 16.

23 Archivo Histórico del Instituto de Antropología e Historia de México. Leg 40 (11), f. 164.

24 AGNM. Convención Revolucionaria: Secretaría de Fomento, leg. 7, "Exposición de los motivos que sirvieron de fundamento a la formación del presupuesto... ," pp. 1–3.

25 Barrera Fuentes, *Crónicas y debates*, I, 617, 619–20; II, 71–72.

26 *La Convención* (24 March 1915).

27 *La Convención* (17 November 1914).

28 AGNM. Convención Revolucionaria: leg. 7, "Memorial de los vecinos del pueblo Atoyac."

29 AGNM. Convención Revolucionaria: leg. 7, "A la Soberana Convención Revolucionaria. Queja de R. González de 26/V/1915."

30 *La Convención* (22 December 1914; 4 January 1915).

31 AGNM. Convención Revolucionaria: Diversos asuntos (1915), leg. 7, "Delegado A. San Martín al Secretariado de la Convención, 26/VI/1915."

32 This document produced no results; in the upper left-had corner in pencil is written "Al archivo."

33 *La Convención* (7 June 1915).

34 *La Convención* (22 May 1915).

35 *La Convención* (24 March 1915).

36 AGNM. Convención Revolucionaria: Diversos asuntos, leg. 7.

37 *La Convención* (25 January, 6 March, and 21 May 1915).

38 *La Convención* (26 May, 1915).
39 *Planes políticos y otros documentos*, pp. 116–22.
40 *La Convención* (8 June 1915).
41 Amaya C., *La soberana convención revolucionaria*, pp. 442–43.
42 *Planes políticos y otros documentos*, pp. 123–24.
43 Ibid., pp. 125–27.
44 *La Convención* (4, 7, 8, and 9 June 1915).
45 *La Convención* (2 June 1915).
46 *La Convención* (15 June 1915).
47 *La Convención* (21 June 1915).

17 FROM THE "BIG STICK" TO THE "GOOD NEIGHBOR" POLICY

E. L. NITOBURG

THE HISTORY of U.S. foreign policy between the two world wars, particularly in Latin America, is the subject of scores of works by American bourgeois historians and publicists. Special attention in this field is devoted to the so-called "Good Neighbor Policy," which, from the point of view of the governing circles in the United States, was most successful and yielded the greatest results.[1] In discussing the factors which determined the nature of U.S. foreign policy, however, bourgeois historians as a rule ignore completely or try to minimize in every way possible the role in events of the popular masses. One would look in vain in their works for any indication of the workers' struggle or of the national-liberation movement and its influence on the forms and methods of U.S. foreign policy.

As yet, Soviet historical literature contains no special studies devoted to the "Good Neighbor Policy" as a whole. There are only articles dealing with partial aspects of this subject, as well as sections of more general works. In the present article the author attempts to analyze a specific question, namely, the genesis of U.S. Latin American policy during the period between the two world wars, the premises or factors which necessitated changes in this policy, and the enunciation of the "Good Neighbor Policy."[2]

During the fifteen years which elapsed from the Spanish American War to the First World War, the United States developed at a tremendous rate and in economic might greatly outstripped England and Germany. The war of 1914–18 was gigantic business for American monopolies. From a country which imported

Originally published as "Ot politiki 'bol'shoi dubinki' k politike 'dobrogo soseda,'" in I. R. Grigulevich et al., eds., *Ot Aliaski do Ognennoi Zemli,*† pp. 23–48.

capital, the United States became a capital exporter; from a debtor nation, it became a creditor nation. Soon after the war, American capital moved to conquer the world. American long-term capital investments abroad, which in 1914 comprised 3.5 billion dollars, increased by 1929 to 14.5 billion dollars.[3] Total U.S. foreign trade turnover grew during this time from 4.3 to 9.6 billion dollars.

By 1929 the United States produced one-half of the total industrial output of the capitalist world. The problem of markets, therefore, became especially acute for American monopolies, and they waged a struggle in all parts of the world for markets, capital investments, sources of raw materials, and spheres of influence. But as before, a special place in this struggle was reserved for their own "backyard"—Latin America.

The First World War opened up Latin America, particularly South America, which found itself cut off from Europe, to the captial and goods of the United States. Between 1913 and 1919, capital investments of the United States in Latin America grew from 1.2 billion dollars to 2.4 billion dollars. In 1924 they constituted 3.7 billion dollars, and in 1929 surpassed 5.5 billion dollars, almost equalling British investments.[4] U.S. exports to Latin America tripled from 1913 to 1919. By 1929, U.S. trade with Latin America had increased 5.6 times in comparison with 1913, surpassing the Latin American trade of England, France, and Germany combined.[5]

Under the Harding and Coolidge administrations, the commercial and financial expansion of American capital received wider support from the Department of State than at any other time. Loans were granted on the condition that recipient governments employ American financial and military advisors and agree in the future not to negotiate loans in Europe.[6]

The nature and methods of the postwar expansion of American monopolistic capital in the Western Hemisphere were decisively influenced by the shift which began at this time in the center of gravity of Wall Street's expanionist activities from the already-dominated Caribbean region to South America. By the end of the First World War, the Caribbean had been converted into an American lake surrounded by U.S. military bases. The Panama Canal had been built, Haiti and the Dominican Republic were occupied by American marines, and American troops were likewise present in Cuba, Nicaragua, and Panama. The Caribbean region had become almost a monopoly preserve of American capital.[7] Having established its supremacy in the Caribbean region and, following the war, become the most powerful capitalist state, the United States passed to the next phase of the struggle for hegemony in the Western Hemisphere.

Statistical data verify that during the period from 1914 to 1929 there was an increase in South America's share in the total export of U.S. capital and trade to Latin America. In 1921, 10.1 percent of total U.S. exports went to the countries of the Caribbean and 6.8 percent to ten countries in South America, while in 1930 these figures were respectively 8.4 percent and 9.4 percent, although the specific overall weight of Latin America in total U.S. exports changed little (17 percent in 1921, 18 percent in 1930).[8]

Distribution of U. S. Capital Investments in Latin America
(in %)[9]

Year	10 Countries of the Caribbean Region	10 Countries of South America	Total
1913	86	14	100
1929	41	59	100

However, in the case of the larger countries of South America, which economically were still fairly independent of the United States, it was not possible to use open armed intervention as employed in the small countries of the Caribbean. Moreover, in the intervening hundred years since the South American republics had become independent, British capital had firmly entrenched itself and certainly had no intention of yielding its position without a struggle.

It is therefore no accident that from the outset American penetration of South America by and large took the form of financial expansion. The key factor in the financial enslavement of South America during this period was not so much direct capital investments, but rather loans. On the eve of the depression of 1929–33, 56.7 percent of direct U.S. capital investments in Latin America still went to the Caribbean region, 43.3 percent to South America. On the other hand, of all U.S. loans to the Latin American countries, 22.3 percent went to the Caribbean and 77.7 percent to South America.[10]

Following the defeat of Germany in the First World War, British imperialism found itself faced with a new, even more powerful rival—the imperialism of the United States—and the entire period from 1918 to the beginning of the 1930s was characterized by a sharp Anglo-American struggle for primacy in the capitalist world. In large measure this rivalry centered on the struggle for the oil, tin, copper, rubber, and cotton of South America.

Inch by inch, in a pertinacious struggle, American capital forced English capital out, and by 1929 the economic position of the United States in such countries as Venezuela, Colombia, Ecuador, and Bolivia was definitely stronger than the English position. In Chile and Peru it was approximately equal, while in Argentina, Brazil, Uruguay, and Paraguay it was weaker.[11] In trade with South America the United States surpassed England, increasing its exports 3.5 times and imports 2.8 times between 1913 and 1928, whereas English exports during these years grew only 28 percent, and imports 71 percent.[12] U.S. capital investments in South America in 1929, however, were still only half the total English investments.[13]

Economic rivalry was interwoven with a struggle for political influence, expressed in competition among various local bourgeois-landowning cliques and numerous governmental upheavals in the South American countries, as well as in conflicts between these countries. The imperialists of the United States and England kindled old boundary disputes and encouraged longstanding rivalries between Argentina, Brazil, and Chile over influence in South America.[14]

The commercial and financial expansion of American capital throughout the world created a serious threat to England's position in the world economy and politics, leading to an aggravation of Anglo-American relations. In the struggle against its American rival, English imperialism skillfully used the hatred of "Yankee imperialism" which existed among the broad popular masses in Latin America.

The opposition of British imperialism and its support of resistance by the ruling circles of a number of South American countries to U.S. expansion in the Western Hemisphere, together with the shift in the center of gravity of this expansion from the Caribbean to South America, unquestionably played a role in Washington's gradual renunciation of its former openly imperialistic policy in Latin America. A still more important factor, which forced U.S. ruling circles to change in the 1930s to new, more-disguised forms of Latin American policy and more flexible methods of "penetration" and control, was the steady rise of the national-liberation and antiimperialist movement in all the countries of Latin America and of a democratic labor movement in the United States itself.

A sharp reduction at the end of the First World War in foreign demand for foodstuffs and raw materials from Latin America caused grave hardships to agriculture and industry in the area. Living conditions for the great masses worsened drastically, and the people's hatred of imperialism and local exploiters increased even more. The October Revolution, writes William Z. Foster, "gave a new glimpse of light and hope to the myriads of oppressed and exploited workers and peasants in all the countries of the Western Hemisphere, from Canada to Argentina. Thenceforth, the lessons and inspiration of the Russian Revolution were fated to exercise an important influence upon the economic and political struggles of the oppressed masses everywhere in the New World."[15]

The fact that the transition of American finance captial to an active struggle for world hegemony coincided with the onset, development, and intensification of the crisis of capitalism complicated enormously the realization of the plans of the Wall Street magnates. In 1918–21, Latin America was shaken by profound social shocks. A powerful wave of strikes enveloped many Latin American countries. Armed uprisings broke out in a number of regions of Brazil, Mexico, Argentina, and Chile. In an atmosphere of revolutionary upsurge, Communist parties sprang up in Mexico (1919), Argentina and Uruguay (1920), Chile and Brazil (1922), and Cuba (1925), while Communist groups appeared in some other countries.[16]

Masses of peasants also rose up. They could not but relate their struggle for land to the struggle against imperialism, which cruelly exploited their labor on the plantations, destroyed established patterns of peasant economy, and hastened the pauperization and impoverishment of the peasantry. Tens of thousands of people took part in the revolt against the American occupiers of Haiti, which began in 1919 and lasted for more than a year. With rare exceptions, however, the peasant movement remained spontaneous.[17] The revolutionary wave of these years attracted also petty-bourgeois elements, students (the movement for university reforms extended to practically all countries of Latin America), soldiers, and even part of the officer corps (Brazil).[18]

In Argentina, Mexico, Brazil, and Chile national capital became firmly established during the war years, as the national bourgeoisie increasingly sought economic independence. The postwar upsurge of the national-liberation movement embraced also a considerable part of the middle sector of the national bourgeoisie, who had been thwarted by the pressure of imperialist monopolies. They demanded independent development of their countries' raw materials and defense of fledgling national industries through the introduction of protectionist tariffs. The circles of the bourgeoisie that were commited to English capital for the promotion of their own interests played on the masses' hatred of Yankee imperialism. This paved the way for a revival of "pan-Hispanist" propaganda. Hostile attacks against the United States increased in the Latin American bourgeois press. During these years all Latin America was swept by a wave of protest against the continued occupation of Haiti, the Dominican Republic, Panama, and Nicaragua by American marines and against the Americans' shooting of hundreds of protesting Haitian peasants—protest which was reflected in the actions of official circles in some Latin American countries.[19]

The revolutionary and national-liberation movement in Latin America continued in the second half of the 1920s. Increased production in the capitalist countries during this period so heightened competition for Latin American markets that fledgling national industries were not always able to survive. New pressure from foreign monopolies and internal social advances, particularly the numerical growth of the proletariat and its increased role in the national-liberation struggle, led to a heightening of anti-imperialist sentiments among the popular masses.

Strikes and peasant and student disturbances continued in most Latin American countries. In 1924 workers in São Paulo, together with the local garrison, rose in rebellion, seizing and holding for almost three weeks this, the second-largest city in South America. This was followed by the legendary march of the "Prestes column," which lasted more than three years and, fighting engagements throughout Brazil, covered 25,000 kilometers, leaving a profound impression on the consciousness of the Brazilian people, who gave to Luis Carlos Prestes the name of Knight of Hope.[20]

The young Communist parties of the Latin American countries continued their efforts to organize and educate the working class and to unite it. In 1926 the Chilean Communists gained ten seats in the Parliament, including two in the Senate. The trade union movement reached a more advanced stage. In a number of countries there appeared national labor organizations, and in 1929 there was formed a united left-wing labor organization—the Latin American Confederation of Trade Unions (LACTU).[21]

Anti-imperialist sentiments were rising even in the ranks of the petty bourgeoisie. The duplicity and vacillation of the middle national bourgeoisie became ever more obvious. The growth of commerce and industry in the larger countries of Latin America and the competition of foreign monopolies pushed the national bourgeoisie into the ranks of the liberation movement. At the same time, the growth of class consciousness and organization of the proletariat, as well as the latter's mounting role in the national-liberation movement, frightened the national bourgeoisie, fearful of the revolutionary activity of the masses, and forced it to collaborate with the imperialists. Moreover, the interests of a certain part of the national bourgeoisie coincided with those of the upper, primarily intermediary and usurious bourgeoisie, intimately tied to foreign capital, and the local agrarian oligarchy.

Nevertheless, as national capital developed and influenced the actions of the ruling circles of the Latin American countries, Washington found it increasingly necessary to take this circumstance into consideration when elaborating policy. Anti-American sentiments in Latin America became so strong that for the first time they were openly aired even at sessions of the Pan-American conferences. "Between the fourth Pan-American conference and the fifth," testifies William Z. Foster, "there was a gap of thirteen years (from 1910 to 1923), and when the fifth conference did meet, it was powerless to make any important decisions."[22]

The liberation struggle of the Latin American peoples during the 1920s reached its height in Nicaragua. The selfless fight of the Nicaraguan patriots led by Augusto Sandino—"general of the free people," as Henri Barbusse called him—against the North American occupation forces became a living embodiment of the unity of the peoples of Latin America. The chief of staff of Sandino's popular revolutionary army was a Venezuelan, Carlos Aponte; the generals of this army were the Salvadoran José León Díaz; the Hondurans Juan Pablo Umansor, Porfirio Sánchez, and Simón González; the Guatamalan María Manuel Girón Ruano; the Mexican Manuel Chávarri, and so on. Freedom-fighters from many Latin American countries fought in Sandino's detachments, among them one of the present leaders of the Venezuelan Communist Party, Gustavo Machado.[23]

The Nicaraguans' heroic resistance of the North American occupation forces made a tremendous impression on all the countries of the Western Hemisphere, immediately highlighting, as if by a powerful projector, the nature of the interrelationship between the peoples of Latin America and U.S. imperialism. The new imperialist intervention produced an outburst of indignation. From Río Grande del Norte to the prairies of Patagonia, the entire continent was swept by a wave of protest meetings and demonstrations. The Mexican Congress condemned the actions of the United States. In a number of countries funds began to be collected to purchase arms for the Nicaraguan patriots.[24] Intervention in Nicaragua also produced mass protests by workers and other democratic organizations in the United States and sharp criticism of the Coolidge administration even in the American Congress.[25] As a result, the Sixth Pan-American Conference, held in Havana in early 1928, was conducted in an extremely tense atmosphere. For the first time, delegates from a majority of the Latin American countries openly demanded a formal ban on armed intervention.

The Havana Conference (and even conservative American historians are forced to recognize this) left a very distressing impression on Latin America, where it intensified even more suspicion, fear, and animosity toward the United States. "Never before have the peoples of Latin American been more bitter toward the United States than they are now," wrote J. F. Rippy in 1928.[26] The conference seriously undermined the prestige of the United States and demonstrated to the Washington politicians that the edifice of Pan-Americanism which they had created over a forty-year period had developed a crack.

The stubborn armed resistance of little Nicaragua against the interventionists, together with the results of the Sixth Pan-American Conference (for Washington extraordinarily alarming) clearly indicated a crisis in the relations between Latin America and the United States. In the new conditions of a total crisis of capitalism and the emergence of a mass anti-imperialist movement in Latin America, continued reliance on the blatantly imperialist "Big Stick Policy" of the era of Teddy Roosevelt and William Howard Taft led the Latin American policy of the United States into a dead end. Already at that time, and in subsequent years, bourgeois historians of all political shadings as well as U.S. politicians were forced to recognize this fact.[27]

By mid-1928 the need for changes in Latin American policy had become obvious to many representatives of the ruling elite in the United States, since the old policy threatened to isolate the United States in Latin America and, consequently, to doom to failure their long-range plans for dominating the Western Hemisphere. In July 1928 the newly elected candidate of the Democratic Party to the post of governor of the State of New York, Franklin Delano Roosevelt, wrote in *Foreign Affairs* that the question of Latin America was "the most important of all," and sounded a warning about the failure of American diplomacy at the Havana Conference and in Latin America generally: "Never before in our history have we had fewer friends in the Western Hemisphere than we have today. . . . The time has come when we must accept . . . new principles." The present "lack of policy [cannot] be approved. The time is ripe," he wrote, "to start another chapter."[28]

In Republican Party circles, too, many began to realize by this time the need for decisive changes in Latin American policy. Ogden L. Mills, a prominent Republican businessman and millionaire, who soon after became Secretary of the Treasury during the presidency of Herbert Hoover, wrote about this in the same July issue of *Foreign Affairs*. In expressing his views on the Republicans, Walter Lippmann, one of the most prominent political analysts, also wrote about this.[29] In 1928 Benjamin Sumner Welles, formerly for many years head of the Latin American section of the Department of State, demanded a "new," "constructive" Latin American policy which would prevent "the rise of motives for revolution and anarchy." He called for the discarding of openly imperialist policy methods and a wider use of such a convenient instrument of Latin American policy as Pan-Americanism.[30]

A comparison of the views of the above-noted American bourgeois statesmen and publicists shows that already in 1928 all of them considered it necessary above all to repudiate the method of open armed intervention by the United States and to substitute the more disguised and flexible method of "collective intervention," which amounted to intervention by the same United States "with the consent" of several Latin American governments.[31] Another proposed change in Latin American policy concerned the Monroe Doctrine, which Washington usually invoked to "justify" its policy of intervention. The Latin Americans had long ago demanded that the United States repudiate the Doctrine. The governments of Chile, Costa Rica, Colombia, and even Cuba opposed its inclusion in the charter of the League of Nations. Argentina, Mexico, Honduras, and El Salvador formally refused to recognize it. Counting, however, on the creation of a bloc of Western Hemisphere countries subservient to Washington based precisely on President Monroe's declaration of 2 December 1823 that Europe should not meddle in the affairs of America and did not have the right to establish new colonies there, the United States sought by every means to keep the Monroe Doctrine in its arsenal, even at the price of "purging" it of many later "corollaries" (such as the Roosevelt "corollary" on the "right of the United States to intervene to maintain order"). This point of view was shared by Sumner Welles and Democrat Franklin Roosevelt (who felt that the Doctrine should not only be preserved but also "Pan-Americanized," that is, utilized as a basis for "cooperation" with the ruling circles of the Latin American countries), as well as Republican Ogden Mills.[32]

Finally, one of the most widespread demands was to devote special attention to the U.S. diplomatic service in Latin America, where only the most experienced and adroit diplomats, specially trained in the Latin American "area," were to be sent.[33]

Thus both Democratic and Republican proponents of a "new," "constructive" Latin American policy had in mind merely a change of external forms, utilizing the "flexible" and disguised methods and means of "influence" best suited to the altered circumstances. But the goal and nature of this policy remained as before: the economic and political domination of Latin America by the United States and conversion of the area into a dependable "back yard," a source of raw materials and a bridgehead for the coming struggle of Wall Street magnates to dominate the world.[34]

There can be no doubt that the unexpected attempt by "Uncle Sam" to hide behind the backs of the Latin American governments in order to crush revolutionary movements in any of the Latin American republics, and the effort to "purge" the Monroe Doctrine of the most recent, blatantly imperialistic "strata," were necessitated primarily by the rapid growth of the national-liberation struggle among Latin America's popular masses. The growing resistance of the Latin American peoples, increased antiimperialist sentiments among the popular masses of the United States, and the intrigues of British imperialism in South America were basic factors which in the final analysis led in a few years to a revision of U.S. imperialist policy toward the countries of Latin America and to President Franklin Roosevelt's proclamation of the so-called Good Neighbor Policy.[35]

Thus by the middle of 1928 it had become clear to some politicians, leaders in the Democratic Party, that the forms and methods of the United States' Latin American policy required changes. This matter occupied a prominent place in the Democratic Party's pre-election campaign in 1928 and was included in its election platform. As for the Republicans, their presidential candidate, Herbert Hoover, also roundly "condemned" intervention and imperialist policy in his pre-election speeches.[36] On his initiative a special document was even prepared at the end of 1928, the "Clark Memorandum," which furthur "purged" the Monroe Doctrine so as to convince the Latin Americans that it had nothing in common with imperialism, in no way justified U.S. intervention, and, in general, referred to the European, rather than the Latin American policy of the United States.[37] It thus officially repudiated a whole series of declarations by numerous U.S. presidents and secretaries of state, and in fact tacitly acknowledged the failure of the Monroe Doctrine as the basis of a Latin American policy. Washington resorted to this only in order to preserve the Doctrine in the arsenal of American diplomacy until such time as it might again be needed. This memorandum was not published, however, until 1930.[38]

In his introductory presidential message to Congress, and subsequently, Hoover repeatedly assured the Latin Americans of "the United States' repudiation of imperialism" and any kind of "foreign domination."[39] But it is difficult to say whether the Hoover administration would actually have gone beyond these loud declarations, of which Latin Americans had long ago tired, were it not for the fact that in the fall of 1929, in the words of William Foster, American "consumptive prosperity" came to an end and a world economic crisis began which intensified even more the contradictions between Latin America and the United States.

The economic crisis of 1929–33, which grew out of the general crisis of capitalism, was unequaled in force and duration. It struck hardest at the leading capitalist country, the United States. The unprecedented stock market crash on Wall Street was followed by the ruin and closing of thousands of industrial and commercial enterprises in the United States. In 1932 the volume of industrial production fell below what it had been before the war, and was only 53.8 percent of the 1929 level. Prices of agricultural products dropped catastrophically. Ruined farmers filled the ranks of the unemployed, whose number in the United States fluctuated during these years between eleven and seventeen million people. Class conflicts sharpened. In contrast to previous years, even unorganized workers participated in strikes. The movement of the unemployed assumed enormous proportions. Over 1.5 million people participated in demonstrations against unemployment in March 1930.

The crisis not only dealt a heavy blow to the entire American economic and social system but also weakened the position of United States imperialism throughout the world. The exportation of capital from the United States almost stopped. Old capital investments became worthless. Foreign trade rapidly shrank. Moreover, while world trade as a whole declined 67.7 percent during 1929–32, and that of England 45 percent, the foreign trade of the United States declined 70 percent.[40] In 1930 the United States adopted one of the most restrictive customs codes in its entire history, the Smoot-Hawley Tariff Act. This aroused reciprocal actions by a majority of capitalist countries. England abandoned the gold standard and moved to protectionism.

The crisis further intensified imperialist and particularly Anglo-American contradictions. The economy of the United States suffered from it much more than did that of England. By the spring of 1933, the volume of industrial production in the United States had been reduced by 60 percent in comparison with 1929, but in England by only 8 percent. During the years of crisis, England regained first place in world trade. American capital investments abroad, particularly in Latin America, depreciated much more than English investments.[41]

English imperialism conducted a fierce counterattack in these years against its American rival. This applied in the first instance to South America, where in the early thirties English capital succeeded temporarily in regaining part of the ground lost during the First World War and in the postwar decade.[42] The United States' share of Latin American imports during the depression years dropped from 38.7 percent to 29.2 percent, while England's share increased from 14.9 percent to 18.1 percent, Germany's from 10.8 percent to 11.5 percent, Japan's from 0.5 percent to 1.8 percent, and so on. In 1932 alone, Latin America reduced its trade with the United States by 42 percent, but with England by only 11 percent.[43]

Although the main imperialist contradictions of the depression period continued to be those between the United States and England, all the other imperialist conflicts likewise became more acute during these years. Attempts by the imperialists to resolve their difficulties at the expense of the Soviet Union through an anti-Soviet "crusade" failed. The ruling circles of Japan and Germany, who were interested in revising the Versailles-Washington system of treaties, openly began preparing for a new world war. In 1931 a hotbed of war was created in the Far East, and in 1933 another in Europe.

It was precisely in the years of economic crisis that Japanese imperialism began to penetrate the Latin American countries. Japan's trade expansion into Latin America grew rapidly and provoked widespread responses of alarm in the United States, even more so as it was accompanied by propaganda directed against "Yankee imperialism."[44] Comintern documents reported: "Japanese imperialism has recently heightened its activity, as seen in the considerable increase in Japanese commerce with South America and the Caribbean, Japanese emigration, and the expansion of military and political ties with a number of bourgeois landowner groups in Mexico, Brazil, and several other countries."[45] No less serious was the alarm caused in Washington by the growing penetration of Latin America by German imperialism.

All this verified once more the unusual difficulties faced by U.S. monopolies in the countries of South America and underscored the need for changes in Washington's Latin American policy which would promote a successful expansion of U.S. imperialism in the southern part of the American continent. The world economic crisis exposed even more the contraditions between the imperialist powers and the colonial and dependent countries. The dominance of foreign capital and precapitalist economic forms gave rise to an especially acute crisis in Latin America. A sharp drop in world prices for minerals and agricultural produce, as well as a reduction in their exportation to Europe and the United States, led in Latin America to the shutting down of mines and factories, to the destruction of millions of sacks of coffee, wheat, bananas, and corn, and to hunger and unemployment among the popular masses.

As a result of the one-crop system imposed by the imperialists, the economy of the Latin American countries found itself totally dependent on the exportation of one or two raw products. Their exports having been reduced by approximately two-thirds, these countries were deprived of the possibility of importing many food products necessary for the population's existence. In response to the Smoot-Hawley Tariff Act, which in the words of *Time* magazine's foreign editor [Charles] Wertenbaker "helped Latin American to plunge into the abyss of the crisis"[46] and almost closed the U.S. domestic market to its products, the Latin American countries also increased tariff barriers, introduced import quotas, established currency controls, stopped payments of debts, and began to negotiate commercial clearing accords with the European countries and Japan.[47] As a result, while from 1929 to 1932 the total foreign trade of the United States was reduced by two-thirds, its trade with Latin America shrank by almost three-fourths.[48] By 1936 American capital invested in foreign securities worldwide had devalued to 38.3 percent of its original value, and in Latin America to 76–77 percent.[49]

An important result of the crisis in the larger countries of Latin America was a further increase in the tendency to create a national industry (textiles, cement, shoes, food, etc.) shielded by protective tariffs, to reduce dependency on monoculture, and to limit the almost uncontrolled interference of foreign capital in their economy by means of special legislation and taking advantage of conflicts among the imperialists.[50]

These changes for the better indicated the strength and influence of Latin America's young national bourgeoisie on the policies of military-landowning circles and aroused growing concern in Washington. During the years of the crisis the standard of living of the laboring masses in Latin America dropped to an unprecedented level. Unemployment, famine, ruin, and imperialistic oppression drove millions of workers to revolutionary demonstrations and struggle against local reaction and foreign capital.

During these years, political struggle was far more acute in Latin America then in the United States. Impoverished peasants, striking laborers and unemployed workers, ruined petty bourgeoisie, progressive intellectuals, and students demanded the withdrawal from their countries of American soldiers, tax collectors, and advisors, and the liquidation of their dependence on foreign capital. The anti-imperialist movement of the masses fused with the struggle against the dictatorship of the military-landholding cliques. In the words of William Foster, "the situation there was fraught with revolution."[51]

In degree and force, the revolutionary upsurge in Latin America during the depression years was led respectively by Peru (1931), Chile (1932), and Cuba (1933), where the anti-imperialist movement assumed a truly mass character. The proletariat played an ever more prominent role in the popular movement, consolidating it, giving it stability and a consistent character. Strikes assumed a scope never before seen in Latin America, and most class battles of Latin America's proletariat in 1929–33 were markedly political and aggressive in nature.[52]

During the years of economic crisis the agrarian movement was notable for its scope and forms of struggle. Strikes on plantations were increasingly widespread. From partial demands and petitions of complaint, the peasants began more and more often to move toward land seizures. This gave the movement a political character. A guerrilla movement developed in Brazil, Argentina, and Cuba. On the whole, as the crisis of 1929–33 deepened, peasant reserves were ever more widely and actively drawn into the anti-imperialist revolution.[53]

The urban petty bourgeoisie took an active part in the revolutionary movement from the very first years of the economic crisis, that is, handicraftsmen, office workers, small merchants, and intellectuals. By the end of the crisis, revolutionary actions on the part of the petty bourgeoisie had become commonplace throughout Latin America. But they reached their greatest height and intensity in Chile, Cuba, and Brazil. The drawing of the broadest segments of the petty bourgeoisie into a single stream of national-liberation struggle was of enormous significance, for winning the working masses of the petty bourgeoisie over to the side of the proletariat is a major consideration in a revolution.

The liberation movement of the broad popular masses was reflected in a revolutionized army and navy. Soldiers' and sailors' revolts took place in Peru (the insurrection of the fifth regiment in Lima in 1931 and the revolt of two cruisers in 1932); in Chile (a number of insurrections in the army and navy in 1931–32); in Argentina (army and naval revolts in 1933); and in Cuba (1933 and 1934). In Brazil, the garrison in the city of Paraiba revolted. Later (1931) in the north of the country, in Pernambuco, soldiers arrested officers and seized banks, the telegraph, and the post office, taking power into their own hands.[54]

"In all these Latin American struggles," writes Foster, "the young Communist parties took a decisive part. They were everywhere giving leadership to the starving and outraged masses of workers, students, and peasants."[55] In directing the revolutionary struggle of the masses, the Communist parties were themselves tempered by the struggle to free themselves from the influence of national reformism and petty-bourgeois ideology. A number of major economic and political battles were carried on under the guidance of the Communist parties of Cuba, Brazil, Argentina, Chile, and El Salvador.

Frightened by the extent of the liberation movement of the Latin American peoples, local reactionaries and the imperialists feverishly threw together various counterrevolutionary blocs of bourgeois-landholding parties, the Catholic Church, and the military. In order to suppress the revolutionary movement of the popular masses, they sought by means of military coups to place more "reliable," "stronger" people in power and to establish a dictatorial regime capable of crushing mass movements. During the four depression years, there were over forty coups and attempted coups in Latin America. It was precisely at this time that a majority of the bloody dictatorships which existed in Latin America in the 1930s and early 1940s were established.

The sharply heightened anti-imperialism of the Latin American peoples' national-liberation movement, itself a part of the worldwide process whereby oppressed peoples were being revolutionized, and also the temporary weakening of the economic position of the United States in Latin America and especially South America, caused alarm in the ruling circles of the United States, forcing the Hoover administration to make a number of changes in the methods and forms of U.S. Latin American policy. Specifically, in March 1930 the "Clark

Memorandum'' was published, annulling the ''Roosevelt Corollary'' to the Monroe Doctrine, which had formed that basis of a policy of armed intervention; the U.S. military administration in Haiti was abolished and negotiations undertaken on the withdrawal from there of American troops; the U.S. Marines were withdrawn from Nicaragua; the United States announced its repudiation of military occupation ''to protect the property of American citizens,'' and once more limited the principle of nonrecognition of ''unconstitutional'' governments to the five Central American countries, as had been the case up until the presidency of Woodrow Wilson.[56]

All these tactical changes, however, were unavoidable, and by no means meant an unconditional renunciation of force, but merely some limitation thereof. The Hoover government made them not in good faith, but under pressure of circumstances. These changes were aimed at creating a semblance of ''voluntary concession'' to the peoples of the Latin American countries on the part of the United States. It is no accident that almost all of them were limited solely to a negative smoothing over of ''old grievances'' in what had already become a frankly odious ''Caribbean policy.''

In these new conditions, the Hoover government was forced to renounce some methods and forms of the ''old policy.'' But this government and its backers, blinded by class hatred of the popular masses, proved to be congenitally incapable, because of their narrow political point of view, of sacrificing even a small part of their immediate benefits for the sake of the wider interests and perspectives of American monopolistic capital as a whole, which already at that time was demanding a much more farsighted Latin American policy.

By late 1932 to early 1933, the anti-imperialist movement and hostility toward Yankee imperialism reached unprecedented levels in Latin America.[57] But the narrow-minded politicians of the Republican Old Guard did not wish to see this, obviously underestimating the strength and scope of the broad-based liberation movement and the degree of animosity toward the United States, not only of the popular masses but also of part of the prosperous classes of Latin America. They likewise underestimated the total need—from the point of view of the interests of American monopolies—to remove or at least weaken these factors as quickly as possible, since they regarded them as temporary and transitory. For this reason the ''concessions,'' too, were exceedingly moderate and designed for only a short time.

Meanwhile, the more farsighted and sober-thinking people in American ruling circles became increasingly aware of the threat to the interests and future perspectives of American captial which the rapid rise of the national-liberation movement and growing animosity toward the United States presented in Latin America. With mounting insistence these circles advocated introducing in U.S. Latin American policy well-planned, long-range changes which would make it possible, first, to pacify and deceive the Latin American peoples for a more or less extended period of time, to throw dust in their eyes concerning U.S. "good will" and "repudiation" of the policy of intervention; second, to achieve close "cooperation" with the ruling classes of Latin America for a combined struggle against the democratic forces; and third, to try in this way to force out the imperialist rivals and establish monopoly control by the magnates of Wall Street over the extensive markets and reserves of strategic raw materials in Latin America.[58]

In the U.S. presidential elections of 1932 the Democratic Party candidate, Franklin D. Roosevelt, was elected and on March 4, 1933 assumed the office of president. His administration came to power at the culmination of the depression. In February 1933 the United States was swept by a wave of bank crashes. American foreign trade was in a state of disarray; the exchange rate of the dollar was falling; the United States was rapidly losing world markets. The export of capital was all but discontinued. Unemployment reached enormous dimensions. Class conflicts became more pronounced.

The rise of the workers movement in the United States and of the liberation movement in the colonies and dependent countries exerted its influence upon the American bourgeoisie, forcing it to give thought to a change in its methods of domination. Despite the severe economic crisis, U.S. monopolists were not about to abandon their plans to establish American hegemony in the world. On the contrary, the whole course of historical development, and above all the deepening of the general crisis of capitalism, incited them to fight for hegemony.

The new government was confronted with the gravest tasks: to lead the United States out of the crisis with the fewest possible losses; to put an end to the growth of the revolutionary movement and strengthen the shaky authority of "American democracy"; to succeed in arming for a new, impending world conflict; and to create the foreign policy preconditions for a successful implementation of the American monopolies' plans for world hegemony.[59]

The attempt to stifle the growth of the mass revolutionary movement and to weaken somewhat the recurrence of crises in the country's economy resulted in a series of reforms known as the New Deal. The facts have shown that the New Deal strengthened even further the positions of the leading financial groups and that the period of Roosevelt's administration was characterized by an unprecedented concentration of capital in the United States and an unusual growth in the profits of American monopolists. At the same time, in this very period U.S. armaments reached unprecedented levels for peacetime.

But although the government was able to tame the reformist trade union leaders, it did not succeed in stopping the growth of the labor movement. The White House, therefore, was forced to reckon with the mood of the broad masses and with an organized working class, not only in the sphere of purely domestic policy, but also in the field of governmental foreign policy.

A special role in U.S. preparations for the impending war was played by Latin America, one of the richest reserves of raw materials in the capitalist world. Even before the economic crisis of 1929–33, FDR, like many other American political leaders, clearly grasped the enormous importance of complete control over Latin America for the success of a further struggle by U.S. monopolies for world hegemony. The desire to utilize the resources and strategic position of Latin America in the impending encounter between the imperialist powers was hindered by the hostility toward Yankee imperialism felt by not only the masses but also a part of the ruling circles in the Latin American countries. Already in 1928 this had forced Roosevelt, as well as Sumner Welles and other American political leaders, publicists, and historians, to suggest the urgent necessity of changing the forms and methods of U.S. Latin American policy and adopting more effective methods of expansion.[60] The depression of 1929–33 only confirmed this necessity.

The crisis had forced the Hoover administration to take the first timid steps toward a change in the forms of U.S. policy in Latin America, but almost nothing was changed. Moreover, as a result of the crisis and the inflexible policy of the Hoover government, by 1933 tendencies inimical to the interests of American imperialism had increased noticeably among ruling circles in the South American countries. At the end of 1932 the Argentine government advanced the Lamas Pact, the object of which was to weaken U.S. influence in the Pan-American Union and the countries of South America. Supported by British imperialism, Argentina attempted to form a customs union directed against the United States.[61]

The press reported a rapid increase in Latin American hostility toward the United States and even the possibility of a refusal to convene the Seventh Pan-American Conference, scheduled for December, 1933.[62] "When President Roosevelt first took office in March 1933, at the depth of the great economic crisis," notes Foster, "political and economic relations between the United States and Latin America were tense. . . . Obviously, a shift in United States imperialist policy in Latin America was absolutely necessary."[63]

Such a turn of events threatened to frustrate Washington's long-range plans in Latin America. Even before assuming the presidency, Roosevelt devoted special attention to the problem of relations with the Latin American countries, which he regarded as a "back yard" and reserve of the United States.[64] In his inaugural address to the Congress on 4 March 1933, he promised that his administration would pursue "the policy of the good neighbor—the neighbor who resolutely respects himself and, because he does so, respects others—the neighbor who respects his obligations and respects the sanctity of his agreements in and with a world of neighbors."[65] A month later, on 12 April 1933, addressing a special session of the governing board of the Pan-American Union on his Latin American policy, Roosevelt declared that "the essential qualities of a true Pan-Americanism must be the same as those which constitute a good neighbor," and for the first time suggested the need to "Pan-Americanize" the Monroe Doctrine, stating that it was a "Pan-American doctrine of continental self-defense" of the peoples of the American republics.[66]

Such pronouncements on "good neighborliness," "respect for the rights of small nations," and so on, repeated from time to time over the years, were made with a view to dulling the vigilance of the Latin American peoples, and lulling and weakening their resistance to the expansion of American capital. They were also designed to deceive the popular masses in the United States, the majority of whom were of anti-imperialist inclination, as well as the masses in other countries of the world. "The appeal to democratic feelings," notes a bourgeois historian, "was an important phase of the 'Good Neighbor' policy of F. D. Roosevelt and C. Hull."[67]

But the "Good Neighbor Policy" was not limited, as is known, to words alone. The Latin Americans had heard similar assurances many times, ever since Woodrow Wilson's time, and they had long ago ceased to believe them. The Roosevelt administration acted more subtly, more energetically, on a large scale. As early as 1933–36, it put an end to a number of the most blatant acts of the "old policy": the Platt Amendment in Cuba and a similar formal "right" of armed intervention by the United States in Haiti and Panama; after twenty years of occupation, it finally recalled the American marines from Haiti; it signed a convention renouncing armed intervention and interference in the affairs of other countries; it quietly consented to annul the treaty of 1923 forced on the countries of Central America by the United States; and so on.

Washington also made a number of other concessions, partially abandoning the "antiquated" and crude practice of open military pressure and military occupation. "While the 'good neighbor' policy by no means lived up to its name, the fact is that it did have a certain positive effect on U.S. relations with other countries in this part of the globe. True, the U.S. government did not relinquish its interventionist practices, and in many instances engaged in unsavory intrigues and rigged elections (using its traditional ties with the local oligarchy), but the Roosevelt administration nevertheless avoided such crude methods as landing marines and imposing its own solutions."[68] All this undoubtedly represented a definite concession to the national-liberation movement, and precisely for this reason the peoples of Latin America welcomed the "Good Neighbor Policy," especially the principle of nonintervention, as a victory over the barbarian dictatorial policy to which the United States had adhered for many years.

The new treaties and accords concluded with the Latin American countries during the 1930s were to replace the "obsolete" forms of American control in these countries by more disguised and flexible forms, such as financial control, control over foreign trade, the creation of puppet dictatorships in the small countries of the Caribbean supported by local mercenaries trained and controlled by Washington, and so on. "In place of their Leonard Woods, Charles Magoons, and other occupation generals," writes the prominent Mexican publicist Mario Gil, "they promoted in Cuba and in all the other 'economically occupied' countries subject to their colonialist policies various generations of creole overlords: the Menocales, Estrada Cabreras, Gerardo Machados, Chamorros, Samozas, Trujillos, Miguel Alemanes, Úbicos, Pérez Jiménez, Castillo Armas, Batistas, Idígoras, etc., etc., who, in addition to being more effective, proved less expensive, as they were paid for by their own people."[69] However, the old and tested methods of "influence" were not overlooked—supplying arms, sending military and other missions, advisors, and so forth. But with respect to especially important strategic regions, the United States continued to maintain full military control (Panama, Cuba, etc.).

Under pressure from the most reactionary circles of monopolists, the Roosevelt government would undoubtedly have been less prone to demonstrate its "good neighborliness" after 1933–34 had the mid-1930s not been marked by the further revolutionizing of Latin America's working masses. Moreover, in light of the growing worldwide struggle of progressive forces against the intervention of the fascist powers in Abyssinia and Spain, the movement in Latin America against the interventionist policies of the United States acquired new resonance. The rising anti-imperialist movement forced Washington and the Wall Street magnates to cover their expansionist policy in the Latin American countries with a further smoke screen of "good neighborliness."

Another factor which also influenced the forms of U.S. Latin American policy on the eve of the Second World War was the rapid economic and political penetration of the Latin American countries by Italian, Japanese, and especially German imperialism. The political and economic conquest by Hitler Germany of any one of the countries in South America would have signified the creation of a German bridgehead in the Western Hemisphere and a serious disruption of the plans nurtured by American monopolies to establish complete control over the region. In the mid-1930s, as a result of Japan's incursion into China and the mounting aggression of Germany and Italy in Europe, Anglo-American rivalry throughout the world began for a time to lose its overriding significance. While not ceasing, in Latin America it was nonetheless overshadowed in this period by the American-German rivalry.[70]

In its struggle against the penetration of German and Italian imperialism, Washington was not opposed to drawing on the support of democratic forces in Latin America and to taking advantage of the antifascist mood of the masses. But although, objectively, the opposition of U.S. ruling circles to Hitler's expansion in Latin America was of a progressive nature, it had nothing to do with a real defense of the interests of the Latin American peoples, as professed by many American historians and publicists, nor did it contradict Washington's general policy of "nonintervention" in other parts of the world. The ruling circles in the United States proceeded wholly from considerations of a defense of personal interests and of plans directed toward preserving and further expanding the position of American monopolistic capital in the Western Hemisphere. The "Good Neighbor Policy" was by no means directed against the ideology and practice of fascism as such, but against German and Italian imperialism competing with its American rival for "primacy" and control in Latin America. "The Roosevelt administration saw in the growing fascist penetration of South America not only a German and Italian threat to the form of government of the Latin American states," testify the authors of *A History of American Foreign Policy*, "but the undermining of our influence in that region as well."[71]

As for local dictatorships of a semifascist and fascist type, Washington, the "good neighbor," supported them, a fact about which both the democratic and bourgeois American press wrote.[72] Roosevelt himself once said of Dominican dictator Rafael Trujillo: "He may be a son-of-a-bitch, but he's our son-of-a-bitch."[73]

The interests not only of latifundists but also of bankers, prominent merchants, and businessmen, who constituted a considerable part of the ruling classes in the Latin American countries, managed by this time to link themselves to the interests of monopolies active in these countries. From the very outset, the "Good Neighbor Policy" sought the "collaboration" of American imperialism with local bourgeois-landowning circles in the struggle against the democratic and national-liberation movement in Latin America, which alone waged a consistent struggle there against fascism. It rested on the "weakness of the ruling classes of the Latin American countries, who were incapable of solving any problems, and appealed to the Wall Street bankers and Washington for 'aid,' to come and exploit their people and to subdue them by force if in the course of an agrarian and anti-imperialist revolution they should attempt to end the regime of oppression and poverty."[74] This policy took into account the common class interests of the Latin American ruling circles and American monopolists, and it unquestionably expanded somewhat the social basis of U.S. support in the Latin American countries. At the same time, the local ruling cliques in a number of these countries became direct agents of imperialism, vitally interested in preserving the dictatorships which terrorized the masses and allowed foreign capital to continue to exploit Latin America.

Behind the "Good Neighbor Policy," in addition to the desire to eliminate completely English, German, and other rivals, there always was a desire to weaken as much as possible the anti-imperialist resistance of the Latin American peoples, without which it was unthinkable to convert the region into a source of colonial superprofits, a supplier of inexpensive raw materials, and a strategic U.S. bridgehead in the impending Second World War.

Hiding behind the screen of "good neighborliness," the U.S. government succeeded in achieving definite successes in its Latin American policy as early as the eve of the Second World War. Precisely because of this, with touching

unanimity, the Federal Congress almost always supported the government's
Latin American policy in the thirties. Even the most rabid isolationists zealously
advocated "inter-American unity." The Western Hemisphere had long been
viewed by U.S. monopolists as "theirs" and was placed above all differences
concerning "isolation" and "international cooperation."[75]

It would be incorrect to forget that at a specific point—in the years when the
fascists were preparing for the Second World War, and especially during the war,
when the fascist threat to the countries of Latin America became a reality—the
solidarity and extensive collaboration of these countries with the United States
were temporarily and objectively of a progressive nature. And in this respect, the
"Good Neighbor Policy," by promoting the victory of the democratic coalition
over the fascist bloc, without question was of definite, positive significance.[76]
But this circumstance did not at all indicate a repudiation by U.S. ruling circles
of their plans to continue strengthening their positions in Latin America. The
events of the forties testify that the "Good Neighbor Policy" justified the hopes
of the Wall Street magnates: during the war years it helped them increase their
influence and control in the Western Hemisphere, and after the war helped them
to create a bloc of Latin American countries subservient to Washington.

Thus forced to make serious concessions and to change sharply the forms of its
policy, American imperialism by no means abandoned its former objectives of
political enslavement and economic exploitation of the countries of Latin
America. Precisely in order to achieve these aims in conditions of a rapidly
growing national-liberation movement and competition with other imperialist
powers, in 1933 U.S. ruling circles enunciated the "Good Neighbor Policy."

NOTES

1 "The United States," asserts Edward Guerrant, "has never had a foreign policy
toward any area that was more successful than the Good Neighbor Policy was from
1933 to 1945." See Edward O. Guerrant, *Roosevelt's Good Neighbor Policy* (Al-
buquerque, 1950), p. 212.
2 This question is interesting, too, in connection with the debate which has gone on in
the United States for years as to which administration originated the Good Neighbor
Policy. Even "reactionaries like Hoover and Dewey," testifies William Z. Foster,
"vied with each other in claiming the authorship of this successful imperialist policy." See William Z. Foster, *Outline Political History of the Americas* (New York,
1951), p. 433. Some American historians link the Good Neighbor Policy to the names
of Franklin Roosevelt and Sumner Welles, others feel that Roosevelt "successfully"
and with "great fanfare" effected a change in U.S. Latin American policy already
initiated by the Hoover and even Coolidge administrations. See C. A. Thomson,

"Toward a New Pan-Americanism," *Foreign Policy Reports* 12, no. 16 (1936), 203; J. Fred Rippy, *Latin America in World Politics: An Outline Survey*, 3rd ed. (New York, 1938), p. 283; idem, *The Caribbean Danger Zone* (New York, 1940), p. 251; Carleton Beals, *The Coming Struggle for Latin America* (Philadelphia, 1938), pp. 226–27; Allan Nevins, *America in World Affairs* (New York, 1942), p. 71; Samuel Guy Inman, *Latin America: Its Place in World Life*, rev. ed. (New York, 1942); p. 394; Allan Nevins and Louis M. Hacker, *The United States and Its Place in World Affairs, 1918–1943* (Boston, 1943), pp. 384–85; Samuel F. Bemis, *The Latin American Policy of the United States: An Historical Interpretation* (New York, 1943), p. 221; R. A. Humphreys, *The Evolution of Modern Latin America* (New York, 1946), p. 133; Guerrant, *Roosevelt's Good Neighbor Policy*, p. 212; Alexander De Conde, *Herbert Hoover's Latin American Policy* (Stanford, California, 1951), pp. xi–xii, 51; Robert H. Ferrell, *American Diplomacy in the Great Depression: Hoover-Stimson Foreign Policy, 1929–1933* (New Haven, 1957), pp. 216, 218, 220, 289; Bryce Wood, *The Making of the Good Neighbor Policy* (New York, 1961), pp. 3–9.

3 According to Cleona Lewis, even in 1929 they comprised seventeen billion dollars. See Cleona Lewis, *America's Stake in International Investments* (Washington, 1938), p. 606.

4 Ibid., p. 606.

5 Benjamin Harrison Williams, *American Diplomacy, Policies and Practice* (New York, 1936), p. 90.

6 Wood, *The Making of the Good Neighbor Policy*, p. 3.

7 See Memorandum, Dana Munro to Sumner Welles, 28 February 1922, National Archives (Washington, D.C.—cited hereafter as NA), 711.13 [59; Memorandum, Sumner Welles and others: "Summary of Questions Pending Between the United States and the Republics of Latin America," 27 February 1922, NA, 710.11] 568.

8 Nevins and Hacker, *The United States and Its Place in World Affairs*, p. 185.

9 Max Winkler, *Investments of United States Capital in Latin America* (Boston, 1928), pp. 275, 278; W. Feurlein and E. Hannan, *Dollars in Latin America* (New York, 1941), p. 54; João F. Normano, *The Struggle for South America: Economy and Ideology* (Boston, 1931), p. 54.

10 Charles E. Hughes, *Our Relations to the Nations of the Western Hemisphere* (Princeton, New Jersey, 1928), pp. 58–59.

11 P. Olson and C. Hikman, *Economía internacional latinoamericana* (Mexico, 1945), p. 115.

12 Normano, *The Struggle for South America*, pp. 32–33.

13 J. Fred Rippy, *Historical Evolution of Hispanic America* (New York, 1944), p. 529; Normano, *The Struggle for South America*, p. 54.

14 L. Denni, *Amerika zavoevyvaet Britaniiu* (Moscow, 1930), pp. 84–85; J. Fred Rippy, *South America and Hemisphere Defense* (Baton Rouge, 1941), p. 47; Clarence H. Haring, *South America Looks at the United States* (New York, 1928), pp. 15–16.

15 Foster, *Ocherk politicheskoi istorii Ameriki* (Moscow, 1953), p. 517.

16 For detailed discussion of the labor movement in these years in Soviet literature see N. M. Lavrov, *Rabochee i natsional'no-osvoboditel'noe dvizhenie v strankakh Latinskoi Ameriki na pervom etape obshchego krizisa kapitalizma* (Moscow, 1956), pp. 6–20; V. I. Ermolaev et al., eds., *Ocherki istorii Argentiny*, † pp. 301–17; M. S.

Al'perovich and N. M. Lavrov, eds., *Ocherki novoi i noveishei istorii Meksiki,*† pp. 316-20; V. I. Ermolnev et al., eds., *Ocherki istorii Brazilii,*† pp. 260-71; E. L. Nitoburg, *Politika amerikanskogo imperializma na Kube, 1918-1939,* † pp. 31-36; Hernán Ramírez Necochea, "Pod'ëm rabochego dvizheniia v Chili v 1917-1922 gg.," *NNI,* no. 5 (September–October 1960), 46-47; etc.

17 *Ocherki istorii Brazilii,* pp. 271-73; Chester Lloyd Jones, *Caribbean Since 1900* (New York, 1936), p. 165; Ludwell L. Montague, *Haiti and the United States, 1714-1938* (Durham, North Carolina, 1940), pp. 233, 235.

18 In Brazil, under the leadership of progressive elements among petty-bourgeois officers who had introduced democratic freedoms into the country, there occurred in the early 1920s armed uprisings in a number of cities, including the heroic revolt of the garrison of the Copacabana fortress in the capital. See *Ocherki istorii Brazilii,* pp. 274-76.

19 Sumner Welles, *Naboth's Vineyard: The Dominican Republic, 1844-1924,* 2 vols. (New York, 1928), II, 829-30.

20 Jorge Amado, *Luiz Karlos Prestes* (Moscow, 1951), pp. 103-5, 113, 214; A. Lur'e, *Geroi brazil'skogo naroda* (Moscow, 1939); *Ocherki istorii Brazilii,* pp. 284-90.

21 *Vop Ist.,* no. 9 (September 1949), 87; *Mirovoe Khoziaistvo i mirovaia politika,* no. 2 (1939), 117; *Kommunisticheskii Internatsional,* nos. 16-17 (1930), 32; *Agrarnye problemy,* no. 3 [7] (1928), 188.

22 Foster, *Ocherk,* p. 364.

23 Gregorio Selser, *Sandino, general de hombres libres,* 2 vols. (Havana, 1960), I, 137, 155, 159, 275.

24 Manuel Ugarte, "Dangers Latent in Our Latin-American Policy," *CH* 26, no. 6 (September, 1927), 899-900; Rippy, *Historical Evolution of Hispanic America,* p. 538.

25 "The policy and pronouncements of Kellogg and Coolidge were greeted by a cyclone of remonstrance both in Congress and in the press," testifies an American historian, supporting this assertion with over twenty references from congressional records and the U.S. press. See Rippy, *Caribbean Danger Zone,* p. 248.

26 Rippy, *Latin America in World Politics,* p. 253.

27 Haring, *South America Looks at the United States,* pp. 10-11; Dana G. Munro, *The Latin American Republics* (New York, 1942), pp. 502, 509; John T. Humphrey, *The Inter-American System: A Canadian View* (Toronto, 1942), p. 42; A. Robles, *La Panamericanisme et la politique de bon voisinage* (Paris, 1938), pp. 33-34; Wood, *The Making of the Good Neighbor Policy,* pp. 5-6. Sumner Welles, *The Times for Decision* (New York, 1944), pp. 177-78.

28 Franklin D. Roosevelt, "Our Foreign Policy: A Democratic View," *FA,* VI, no. 4 (July, 1928), 583-84, 586.

29 Walter Lippmann, "Second Thoughts on Havana," *FA* 6, no. 4 (July, 1928), 552-53; Ogden L. Mills, "Our Foreign Policy: A Republican View," *FA* 6 no. 4 (July, 1928), 566-67.

30 He set forth his own "credo" in the concluding chapter of his book on the history of the Dominican Republic. See Welles, *Naboth's Vineyard,* II, 936-37.

31 Lippmann, "Second Thoughts on Havana," pp. 550-55; Roosevelt, "Our Foreign Policy: A Democratic View," pp. 584-86; Welles, *Naboth's Vineyard,* II, 931-32. It is characteristic that such a "coincidence" of views on the matter of intervention

occurred in those years among historians of the most diverse shades (Norton, Buell, Moon, etc.). See Chester L. Jones, Henry K. Norton, and Parker T. Moon, *The United States and the Caribbean: American Policies Abroad. Opinions expressed for the Chicago Council of Foreign Relations* (Chicago, 1929); also *AAAPSS*, July 1928, pp. 73 ff.

32 Welles, *Naboth's Vineyard*, II, 923, 925; Mills, "Our Foreign Policy," pp. 556–67; Roosevelt, "Our Foreign Policy: A Democratic View," pp. 576, 581. In 1927–28, the chairman of the Senate commission for foreign affairs, Borah, a member of this commission, Shipstead, and the historians Samuel Guy Inman and C. P. Hawland also declared the need to "revive the original doctrine." See *Congressional Record: Proceedings and Debates of the Second Session of the Sixty-Ninth Congress of the United States of America*, 68, pt. 2 (January 7 to January 26, 1927), Senate (Thursday, January 13, 1927), 1555–56; Samuel Guy Inman, "The Monroe Doctrine As an Obsolete Principle," *CH* 26, no. 6 (September 1927), 881; Henrik Shipstead, " 'Dollar Diplomacy' in Latin America," *CH* 26 no. 6 (September 1927), 886–87; C. P. Hawland, *Survey of American Foreign Relations, 1928* (New Haven, 1929), p. 55.

33 Lippmann, "Second Thoughts on Havana," p. 554; Samuel Guy Inman, *Problems in Pan-Americanism* (New York, 1925), pp. 320–22; Haring, *South America Looks at the United States*, p. 123; Munro, *The Latin American Republics*, pp. 26–27.

34 The above-mentioned authors also wrote about this with varying degrees of frankness. Thus, citing the words of Palmerston that "in diplomacy the tone is everything—it makes the song," i.e. the form, Clarence Haring went on to quote an editorial which appeared in *The New York Times* on 14 January 1927: "This truth we have unhappily failed to recognize and live up to in our recent dealings with our neighbors to the south." [See Haring, *South America Looks at the United States*, p. 58, n. 13.] Dana Munro also wrote that "the existing difference of opinion relates more to the form in which we ought to carry out our policy than to this policy itself." See Dana Munro, *Relations Between Central America and the United States* (New York, 1934), p. 25. Finally, Franklin Roosevelt himself, speaking of the interventions in Haiti and the Dominican Republic, felt it necessary to state: "It is not that assistance of some sort was not necessary (i.e. U.S. intervention—E.N.); it was the method which was wrong." See Roosevelt, "Our Foreign Policy: A Democratic View," p. 583.

35 Foster, *Ocherk*, pp. 364–65.

36 Armando Roa, *Roosevelt, the Executive Dictator* (Havana, 1933), pp. 28–29; Jones, Norton, and Moon, *The United States and the Caribbean*, pp. 146, 149–50; Welles, *The Time for Decision*, p. 189.

37 Joshua R. Clark, *Memorandum on the Monroe Doctrine*, December 17, 1928 (Washington, 1930), pp. xix, xxi, xxiv.

38 De Conde, *Herbert Hoover's Latin American Policy*, pp. 48–49.

39 Thomas A. Bailey, *A Diplomatic History of the American People* (New York, 1944), p. 730.

40 John Holladay Latané and David W. Wainhouse, *A History of American Foreign Policy*, 2nd ed. rev. (New York, 1940), p. 819.

41 Cleona Lewis, *Strany-dolzhniki i strany-kreditory, 1938–1944* (Moscow, 1947), p. 74; A. S. Kodachenko, *Anglo-amerikanskaia bor'ba za rynki sbyta (1929–1933)* (Moscow, 1959), p. 43.

42 Vernon L. Phelps, *The International Economic Position of Argentina* (Philadelphia, 1938), p. 181.

43 German trade with Latin America began to grow especially rapidly in the mid-1930s, already after Hitler and his supporters had come to power. Thus, Germany's share in Latin American imports was 3.7% in 1920, 10.8% in 1929, 11.5% in 1933, and 17.1% in 1938. See Richard K. Showman and Lyman S. Judson, *The Monroe Doctrine and the Growth of Western Hemisphere Solidarity* (New York, 1941), p. 195.

44 From 1929 to 1937, Japanese exports to Latin America increased five times; in the case of Panama, they increased twenty times, and in that of the Dominican Republic, even thirty times. See *La Prensa* (New York), 1 November 1933; "Japanese Trade Advance," *CH* 40, no. 3 (June 1934), 341; "Japanese Trade Invasion," *CH* 40, no. 4 (July 1934), 476; "Latin America and Japan," 42, no. 1 (April 1935), 76. See also João F. Normano and Antonello Gerbi, *The Japanese in South America: An Introductory Survey with Special Reference to Peru* (New York, 1943), pp. 11–15, 32–34.

45 *Kommunisticheskii Internatsional pered VII Vsemirnym kongressom: Materialy* (Moscow, 1935), p. 390.

46 Charles Wertenbaker, *A New Doctrine for the Americas* (New York, 1941), p. 75.

47 Nicholas J. Spykman, *America's Strategy in World Politics* (New York, 1942), p. 75; Feurlein and Hannan, *Dollars in Latin America*, p. 19.

48 Committee on Latin American Policy, Foreign Policy Association, and World Peace Foundation, *Recommendations as to the Pan American Conference at Montevideo* (New York and Boston, 1933), p. 10.

49 Lewis, *America's Stake in International Investments*, p. 414.

50 George Wythe, "The New Industrialism in Latin America," *JPE* 45, no. 2 (April 1937), 207–28.

51 Foster, *Ocherk*, p. 586.

52 On the labor movement in Latin America in the period 1929–1933, see Lavrov, *Rabochee i natsional'no-osvoboditel'noe dvizhenie v stranakh Latinskoi Ameriki*, pp. 32, 34–35; *Ocherki istorii Argentiny*, pp. 352–53, 370; *Ocherki istorii Brazilii*, pp. 309, 321–24; *Ocherki novoi i noveishei istorii Meksiki*, pp. 380–81; E. L. Nitoburg, *Politika amerikanskogo imperializma na Kube*, pp. 107–12, 130–32, 171–76, 197–98, 205–8, 243–46 ff.

53 On the peasant movement, see *Ocherki novoi i noveishei istorii Meksiki*, pp. 381–82; *Ocherki istorii Brazilii*, pp. 325–26; Nitoburg, *Politika amerikanskogo imperializma*, pp. 114, 132, 170–71, 206, 244–45; *NNI*, no. 1 (January–February 1958), 53; United States, Department of State, *Foreign Relations of the United States, Diplomatic Papers, 1932*, 5 vols. (Washington, 1948), V, 613–22, 709–31.

54 *Kommunisticheskii Internatsional*, no. 9 (1935), 41; B. I. Koval, "Klassovaia bor'ba v Brazilii v period mirovogo ekonomicheskogo krizisa 1929–1933 godov," *NNI*, no. 1 (1958), 52; *Ocherki istorii Brazilii*, pp. 324–25.

55 Foster, *Ocherk*, pp. 570–71.

56 United States, Department of State, *Press Releases:* 15 and 22 November 1930; 18 and 25 June, 4 July and 15 August 1931; 15 October 1932; 7 January 1933. See also Henry L. Stimson, *The United States and the Other American Republics* (Washington, 1931), pp. 6–12.

57 Such is the view of many bourgeois historians and of the Latin American press (Still-water, *As Our Neighbors See Us* [1940], pp. 141–42).

58 One such statement was an article by Norman Davis, who was advisor to Franklin Roosevelt, U.S. representative at the disarmament conference, and an associate of the Morgan financial group. His views coincided with those of Roosevelt and Welles. See Norman H. Davis, "Wanted: A Consistent Latin American Policy," *FA* 9, no. 4 (July, 1931), 547–68.

59 William Appleman Williams, *Tragediia amerikanskoi diplomatii* (Moscow, 1960), pp. 125–26.

60 Roosevelt, writes the prominent Cuban scholar and statesman, Carlos Rafael Rod-ríguez, "understood that to consider as the best guarantee of North American interests in Latin America the tyrannies established there during the Harding and Coolidge administrations was tantamount to suicide. He also understood—opportunely for imperialism—that the greatest benefit would be derived not from flagrant robbery of the Latin American countries, but rather through a system in which "aid" given by North America would be recovered many times over, and which would not cause the same discontentment among the Latin American peoples as had the policies of the Republican administration." See Carlos Rafael Rodríguez, *La "Misión Welles": La lucha antiimperialista en Cuba* (Havana, 1960), II, 24.

61 Walter Lippmann and W. O. Scroggs, *The United States in World Affairs—1933* (New York, 1934), p. 192.

62 *The Times* (London), 4 and 11 February 1933; *Pravda*, 6 and 13 February 1933.

63 Foster, *Ocherk*, p. 597.

64 Welles, *The Time for Decision*, p. 192.

65 Franklin D. Roosevelt, *The Public Papers and Addresses of Franklin D. Roosevelt*, vol. II, *The Year of Crisis* (New York, 1938), p. 14.

66 Ibid., pp. 129–31.

67 Rippy, *South America and Hemisphere Defence*, p. 10.

68 *Problemy mira i sotsializma*, no. 6 (1965), 2. The progressive American publicist Herman Olden has likewise written on this: "While on the whole the basic imperialist relationship did not change and, in fact, U.S. economic and political penetration increased during this period, the Good Neighbor Policy did mark a change from the policies of open armed intervention. Throughout the years of the New Deal ... [and since], not a single marine landed on the shores of a Latin American country to impose the will of U.S. monopolies, although ... other effective means of direct intervention were used." Herman Olden, *U.S. over Latin America* (New York, 1955). p. 7.

69 Mario Gil, *Kuba—da! Yanki—net!* (Moscow, 1961), p. 65.

70 Already in 1937 Germany had supplanted England, occupying first place as an expor-ter of industrial goods to Brazil and Paraguay, and second place in fourteen other Latin American countries. German economic influence in Argentina became especially pronounced.

71 Latané and Wainhouse, *A History of American Foreign Policy*, p. 863.

72 "Does the Good Neighbor Policy not mean," questioned the *New York Post* after the outbreak of the antifascist war, "that the United States is the good neighbor of any fascist who in word is prepared to respect democratic principles?" See the *New York Post*, 1 February 1944.

73 R. Smith, *The United States and Cuba: Business and Diplomacy, 1917–1960* (New York, 1960), p. 184.
74 Luis Carlos Prestes, "Latinoamerikanskie narody boriutsia protiv imperializma SShA," *Pravda,* 4 September 1949.
75 Foster, *Ocherk,* pp. 599, 601.
76 Ibid., pp. 619–20.

BIBLIOGRAPHY
CONTRIBUTORS
INDEX

BIBLIOGRAPHY

THE FOLLOWING annotated bibliography seeks to provide added insight into the nature and scope of Soviet historical writings on Latin America. While it reflects a long process of review and selection, it is a representative listing only, and makes no pretension to completeness. As a working principle, I have limited it to books reflective of scholarship, and in the case of articles, to selections from scholarly journals and to individual contributions appearing in edited works other than those listed below. Selection of both books and articles has been limited further to materials directly available to me.

A word about the annotations is also in order. Despite the real difficulty of providing insight into scholarly work in the space of a few lines, it seemed that some commentary, however brief, would serve a useful purpose. Inasmuch as the Western, non-Marxist scholar is especially interested in the quality of Soviet historiography, and whereas sources are a key indicator of quality, attention has been focused on this aspect of the entries. Wherever relevant, comments have also been made on the scope, thesis, and organization of the listed works. Annotations of articles vary from commentary on sources and content to mere translation of titles, where this has been deemed sufficient.

Books

Al'perovich, M. S. *Ispanskaia Amerika v bor'be za nezavisimost'* [Spanish America in the struggle for independence]. Moscow: Nauka, 1971. Volume appearing in a popular history series published by the USSR Academy of Sciences; general, somewhat traditional, but scholarly discussion of Spanish American independence; illustrated and annotated; includes brief bibliography of supplementary Russian-language readings.

_____. *Revoliutsiia i diktatura v Paragvae (1810–1840)* [Revolution and dictatorship in Paraguay (1810–1840)]. Moscow: Nauka, 1975. Serious monograph on the Francia period; draws on exhaustive selection of published primary sources as well as relevant secondary material. This is an important contribution to the existing literature on nineteeth-century Paraguay.

_____. *Sovetskaia istoriografiia stran Latinskoi Ameriki* [Soviet historiography of the Latin American countries]. Moscow: Nauka, 1968. An important summary review of Soviet scholarship in the field of Latin American history by a leading Soviet historian.

_____. *Voina za nezavisimost' Meksiki (1810–1824)* [Mexico's war of independence (1810–1824)]. Moscow: Nauka, 1964. An important Marxist treatment of this topic. The author views Mexico's war of independence as fundamentally a bourgeois revolution which, while failing to produce radical socioeconomic transformations, nonetheless secured political independence and undermined the existing feudal colonial order, thereby hastening the development of capitalist relations and the country's incorporation into the world economic system. Based on a broad selection of published sources as well as materials from the historical archives of the USSR Ministry of Foreign Affairs. Includes extensive bibliography.

Al'perovich, M. S., V. I. Ermolaev, M. F. Kudachkin, and N. M. Lavrov., eds. *Ocherki istorii Chili* [Essays on the history of Chile]. Moscow: Nauka, 1967. General survey of Chilean history from pre-Columbian times to the Christian-Democratic presidential victory of 1964. Includes an historiographical essay, a chronology of important dates, and a lengthy bibliography. The presidential elections of 1964, the authors conclude, showed that Chile faced "a serious struggle between democratic forces seeking to introduce radical change and the forces of reaction, domestic and foreign, who defend the old order and their own privileges."

Al'perovich, M. S., and N. M. Lavrov, eds. *Ocherki novoi i noveishei istorii Meksiki, 1810–1945* [Essays on the modern and contemporary history of Mexico, 1810–1945]. Moscow: Izdatel'stvo sotsial'no-ekonomicheskoi literatury, 1960. General survey of modern Mexican history from the late eighteenth century to 1945. The first such work in Marxist literature. Includes background chapter on pre-Columbian and colonial periods; also a chronology of important dates and a lengthy bibliography.

Al'perovich, M. S., and B. T. Rudenko. *Meksikanskaia revoliutsiia 1910–1917 gg. i politika SShA* [The Mexican Revolution of 1910–1917 and U.S. policy]. Moscow: Sotsekgiz, 1958. The first work of scholarship in Soviet historical literature on this subject, written by two leading specialists in the modern history of Mexico, and based on a broad selection of published sources. The authors argue that the Mexican Revolution constituted a popular struggle against the reaction of church and landed interests and foreign (primarily

American) imperialism, its immediate objectives being land, the liquidation of feudal vestiges, and the institution of democratic reforms.

Al'perovich, M. S., and L. Yu. Slëzkin. *Novaia istoriia stran Latinskoi Ameriki* [The modern history of the Latin American countries]. Moscow: Vysshaia Shkola, 1970. Well written, but unevenly organized university-level textbook spanning the nineteenth and twentieth centuries.

Bashilov. V. A. *Drevnie tsivilizatsii Peru i Bolivii* [The ancient civilizations of Peru and Bolivia]. Moscow: Nauka, 1972. A detailed inquiry by a leading Soviet specialist into the ancient history of the Central Andes. It examines the two-thousand-year period from the first millenium B.C. to the founding of the Incan state and is based on a judicious selection of available sources. Profusely illustrated. Includes a useful historiographical essay on the development and state of the field, and an extensive bibliography.

Belen'kii, A. B. *Razgrom meksikanskim narodom inostrannoi interventsii (1861–1867)* [The rout of foreign intervention by the Mexican people (1861–1867)]. Moscow: Izdatel'stvo Akademii nauk SSSR, 1959. Generally factual treatment of the topic based on broad selection of published sources.

Bertel's, D. E., B. N. Komissarov, and T. I. Lysenko, comps., L. A. Shur, ed., *Materialy ekspeditsii akademika Grigoriia Ivanovicha Langsdorfa v Braziliiu v 1821–1829 gg.: Nauchnoe opisanie* [Materials from the expedition of Grigorii Ivanovich Langsdorf to Brazil (1821–1829): a scholarly description]. Leningrad: Izdatel'stvo Nauka, Leningrad branch, Akademiia nauk SSSR, Arkhiv, Trudy (Vyp. 25), 1973. Preliminary description and inventory of expedition materials preserved in Soviet repositories. Entries in original language, with Russian translations of foreign-language titles. All materials described as to content, format, and location. Contains name, subject, and geographic indexes. Duplicate table of contents in Portuguese. Includes reproductions of graphic material.

Dabagian, E. S. *Natsional-reformizm v sovremennoi Venesuele. Partiia "Demokraticheskoe deistvie": Ideologiia i politika* [National-reformism in contemporary Venezuela. The "Democratic Action" party: ideology and politics]. Moscow: Nauka, 1972. Detailed political history of Acción Democrática, based on extensive selection of primary and secondary sources. Also treats party ideology and recent AD approaches to issues of industrialization, agrarian reform, labor, and foreign policy.

Dridzo, A. D. *Yamaiskie maruny: Istoriko-etnograficheskii ocherk* [The Jamaican maroons: an historico-ethnographic essay]. Moscow: Nauka, 1971. A scholarly introduction to the problem of runaway slave communities in eighteenth-century Jamaica. Of particular interest for the comparative history of New World slavery. Includes an essay on sources, but lacks a bibliography.

Efimov, A. V., and I. R. Grigulevich, eds. *Kuba: Istoriko-etnograficheskie ocherki* [Cuba: historico-ethnographic essays]. Moscow: Izdatel'stvo

Adakemii nauk SSSR, 1961. An important volume for the study of the history of the Cuban Revolution. Includes original contributions by Guevara, Núñez Jiménuz, Rivera de la Calle, and Juan Marinello, as well as articles by E. V. Ananova, M. A. Okuneva, A. D. Dridzo, I. R. Grigulevich, L. A. Shur, and other Soviet specialists.

Efimov, A. V., I. R. Grigulevich, and S. A. Gonionskii, eds. *Natsii Latinskoi Ameriki: Formirovanie, razvitie* [The nations of Latin America: their formation and development]. Moscow: Nauka, 1964. A major collection of articles on the general problem of national consolidation in Latin America. Themes range from the "antinational character of Pan Americanism" to linguistic peculiarities in Brazilian Portuguese and Argentine Spanish, the ethno-history of the Amazon basin, national consolidation among the Quechua Indians, and nationalistic features in the poetry of Peru. Within these broad parameters, there are contributions dealing specifically with Cuba, Mexico, Brazil, Uruguay, British Guiana, Panama, and Central America. The volume also includes a lengthy piece about Paraguay by Oscar Kreidt, former secretary general of the Paraguayan CP.

Efimov, A. V., I. R. Grigulevich, and S. A. Tokarev, eds. *Narody Amerikil* Vol. II. *Tsentral'naia i Yuzhnaia Amerika* [The peoples of America: Central and South America]. Moscow: Izdatel'stvo Akademii nauk SSSR, 1959. The standard Soviet reference work on the ethno-history of Latin America. Part of a larger series entitled The Peoples of the World. Two chapters provide a general discussion of Spanish and Portuguese colonization. Volume includes maps, numerous illustrations, bibliography, and a glossary of terms.

Ermolaev, V. I., M. S. Al'perovich, and L.Yu. Slëzkin, eds. *Ocherki istorii Brazilii* [Essays on the history of Brazil]. Moscow: Izdatel'stvo sotsial'no-ekonomicheskoi literatury, 1962. General survey of Brazilian history from discovery to the presidency of João Goulart. Includes an historiographical essay, a chronology of important dates, and a lengthy bibliography. The authors conclude that in light of the political crisis of 1961, the Brazilian army "no longer constituted a reliable support of the ruling handful of local and foreign exploiters."

Ermolaev, V. I., N. M. Lavrov, and A. I. Shtrakhov, eds. *Ocherki istorii Argentiny* [Essays on the history of Argentina]. Moscow: Izdatel'stvo sotsial'no-ekonomicheskoi literatury, 1961. General survey of Argentine history from the colony to the fall of Perón, the first such work in Marxist literature. Includes a chronology of important dates, plus an extensive bibliography. The authors conclude that the so-called Liberating Revolution of September 1955 failed to liberate the Argentine people; rather power passed "from reactionary nationalists into the hands of those who defend the interests of bourgeois-landholding elites and foreign imperialism."

Garanin. F. A. *Narodnyi front v Chili, 1936–1941* [The Popular Front in Chile, 1936–1941]. Moscow: Nauka, 1973. Scholarly monograph based on a varied but far from exhaustive selection of sources. Author stresses internal origins of the Popular Front, by and large ignoring pertinent international factors. Only passing references to the Comintern; no mention of concurrent events in Brazil. This volume takes special issue with the interpretations of Alba, Alexander, Halperin, and Ravines.

Glinkin, A. N. *Noveishaia istoriia Brazilii, 1939–1959* [The recent history of Brazil, 1939–1959]. Moscow, IMO, 1961. Lengthy survey of the political, social, and economic history of Brazil during the Second World War and the postwar period. Special attention given to the problem of economic dependency. Based on broad selection of published sources.

Gonionskii, S. A. *Istoriia panamskoi "revoliutsii"* [The history of the Panamanian "revolution"]. Moscow: IMO, 1958. Generally superficial, sparsely documented treatment of a significant chapter in the history of inter-American relations, i.e. the creation of Panama as an independent republic, by a former Soviet diplomat.

————. *Latinskaia Amerika i SShA, 1939–1959: Ocherki istorii diplomaticheskikh otnoshenii* [Latin American and the United States, 1939–1959: essays on the history of diplomatic relations]. Moscow: IMO, 1960. Detailed examination of two decades of U.S. efforts "to establish undisputed political, economic, military, and ideological dominion in the countries of Latin America." Author perceives an impending crisis in inter-American relations and points to signs of a weakening U.S. position in the hemisphere, accompanied by a corresponding rise in the influence of the socialist countries. Based on an extensive selection of published sources. Includes bibliographic essay and complete bibliography.

————. *Ocherki noveishei istorii stran Latinskoi Ameriki* [Essays on the recent history of the Latin American countries]. Moscow: Prosveshchenie, 1964. Overview of the postwar period (1945–1963). Volume comprises an introduction and essays on twenty Latin American republics. Written for students and non-specialists. Lacks references and bibliography.

Gonionskii, S. A., and I. F. Khoroshaeva, eds. *Natsional'nye protsessy v Tsentral'noi Amerike i Meksike* [National processes in Central America and Mexico]. Moscow: Nauka, 1974. A collection of scholarly articles on diverse aspects of national formation in Middle America, based on a wide variety of sources, including scattered archival materials. While raising some interesting questions about the historical development of nations in this region, the book reflects a lack of conceptual precision with relation to national formation as an historical process.

Grigor'ian, Yu. M. *Germanskii imperializm v Latinskoi Amerike (1933–1945)* [German imperialism in Latin America (1933–1945)]. Moscow: Nauka, 1974. Solid monograph based on extensive selection of sources, including unpublished materials from the Deutsches Zentralarchiv in Potsdam. Bibliography; index of names; complete footnoting.

Grigulevich, I. R. *"Miatezhnaia" tserkov' v Latinskoi Amerike* [The "insurrectionary" church in Latin America]. Moscow: Nauka, 1972. An inquiry into the recent history of revolutionary militancy in Latin America among representatives of organized religion. Written by one intimately familiar with both the area and the subject, this volume contains valuable material. Includes chaper on religious syncretism and the Afro-Christian cults which bears little relation to the stated topic. Based on varied although far from exhaustive selection of sources.

Grigulevich, I. R., R. V. Kinzhalov, and I. F. Khoroshaeva, eds. *Bartolome de Las-Kasas: K istorii zavoevaniia Ameriki. Sbornik statei* [Bartolomé de las Casas: toward a history of the conquest of America. A collection of articles]. Moscow: Nauka, 1966. A collection of scholarly articles commemorating the four-hundredth anniversary of the death of Las Casas. Topics treated include Spain in the age of discovery (E. E. Litavrina), the Las Casas-Motolinía dispute (I. F. Khoroshaeva), Mayan theatrical presentations as described in the writings of Las Casas (Yu. V. Knorozov), Las Casas and the Black Legand (L. Yu. Slëzkin), the Las Casas researches of Lewis Hanke (S. Ya. Serov), and the literary legacy of Las Casas (V. L. Afanas'ev). Also includes a detailed bibliography of works by and about Las Casas housed in Soviet repositories.

Grigulevich, I. R., I. A. Zolotarevskaia, R. F. Ivanov, and E. L. Nitoburg, eds. *Ot Aliaski do Ognennoi Zemli: Istoriia i etnografiia stran Ameriki* [From Alaska to Tierra del Fuego: history and ethnography of America]. Moscow: Nauka, 1967. A festschrift in honor of the prominent Soviet Americanist A. V. Efimov. Includes wide range of scholarly contributions spanning the Western Hemisphere from Greenland to Chile. Of the volume's thirty-one articles, seventeen deal with Latin America.

Grinevich, E. A. *Stranitsy istorii Kuby (1939–1952 gg.)* [Pages of Cuban history (1939–1952)]. Moscow: Mezhdunarodnye otnoshennia, 1964. Semipopular, semischolarly volume based on a variety of primary and secondary sources. Sparsely documented. No bibliography.

Guliaev, V. I. *Amerika i Staryi Svet v dokolumbovu epokhu* [America and the Old World in the pre-Columbian era]. Moscow: Nauka, 1968. Volume appearing in a popular history series published by the USSR Academy of Sciences. General but scholarly discussion of the problem of pre-Columbian contacts between the New World and the Old—*Old World* being used in the broader sense to mean Asia as well as Europe. Documentation includes numerous diagrams and photographic reproductions.

———. *Drevneishie tsivilizatsii Mezoameriki* [The oldest civilizations of Middle America]. Moscow: Nauka, 1972. A sound overview of the Teotihuacan, Zapotec, Olmec, and Mayan civilizations. Includes brief history of Middle American archeology, together with chapters on the earliest inhabitants of the region and the development of pre-Columbian argriculture. Extensively illustrated. Contains full bibliography, as well as a summary in Spanish.

Il'ina, N. G. *Politicheskaia bor'ba v Kolumbii (1946–1957)* [Political struggle in Colombia (1946–1957)]. Moscow: Nauka, 1968. Narrative approach to the politics of *violencia*. Although this volume contains some interesting material, treatment of the topic is generally inadequate. Author reveals excessive subjectivity in her discussion of the role of the Columbian Communist Party, and the use of available documentation is frequently unsound. Book contains lengthy but incomplete bibliography and a review essay on sources and literature.

Kinzhalov. R. V. *Kul'tura drevnykh maiia* [The culture of the ancient Maya]. Leningrad: Nauka, 1971. A thorough overview of the topic by an eminent scholar of pre-Columbian civilizations. Volume includes a detailed review of sources and literature, as well as an exhaustive bibliography.

Knorozov, Yu. V. *Pis'mennost' indeitsev maiia* [Maya Indian writing]. Moscow and Leningrad: Izdatel'stvo Adademii nauk SSSR, 1963. The principal exposition of the author's controversial analysis of the ancient Mayan writing system. In addition to purely analytic chapters, this long work contains Mayan texts of the colonial period with Russian translations, a short dictionary of ancient Mayan, a catalog of Mayan graphemes, and photographic reproductions of ancient Mayan hieroglyphic texts, including complete copies of the Dresden, Paris, and Madrid manuscripts.

————. *Sistema pis'ma drevnykh maiia* [The writing system of the ancient Mayas]. Moscow: Izdatel'stvo Akademii nauk SSSR, 1955. A preliminary exposition of the author's analysis of the Mayan writing system. Volume includes a full Spanish translation of the Russian text.

Korolëv. N. V. *Strany Latinskoi Ameriki v mezhdunarodnykh otnosheniiakh (1898–1962 gg.)* [The Latin American countries in international relations (1898–1962)]. Kishinëv: Kartia Moldoveniaske, 1962. Major volume based on a relatively wide selection of primary and secondary sources. Treats the general theme of Latin America as an object of competition among the leading capitalist powers and the area's resultant struggle for economic and political independence.

————. *Strany Yuzhnoi Ameriki i Rossiia (1890–1917 gg.)* [The South American countries and Russia (1890–1917)]. Kishinëv: Shtiintsa, 1972. A modest volume which nonetheless makes a significant contribution to the history of Russo-Latin American relations. Author focuses on economic ties, Russian emigration, and tsarist diplomacy. Based almost entirely on unpublished Russian archival sources.

Koval, B. I. *Istoriia brazil'skogo proletariata (1857–1967)* [History of the Brazilian proletariat (1858–1967)]. Moscow: Nauka, 1968. A scholarly study of Brazilian labor history. In contrast to non-Marxist treatments of this topic, the author gives special emphasis to the rise of organized labor in the nineteeth and early twentieth centuries. Based on an extensive selection of printed sources.

Larin (pseud.), N. S. [N. S. Leonov]. *Bor'ba tserkvi s gosudarstvom v Meksike (Vosstanie "kristeros" v 1926–1929 gg.)* [The church-state struggle in

Mexico (the "Cristeros" uprising of 1926-1929)]. Moscow: Nauka, 1965. An essentially narrative history of the Cristeros Rebellion, based on a varied, but limited selection of sources. At issue, the author argues, was the triumph of Mexico's bourgeois-democratic revolution of a decade before, which the Catholic Church sought to destroy and the mass of Mexican society succeeded in preserving.

Lavretskii (pseud.), I. [I. R. Grigulevich]. *Ernesto Che Gevara* [Ernesto Che Guevara]. Moscow: Molodaia gvardiia, 1972. A long, sympathetic biography by a scholar and seasoned revolutionary intimately familiar with Latin American realities. Semipopular in format, yet important for the specialist. Includes Cuban reminiscences of Anastas Mikoyan; also numerous photographs.

Lavrov, N. M. *Meksikanskaia revoliutsiia 1910-1917 gg.* [The Mexican Revolution of 1910-1917]. Moscow: Nauka, 1972. Scholarly treatment of an important, still fertile topic. Mexican Revolution is viewed as a bourgeois-democratic, anti-imperialist struggle which created conditions favorable to national development, furthered, in turn, by the Cardenas reforms of the 1930s. The author is the first Soviet historian to make significant use of Latin American archival sources (outside of Cuba); volume draws on materials housed in the Archivo General de la Nación and the Archivo General de la Secretaría de Relaciones Exteriores, as well as the historical archives of the Soviet Ministry of Foreign Affairs. Includes an extensive bibliography.

Lavrov, N. M., A. I. Shtrakhov, and B. I. Koval, eds. *Voina za nezavisimost' v Latinskoi Amerike (1810-1826). Sbornik statei* [The war of independence in Latin America (1810-1826): a collection of articles]. Moscow: Nauka, 1964. Collection includes significant contributions on the independence movement in Brazil (V. I. Ermolaev), Cuba (A. M. Zorina), and the River Plate (A. I. Shtrakhov), Brazilian slavery on the eve of independence (B. I. Koval), U.S. responses to the independence movement (N. N. Bolkhovitinov), and the international politics of recognition (L. Yu. Slëzkin).

Magidovich, I. P. *Istoriia otkrytiia i issledovaniia Tsentral' noi i Yuzhnoi Ameriki* [The history of the discovery and exploration of Central and South America]. Moscow: Mysl', 1965. A lengthy survey history of the exploration of Latin America down to the early twentieth century. Central America as used by the author in the title embraces Mexico and the Caribbean. Volume includes substantial bibliography.

Manizer, G. G. *Ekspeditsiia akademika G. I. Langsdorfa v Braziliiu, 1821-1828* [The expedition of academician G. I. Langsdorf to Brazil, 1821-1828]. Moscow: Geografgiz, 1948. The first major study of the Langsdorf expedition based on expedition records and related materials; author focuses on expedition's contribution to the fields of ethnography and linguistics. See Chapter 11 above, B. N. Komissarov, "The Archive of the G. I. Langsdorf Expedition to Brazil (1821-1829)."

Miroshevskii, V. M. *Osvoboditel'nye dvizheniia v amerikanskikh koloniiakh Ispanii ot ikh zavoevaniia do voiny za nezavisimost' (1492–1810 gg.)* [Liberation movements in Spain's American colonies from their conquest to the war of independence (1492–1810)]. Moscow and Leningrad: Izdatel'stvo Akademii nauk SSSR, 1946. The first scholarly monograph by a Soviet historian on a Latin American topic. Examines the independence movement as a prolonged process embracing the entire colonial period. Based on a varied, if limited, selection of sources.

Nitoburg, E. L. *Politika amerikanskogo imperializma na Kube, 1918–1939* [The policy of American imperialism in Cuba, 1918–1939]. Moscow: Nauka, 1965. An important, well-documented work based on both Soviet and foreign sources, including pertinent U.S. government publications. Of particular interest is the author's use of materials housed in the Central State Archives of the Soviet Union, the USSR State Museum of the Revolution, and the archives of the Soviet Ministry of Foregin Affairs. Volume includes an extensive bibliography.

Poiarkova, N. T. *Kolonial'naia politika SShA v Puerto-Riko: Problemy "svobodno-prisoedinivshegosia" gosudarstva* [The colonial policy of the United States in Puerto Rico: problems of a "free associated" state]. Moscow: Nauka, 1969. Overview of U.S.-Puerto Rican relations stressing the island's continuing colonial staus under the guise of commonwealth. Based on varied selection of sources, including U.N. publications, U.S. government documents, and the Puerto Rican press (e.g. *Claridad, El Imparcial, El Mundo, San Juan Star*). Reflects considerable familiarity with the recent political history of the island, although little is said about the mainland aspects of that history.

Potokova, N. V. *Agressiia SShA protiv Meksiki. 1846–1848* [The U.S. aggression against Mexico, 1846–1848]. Moscow: Isdatel'stvo sotsial'no-ekonomischeskoi literatury, 1962. Pro-Mexican narrative account of the Mexican-American War based on modest selection of printed sources; no bibliography.

Revunenkov, V. G. *Istoriia stran Latinskoi Ameriki v noveishee vremia* [The history of the Latin American countries in recent times]. Moscow: Vysshaia shkola, 1963. First Soviet university textbook on twentieth-century Latin America. Comprises introduction, ten country chapters (Argentina, Bolivia, Brazil, Chile, Colombia, Cuba, Guatemala, Mexico, Peru, Venezuela), and short bibliography of supplementary titles. Introduces elements of a Marxist periodization, but generally treats traditional themes and problems.

Shishkina, V. I. *Sotsial'no-politicheskie vzgliady Khose Marti* [The socio-political views of José Martí]. Moscow: Izdatel'stvo Moskovskogo universiteta, 1969. Modest study based mainly on the writings of Martí. Author concludes that if Martí lacked a fully Marxist understanding of the problems facing Cuba and Latin America in the final decades of the nineteenth century, he nonetheless perceived those problems in their broad outlines and took realistic steps to resolve them in accord with the realities of the day.

Shul'govskii, A. F. *Meksika na krutom povorote svoei istorii (Osvoboditel' naia i antiimperialisticheskaia bor' ba meksikanskogo naroda v 30-e gody i problema vybora Meksikoi puti sotsial' nogo razvitiia)* [Mexico at a critical juncture of its history (the liberation and anti-imperialist struggle of the Mexican people in the 1930s and Mexico's search for a way to social development)]. Moscow: Prosveshchenie, 1967. A long history of the Cárdenas years based on a varied selection of printed sources. Author posits decisive significance in the struggle of democratic, progressive forces to bring about social changes which would allow Mexico to move down a noncapitalist path to national development—an effort, in his view, that failed because of the isolation of democratic revolutionaries from key segments of Mexican society.

Shul'govskii, A. F., M. I. Bylinkina, D. A. D'iakonov, R. A. Molochkova, and S. I. Semënov, eds. *Problemy ideologii i natsional' noi kul'tury stran Latinskoi Ameriki* [Problems of ideology and the national culture of the Latin American countries]. Moscow: Nauka, 1967. Collection of articles by Soviet and Latin American authors on the development of Latin American social thought. Emphasis on the precursors of Marxist-Leninist thought in Latin America.

Shur, L. A., comp. *K beregam Novogo Sveta: Iz neopublikovannykh zapisok russkikh puteshestvennikov nachala XIX veka* [To the shores of the New World: from the unpublished notes of early nineteenth-century Russian travelers]. Moscow: Nauka, 1971. Journals of three Russian mariners who visited various parts of Latin America during the independence and immediate post-independence periods. Published with detailed explanatory notes.

_____. *Rossiia i Latinskaia Amerika: Ocherki politicheskikh, ekonomicheskikh i kul' turnykh otnoshenii* [Russia and Latin America: essays on their political, economic, and cultural relations]. Moscow: Mysl', 1964. An overview of Russo-Latin American contacts from the eighteenth through early twentieth centuries. Suggests that such ties were more varied than previously realized.

Sizonenko, A. I. *Ocherki istorii sovetsko-latinoamerikanskikh otnoshenii, 1924–1970 gg.* [Essays on the history of Soviet-Latin American relations, 1924–1970]. Moscow: Nauka, 1971. A survey history of Soviet-Latin American relations whose interest lies as much in its interpretation of factual material as in the factual material itself. Author seeks to demonstrate that in its dealings with Latin America, "the USSR has always adhered strictly and consistently to the Leninist principle of peaceful coexistence among states of differing social orders."

Slëzkin, L. Yu. *Istoriia Kubinskoi respubliki* [A history of the Republic of Cuba]. Moscow: Nauka, 1966. A general history of Cuba from emancipation through 1962. Based on a variety of sources, including materials from Cuban and Soviet archives. Contains an extensive bibliography.

————. *Politika SShA v Yuzhnoi Amerike, 1929–1933* [U.S. policy in South America, 1929–1933]. Moscow: Isdatel'stvo Akademii nauk SSSR, 1956. Author argues that the great depression of 1929–33 produced an aggressive expansion of U.S. economic domination in South America. Based on broad selection of primary and secondary sources.

————. *Rossiia i voina za nezavisimost' v Ispanskoi Amerike* [Russia and the war of independence in Spanish America]. Moscow: Nauka, 1964. An important scholarly contribution to the literature on the international politics of Latin American independence. Draws heavily on previously unused Russian archival materials. Author argues that while tsarist attitudes toward colonial emancipation varied from 1810 to 1826, at no time did Russia stray from a de facto position of neutrality. See chapter 8 above, L. Yu. Slëzkin, "The Congress of Aix-la-Chapelle and the Pacification of Spain's Colonies in America: The Position of Tsarist Russia."

————. *Zemlia Sviatogo Kresta: Otkrytie i zavoevanie Brazilii* [Land of the Holy Cross: the discovery and conquest of Brazil]. Moscow: Nauka, 1970. Volume appearing in a popular history series published by the USSR Academy of Sciences. Narrative account of the early colonial history of Brazil from discovery to the expulsion of the French from Guanabara Bay in 1567. Illustrated and annotated. Contains short bibliography of supplementary Russian-language readings on the history of New World discovery.

Sozina, S. A. *Muiski: Eshchë odna tsivilizatsiia drevnei Ameriki* [The Mwiskas: yet another ancient American civilization]. Moscow: Latin American Institute, USSR Academy of Sciences, 1969. Scholarly introduction to Chibcha civilization by a young Soviet historian, based on Spanish chronicles and the relevant secondary literature. The first work dealing with the Chibchas written in the Russian language.

Vladimirov, L. S. *Diplomatiia SShA v period amerikano-ispanskoi voiny 1898 g.* [U.S. diplomacy during the Spanish American War of 1898]. Moscow: Izdatel'stvo politicheskoi literatury, 1957. Author argues that the Spanish American War marked the beginning of a new historical period—the age of imperialist wars and the repartition of the world among the leading capitalist powers; in a Leninist frame of reference, it was the world's first imperialist conflict. This volume rests on a varied but far from exhaustive selection of sources, including materials from the historical archives of the Soviet Ministry of Foreign Affairs and published U.S. government documents of the period.

Vol'skii, V. V., ed. *SSSR i Latinskaia Amerika, 1917–1967* [The USSR and Latin America, 1917–1967]. Moscow: Mezhdunarodnye otnosheniia, 1967. Four essays dealing with (1) the impact of the Russian October Revolution on the revolutionary movement in Lain America, (2) diplomatic, economic, and cultural ties, (3) Soviet-Cuban relations, and (4) Latin American studies in the USSR.

————, I. R. Grigulevich, Yu. V. Dashkevich, and L. Yu. Slëzkin, eds. *Latinskaia Amerika v proshlom i nastoiashchem: Sbornik statei po ekonomike, istorii i kul'ture stran Latinskoi Ameriki* [Latin America past and present: collection of articles on the economy, history, and culture of the Latin American countries]. Moscow: Izdatel'stvo sotsial'no-ekonomicheskoi literatury, 1960. An early collection of articles by Soviet and Latin American specialists. Contributions of interest by Soviet historians treat the Inconfidência Mineira (A. M. Khazanov), eighteenth- and early nineteenth-century Latin America as seen in the Russian periodical press (L. A. Shur), and the early phases of Latin American independence as viewed by tsarist diplomats (L. Yu. Slëzkin). Also includes a review article on the study of Latin American history in the USSR (M. S. Al'perovich).

Zorina, A. M. *Iz geroicheskogo proshlogo kubinskogo naroda* [From the heroic past of the Cuban people]. Moscow: Izdatel'stvo Akademii nauk SSSR, 1961. A scholarly study of the Cuban independence movement from 1868 to 1898. Author focuses attention on socio-economic aspects of the movement. Analysis based on published sources as well as unpublished materials from the historical archives of the Soviet Navy and Ministry of Foreign Affairs. Includes a detailed discussion of sources and a solid bibliography.

————. *Revoliutsionnoe dvizhenie na Kube, 1917–1925* [The revolutionary movement in Cuba, 1917–1925]. Moscow: Nauka, 1971. A brief study of the impact of the Russian October Revolution on the Cuban labor and revolutionary movements—an event, the author argues, which profoundly influenced the whole development of the revolutionary process in Cuba. Sources include materials from the Archivo Nacional de Cuba and the Archivo Histórico Regional in Santiago de Cuba; no bibliography.

Zubok, L. I. *Imperialisticheskaia politika SShA v stranakh Karibskogo basseina, 1900–1939* [U.S. imperialist policy in the countries of the Caribbean basin, 1900–1939]. Moscow: Izdatel'stvo Akademii nauk SSSR, 1948. A seminal Marxist study of U.S. expansionism in Middle America and the Caribbean; volume based on broad selection of printed sources; includes maps and an exhaustive bibliography.

Articles

Afanas'ev, V. L. "Bartolome de Las Kasas—oblichitel' ispanskikh kolonizatorov (K 400-letiiu so dnia smerti)" (Bartolome de las Casas—accuser of the Spanish colonizers (on the 400th anniversary of his death)], *NNI*, no. 3 (May–June 1966), 60–72.

———. "Bartolome de Las Kasas i ego vremia" [Bartolomé de las Casas and his time]. In Bartolome de Las Kasas, *Istoriia Indii* [Historia de las Indias], pp. 7–50. Leningrad: Nauka, Leningrad branch, 1968. Introductory article to edited Russian translation of Las Casas' *Historia de las Indias*. Measured treatment of the "Black Legend" theme by a sound scholar and recognized Las Casas specialist.

Aleksin, A. "SShA i Chili v gody vtoroi mirovoi voiny" [The United States and Chile in the years of the Second World War]. *NNI*, no. 6 (November–December 1970), 78–91. Author argues that the specific conditions of the Second World War permitted an expansion of U.S. economic, political, and military interests in Chile; based almost entirely on documents contained in *Foreign Relations of the United States* series.

Al'perovich, M. S. "Diktatura Fransii v osveshchenii istorikov Yuzhnoi Ameriki" [The Francia dictatorship as interpretated by South American historians]. *LA*, 6 (November–December 1973), 121–34. Balanced historiographical review of the literature.

———. "K voprosu o chislennosti indeiskogo naseleniia Meksiki v kolonial'nyi period" [On the size of the Indian population in colonial Mexico]. *SE*, no. 3 (1962), 71–80. Review of the literature.

———. "Meksikanskaia istoriografiia (1918–1964)" [Mexican historiography, 1918–1964]. In I. S. Galkin et al. eds., *Istoriografiia novoi i noveishei istorii stran Evropy i Ameriki* [Historiography of the modern and recent history of the countries of Europe and America], pp. 552–61. Moscow: Izdatel'stvo Moskovskogo universiteta, 1968. Review article written for Soviet university students.

———. "Miranda i 'Velikaia Kolumbiia'" [Miranda and "Grand Colombia"]. *NNI*, no. 4 (July–August 1966), 56–66. Perceptive analysis of Miranda's role as precursor of Spanish American independence and intellectual forerunner to the political thought of Bolívar.

———. "O kharaktere i formakh ekspluatatsii indeitsev v amerikanskikh koloniiakh Ispanii (XVI–XVIII veka)" [On the nature and forms of exploitation of Indians in Spain's American colonies (16th–18th centuries)]. *NNI*, no. 2 (March–April 1957), 49–68.

———. "Velikaia frantsuzskaia revoliutsiia XVIII veka i ispanskie kolonii v Amerike" [The great French revolution of the eighteenth century and the Spanish colonies in America]. *NNI*, no. 1 (January–February 1965), 26–40.

Al'perovich, M. S., V. I. Ermolaev, I. R. Lavretskii, and S. I. Semënov. "Ob osvoboditel'noi voine ispanskikh kolonii v Amerike (1810–1826)" [On the war of independence in the Spanish American colonies, 1810–1826]. *Vop. Ist.*, no. 11 (November 1956), 52–71. A seminal article signalling a turn away from Stalinist subjectivism in Soviet approaches to Latin American history.

Outlines broad parameters for analyzing the fall of colonial rule in Spain's New World possessions, suggesting a multicausal explanation, while at the same time stressing the primacy of internal socio-economic conditions.

Ananova, E. V. "Dominikanskaia tragediia. I. Tiraniia Trukhil'o" [The Dominican tragedy. Pt. I: the tyranny of Trujillo]. *NNI*, no. 4 (July–August 1965), 34–53.

————. "Dominikanskaia tragediia. II. Respublika na pereput'e" [The Dominican tragedy. Pt. II: the republic at the crossroads]. *NNI*, no. 5 (September–October 1965), 64–81.

————. "Vooruzhënnaia interventsiia SShA v Dominikanskoi respublike" [U.S. military intervention in the Dominican Republic]. *NNI*, no. 6 (November-December 1968), 42–57, and no. 1 (January-February 1969), 24–37.

Anikin, A. S. "Ekspansiia severoamerikanskogo imperializma v Chili v gody 'kholodnoi voiny'" [The expansion of North American imperialism in Chile during the "cold war" years]. *Vop. Ist.*, no. 7 (July 1971), 66–80. Based on published documents, press accounts, and a varied selection of secondary sources.

Antonov, Yu. A. "Dvizhenie tenentistov (Vooruzhënnaia bor'ba demokraticheskikh sil brazil'skoi armii v 1922–1930 gg.)" [The *tenentes* movement (the armed struggle of democratic forces in the Brazilian army in the years 1922—1930)]. *NNI*, no. 3 (May–June 1966), 89–99.

Arutonov, S. A. "Yapontsy v Brazilii" [The Japanese in Brazil]. *RN*, no. 2 (1972), 256–65. Overview based on available published literature.

Bolkhovitinov, N. N. "Voina Latinskoi Ameriki za nezavisimost' i pozitsiia Rossii" [Latin America's war for independence and the position of Russia]. *Vop. Ist.*, no. 11 (November 1965), 153–59.

————, comp. "Otnoshenie Rossii k nachalu voiny Latinskoi Ameriki za nezavisimost'" [Russia's attitude toward the start of the war for independence in Latin America]. *IA*, no. 3 (1962), 120–31. Seven previously unpublished documents from the Central State Historical Archives of the USSR (Leningrad) and the Russian Foreign Policy Archives (Moscow), together with notes and introductory article (written in collaboration with L. Yu. Slëzkin) evidencing Russian pre-1815 interest in direct trade ties with the insurgent Spanish American colonies.

Dmitrieva, V. D. "Probuzhdenie severo-vostoka (O nekotorykh osobennostiakh krest'ianskogo dvizheniia v Brazilii v kontse 50-kh - nachale 60-kh godov" [The awakening of the Northeast (some features of the peasant movement in Brazil in the late 1950s and early '60s)]. *NNI*, no. 5 (September–October 1968), 85–96.

Dridzo, A. D. "Gonduras na rannem etape formirovaniia natsii" [Honduras in the early stages of national formation]. *LA*, no. 4 (July–August 1973), 79–86.

General discussion of the process of national consolidation in nineteenth-century Honduras, based on contemporary as well as modern works.

————. "K voprosu o chislennosti indeitsev Yamaiki pered nachalom kolonizatsii" [On the size of the indigenous population of Jamaica at the onset of colonization]. *SE,* no. 3 (1966), 139–44. Intelligent analysis of available literature; author concludes that native population must have numbered between 200,000 and 300,000 Amerinds.

Ermolaev, V. I. "Kompartiia Argentiny—pervaia sektsiia III Internatsionala v Latinskoi Amerikie" [The Communist Party of Argentina: first section of the Third International in Latin America]. *NNI,* no. 3 (May-June 1959), 49–66. Overview of Argentine CP through the 1920s, based entirely on readily available published sources.

————. "Nekotorye voprosy osvoboditel'noi bor'by amerikanskikh kolonii Ispanii i Portugalii (K 150-letiiu nachala voiny za nezavisimost' 1810–1826 gg.)" [Some problems of the independence struggle of the American colonies of Spain and Portugal (on the 150th anniversary of the war for independence of 1810–1826)]. *NNI,* no. 3 (May–June 1960), 23–37. Historiographical piece which also draws on primary source materials, including unpublished manuscripts in Russian Foreign Policy Archives (Moscow). Author takes particular issue with foreign scholars who depict Brazilian independence movement as a peaceful process in alleged contrast to what occurred in Spanish America.

Ganelin, R. Sh. "Iz istorii ekonomicheskikh sviazei Rossii a Meksikoi i Brazilii v seredine XIX veka" [From the history of Russian economic ties with Mexico and Brazil in the mid-19th century]. *NNI,* no. 6 (November–December 1963), 59–64.

————. "Popytki razvitiia ekonomicheskikh sviazei mezhdu Rossiei i stranami Latinskoi Ameriki v kontse XIX - nachale XX v." [Attempts to develop economic ties between Russia and the countries of Latin America in the late nineteenth and early twentieth century]. In M. P. Viatkin, R. Sh. Ganelin, and A. A. Fursenko, eds., *Monopolii i inostrannyi kapital v Rossii* [Monopolies and foreign capital in Russia], pp. 315–58. Moscow and Leningrad: Izdatel'stvo Akademii nauk SSSR, 1962. Author argues that Russia sought partially to reduce its dependence on foreign capital by promoting direct trade with Latin America, an effort which failed. Based primarily on manuscript holdings of Central State Historical Archives (Leningrad), Soviet Ministry of Foreign Affairs (Moscow), and Naval Archives of the USSR (Leningrad).

Glinkin, A. N. "Istoriografiia v Brazilii (1918–1964)" [Historiography in Brazil, 1918–1964]. In I. S. Galkin et al., eds., *Istoriografiia novoi i noveishei istorii stran Evropy i Ameriki* [Historiography of the modern and recent history of the countries of Europe and America], pp. 538–51. Moscow: Izdatel'stvo Moskovskogo universiteta, 1968. Review article written for Soviet university students.

————. "Latinskaia Amerika i mirovoi istoricheskii protses v XIX-XX vv."
[Latin America and the world historical process in the nineteenth and twentieth
centuries]. *LA,* no. 3 (May–June 1971), 18–34. Complete version of paper
delivered in August 1970 at Thirteenth International Congress of Historical
Sciences (Moscow).

Gonionskii, S. A. "Dinastiia tiranov Somosa" [The dynasty of Somoza tyrants].
NNI, no. 1 (January–February 1973), 136–45, and no. 2 (March–April 1973),
128–37. Modestly documented narrative account.

————. "Vosstanie komuneros v Novoi Granade (1781 g.)" [The *comuneros*
rebellion of 1781 in New Granada]. *NNI,* no. 1 (January–February 1971),
149–57. Brief overview of *comuneros* rebellion by a scholar who has spent
time in Colombia. Author concludes that the *comuneros* movement was
separatist in nature. Although this conclusion allegedly rests on a study of
documents in Colombian archives and the Colombian National Library, the
article cites no manuscript sources and is based almost entirely on Lucas
Molano Díaz' *Proceso y sinopsis de la independencia de Colomiba* (Cali,
1960), and Indalecio Liévano Aguirre's *Los grandes conflictos sociales y
económicos en nuestra historia,* 4 vols. (Bogota, 1961).

Grigor'ev, V. G. "Amerikanskii imperializm i kubinskaia revoliutsiia (1959
g.-aprel' 1961 g.)" [American imperialism and the Cuban Revolution
(1959–April 1961)]. *NNI,* no. 1 (January–February 1967), 58–66.

Grigor'ian, Yu. M. " 'Tretii raikh' v bor'be za latinoamerikanskii rynok" [The
"Third Reich" in the struggle for the Latin American market]. *LA,* no. 6
(November–December 1971), 128–38. Author presents interesting material
drawn from variety of sources, including holdings of Deutsche Zentralarchiv
(Potsdam), but fails to cite related researches of Katz, Hell, and Kannapin.

Grigulevich, I. R. "Istoriografiia Kuby (1959–1964)" [The Historiography of
Cuba, 1959–1964]. In I. S. Galkin et al., eds., *Istoriografiia novoi i noveishei
istorii stran Evropy i Ameriki* [Historiography of the modern and recent history
of the countries of Europe and America], pp. 401–6. Moscow: Izdatel'stvo
Moskovskogo universiteta, 1968. Review article written for Soviet university
students.

Gromyko, A. A. "Karibskii krizis" [The Caribbean crisis]. *Vop. Ist.,* no. 7 (July
1971), 135–44, and no. 8 (August 1971), 121–29. Official Soviet account of
the Cuban missile crisis by the son of Soviet Foreign Minister Andrei
Gromyko. Extensively documented, including much material from Soviet
Foreign Ministry archives. Stresses diplomacy and international politics, with
relatively little attention to military dimensions of the crisis. A key source for
the history of this important event.

Guber, A. A. "Problemy natsional'no-osvoboditel'noi bor'by v Latinskoi
Amerike (1810–1826 gg.) v trudakh sovetskikh istorikov" [Problems of the
national-liberation struggle in Latin America (1810–1826) in the writings of
Soviet historians]. *NNI,* no. 1 (January–February 1970), 32–38.

Guber, A. A., and N. M. Lavrov. "K 150-letiiu voiny za nezavisimost' Latinskoi Ameriki" [On the 150th anniversary of Latin America's war for independence]. *NNI*, no. 4 (July–August 1960), 11–18. Historiographical essay.

Gus'kov, A. V. "Bor'ba rabochego klassa Chili za edinstvo antiimperialisticheskikh sil v 1934–1939 gg: Sozdanie i pobeda narodnogo fronta" [The struggle of the Chilean working class for the unification of antiimperialist forces in 1934–1939: the creation and triumph of the popular front]. *UZIGPI*, vol. 43 (Voprosy istorii, 1967), 63–105. Chronological continuation of the following article. Here greater emphasis is placed on the labor movement than on the Chilean Communist Pary, although the affairs of the latter are touched upon as well. A fundmental article for the history of the Chilean Popular Front.

————. "Obostrenie klassovoi bor'by v Chili v period mirovogo ekonomicheskogo krizisa 1929–1933 gg.: 'Sotsialisticheskaia respublika' " [The intensification of class struggle in Chile during the world economic crisis of 1929–1933: the "Socialist Republic"]. *UZIGPI*, vol. 43 (Voprosy istorii, 1967), 3–62. An important article for the history of the Communist movement in Chile. Sheds some light on factional splits. Brief discussion of the founding and initial development of Chilean CP in 1920s. Based on varied, although by no means exhaustive, selection of sources.

Ioffe, A. E. "SSSR i Latinskaia Amerika (Kul'turnye sviazi do vtoroi mirovoi voiny" [The USSR and Latin America (Cultural ties before the Second World War)]. *NNI*, no. 3 (May–June 1967), 81–89.

————. "SSSR i Latinskaia Amerika (Politicheskie i ekonomicheskie otnosheniia do vtoroi mirovoi voiny" [The USSR and Latin America (Political and economic ties before the Second World War)]. *NNI*, no. 5 (September–October 1965), 79–88.

Ivanov, G. I. "Enkom'enda v Meksike i vosstaniia indeitsev v XVI veke" [The *encomienda* in Mexico and Indian uprisings in the sixteenth century], *UZIGPI*, vol. 35 (Voprosy vseobshchei istorii, 1964), 99–157. An example of serious historical writing by a scholar outside the traditional centers of Russian culture and research. Like the following articles by the same author, this one is based on a varied selection of key published sources.

————. "Meksika vo vtoroi polovine XVIII v.: Ispanskii kolonializm i indeitsy" [Mexico in the second half of the eighteenth century: Spanish colonialism and the Indians]. *UZIGPI*, vol. 58 (Voprosy vseobshchei istorii, 1970), 3–44.

————. "Narodnye vosstaniia v Meksike vo vtoroi polovine XVII veka" [Popular uprisings in Mexico in the second half of the seventeenth century]. *NNI*, no. 1 (January–February 1964), 57–72. Author argues that numerous Indian uprisings of the late seventeenth century prepared the ground for independence in the early nineteenth century.

————. "Peonazh v Meksike v XVI–XVIII vv. (Ispanskii kolonializm i dol-govoe rabstvo)" [Peonage in Mexico in the sixteenth through eighteenth centuries (Spanish colonialism and debt slavery)]. *UZIGPI*, vol. 43 (Voprosy vseobshchei istorii, 1967), 147–223. A seminal Marxist treatment of an important colonial topic: author traces the emergence of debt peonage as an offshoot of *repartimiento* from 1550s to 1630s, the substitution of debt peonage for *repartimiento* from 1630s to 1750s, and the gradual replacement of debt peonage by wage labor from 1750s to 1820s. Profusely documented; draws heavily on key published Spanish-language documentation, as well as principal secondary sources in English, Spanish, and French.

————. "Repartim'ento v Meksike v XVI–XVIII vv.; iz istorii feodal'no-kolonial'noi ekspluatatsii indeiskogo naseleniia" [The *repartimiento* in Mexico in the sixteenth through eighteenth centuries; from the history of the feudal-colonial exploitation of the Indian population]. *UZIGPI*, vol. 35 (Voprosy vseobshchei istorii, 1964), 158–95. General discussion based on the relevant published documents.

Khazanov, A. M. "K voprosu o negritianskom gosudarstve Palmares v Brazilii" [The Negro state of Palmares in Brazil]. *NNI*, no. 2 (March–April 1958), 13–31.

————. "Portugal'skaia rabotorgovlia (Stranitsy istorii kolonializma)" [The Portuguese slave trade (pages from the history of colonialism)]. *NNI*, no. 4 (July–August 1968), 55–68. Interpretive article based on varied but not extensive selection of sources. Anti-Freyre in thrust, although Freyre is not cited directly. In essence, an attack on recent Portuguese versions of the Freyre thesis designed to justify Portugal's continuing presence in Africa.

Komissarov, B. N. "Braziliia pervoi chetverti XIX veka v opisaniiakh russkikh moreplavatelei" [Brazil as described by Russian mariners in the first quarter of the nineteenth century]. *VLU*, no. 14 (Seriia istorii, iazyka i literatury), vyp. 3 (1961), 43–54.

————, comp. "Braziliia v opisaniiakh uchastnikov russkoi ekspeditsii 1821–1829 godov" [Brazil in the accounts of participants in the Russian expedition of 1821–1829]. *NNI*, no. 3 (May–June 1966), 115–27. Excerpts from unpublished manuscripts housed in Archives of the USSR Academy of Sciences (Leningrad). Introduction and explanatory notes.

————. "Materialy ekspeditsii G. I. Langsdorfa 1821–1829 godov kak istochnik po istorii Brazilii" [Materials from the G. I. Langsdorf expedition of 1821–1829 as a source for the history of Brazil]. *NNI*, no. 1 (January–February 1968), 139–50.

————. "Ob otnoshenii Rossii k voine Ispanskoi Ameriki za nezavisimost' (po materialam arkhiva V. M. Miroshevskogo)" [On Russia's attitude toward the Spanish American war for independence (based on materials in the V. M. Miroshevskii archive)]. *VLU*, no. 8 (Seriia istorii, iazyka i literatury), vyp. 2 (1964), 60–71. Posthumous publication of article by V. M. Miroshevskii.

Koval, B. I. "K voprosu o sotsial'no-ekonomicheskom razvitii Brazilii v seredine XIX veka" [On the socio-economic development of Brazil in the mid-nineteenth century]. *Vop. Ist.*, no. 2 (February 1963), 112–21. Intelligent discussion of clash between decaying slaveholding order and expanding capitalist relations; draws on relevant secondary literature.

Koval, B. I., and N. S. Konovalova. "Oktiabr'skaia revoliutsiia i nachalo novogo etapa rabochego dvizheniia v stranakh Latinskoi Ameriki" [The October Revolution and the start of a new stage in the Latin American labor movement]. *NNI*, no. 4 (July–August 1967), 18–30. Based on varied selection of printed sources.

Kovalev, E. V. "Khristianskie demokraty i problema agrarnoi reformy v Chili" [The Christian Democrats and the problem of agrarian reform in Chile]. *Vop. Ist.*, no. 6 (June 1969), 80–95.

Krauts, K. A. "Palmares: Osvoboditel'noe dvizhenie rabov v Brazilii XVII v. (istochnik, trudy, problemy)" [Palmares: the slave emancipation movement in seventeenth-century Brazil (sources, scholarship, problems)]. *LA*, no. 3 (May–June 1971), 185–95.

Larin (pseud.), N. S. [N. S. Leonov]. "Iz istorii osvoboditel'noi bor'by naroda Nikaragua protiv vooruzhёnnoi interventsii SShA v 1927–1933 godakh" [From the history of the Nicaraguan people's liberation struggle against the military intervention of the United States in the years 1927–1933)]. *Vop. Ist.*, no. 8 (August 1961), 86–96. General account of Sandino movement based on printed sources.

Lavrov, N. M. "Politicheskaia bor'ba v Chili v kontse XIX nachale XX veka" [Political struggle in Chile in the late nineteenth and early twentieth century]. *NNI*, no. 5 (November–December 1966), 51–59. Brief narrative account based on varied selection of published sources.

Lukin, B. V. "Sviazi Mirandy s rossiiskoi diplomaticheskoi missiei v Londone (Po materialam ego neizvestnykh pisem)" [Miranda's ties with the Russian diplomatic mission in London (based on his unpublished letters)]. *NNI*, no. 4 (July–August 1966), 67–73. Seven previously unpublished letters (in Russian translation) written by Francisco de Miranda between 1791 and 1800; introduction and explanatory notes.

Malkov, A. P., and V. M. Marchenko, "Deiatel'nost' 'Yuzhamtorga' (K istorii ekonomicheskikh otnoshenii mezhdu SSSR i stranami Latinskoi Ameriki)" [The activities of "Yuzhamtorg" (toward a history of economic relations between the USSR and the countries of Latin America)]. *NNI*, no. 4 (July–August 1968), 82–88.

Matveeva, N. R. "Braziliia i strany La Platy posle Paragvaiskoi voiny, 1864–1870" [Brazil and the Platine countries after the Paraguayan War, 1864–1870], *UZKPI*, vol. 35 (1963), 246–82.

—————. "Kolonial'naia ekspansiia Anglii v Paragvae (Iz istorii paragvaisko-angliiskikh otnoshenii v 40-50-kh godakh XIX veka)" [England's colonial expansion into Paraguay (from the history of Anglo-Paraguayan relations in the 1840s and '50s)]. *UZKGPI*, vol. 26 (Kafedra istorii, 1962), 215–50. A study of unsuccessful attempts by English capital to penetrate Paraguay during the first half of the nineteenth century, based on a relatively broad selection of primary and secondary sources.

————. "Pervye popytki ustanovleniia otnoshenii SShA s Paragvaem (40-e gody XIX veka)" [Initial U.S. efforts to establish relations with Paraguay (1840s)], *UZKPI*, vol. 38 (1964), 382–434.

Moriakov, V. I. "Russkii perevod 'Istoriia obeikh Indii' Reinalia" [A Russian translation of Raynal's "History of the Two Indies"]. *VMU*, series 9 (History), no. 1 (January–February 1972), 55–68.

Nikirov (pseud.), B. S. [B. S. Nikiforov]. "Iz istorii rabochego dvizheniia na Kube" [From the history of the labor movement in Cuba]. *Vop Ist.*, no. 9 (September 1961), 103–15. Discussion of the period 1944–48, based mainly on Cuban press.

Nitoburg, E. L. "Dokumenty po istorii osvoboditel'nogo dvizheniia na Kube (Obzor kollektsii dokumentov v Gosudarstvennom muzee revoliutsii SSSR)" [Documents on the liberation movement in Cuba (a review of documents in the USSR State Museum of the Revolution)]. *NNI*, no. 2 (March–April 1966), 83–94.

Petukhov, V. I. "Nastuplenie inostrannykh monopolii v Yuzhnoi Amerike posle tikhookeanskoi voiny 1879–1884 godov" [The offensive of foreign monopolies in South American after the 1879–1884 War of the Pacific]. *NNI*, no. 1 (January–February 1970), 115–25.

————. "Posledniaia interventsiia Ispanii v Yuzhnoi Amerike (1863–1866)" [Spain's last intervention in South America (1863–1866)], *Vop. Ist.*, no. 7 (July 1970), 79–94. Well-documented narrative account based on available published sources.

Poiarkova, N. T. "K izucheniiu Latinskoi Ameriki v SShA" [Latin American studies in the United States]. *LA*, no. 1 (January–February 1973), 116–24. Author relates growth of Latin American studies in the United States to the imperatives of U.S. involvement in Latin America.

Poliakov, B. A. "Osvoboditel'noe dvizhenie v Peru v 1945–1948 gg." [The liberation movement in Peru in the years 1945–1948]. In R. F. Ivanov and M. S. Al'perovich, eds., *Rabochee i natsional'no-osvoboditel'noe dvizhenie v stranakh Ameriki* [The labor and national-liberation movement in the countries of America], pp. 279–323. Moscow: Nauka, 1967. Detailed discussion of political process based on wide selection of printed sources. Article focuses on the role of APRA and Communist Party of Peru.

Rudenko, B. T. "Rikardo Flores Magon i revoliutsionno-demokraticheskoe techenie v meksikanskoi revoliutsii 1910–1917 gg." [Ricardo Flores Magón and the democratic-revolutionary current in the Mexican Revolution of 1910–1917]. *LA*, no. 2 (March–April 1973), 92–108.

———. "Sotsial'naia struktura meksikanskogo obshchestva nakanune revoliu-tsii 1910–1917 gg." [The social structure of Mexican society on the eve of the Revolution of 1910–1917]. *Vop. Ist.*, no. 11 (November 1970), 65–79. Suggestive class analysis of pre-Revolutionary Mexico from a Leninist perspective.

Rybalkin, I. E. "Grazhdanskaia voina 1948 goda v Kosta-Rike" [The 1948 civil war in Costa Rica]. *NNI*, no. 4 (July–August 1959), 55–71. Based largely on periodical accounts, with emphasis on the role of U.S. business interests.

Semënov, S. I., and A. F. Shul'govskii. "Rol' Khose Karlosa Mariategi v sozdanii Kommunisticheskoi partii Peru" [The role of José Carlos Mariátegui in the creation of the Peruvian Communist Party]. *NNI*, no. 5 (September–October 1957), 68–85. Important article for the study of this specific problem. Authors stress flexibility of Mariátegui's ideology and his ability to adapt Marxist-Leninist theory to the concrete realities of Latin America. Based on varied documentation.

Serov, S. Ya. "Rasovaia problema v rabotakh Alekhandro Lipshutsa" [The race problem in the works of Alejandro Lipschutz]. *RN*, no. 1 (1971), 104–16.

Shavlokhava, T. N. "Federal'naia voina v Venesuele" [The War of Federation in Venezuela]. *VMU*, series 9 (History), no. 5 (1969), 19–34. Scholarly treat-ment based on varied selection of printed sources.

Shtrakhov, A. I. "O nesostoiatel'nosti konservativno-klerikal'nykh kontseptsii ispanskikh kolonial'nykh poriadkov na La-Plate" [Untenable clerical-conservative conceptions of the Spanish colonial system in the River Plate]. *NNI*, no. 3 (May–June 1973), 82–90. Critical review of "white legend" appraisals of Spanish colonialism in Argentine historiography.

———. "Osvoboditel'naia bor'ba naroda La-Platy v 1810–1816 godakh" [The Platine people's struggle for independence in the years 1810–1816]. *NNI*, no. 4 (July–August 1960), 19–35. Lengthy interpretive article based largely on published secondary sources.

Shul'govskii, A. F. "Proletarskaia revoliutsiia v Rossii i anti-imperialisticheskoe dvizhenie v Latinskoi Amerike" [The proletarian revolution in Russian and the anti-imperialist movement in Latin America]. *Vop. Ist.*, no. 11 (November 1976), 92–106. Discussion of the impact of Russian October Revolution on Latin America in 1920s, based on a limited selection of printed sources.

Shur, L. A. "Iz istorii ustanovleniia diplomaticheskikh otnoshenii Rossii so stranami Latinskoi Ameriki" [From the history of the founding of Russian diplomatic relations with the countries of Latin America]. *Vop. Ist.*, no. 8 (August 1964), 211–15.

———. "Kul'turnye i literaturnye sviazi Rossii i Brazilii v XVIII-XIX vv." [The cultural and literary ties of Russia and Brazil in the eighteenth and nineteenth centuries]. In A. V. Efimov et al., eds., *Braziliia: Ekonomika, politika, kul'tura* [Brazil: Economics, politics, culture], pp. 473–512. Moscow: Nauka, 1963.

————. "Latinoamerikanskie literatury v Rossii v nachale XIX v." [The literatures of Latin America in early nineteenth-century Russia]. In M. P. Alekseev, ed., *Mezhdunarodnye sviazi russkoi literatury: Sbornik statei* [The international ties of Russian literature: a collection of articles], pp. 175–91. Moscow and Leningrad: Izdatel'stvo Akademii nauk SSSR, 1963. Author describes the growth of Russian knowledge about Latin America, as well as the influence of Latin American literature in Russia.

————. "Materialy russkikh puteshestvennikov XVIII-XIX vv. kak istochnik po geografii, istorii i etnografii stran Latinskoi Ameriki" [The papers of eighteenth- and nineteenth-century Russian travelers as a source for the geography, history, and ethnography of the Latin American countries]. *IVGO*, vol. 100 (1968), 230–36.

————. "Putevye zapiski i dnevniki russkikh puteshestvennikov kak istochnik po istorii Kalifornii (pervaia polovina XIX v.)" [The travel notes and diaries of Russian travelers as a source for the history of California (first half of the nineteenth century)]. *Amerikanskii ezhegodnik* (1971), 295–319. Translated by James R. Gibson and published under the title "Russian Travel Notes and Journals As Sources for the History of California, 1800–1850," *CHQ* 52, no. 1 (Spring 1973), 38–63.

————. "Russkie puteshestvenniki v Chili v XIX v. (O russkikh istochnikakh po istorii i etnografii Chili)" [Russian travelers in Chile in the nineteenth century (on Russian sources for the history and ethnography of Chile)]. In S. A. Gonionskii et al., eds., *Chili: Politika, ekonomika, kul'tura* [Chile: politics, economics, culture], pp. 338–54. Moscow: Nauka, 1965. Well-documented review of Russian source materials relating to nineteenth-century Chile.

Slëzkin, L. Yu. "Istoriografiia kubinskoi revoliutsii (vozniknovenie i stanovlenie)" [Historiography of the Cuban Revolution (its origins and formation)]. In G. N. Sevost'ianov, ed., *Amerikanskaia istoriografiia vneshnei politiki SShA, 1945–1970* [American historiography of U.S. foreign policy, 1945–1970], pp. 348–93. Moscow: Nauka, 1972.

————. "Revoliutsiia negrov-rabov na ostrove San-Domingo (Gaiti) v 1791–1803 gg." [The Negro slave revolution of 1791–1803 on the island of Santo Domingo (Haiti)]. In *UZNNI*, vyp. 2 (91956), 134–206. Narrative account of revolutionary events in Haiti based on limited selection of published sources. Impact of Haitian independence on other colonial areas stressed. Author concludes that independence struggle in Haiti constituted "one of the most unique bourgeois revolutions in history and the most radical revolution to occur in the Western Hemisphere during the early 19th century."

Smolenskii, V. "SShA i tikhookeanskaia voina 1879–1884 gg. (Istoriia odnoi nesostoiavsheisia interventsii)" [The United States and the War of the Pacific of 1879–1884 (the history of an unconsummated intervention)]. *NNI*, no. 3 (May–June 1967), 16–30. Study of U.S. national interests, based in part on published Congressional documents.

Sokolov, A. A. "Meksikanskaia kommunisticheskaia partiia v bor'be za edinstvo rabochego dvizheniia strany (1919–1929 gg.)" [The Mexican Communist Party in the struggle to unite labor (1919–1929)], *VMU*, series 9 (History), no. 5 (September–October 1971), 45–59. Fundamental article for the early history of the Mexican Communist Party. Based on wide range of primary sources, including archival materials housed in Central State Archives of the USSR and the USSR State Museum of the Revolution.

––––––. "Meksikanskaia regional'naia rabochaia konfederatsiia i rezhim 'revoliutsionnogo kaudil'izma' (1920–1928 gg.)" [The Mexican Regional Labor Confederation and the regime of "revolutionary caudillismo" (1920–1928)], *VMU*, series 9 (History), no. 1 (January–February 1971), 17–38. Well-researched article based on wide range of primary sources, including materials housed in the USSR State Museum of the Revolution.

Sokolova, Z. I. "Istoriia vos'midesiati dvukh s 'Granmy'" [The history of the eighty-two of the "Granma"]. *NNI*, no. 4 (July–August 1967), 54–60. Account of initial armed encounters with Batista forces in late 1956–early 1957, based on available printed sources.

Sotnikova, T. P. "Agrarnyi vopros na vtorom etape voiny za nezavisimost' v Venesuele (1816–1826 gg.)" [The agrarian question in the second stage of Venezuela's war for independence, 1816–1826]. *UZYGPI*, vyp. 76 (History, 1970), 90–102. Relatively superficial article based mainly on the documentary collection *Materiales para el estudio de la cuestión agraria en Venezuela, 1800–1830* (Caracas, 1964). Author's conclusion: "The war of independence failed to resolve the agrarian question; the problems of latifundia and a landless peasantry persisted into the nineteenth century."

Stoliarov, V. I. "Predposylki voiny za nezavisimost' Vanesuely" [The causes of Venezuela's war of independence]. *LA*, no. 1 (January–February 1970), 64–78. Interpretive article based on variety of printed sources and relevant secondary literature; author argues that independence was not the work of creole elites, but rather resulted from a complex of causes.

––––––. "Provozglashenie nezavisimosti Venesuely" [The declaration of Venezuelan independence]. *NNI*, no. 4 (July–August 1971), 61–72. Narrative account based on varied selection of published primary sources.

Sukhomlinov, V. F. "Ob ustanovlenii russko-brazil'skikh otnoshenii" [On the establishment of Russo-Brazilian relations]. *NNI*, no. 2 (March–April 1965), 89–96. Article focuses on period 1812–1821, with brief references to question of foreign recognition. Based primarily on diplomatic correspondence housed in Russian Foreign Policy Archives (Moscow).

Svet, Ya. M., and L. A. Shur. "Russko-latinoamerikanskie otnosheniia XVI–XIX vv. v osveshchenii zarubezhnykh issledovatelei" [Russo-Latin American relations in the sixteenth to nineteenth centuries as viewed by foreign scholars]. *LA*, no. 6 (November–December 1970), 138–59. Historiographical review.

Ternovoi, O. S. "Natsional'nyi geroi Kuby Khose Marti—borets protiv imperializma SShA" [Cuban national hero José Martí: fighter against U.S. imperialism]. *NNI*, no. 1 (January–February 1962), 46–54.

Tivikova, A. A. "Sozdanie kubinskoi revoliutsionnoi partii (1890–1892 gg.)" [The formation of the Cuban Revolutionary party, 1890–1892]. *VLU*, no. 2 (History, Language, Literature), vyp. 1 (1973), 144–48. Brief narrative article based on *Obras completas* of José Martí and manuscript holdings of Archivo Nacional de Cuba (Havana).

Tomanovskaia, O. S. "Bartolome de Las Kasas i vozniknovenie rabstva negrov v Vest-Indii" [Bartolomé de las Casas and the origin of Negro slavery in the West Indies]. *LA*, no. 1 (January–February 1972), 124–38. Sparsely documented interpretive article.

Yanchuk, I. I. "Amerikanskaia burzhuaznaia istoriografiia o politike 'dobrogo soseda' v gody vtoroi mirovoi voiny" [American bourgeois historiography of the "Good Neighbor Policy" during the Second World War]. *LA*, no. 3 (May–June 1972), 168–74. Historiographical review.

———. "Politika SShA v stranakh Latinskoi Ameriki v nachale vtoroi mirovoi voiny (sentiabr' 1939 g. - aprel' 1940 g.)" [U.S. policy in the countries of Latin America at the beginning of the Second World War (September 1939–April 1940)]. In R. F. Ivanov and M. S. Al'perovich, eds., *Rabochee i natsional'no-osvoboditel'noe dvizhenie v stranakh Ameriki* [The labor and national-liberation movement in the countries of Latin America], pp. 220–78. Moscow: Nauka, 1967.

———. "SShA na gavanskoi konferentsii 1940 goda" [The United States at the Havana Conference of 1940]. *NNI*, no. 1 (January–February 1966), 89–96. Brief account of the Havana Conference based on relevant published documentation. Author treats the conference as a prelude to the creation of the OAS and as an example of how the United States used the doctrine of Pan-Americanism to further U.S. domination of the hemisphere.

Zorina, A. M. "K voprosu o genezise kapitalizma na Kube v XIX veke" [The genesis of capitalism in Cuba in the 19th century]. *NNI*, no. 3 (May–June 1972), 25–37. General discussion based on a varied but far from exhaustive selection of published sources.

———. "Natsional'no-osvoboditel'noe dvizhenie na Kube v 1895–1898 gg." [The national-liberation movement in Cuba in the years 1895–1898]. *UZNNI*, vyp. III (1957), 95–153. An early contribution by a leading Soviet specialist in nineteenth-century Cuban history. Generally balanced treatment of a controversial topic. Author argues that U.S. intervention produced the first imperialist war (in a Leninist sense), thereby initiating the process of repartitioning the world among the major capitalist powers, a process in which U.S. hegemony was extended to Cuba. Based on a varied selection of published sources, although conspicuously little use was made of pertinent newspaper and periodical accounts.

Zubritskii, Yu. A. "Avantiura Uokera (Iz istorii agressii SShA v Tsentral'noi Amerike)" [The Walker adventure (from the history of U.S. aggression in Central America)]. *NNI*, no. 1 (January–February 1968), 49–61. Modestly documented narrative account.

CONTRIBUTORS

AL'PEROVICH, Moisei Samuilovich (b. 22 November 1918). Senior research scholar, Institute of World History of the USSR Academy of Sciences (Moscow); Doctor of Historical Sciences; specialist in the modern history of Latin America; research focuses on independence, modern Mexico, nineteenth-century Paraguay, and various problems of historiography.

BOLKHOVITINOV, Nikolai Nikolaevich (b. 26 October 1930). Senior research scholar, Institute of World History of the USSR Academy of Sciences (Moscow); Doctor of Historical Sciences; specialist in modern U.S. and Latin American history; research focuses on Russo-American relations in the eighteenth and nineteenth centuries.

EFIMOV, Aleksei Vladimirovich (1896–1971). Prominent Soviet historian, ethnographer, and historical geographer; scholarly interests focused on the Western Hemisphere; numerous works on the history and peoples of both Anglo and Latin America; also, noteworthy research on the history of Russian exploration and discovery; as noted in the Introduction, an influential figure in the formation of the Soviet historical profession; during the final fifteen years of his life, head of the American division of the Institute of Ethnography of the USSR Academy of Sciences (Moscow).

ERMOLAEV, Vasilii Ivanovich (1916–1974). At the time of his death, head of Cuban division, Latin American Institute of the USSR Academy of Sciences (Moscow); Candidate in Historical Sciences; Docent; specialist in modern and contemporary Latin American history; research focuses on the history of the labor and communist movements in Latin America.

KINZHALOV, Rostislav Vasil'evich (b. 15 July 1920). Senior research scholar and head of American division, Institute of Ethnography of the USSR Academy of Sciences (Leningrad branch); Doctor of Historical Sciences; pre-Columbian specialist; research focuses on the ancient Maya.

KOMISSAROV, Boris Nikolaevich (b. 8 December 1939). Lecturer, Leningrad State University; Candidate in Historical Sciences; specialist in modern and contemporary Latin American history; research focuses on early nineteenth-century Brazil and Russian source materials pertaining thereto.

KOVAL, Boris Iosifovich (b. 5 June 1930). Professor, Academy of Social Sciences attached to the Central Committee of the CPSU; Doctor of Historical Sciences; specialist in the modern and contemporary history of Latin America, primarily Brazil; research focuses on labor and national-liberation movements.

LAVROV, Nikolai Matveevich (b. 2 August 1915). Head of Latin American division, Institute of World History of the USSR Academy of Sciences (Moscow); Doctor of Historical Sciences; specialist in modern Latin American history; research focuses on modern Mexico.

NITOBURG, Eduard L'vovich (b. 28 December 1918). Senior research scholar, Institute of Ethnography of the USSR Academy of Sciences (Moscow); Doctor of Historical Sciences; specialist in modern Latin American history; research focuses on U.S. policies in Cuba between the two world wars; recent work deals with blacks in Cuba and the United States.

SHUL'GOVSKII, Anatolii Fëdorovich (b. 11 November 1926). Head of division of labor and national-liberation movement, Latin American Institute of the USSR Academy of Sciences (Moscow); Doctor of Historical Sciences; Professor; specialist in modern and contemporary Latin American history; research interests focus on intellectual history, labor and national-liberation movements, and the modern history of Mexico.

SHUR, Leonid Avelevich (b. 11 September 1930). Research scholar, Institute of Ethnography of the USSR Academy of Sciences (Moscow); Candidate in Philological Sciences; specialist in eighteenth- and nineteenth-century Latin American history; bibliographer; research focuses on Russian travel literature and other original Russian sources pertaining to Latin America, including California in the Spanish and Mexican periods.

SLËZKIN, Lev Yur'evich (b. 17 June 1920). Senior research scholar, Institute of World History of the USSR Academy of Sciences (Moscow); Doctor of Historical Sciences; specialist in colonial and early modern history of the Western Hemisphere; research has focused on Latin American independence; more recently, interests have centered on the English colonies, with a view to an eventual comparative colonial history of the Americas.

ZORINA, Adelaida Mikhailovna (1910-1977). Senior research scholar, Institute of World History of the USSR Academy of Sciences (Moscow); Candidate in Historical Sciences; Docent; specialist in modern Latin American history; research focuses on nineteenth- and early twentieth-century Cuba.

INDEX

DESIGNED BY IRVING PERKINS
COMPOSED BY THE COMPOSING ROOM, INC., GRAND RAPIDS, MICHIGAN
MANUFACTURED BY CUSHING-MALLOY, INC., ANN ARBOR, MICHIGAN
TEXT IS SET IN TIMES ROMAN, DISPLAY LINES IN TIMES ROMAN AND CASLON

Library of Congress Cataloging in Publication Data
Main entry under title:
Soviet historians on Latin America.
(Publication—Conference on Latin American History; no. 5)
Bibliography: p.
1. Latin America—History—Addresses, essays,
lectures.   2. Latin America—Historiography—Addresses,
essays, lectures.   3. Latin America—Relations (general)
with Russia—Addresses, essays, lectures.   4. Russia—
Relations (general) with Latin America—Addresses,
essays, lectures.   I. Bartley, Russell, H.   II. Conference on Latin American History.   III. Series: Conference on American History. Publications; no. 5.
F1410.S68 1978   980′.007′2047   76-53648
ISBN 0-299-07250-9